5 STEPS TO A 5

AP Biology

2024

5 STEPS TO A 5

AP Biology
2024

Mark Anestis • Kelcey Burris

McGraw Hill

New York Chicago San Francisco Athens London Madrid
Mexico City Milan New Delhi Singapore Sydney Toronto

1 2 3 4 5 6 7 8 9   LHS   28 27 26 25 24 23
1 2 3 4 5 6 7 8 9   LHS   28 27 26 25 24 23   (Elite Student Edition)

ISBN   978-1-265-27379-8
MHID   1-265-27379-0

e-ISBN   978-1-265-27424-5
e-MHID   1-265-27424-X

ISBN   978-1-265-27522-8 (Elite Student Edition)
MHID   1-265-27522-X

e-ISBN   978-1-265-27536-5 (Elite Student Edition)
e-MHID   1-265-27536-X

Trademarks: McGraw Hill, the McGraw Hill logo, *5 Steps to a 5*, and related trade dress are trademarks or registered trademarks of McGraw Hill and/or its affiliates in the United States and other countries and may not be used without written permission. All other trademarks are the property of their respective owners. McGraw Hill is not associated with any product or vendor mentioned in this book.

AP, Advanced Placement Program, and *College Board* are registered trademarks of the College Board, which was not involved in the production of, and does not endorse, this product.

The series editor was Grace Freedson, and the project editor was Del Franz.

Series design by Jane Tenenbaum.

McGraw Hill products are available at special quantity discounts to use as premiums and sales promotions, or for use in corporate training programs. To contact a representative, please visit the Contact Us pages at www.mhprofessional.com.

McGraw Hill is committed to making our products accessible to all learners. To learn more about the available support and accommodations we offer, please contact us at accessibility@mheducation.com. We also participate in the Access Text Network (www.accesstext.org), and ATN members may submit requests through ATN.

CONTENTS

Preface ix
Acknowledgments xi
About the Authors xiii
Introduction: The Five-Step Program xv
Course Framework xix

STEP 1 Set Up Your Study Program

1 **What You Need to Know About the AP Biology Exam** 3
   Background of the Advanced Placement Program 3
   Who Writes the AP Biology Exam 4
   The AP Grades and Who Receives Them 4
   Reasons for Taking the AP Biology Exam 4
   Questions Frequently Asked About the AP Biology Exam 5

2 **How to Plan Your Time** 8
   Three Approaches to Preparing for the AP Biology Exam 8
   Calendar for Each Plan 10

STEP 2 Determine Your Test Readiness

3 **Take a Diagnostic Exam** 15
   Diagnostic Exam: AP Biology: Section I 19
   Answers and Explanations 29
   Free-Response Grading Outline 33
   Scoring and Interpretation 36

STEP 3 Develop Strategies for Success

4 **How to Approach Each Question Type** 39
   Multiple-Choice Questions 40
   Free-Response Questions 40

STEP 4 Review the Knowledge You Need to Score High

5 **Chemistry of Life** 47
   Introduction 47
   Elements, Compounds, Atoms, and Ions 47
   Water 49
   Macromolecules 51
   Nucleic Acids 56
   pH: Acids and Bases 57
   Review Questions 58
   Answers and Explanations 59
   Rapid Review 60

6 Cell Structure and Function   61
Introduction   62
Types of Cells   62
Endosymbiotic Theory   62
Organelles   63
Cell Size   65
Cell Membranes: Fluid Mosaic Model   65
Types of Cell Transport   67
Water Potential   69
Review Questions   71
Answers and Explanations   73
Rapid Review   74

7 Cellular Energetics   76
Introduction   77
Enzymes   77
Cellular Energy   79
Aerobic Respiration   80
Anaerobic Respiration   86
The Players in Photosynthesis   88
The Reactions of Photosynthesis   89
Types of Photosynthesis   94
Review Questions   96
Answers and Explanations   98
Rapid Review   99

8 Cell Communication and Cell Cycle   102
Introduction   102
Cell Communication   103
Signaling   103
Signal Transduction Pathway   104
Phosphorylation   104
Secondary Messengers   105
Cell Division in Prokaryotes   106
The Cell Cycle   106
Mitosis   107
Control of Cell Division   108
Apoptosis   109
Feedback   109
Homeostasis   109
Review Questions   110
Answers and Explanations   111
Rapid Review   111

9 Heredity   114
Introduction   115
Haploid Versus Diploid Organisms   115
Meiosis   115
Some Important Terms to Know   118
Sources of Cell Variation   119
Mendel and His Peas   119
Non-Mendelian Genetics   121

Intermediate Inheritance   121
Other Forms of Inheritance   122
Sex Determination and Sex Linkage   124
Linkage and Gene Mapping   125
Heads or Tails?   126
Pedigrees   126
Common Disorders   128
Chromosomal Complications   129
Review Questions   130
Answers and Explanations   133
Rapid Review   135

10 Molecular Genetics   137
Introduction   137
The Central Dogma   138
Replication of DNA   138
Telomeres   143
Transcription of DNA   144
RNA Processing   146
Translation of RNA   148
Gene Regulation   152
Cell Specialization   156
Mutations   157
The Genetics of Viruses   160
The Genetics of Bacteria   161
Biotechnology   162
Review Questions   165
Answers and Explanations   166
Rapid Review   167

11 Evolution   170
Introduction   171
Definition of Evolution   171
Natural Selection   174
Lamarck and Darwin   174
Adaptations   175
Types of Selection   175
Evolution Patterns   177
Sources of Variation   177
Speciation   178
When Evolution Is Not Occurring: Hardy-Weinberg Equilibrium   180
The Evidence for Evolution   182
Phylogeny   182
Key Ideas   183
Macroevolution   185
Origins of Life on Earth   186
Review Questions   189
Answers and Explanations   190
Rapid Review   190

12 Ecology 193
Behavioral Ecology 194
Types of Animal Learning 194
Animal Movement 195
Animal Communication 198
Ecology 199
Population Ecology and Growth 199
Life History Strategies 202
Biological Communities 204
Trophic Levels 207
Biomes 210
Biogeochemical Cycles 211
Disruptions to Ecosystem 212
Review Questions 213
Answers and Explanations 215
Rapid Review 217

13 Laboratory Review 220
Introduction 220
Investigation 1: Artificial Selection 221
Investigation 2: Mathematical Modeling: Hardy-Weinberg 221
Investigation 3: Comparing DNA Sequences to Understand Evolutionary Relationships with BLAST 223
Investigation 4: Diffusion and Osmosis 224
Investigation 5: Photosynthesis 228
Investigation 6: Cellular Respiration 230
Investigation 7: Cell Division: Mitosis and Meiosis 231
Investigation 8: Biotechnology: Bacterial Transformation 234
Investigation 9: Biotechnology: Restriction Enzyme Analysis of DNA 235
Investigation 10: Energy Dynamics 237
Investigation 11: Transpiration 238
Investigation 12: Fruit Fly Behavior 240
Investigation 13: Enzyme Activity 241
Review Questions 243
Answers and Explanations 244
Rapid Review 245

STEP 5 Build Your Test-Taking Confidence

AP Biology Practice Exam 1 251
AP Biology Practice Exam 2 275

Bibliography 297
Websites 299
Glossary 301

PREFACE

Hello, and welcome to the new edition of the AP Biology review book that promises to be the most fun you have ever had!!!! Well, OK. . . . It will not be the most fun you have ever had . . . but maybe you will enjoy yourself a little bit. If you let yourself, you may at least learn a lot from this book. It contains the major concepts and ideas to which you were exposed over the past year in your AP Biology classroom, written in a manner that, we hope, will be pleasing to your eyes and your brain.

Many books on the market contain the same information that you will find in this book. However, we have approached the material a bit differently. We have tried to make this book as conversational and understandable as possible. We have had to review for countless standardized tests and cannot think of anything more annoying than a review book that is a total snoozer. In fact, we had this book "snooze-tested" by more than five thousand students, and the average reader could go 84 pages before falling asleep. This is better than the "other" review books whose average snooze time fell within the range of 14–43 pages. OK, we made up those statistics . . . but we promise that this book will not put you to sleep.

While preparing this book, we spoke to 154,076 students who had taken the AP exam and asked them how they prepared for the test. They indicated which study techniques were most helpful to them and which topics in this book they considered *vital* to success on this test. Throughout the book there are notes in the margins with these students' comments and tips. Pay heed to these comments because these folks know what they are talking about. They have taken this test and may have advice that will be useful to you.

We are not going to mislead you into thinking that you do not need to study to do well on this exam. You will actually need to prepare quite a bit. But this book will walk you through the process in as painless a way as possible. Use the study questions at the end of each chapter in Step 4 to practice applying the material you just read. Use the study tips listed in Step 3 to help you remember the material you need to know. Take the two practice tests in Step 5 as the actual exam approaches to see how well the information is sinking in.

Well, it's time to stop gabbing and start studying. Begin by setting up your study program in Step 1 of this book. Take the diagnostic test in Step 2 and look through the answers and explanations to see where you stand before you dive into the review process. Then look through the hints and strategies in Step 3, which may help you finally digest all the information that comes at you in Step 4. Then, we suggest that you kick back, relax, grab yourself a comfortable seat, and dig in. There is a lot to learn before the exam. Happy reading!

ACKNOWLEDGMENTS

This project would not have been completed without the assistance of many dear friends and relatives. To my wife, Stephanie, your countless hours of reading, rereading, and reading once again were of amazing value. Thank you so much for putting in so much time and energy to my cause. You have helped make this book what it is. To my parents and brothers who likewise contributed by reading a few chapters when I needed a second opinion, I thank you. I would like to thank Chris Black for helping me edit and clarify a few of the chapters. I would like to thank Don Reis, whose editing comments have strengthened both the content and the flow of this work. Finally, a big thank-you to all the students and teachers who gave me their input and thoughts on what they believed to be important for this exam. They have made this book that much stronger. Thank you all.

—Mark Anestis

ABOUT THE AUTHORS

MARK ANESTIS was born in Pittsburgh, Pennsylvania, and has lived in Connecticut since the age of six. He graduated from Weston High School in Weston, Connecticut, in 1993 and attended Yale University. While taking science courses in preparation for medical school, he earned a bachelor's degree cum laude in economics. He attended the University of Connecticut School of Medicine for two years and passed the step 1 boards, then chose to redirect his energy toward educating students in a one-on-one environment. He is the founder and director of The Learning Edge, a tutoring company based in Hamden, Connecticut (www.thelearningedge.net). Since January 2000, he has been tutoring high school students all over the globe (online) in math, the sciences, and standardized test preparation (including the SAT, ACT, and SAT Subject Tests).

In addition to this review book, he has coauthored *McGraw Hill's SAT*, *McGraw Hill's PSAT/NMSQT*, and *McGraw Hill's 12 SAT Practice Tests and PSAT*. The author also created the DAILY WORD app (thedailywordapp.net), which allows students to build better vocabularies! The app is available on the App Store.

KELCEY BURRIS is originally from Vancouver, Washington. He earned his bachelor's in biology at Concordia University in Portland, Oregon, and his master's in education from Florida Gulf Coast University in Fort Myers, Florida. He started teaching at Gulf Coast High School in Naples, Florida, in 1999. Kelcey opened Palmetto Ridge High School in 2004 as the science chair before relocating with his family back to Vancouver. He has been the science chair at Union High School since it opened in 2007 and is still there today, teaching AP Biology and AP Computer Science Principles. He has taught AP Biology for 20 years and is an active AP Reader. Kelcey is an AP Biology Consultant for the College Board, training teachers all over the United States and the world, including Guam and Chengdu and Shanghai, China. He enjoys spending time with his daughter and wife.

INTRODUCTION: THE FIVE-STEP PROGRAM

Welcome!

If you focus on the beginning, the rest will fall into place. When you purchase this book and decide to work your way through it, you are beginning your journey to the Advanced Placement (AP) Biology exam. We will be with you every step of the way.

Why This Book?

We believe that this book has something unique to offer you. We have spoken with many AP Biology teachers and students and have been fortunate to learn quite a bit. Teachers helped us understand which topics are most important for class, and students described what they wanted from a test-prep book. Therefore, the contents of this book reflect genuine student concerns and needs. This is a student-oriented book. We did not attempt to impress you with arrogant language, mislead you with inaccurate information and tasks, or lull you into a false sense of confidence through ingenious shortcuts. We have not put information into this book simply because it is included in other review books. We recognize the fact that there is only so much that one individual can learn for an exam. Believe us, we have taken our fair share of these tests—we know how much work they can be. This book represents a realistic approach to studying for the AP exam. We have included very little heavy technical detail in this book. (There *is* some . . . we had to . . . but there is not very much.)

Think of this text as a resource and guide to accompany you on your AP Biology journey throughout the year. This book is designed to serve many purposes. It should:

- Clarify requirements for the AP Biology exam
- Provide you with test practice
- Help you pace yourself
- Function as a wonderful paperweight when the exam is completed
- Make you aware of the five steps to mastering the AP Biology exam

Organization of the Book

We know that your primary concern is to learn about the AP Biology exam. We start by introducing the five-step plan. We then give an overview of the exam in general. We follow that up with three different approaches to exam preparation and then move on to describe some tips and suggestions for how to approach the various sections of the exam. The Diagnostic Exam should give you an idea of where you stand before you begin your preparations. We recommend that you spend 45 minutes on this practice exam.

The volume of material covered in AP Biology is quite intimidating. Step 4 of this book provides a comprehensive review of all the major sections you may or may not have covered in the classroom. Not every AP Biology class in the country will get through the same amount of material. This book should help you fill any gaps in your understanding of the course work.

Step 5 of this book is the practice exam section. Here is where you put your skills to the test. The multiple-choice questions provide practice with the types of questions you may encounter on the AP exam. Keep in mind that they are *not* exact questions taken directly from past exams. Rather, they are designed to focus you on the key topics that often appear on the actual AP Biology exam. When you answer a question we've written in this book, do not think to yourself, "OK . . . that's a past exam question." Instead, you should think to yourself, "OK, the authors thought that was important, so I should remember this fact. It may show up in some form on the real exam." The essay questions are designed to cover the techniques and terms required by the AP exam. After taking each exam, you can check yourself against the explanations of every multiple-choice question and the grading guidelines for the essays.

The material at the end of the book is also important. It contains a bibliography of sources that may be helpful to you, a list of websites related to the AP Biology exam, and a glossary of the key terms discussed in this book.

Introducing the Five-Step Program

The five-step program is designed to provide you with the skills and strategies vital to the exam and the practice that can help lead you to that perfect "Holy Grail" score of 5.

Step 1: Set Up Your Study Program

Step 1 leads you through a brief process to help determine which type of exam preparation you want to commit yourself to:

1. Full-year prep: September through May
2. One-semester prep: January through May
3. Six-week prep: the six weeks prior to the exam

Step 2: Determine Your Test Readiness

Step 2 consists of a Diagnostic Exam, which will give you an idea of what you already know and what you need to learn between now and the exam. Take the test, which is broken down by topic, look over the detailed explanations, and start learning!

Step 3: Develop Strategies for Success

Step 3 gives you strategy advice for the AP Biology exam. It teaches you about the multiple-choice questions and the free-response questions you will face on exam day.

Step 4: Review the Knowledge You Need to Score High

Step 4 is a big one. This is the comprehensive review of all the topics on the AP exam. You've probably been in an AP Bio class all year, and you've likely spent hours upon hours reading through the AP Biology textbooks. These review chapters are appropriate both for quick skimming (to remind yourself of salient points that may have slipped your mind) and for in-depth study (to teach yourself broader concepts that may be new to you.)

Step 5: Build Your Test-Taking Confidence

Ahhhh, the full-length practice tests—oh, the joy! In addition to the Diagnostic Exam, this book has two more full-length practice tests. One of the most effective ways to improve as you prepare for any exam is to take as many practice tests as you can. Sit down and take these tests fully timed, see what you get wrong, and learn from those mistakes. Remember . . . it's good to make mistakes on these exams because if you learn from those mistakes now, you won't make them again in May!

The Graphics Used in This Book

To emphasize particular skills and strategies, we use several icons throughout this book. An icon in the margin will alert you that you should pay particular attention to the accompanying text. We use three icons:

1. This icon points out a very important concept or fact that you should not pass over.

2. This icon calls your attention to a problem-solving strategy that you may want to try.

3. This icon indicates a tip that you might find useful.

Boldfaced words indicate terms that are included in the Glossary at the end of the book. Boldface is also used to indicate the answer to a sample problem discussed in the test. Throughout the book you will find marginal notes, boxes, and starred areas. Pay close attention to these areas because they can provide tips, hints, strategies, and further explanations to help you reach your full potential.

COURSE FRAMEWORK

Overview

This course framework provides a clear and detailed description of the course requirements necessary for student success; it specifies what students must know, be able to do, and understand to qualify for college credit or placement.

This material is printed with permission of the College Board and comes from the AP Biology Course and Exam Description Guide.

Source: AP BIOLOGY COURSE AND EXAM DESCRIPTION Copyright © 2019 The College Board. Reproduced with permission. http://apcentral.collegeboard.com

The course framework includes two essential components:

Science Practices

The science practices are central to the study and practice of biology. Students should develop and apply the described practices on a regular basis over the span of the course.

Course Content

The course content is organized into commonly taught units of study that provide a suggested sequence for the course. These units comprise the content and skills that colleges and universities typically expect students to master to qualify for college credit and/or placement. This content is grounded in big ideas, which are crosscutting concepts that build conceptual understanding and spiral throughout the course.

Science Practices

The following table presents the science practices that students should develop during the AP Biology course. These practices form the basis of many tasks on the AP Biology Exam. The unit guides that follow embed and spiral these practices throughout the course.

Science Practice 1	Science Practice 2	Science Practice 3
Concept Explanation **1**	*Visual Representations* **2**	*Questions and Methods* **3**
Explain biological concepts, processes, and models presented in written format.	Analyze visual representations of biological concepts and processes.	Determine scientific questions and methods.

SKILLS

1.A Describe biological concepts and/or processes.	**2.A** Describe characteristics of a biological concept, process, or model represented visually.	**3.A** Identify or pose a testable question based on an observation, data, or a model.
1.B Explain biological concepts and/or processes.	**2.B** Explain relationships between different characteristics of biological concepts, processes, or models represented visually	**3.B** State the null and alternative hypotheses, or predict the results of an experiment.
1.C Explain biological concepts, processes, and/or models in applied contexts.	a. In theoretical contexts.	**3.C** Identify experimental procedures that are aligned to the question, including
	b. In applied contexts.	a. Identifying dependent and independent variables.
	2.C Explain how biological concepts or processes represented visually relate to larger biological principles, concepts, processes, or theories.	b. Identifying appropriate controls.
		c. Justifying appropriate controls.
	2.D Represent relationships within biological models, including	**3.D** Make observations, or collect data from representations of laboratory setups or results. (Lab only; not assessed)
	a. Mathematical models.	
	b. Diagrams.	**3.E** Propose a new/next investigation based on
	c. Flow charts.	a. An evaluation of the evidence from an experiment.
		b. An evaluation of the design/methods.

Science Practice 4	Science Practice 5	Science Practice 6
Representing and Describing Data 4	*Statistical Tests and Data Analysis* 5	*Argumentation* 6
Represent and describe data.	Perform statistical tests and mathematical calculations to analyze and interpret data.	Develop and justify scientific arguments using evidence.

SKILLS

4.A Construct a graph, plot, or chart (*X,Y; Log Y; Bar; Histogram; Line, Dual Y; Box and Whisker; Pie*).

a. Orientation

b. Labeling

c. Units

d. Scaling

e. Plotting

f. Type

g. Trend line

4.B Describe data from a table or graph, including

a. Identifying specific data points.

b. Describing trends and/or patterns in the data.

c. Describing relationships between variables.

5.A Perform mathematical calculations, including

a. Mathematical equations in the curriculum.

b. Means.

c. Rates.

d. Ratios.

e. Percentages.

5.B Use confidence intervals and/or error bars (both determined using standard errors) to determine whether sample means are statistically different.

5.C Perform chi-square hypothesis testing.

5.D Use data to evaluate a hypothesis (or prediction), including

a. Rejecting or failing to reject the null hypothesis.

b. Supporting or refuting the alternative hypothesis.

6.A Make a scientific claim.

6.B Support a claim with evidence from biological principles, concepts, processes, and/or data.

6.C Provide reasoning to justify a claim by connecting evidence to biological theories.

6.D Explain the relationship between experimental results and larger biological concepts, processes, or theories.

6.E Predict the causes or effects of a change in, or disruption to, one or more components in a biological system based on

a. Biological concepts or processes.

b. A visual representation of a biological concept, process, or model.

c. Data.

AP BIOLOGY

Course Content

Based on the Understanding by Design® (Wiggins and McTighe) model, this course framework provides a clear and detailed description of the course requirements necessary for student success. The framework specifies what students must know, be able to do, and understand, with a focus on the big ideas that encompass core principles, theories, and processes of the discipline. The framework also encourages instruction that prepares students for advanced work in STEM and life science–related majors.

Big Ideas

The big ideas serve as the foundation of the course and allow students to create meaningful connections among course concepts. Often, they are abstract concepts or themes that become threads running throughout the course. Revisiting the big ideas and applying them in a variety of contexts allow students to develop deeper conceptual understandings. Following are the big ideas of the course and a brief description of each:

Big Idea 1: Evolution (Evo)

The process of evolution drives the diversity and unity of life. Evolution is a change in the genetic makeup of a population over time, with natural selection as its major driving mechanism. Darwin's theory, which is supported by evidence from many scientific disciplines, states that inheritable variations occur in individuals in a population. Due to competition for limited resources, individuals with more favorable genetic variations are more likely to survive and produce more offspring, thus passing traits to future generations. A diverse gene pool is vital for the survival of species because environmental conditions change. The process of evolution explains the diversity and unity of life, but an explanation about the *origin* of life is less clear.

In addition to the process of natural selection, naturally occurring catastrophic and human-induced events, as well as random environmental changes, can result in alteration in the gene pools of populations. Scientific evidence supports that speciation and extinction have occurred throughout Earth's history and that life continues to evolve within a changing environment, thus explaining the diversity of life.

Big Idea 2: Energetics (Ene)

Biological systems use energy and molecular building blocks to grow, reproduce, and maintain dynamic homeostasis. Cells and organisms must exchange matter with the environment. Organisms respond to changes in their environment at the molecular, cellular, physiological, and behavioral levels. Living systems require energy and matter to maintain order, grow, and reproduce. Organisms employ various strategies to capture, use, and store energy and other vital resources. Energy deficiencies are not only detrimental to individual organisms, but they can cause disruptions at the population and ecosystem levels. Homeostatic mechanisms that are conserved or divergent across related organisms reflect either continuity due to common ancestry or evolutionary change in response to distinct selective pressures.

Big Idea 3: Information Storage and Transmission (Ist)

Living systems store, retrieve, transmit, and respond to information essential to life processes. Genetic information provides for continuity of life, and, in most cases, this information is passed from parent to offspring via DNA. Nonheritable information transmission influences behavior within and between cells, organisms, and populations. These behaviors are directed by underlying genetic information, and responses to information are vital to natural selection and evolution. Genetic information is a repository of instructions necessary for the survival, growth, and reproduction of the organism. Genetic variation can be advantageous for the long-term survival and evolution of a species.

Big Idea 4: Systems Interactions (Syi)

Biological systems interact, and these systems and their interactions exhibit complex properties. All biological systems comprise parts that interact with one another. These interactions result in characteristics and emergent properties not found in the individual parts alone. All biological systems from the molecular level to the ecosystem level exhibit properties of biocomplexity and diversity. These two properties provide robustness to biological systems, enabling greater resiliency and flexibility to tolerate and respond to changes in the environment.

Units	Exam Weighting
Unit 1: Chemistry of Life	8–11%
Unit 2: Cell Structure and Function	10–13%
Unit 3: Cellular Energetics	12–16%
Unit 4: Cell Communication and Cell Cycle	10–15%
Unit 5: Heredity	8–11%
Unit 6: Gene Expression and Regulation	12–16%
Unit 7: Natural Selection	13–20%
Unit 8: Ecology	10–15%

Spiraling the Big Ideas

The following table shows how the big ideas spiral across units by showing the units in which each big idea appears.

Big Ideas	Unit 1	Unit 2	Unit 3	Unit 4	Unit 5	Unit 6	Unit 7	Unit 8
	Chemistry of Life	Cell Structure and Function	Cellular Energetics	Cell Communication and Cell Cycle	Heredity	Gene Expression and Regulation	Natural Selection	Ecology
Evolution — EVO		❯			❯		❯	❯
Energetics — ENE	❯	❯	❯	❯				❯
Information Storage and Transmission — IST	❯			❯	❯	❯		❯
Systems Interactions — SYI	❯	❯	❯		❯		❯	

Course at a Glance

Plan

The course at a glance provides a useful visual organization of the AP Biology curricular components, including:

- Sequence of units, along with approximate weighting and suggested pacing. Please note, pacing is based on 45-minute class periods, meeting five days each week for a full academic year
- Progression of topics within each unit
- Spiraling of the big ideas and science practices across units

Teach

SCIENCE PRACTICES
Science practices are spiralled throughout the course:

1. Concept Explanation
2. Visual Representations
3. Questions and Methods
4. Representing and Describing Data
5. Statistical Tests and Data Analysis
6. Argumentation

BIG IDEAS
The big ideas spiral across topics and units:

EVO Evolution
IST Information Storage and Transfer
ENE Energetics
SYI Systems Interactions

Assess

Assign the Personal Progress Checks—either as homework or in class—for each unit. Each Personal Progress Check contains formative multiple-choice and free-response questions. The feedback from the Personal Progress Checks shows students the areas where they need to focus.

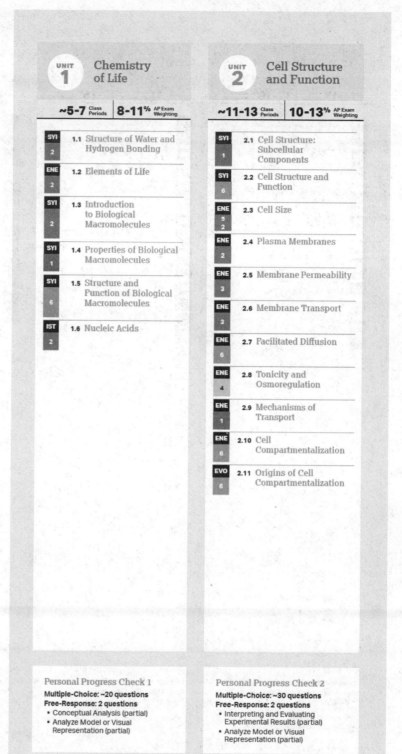

UNIT 1 — Chemistry of Life

~5-7 Class Periods | **8-11%** AP Exam Weighting

SP		Topic
SYI	2	1.1 Structure of Water and Hydrogen Bonding
ENE	2	1.2 Elements of Life
SYI	2	1.3 Introduction to Biological Macromolecules
SYI	1	1.4 Properties of Biological Macromolecules
SYI	6	1.5 Structure and Function of Biological Macromolecules
IST	2	1.6 Nucleic Acids

UNIT 2 — Cell Structure and Function

~11-13 Class Periods | **10-13%** AP Exam Weighting

SP		Topic
SYI	1	2.1 Cell Structure: Subcellular Components
SYI	6	2.2 Cell Structure and Function
ENE	5 / 2	2.3 Cell Size
ENE	2	2.4 Plasma Membranes
ENE	3	2.5 Membrane Permeability
ENE	3	2.6 Membrane Transport
ENE	6	2.7 Facilitated Diffusion
ENE	4	2.8 Tonicity and Osmoregulation
ENE	1	2.9 Mechanisms of Transport
ENE	6	2.10 Cell Compartmentalization
EVO	6	2.11 Origins of Cell Compartmentalization

Personal Progress Check 1

Multiple-Choice: ~20 questions
Free-Response: 2 questions
- Conceptual Analysis (partial)
- Analyze Model or Visual Representation (partial)

Personal Progress Check 2

Multiple-Choice: ~30 questions
Free-Response: 2 questions
- Interpreting and Evaluating Experimental Results (partial)
- Analyze Model or Visual Representation (partial)

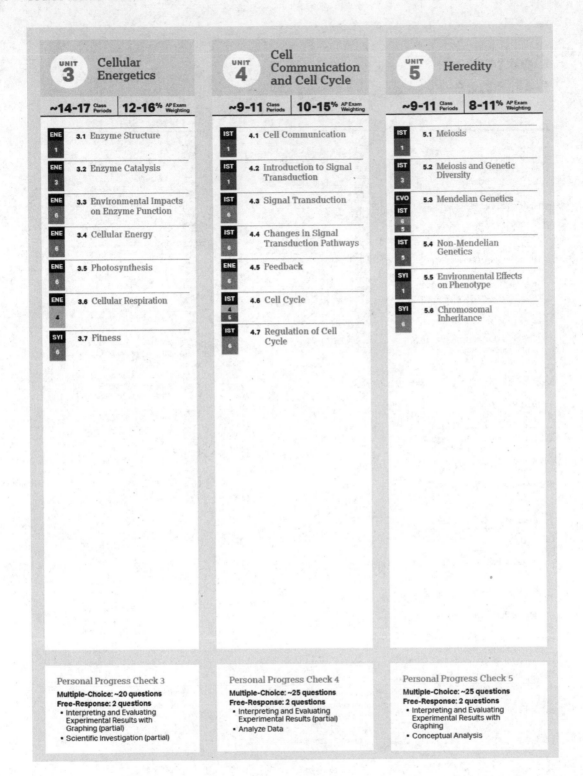

UNIT 3 Cellular Energetics

~14-17 Class Periods | 12-16% AP Exam Weighting

ENE 1	3.1	Enzyme Structure
ENE 3	3.2	Enzyme Catalysis
ENE 6	3.3	Environmental Impacts on Enzyme Function
ENE 6	3.4	Cellular Energy
ENE 6	3.5	Photosynthesis
ENE 4	3.6	Cellular Respiration
SYI 6	3.7	Fitness

Personal Progress Check 3

Multiple-Choice: ~20 questions
Free-Response: 2 questions
- Interpreting and Evaluating Experimental Results with Graphing (partial)
- Scientific Investigation (partial)

UNIT 4 Cell Communication and Cell Cycle

~9-11 Class Periods | 10-15% AP Exam Weighting

IST 1	4.1	Cell Communication
IST 1	4.2	Introduction to Signal Transduction
IST 6	4.3	Signal Transduction
IST 6	4.4	Changes in Signal Transduction Pathways
ENE 6	4.5	Feedback
IST 4 5	4.6	Cell Cycle
IST 6	4.7	Regulation of Cell Cycle

Personal Progress Check 4

Multiple-Choice: ~25 questions
Free-Response: 2 questions
- Interpreting and Evaluating Experimental Results (partial)
- Analyze Data

UNIT 5 Heredity

~9-11 Class Periods | 8-11% AP Exam Weighting

IST 1	5.1	Meiosis
IST 3	5.2	Meiosis and Genetic Diversity
EVO IST 6 5	5.3	Mendelian Genetics
IST 5	5.4	Non-Mendelian Genetics
SYI 1	5.5	Environmental Effects on Phenotype
SYI 6	5.6	Chromosomal Inheritance

Personal Progress Check 5

Multiple-Choice: ~25 questions
Free-Response: 2 questions
- Interpreting and Evaluating Experimental Results with Graphing
- Conceptual Analysis

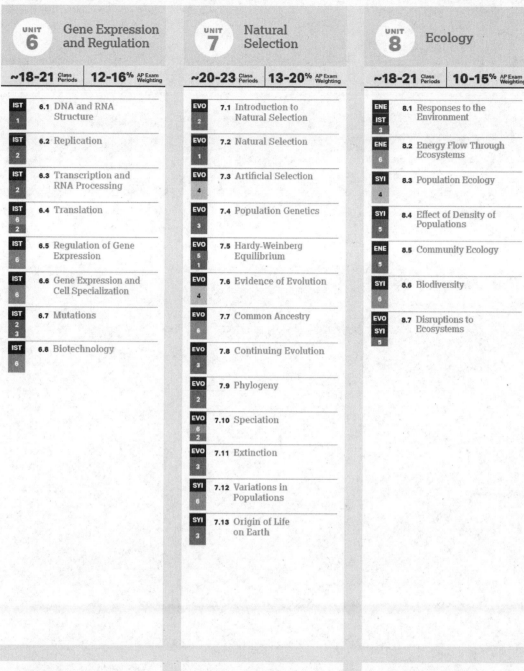

UNIT **6** Gene Expression and Regulation	UNIT **7** Natural Selection	UNIT **8** Ecology
~18-21 Class Periods | 12-16% AP Exam Weighting	~20-23 Class Periods | 13-20% AP Exam Weighting	~18-21 Class Periods | 10-15% AP Exam Weighting
IST 1 — 6.1 DNA and RNA Structure	**EVO** 2 — 7.1 Introduction to Natural Selection	**ENE IST** 3 — 8.1 Responses to the Environment
IST 2 — 6.2 Replication	**EVO** 1 — 7.2 Natural Selection	**ENE** 6 — 8.2 Energy Flow Through Ecosystems
IST 2 — 6.3 Transcription and RNA Processing	**EVO** 4 — 7.3 Artificial Selection	**SYI** 4 — 8.3 Population Ecology
IST 6 2 — 6.4 Translation	**EVO** 3 — 7.4 Population Genetics	**SYI** 5 — 8.4 Effect of Density of Populations
IST 6 — 6.5 Regulation of Gene Expression	**EVO** 5 1 — 7.5 Hardy-Weinberg Equilibrium	**ENE** 5 — 8.5 Community Ecology
IST 6 — 6.6 Gene Expression and Cell Specialization	**EVO** 4 — 7.6 Evidence of Evolution	**SYI** 6 — 8.6 Biodiversity
IST 2 3 — 6.7 Mutations	**EVO** 6 — 7.7 Common Ancestry	**EVO SYI** 5 — 8.7 Disruptions to Ecosystems
IST 6 — 6.8 Biotechnology	**EVO** 3 — 7.8 Continuing Evolution	
	EVO 2 — 7.9 Phylogeny	
	EVO 6 2 — 7.10 Speciation	
	EVO 3 — 7.11 Extinction	
	SYI 6 — 7.12 Variations in Populations	
	SYI 3 — 7.13 Origin of Life on Earth	

Personal Progress Check 6

Multiple-Choice: ~25 questions
Free-Response: 2 questions
- Interpreting and Evaluating Experimental Results
- Analyze Model or Visual Representation

Personal Progress Check 7

Multiple-Choice: ~40 questions
Free-Response: 2 questions
- Interpreting and Evaluating Experimental Results with Graphing
- Analyze Data

Personal Progress Check 8

Multiple-Choice: ~20 questions
Free-Response: 2 questions
- Interpreting and Evaluating Experimental Results with Graphing
- Scientific Investigation

5 STEPS TO A 5™

AP Biology

2024

Set Up Your Study Program

CHAPTER 1 What You Need to Know About the AP Biology Exam
CHAPTER 2 How to Plan Your Time

CHAPTER **1**

What You Need to Know About the AP Biology Exam

IN THIS CHAPTER

Summary: Learn what topics are tested, how the test is scored, and basic test-taking information.

Key Ideas

✪ Some colleges will award credit for a score of 4 or 5.

✪ Multiple-choice questions account for 50 percent of your final score.

✪ Points are no longer deducted for incorrect answers to multiple-choice questions. You should try to eliminate incorrect answer choices and then guess; there is no penalty for guessing.

✪ Free-response questions account for 50 percent of your final score.

✪ Your composite score on the two test sections is converted into a score on the 1-to-5 scale.

Background of the Advanced Placement Program

The Advanced Placement program was begun by the College Board in 1955 to construct standard achievement exams that would allow highly motivated high school students the opportunity to be awarded advanced placement as first-year students in colleges and universities in the United States. Today, more than a million students from every state in the nation and from foreign countries take the annual AP exams in May.

The AP programs are designed for high school students who wish to take college-level courses. In our case, the AP Biology course and exam are designed to involve high school students in college-level biology studies.

Who Writes the AP Biology Exam

After extensive surfing of the College Board website, here is what we have uncovered. The AP Biology exam is created by a group of college and high school biology instructors known as the AP Development Committee. The committee's job is to ensure that the annual AP Biology exam reflects what is being taught and studied in college-level biology classes at high schools.

This committee writes a large number of multiple-choice questions, which are pretested and evaluated for clarity, appropriateness, and range of possible answers. The committee also generates a pool of essay questions, pretests them, and chooses those questions that best represent the full range of the scoring scale, which will allow the AP readers to evaluate the essays equitably.

It is important to remember that the AP Biology exam is thoroughly evaluated after it is administered each year. This way, the College Board can use the results to make course suggestions and to plan future tests.

The AP Grades and Who Receives Them

Once you have taken the exam and it has been scored, your test will be graded with one of five numbers by the College Board:

- A 5 indicates that you are extremely well qualified.
- A 4 indicates that you are well qualified.
- A 3 indicates that you are adequately qualified.
- A 2 indicates that you are possibly qualified.
- A 1 indicates that you are not qualified to receive college credit.

A grade of 5, 4, 3, 2, or 1 will usually be reported by early July.

Reasons for Taking the AP Biology Exam

Why put yourself through a year of intensive study, pressure, stress, and preparation? Only you can answer that question. Following are some of the reasons that students have indicated to us for taking the AP exam:

- For personal satisfaction.
- To compare themselves with other students across the nation.
- Because colleges look favorably on the applications of students who elect to enroll in AP courses.
- To receive college credit or advanced standing at their colleges or universities.
- Because they love the subject.
- So that their families will be really proud of them.

There are plenty of other reasons, but no matter what they might be, the primary reason for enrolling in the AP Biology course and taking the exam in May is to feel good about yourself and the challenges you have met.

Questions Frequently Asked About the AP Biology Exam

Here are some common questions students have about the AP Biology exam and some answers to those questions.

If I Don't Take an AP Biology Course, Can I Still Take the AP Biology Exam?

Yes. Although the AP Biology exam is designed for students who have had a year's course in AP Biology, some high schools do not offer this type of course. Many students in these high schools have also done well on the exam, although they had not taken the course. However, if your high school does offer an AP Biology course, by all means take advantage of it and the structured background it will provide you.

How Is the Advanced Placement Biology Exam Organized?

The exam has two parts and is scheduled to last three hours. The first section is a set of 60 multiple-choice questions. You will have 90 minutes to complete this part of the test.

After you complete the multiple-choice section, you will hand in your test booklet and scan sheet, and you will be given a brief break. The length of this break depends on the particular administrator. You will not be able to return to the multiple-choice questions when you return to the examination room.

The second section of the exam is a 90-minute essay-writing segment consisting of two long free-response questions and four short free-response questions. This section will be split into a 10-minute reading period, followed by an 80-minute writing period. All of the questions will test your understanding of the four big ideas in biology and how science investigators actually work.

Must I Check the Box at the End of the Essay Booklet That Allows AP Staff to Use My Essays as Samples for Research?

No. This is simply a way for the College Board to make certain they have your permission if they decide to use one or more of your essays as a model. The readers of your essays pay no attention to whether or not that box is checked. Checking the box will not affect your grade.

How Is the Multiple-Choice Section Scored?

The scan sheet with your answers is run through a computer, which counts the number of correct answers. The AP Biology questions usually have four choices. A question left blank receives a zero. The very complicated formula for this calculation looks something like this (where $N =$ the number of answers):

$$N_{\text{right}} = \text{raw score}$$

OK, that is not complicated at all.

How Are My Free-Response Answers Scored?

Each of your essays is read by a different, trained AP reader called a *faculty consultant*. The AP/College Board members have developed a highly successful training program for their readers, providing many opportunities for checks and double checks of essays to ensure a fair and equitable reading of each essay.

The scoring guides are carefully developed by a chief faculty consultant, a question leader, table leaders, and content experts. All faculty consultants are then trained to read and score just *one* essay question on the exam. They actually become experts in that one essay question. No one knows the identity of any writer. The identification numbers and names are covered, and the exam booklets are randomly distributed to the readers in packets of 25 randomly chosen essays. Table leaders and the question leader review samples of each reader's scores to ensure that quality standards are constant.

> Free-response question 1: Interpreting and Evaluating Experimental Results is scored on an 8 to 10-point scale
>
> Free-response question 2: Interpreting and Evaluating Experimental Results with Graphing is an 8 to 10-point scale
>
> Free-response question 3: Scientific Investigation is a 4-point question
>
> Free-response question 4: Conceptual Analysis is a 4-point question
>
> Free-response question 5: Analyze Model or Visual Representation is a 4-point question
>
> Free-response question 6: Analyze Data is a 4-point question

How Is My Composite Score Calculated?

This is where fuzzy math comes into play. The folks at the College Board are constantly adjusting the exact formula used to determine your composite score. Here is an example of a conversion they have used in the past, and this will be the conversion you will use to score any tests you do in this book.

The composite score for the AP Biology exam is 120. The free-response section represents 50 percent of this score, which equals 60 points. The multiple-choice section makes up 50 percent of the composite score, which equals another 60 points.

Take your multiple-choice results and plug them into the following formula (keep in mind that this formula was designed for a previous AP Biology exam and could be subject to some minor tweaking by the AP Board):

Number multiple-choice correct ———————

Take your essay results and plug them into this formula:

Total free-response points $\times$ 1.76 = ———————

Your total composite score for the exam is determined by adding the score from the multiple-choice section to the score from the essay section and rounding that sum to the nearest whole number.

How Is My Composite Score Turned into the Grade That Is Reported to My College?

Keep in mind that the total composite scores needed to earn a 5, 4, 3, 2, or 1 change each year. These cutoffs are determined by a committee of AP, College Board, and Educational Testing Service (ETS) directors, experts, and statisticians. The same exam that is given to the AP Biology high school students is given to college students. The various college professors report how the college students fared on the exam. This provides information for the chief faculty consultant on where to draw the lines for a 5, 4, 3, 2, or 1 score. A score of 5 on this AP exam is set to represent the average score received by the college students who scored an A on the exam. A score of a 3 or a 4 is the equivalent of a college grade B, and so on.

Over the years, there has been an observable trend indicating the number of points required to achieve a specific grade. Data released from a particular AP Biology exam show that the approximate range for the five different scores are as follows (this changes from year to year—just use this as an approximate guideline):

- low to mid 90's to 120   5
- low to mid 70's to low to mid 90's   4
- mid 50's to mid 70's   3
- low 30's to mid 50's   2
- 0 to low 30   1

What Should I Bring to the Exam?

Here are some suggestions:

- A simple calculator
- Several pencils and an eraser
- Several black pens (black ink is easier on the eyes)
- A watch
- Something to drink—water is best
- A quiet snack, such as Lifesavers
- Your brain (optional)
- Tissues

What Should I *Avoid* Bringing to the Exam?

You should not bring:

- A jackhammer
- Loud stereo
- Pop rocks
- Your parents

Is There Anything Else I Should Be Aware Of?

You should:

- Allow plenty of time to get to the test site.
- Wear comfortable clothing.
- Eat a light breakfast or lunch.
- Remind yourself that you are well prepared and that the test is an enjoyable challenge and a chance to share your knowledge. Be proud of yourself! You worked hard all year. Once test day comes, there is nothing further you can do. It is out of your hands, and your only job is to answer as many questions correctly as you possibly can.

What Should I Do the Night Before the Exam?

Although we do not vigorously support last-minute cramming, there may be some value to some last-minute review. Spending the night before the exam relaxing with family or friends is helpful for many students. Watch a movie, play a game, gab on the phone, and then find a quiet spot to study. While you're unwinding, flip through your notebook and review sheets. As you are approaching the exam, you might want to put together a list of topics that have troubled you and review them briefly the night before the exam. If you are unable to fall asleep, flip through our chapter on laboratory review (Chapter 13). Within moments, you're bound to be ready to drift off. Pleasant dreams.

CHAPTER 2

How to Plan Your Time

IN THIS CHAPTER

Summary: What to study for the AP Biology exam, depending on how much time you have available, plus three schedules to help you plan your course of study.

Key Ideas

❂ Focus your attention and spend time on those topics that are most likely to increase your score.

❂ Study the topics that you are *afraid* will appear, and relax about those that you know best.

❂ Do not study so widely that you forget to learn the important details of some of the more heavily detailed topics that appear on the AP Biology exam.

Three Approaches to Preparing for the AP Biology Exam

Overview of the Three Plans

No one knows your study habits, likes, and dislikes better than you do. So you are the only one who can decide which approach you want or need to adopt to prepare for the Advanced Placement Biology exam. Look at the brief profiles below. These may help you determine a prep mode.

You're a Full-Year Prep Student (Plan A) if

1. You are the kind of person who likes to plan for everything very far in advance.
2. You arrive at the airport two hours before your flight because "you never know when these planes might leave early."
3. You like detailed planning and everything in its place.
4. You feel that you must be thoroughly prepared.
5. You hate surprises.

You're a One-Semester Prep Student (Plan B) if

1. You get to the airport one hour before your flight is scheduled to leave.
2. You are willing to plan ahead to feel comfortable in stressful situations, but are okay with skipping some details.
3. You feel more comfortable when you know what to expect, but a surprise or two is cool.
4. You're always on time for appointments.

You're a Six-Week Prep Student (Plan C) if

1. You get to the airport just as your plane is announcing its final boarding.
2. You work best under pressure and tight deadlines.
3. You feel very confident with the skills and background you've learned in your AP Biology class.
4. You decided late in the year to take the exam.
5. You like surprises.
6. You feel okay if you arrive 10–15 minutes late for an appointment.

General Outline of Three Different Study Plans

MONTH	PLAN A: FULL SCHOOL YEAR	PLAN B: ONE SEMESTER	PLAN C: SIX WEEKS
September–October	Introduction to material	—	—
November	Chapters 5–6 (Units 1–2)	—	—
December	Chapters 7–8 (Units 3–4)	—	—
January	Chapter 9 (Unit 5)	Chapters 5–6 (Units 1–2)	—
February	Chapter 10 (Unit 6)	Chapters 7–8 (Units 3–4)	—
March	Chapter 11 (Unit 7)	Chapters 9–10 (Units 5–6)	—
April	Chapters 12–13 (Unit 8 & Labs); Practice Exam 1	Chapters 11–13; (Units 7–8 & Labs); Practice Exam 1	Skim Chapters 5–10; all Rapid Review sections; Practice Exam 1
May	Review everything; Practice Exam 2	Review everything; Practice Exam 2	Skip Chapters 11–13; all Rapid Review sections; Practice Exam 2

Calendar for Each Plan

Plan A: You Have a Full School Year to Prepare

Although its primary purpose is to prepare you for the AP Biology exam you will
take in May, this book can enrich your study of biology, your analytical skills,
and your scientific essay-writing skills.

SEPTEMBER–OCTOBER (Check off the activities as you complete them.)
— Determine the study mode (A, B, or C) that applies to you.
— Carefully read Steps 1 and 2 of this book.
— Pay close attention to your walk-through of the Diagnostic Exam.
— Get on the web and take a look at the AP website(s).
— Skim the comprehensive review section (Step 4). (Reviewing the topics covered in this section will be part of your yearlong preparation.)
— Buy a few color highlighters.
— Flip through the entire book. Break the book in. Write in it. Toss it around a little bit . . . highlight it.
— Get a clear picture of what your own school's AP Biology curriculum is.
— Begin to use the book as a resource to supplement your classroom learning.

NOVEMBER (the first 10 weeks have elapsed)
— Read and study Chapter 5, Chemistry of Life.
— Read and study Chapter 6, Cell Structure and Function.

DECEMBER
— Read and Study Chapter 7, Cellular Energetics
— Read and Study Chapter 8, Cell Communication and Cell Cycle.
— Review Chapters 5–6.

JANUARY (20 weeks have elapsed)
— Read and study Chapter 9, Heredity.
— Review Chapters 5–8.

FEBRUARY
— Read and study Chapter 10, Molecular Genetics.
— Review Chapters 5–9.

MARCH (30 weeks have now elapsed)
— Read and study Chapter 11, Evolution.
— Review Chapters 5–10.

APRIL
— Take Practice Exam 1 in the first week of April.
— Evaluate your strengths and weaknesses.
— Study appropriate chapters to correct your weaknesses.
— Read and study Chapter 12, Ecology.
— Read and study Chapter 13, Laboratory Review.
— Review Chapters 1–11.

MAY (first 2 weeks) (THIS IS IT!)
— Review Chapters 5–13—all the material!
— Take Practice Exam 2.
— Score yourself.
— Get a good night's sleep before the exam. Fall asleep knowing that you are well prepared.

GOOD LUCK ON THE TEST!

Plan B: You Have One Semester to Prepare

Working under the assumption that you've completed one semester of biology studies, the following calendar will use those skills you've been practicing to prepare you for the May exam.

JANUARY
— Carefully read Steps 1 and 2 of this book.
— Take the Diagnostic Exam.
— Pay close attention to your walk-through of the Diagnostic Exam.
— Read and study Chapter 5, Chemistry of Life.
— Read and study Chapter 6, Cell Structure and Function.

FEBRUARY
— Read and study Chapter 7, Cellular Energetics.
— Read and study Chapter 8, Cell Communication.
— Review Chapters 5–6.

MARCH (10 weeks to go)
— Read and study Chapter 9, Heredity.
— Read and study Chapter 10, Molecular Genetics.
— Review Chapters 5–8.

APRIL
— Take Practice Exam 1 in the first week of April.
— Evaluate your strengths and weaknesses.
— Study appropriate chapters to correct your weaknesses.
— Read and study Chapter 11, Evolution.
— Read and study Chapter 12, Ecology.
— Read and study Chapter 13, Laboratory Review.
— Review Chapters 5–10.

MAY (first 2 weeks) (THIS IS IT!)
— Review Chapters 5–13, all the material!
— Take Practice Exam 2.
— Score yourself.
— Get a good night's sleep before the exam. Fall asleep knowing that you are well prepared.

GOOD LUCK ON THE TEST!

Plan C: You Have Six Weeks to Prepare

At this point, we assume that you have been building your biology knowledge
base for more than six months. You will, therefore, use this book primarily
as a specific guide to the AP Biology exam.
Given the time constraints, now is not the time to try to expand your
AP Biology curriculum. Rather, you should focus on and refine
what you already know.

APRIL 1–15
— Skim Steps 1 and 2 of this book.
— Skim Chapters 5–7.
— Carefully go over the Rapid Review sections of Chapters 5–9.
— Complete Practice Exam 1.
— Score yourself and analyze your errors.
— Skim and highlight the Glossary at the end of the book.

APRIL 16–MAY 1
— Skim Chapters 8–10.
— Carefully go over the Rapid Review sections of Chapters 8–10.

— Carefully go over the Rapid Review for Chapters 5–7.
— Continue to skim and highlight the Glossary.

MAY (first 2 weeks) (THIS IS IT!)
— Skim Chapters 11–13.
— Carefully go over the Rapid Review sections of Chapters 11–13.
— Complete Practice Exam 2.
— Score and analyze your errors.
— Get a good night's sleep. Fall asleep knowing that you are well prepared.

GOOD LUCK ON THE TEST!

STEP **2**

Determine Your Test Readiness

CHAPTER **3**   Take a Diagnostic Exam

CHAPTER 3

Take a Diagnostic Exam

IN THIS CHAPTER

Summary: In the following pages, you will find a diagnostic exam. It is intended to give you an idea of your level of preparation in biology. After you have completed the test, check your answers against the given answers.

Key Ideas

- ✪ Practice the kind of multiple-choice questions you might be asked on the real exam.
- ✪ Answer questions that approximate the coverage of themes on the real exam.
- ✪ Check your work against the given answers.
- ✪ Determine your areas of strength and weakness.
- ✪ Highlight the concepts to which you must give special attention.

Answer Sheet for Diagnostic Exam in AP Biology

MULTIPLE-CHOICE QUESTIONS

1 Ⓐ Ⓑ Ⓒ Ⓓ	22 Ⓐ Ⓑ Ⓒ Ⓓ	43 Ⓐ Ⓑ Ⓒ Ⓓ
2 Ⓐ Ⓑ Ⓒ Ⓓ	23 Ⓐ Ⓑ Ⓒ Ⓓ	44 Ⓐ Ⓑ Ⓒ Ⓓ
3 Ⓐ Ⓑ Ⓒ Ⓓ	24 Ⓐ Ⓑ Ⓒ Ⓓ	45 Ⓐ Ⓑ Ⓒ Ⓓ
4 Ⓐ Ⓑ Ⓒ Ⓓ	25 Ⓐ Ⓑ Ⓒ Ⓓ	46 Ⓐ Ⓑ Ⓒ Ⓓ
5 Ⓐ Ⓑ Ⓒ Ⓓ	26 Ⓐ Ⓑ Ⓒ Ⓓ	47 Ⓐ Ⓑ Ⓒ Ⓓ
6 Ⓐ Ⓑ Ⓒ Ⓓ	27 Ⓐ Ⓑ Ⓒ Ⓓ	48 Ⓐ Ⓑ Ⓒ Ⓓ
7 Ⓐ Ⓑ Ⓒ Ⓓ	28 Ⓐ Ⓑ Ⓒ Ⓓ	49 Ⓐ Ⓑ Ⓒ Ⓓ
8 Ⓐ Ⓑ Ⓒ Ⓓ	29 Ⓐ Ⓑ Ⓒ Ⓓ	50 Ⓐ Ⓑ Ⓒ Ⓓ
9 Ⓐ Ⓑ Ⓒ Ⓓ	30 Ⓐ Ⓑ Ⓒ Ⓓ	51 Ⓐ Ⓑ Ⓒ Ⓓ
10 Ⓐ Ⓑ Ⓒ Ⓓ	31 Ⓐ Ⓑ Ⓒ Ⓓ	52 Ⓐ Ⓑ Ⓒ Ⓓ
11 Ⓐ Ⓑ Ⓒ Ⓓ	32 Ⓐ Ⓑ Ⓒ Ⓓ	53 Ⓐ Ⓑ Ⓒ Ⓓ
12 Ⓐ Ⓑ Ⓒ Ⓓ	33 Ⓐ Ⓑ Ⓒ Ⓓ	54 Ⓐ Ⓑ Ⓒ Ⓓ
13 Ⓐ Ⓑ Ⓒ Ⓓ	34 Ⓐ Ⓑ Ⓒ Ⓓ	55 Ⓐ Ⓑ Ⓒ Ⓓ
14 Ⓐ Ⓑ Ⓒ Ⓓ	35 Ⓐ Ⓑ Ⓒ Ⓓ	56 Ⓐ Ⓑ Ⓒ Ⓓ
15 Ⓐ Ⓑ Ⓒ Ⓓ	36 Ⓐ Ⓑ Ⓒ Ⓓ	57 Ⓐ Ⓑ Ⓒ Ⓓ
16 Ⓐ Ⓑ Ⓒ Ⓓ	37 Ⓐ Ⓑ Ⓒ Ⓓ	58 Ⓐ Ⓑ Ⓒ Ⓓ
17 Ⓐ Ⓑ Ⓒ Ⓓ	38 Ⓐ Ⓑ Ⓒ Ⓓ	59 Ⓐ Ⓑ Ⓒ Ⓓ
18 Ⓐ Ⓑ Ⓒ Ⓓ	39 Ⓐ Ⓑ Ⓒ Ⓓ	60 Ⓐ Ⓑ Ⓒ Ⓓ
19 Ⓐ Ⓑ Ⓒ Ⓓ	40 Ⓐ Ⓑ Ⓒ Ⓓ	
20 Ⓐ Ⓑ Ⓒ Ⓓ	41 Ⓐ Ⓑ Ⓒ Ⓓ	
21 Ⓐ Ⓑ Ⓒ Ⓓ	42 Ⓐ Ⓑ Ⓒ Ⓓ	

DIAGNOSTIC EXAM: AP BIOLOGY: SECTION I

MULTIPLE-CHOICE QUESTIONS

Time—1 hour and 30 minutes

For the multiple-choice questions that follow, select the best answer and fill in the appropriate letter on the answer sheet.

1. A pH of 10 is how many times more basic than a pH of 7?

   A. 10
   B. 100
   C. 1,000
   D. 10,000

2. Destruction of microfilaments would most adversely affect which of the following?

   A. Cell division
   B. Cilia
   C. Flagella
   D. Muscular contraction

3. Imagine that for a particular species of moth, females are primed to respond to two types of male mating calls. Males who produce an in-between version will not succeed at obtaining a mate and will therefore have low reproductive success. This is an example of

   A. directional selection.
   B. stabilizing selection.
   C. artificial selection.
   D. disruptive selection.

4. Crossover occurs during

   A. prophase of mitosis.
   B. prophase I of meiosis.
   C. prophase II of meiosis.
   D. prophase I and II of meiosis.

5. Which of the following is a specialized feature of plants that live in hot and dry regions?

   A. Stomata that open and close
   B. Transpiration
   C. Photophosphorylation
   D. C_4 photosynthesis

6. A virus that carries the reverse transcriptase enzyme is a

   A. retrovirus.
   B. prion.
   C. viroid.
   D. DNA virus.

7. Ants live on acacia trees and are able to feast on the sugar produced by the trees. The tree is protected by the ants' attack on any foreign insects that may harm the tree. This is an example of

   A. parasitism.
   B. commensalism.
   C. mutualism.
   D. symbiosis.

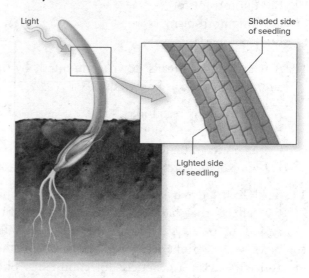

8. What process is taking place in the plant to cause its behavioral and physiological response?

   A. Phototropism
   B. Gravitropism
   C. Photomorphogenesis
   D. Circadian rhythms

9. The vine in the figure above is exhibiting what behavioral response?

A. Gravitropism
B. Phototropism
C. Thigmotropism
D. Photoperiodism

10. A reaction that breaks down compounds by the addition of water is known as

A. a hydrolysis reaction.
B. a dehydration reaction.
C. an endergonic reaction.
D. an exergonic reaction.

11. Sickle cell anemia is a mutation in hemoglobin that affects the shape of red blood cells during periods of low oxygenation. Sickle cell anemia displays recessive inheritance. An expecting mother and father visit a geneticist for counseling. Both parents are carriers of the sickle cell trait. Calculate the likelihood that their child is a carrier.

A. 0.75
B. 0.50
C. 0.25
D. 0.65

12. Dwarfism is an autosomal dominant disease. A couple has sought out genetic counseling as they prepare to start a family. They want to have two biological children. One parent has been diagnosed with dwarfism (Dd); the second parent is healthy (dd). Calculate the probability that both children have dwarfism.

A. 0.25
B. 0.50
C. 0.75
D. 0.15

13. A population of mice is in Hardy-Weinberg equilibrium. The recessive phenotype is found in 1 out of every 2,500 mice. Calculate the percentage of the heterozygous phenotype.

A. 0.02
B. 0.04
C. 0.98
D. 0.40

14. Which of the following is an example of aneuploidy?

A. Cri-du-chat syndrome
B. Chronic myelogenous leukemia
C. Turner syndrome
D. Achondroplasia

15. Among the following choices, which one would most readily move through a selectively permeable membrane?

A. Small, uncharged polar molecule
B. Large, uncharged polar molecule
C. Glucose
D. Sodium ion

16. Which of the following is not a lipid?

A. Steroid
B. Fat
C. Phospholipid
D. Glycogen

17. Which of the following hormones is *not* released by the anterior pituitary gland?

A. Follicle-stimulating hormone (FSH)
B. Antidiuretic hormone (ADH)
C. Growth hormone (GH or STH)
D. Adrenocorticotropic hormone (ACTH)

18. Which of the following is the *least* specific taxonomic classification category?

A. Division
B. Order
C. Family
D. Genus

19. Which cells control the opening and closing of a plant's stomata?

A. Guard cells
B. Collenchyma cells
C. Parenchyma cells
D. Mesophyll cells

20. Imagine that 9 percent of a population of anteaters have a short snout (recessive), while 91 percent have a long snout (dominant). If this population is in Hardy-Weinberg equilibrium, what is the expected frequency (in percent) of the heterozygous condition?

A. 30.0
B. 34.0
C. 38.0
D. 42.0

21. The situation in which a gene at one locus alters the phenotypic expression of a gene at another locus is known as

A. incomplete dominance.
B. codominance.
C. pleiotropy.
D. epistasis.

22. The oxygen produced during the light reactions of photosynthesis comes directly from

A. H_2O.
B. H_2O_2.
C. $C_2H_3O_2$.
D. CO_2.

23. A population of fruit flies is in Hardy-Weinberg equilibrium. The allele for black eyes (B) is dominant to the red allele (b). The recessive phenotype is seen in 36 percent of the population. Calculate the frequency of the dominant allele.

A. 0.40
B. 0.36
C. 0.60
D. 0.18

24. The presence of which of the following organelles or structures would most convincingly indicate that a cell is a eukaryote and not a prokaryote?

A. Plasma membrane
B. Cell wall
C. Lysosome
D. Ribosome

25. Traits that are similar between organisms that arose from a common ancestor are known as

A. convergent.
B. homologous.
C. vestigial.
D. divergent.

26. The process by which a huge amount of DNA is created from a small amount of DNA in a very short amount of time is known as

A. cloning.
B. transformation.
C. a polymerase chain reaction.
D. gel electrophoresis.

27. A compound contains a COOH group. What functional group is that?

A. Carbonyl group
B. Carboxyl group
C. Hydroxyl group
D. Phosphate group

28. Which of the following forms of cell transport requires the input of energy?

A. Diffusion
B. Osmosis
C. Facilitated diffusion
D. Active transport

29. Homologous chromosomes are chromosomes that

A. are found only in identical twins.
B. are formed during mitosis.
C. split apart during meiosis II.
D. resemble one another in shape, size, and function.

30. Which of the following is an incorrect statement about DNA replication?

A. It occurs in the nucleus.
B. It occurs in a semiconservative fashion.
C. Helicase is the enzyme that adds the nucleotides to the growing strand.
D. DNA polymerase can build only in a 5′-to-3′ direction.

31. Warning coloration adopted by animals that possess a chemical defense mechanism is known as

A. cryptic coloration.
B. deceptive markings.
C. aposematic coloration.
D. Batesian mimicry.

32. In a large pond that consists of long-finned fish and short-finned fish, a tornado wreaks havoc on the pond, killing 50 percent of the fish population. By chance, most of the fish killed were short-finned varieties, and in the subsequent generation there were fewer fish with short fins. This is an example of

A. gene flow.
B. bottleneck.
C. balanced polymorphism.
D. allopatric speciation.

33. Which of the following structures would not have developed from the mesoderm?

A. Muscle
B. Heart
C. Kidneys
D. Liver

34. In a certain breed of dog, the allele for red-colored tongue (T) is dominant to the allele for purple tongue (t). A researcher collected data on 48 dogs bred from a cross between a red-tongued dog and a purple-tongued dog. Of the 48 offspring, 36 had red tongues, and 12 had purple tongues. Calculate the chi-squared value for the null hypothesis, assuming that the red-tongued dog was heterozygous for the tongue-color gene.

Chi-Square Significance Table

DEGREE OF FREEDOM (n)	5% PROBABILITY VALUE (P)
1	3.84
2	5.99
3	7.81
4	9.49

A. 24
B. 48
C. 12
D. 6

35. The cyclic pathway of photosynthesis occurs because

A. the Calvin cycle uses more ATP than NADPH.
B. it can occur in regions lacking light.
C. it is a more efficient way to produce oxygen.
D. it is a more efficient way to produce the NADPH needed for the Calvin cycle.

36. Which of the following conditions is an X-linked condition?

A. Hemophilia
B. Tay-Sachs disease
C. Cystic fibrosis
D. Sickle cell anemia

37. The uptake of foreign DNA from the surrounding environment is known as

A. generalized transduction.
B. specialized transduction.
C. conjugation.
D. transformation.

38. Most of the digestion of food occurs in the

A. esophagus.
B. stomach.
C. small intestine.
D. large intestine.

39. You have just come back from visiting the redwood forests in California and were amazed at how *wide* those trees were. What process is responsible for the increase in width of these trees?

A. Growth of guard cells
B. Growth of collenchyma cells
C. Growth of apical meristem cells
D. Growth of lateral meristem cells

40. The trophoblast formed during the early stages of human embryology eventually develops into the

A. placenta.
B. embryo.
C. hypoblast.
D. morula.

41. What biome is known for having the greatest diversity of species?

A. Taiga
B. Temperate grasslands
C. Tropical forest
D. Savanna

42. In hypercholesterolemia, a genetic condition found in humans, individuals who are HH have normal cholesterol levels, those who are hh have horrifically high cholesterol levels, and those who are Hh have cholesterol levels that are somewhere in between. This is an example of

A. dominance.
B. incomplete dominance.
C. codominance.
D. epistasis.

43. The light-dependent reactions of photosynthesis occur in the

A. nucleus.
B. cytoplasm.
C. thylakoid membrane.
D. stroma.

44. Which of the following is a characteristic of an R-selected strategist?

A. Low reproductive rate
B. Extensive postnatal care
C. Relatively constant population size
D. J-shaped growth curve

45. Which of the following statements about mitosis is correct?

A. Mitosis makes up 30 percent of the cell cycle.
B. The order of mitosis is prophase, anaphase, metaphase, and telophase.
C. Single-cell eukaryotes undergo mitosis as part of asexual reproduction.
D. Cell plates are formed in animal cells during mitosis.

46. A vine that wraps around the trunk of a tree is displaying the concept known as

A. photoperiodism.
B. thigmotropism.
C. gravitropism.
D. phototropism.

47. Which hormone is known for assisting in the closing of the stomata and inhibition of cell growth?

A. Abscisic acid
B. Cytokinin
C. Ethylene
D. Gibberellin

48. During the humoral immune response, the following sequence takes place. An antigen invader → B cell meets antigen → B cell differentiates into plasma cells and memory cells → plasma cells produce antibodies → antibodies eliminate antigen. What role does the antigen play in activation and communication with the cells of the immune system?

A. Signal
B. Receptor
C. Signal transduction
D. Cellular response

49. Which reaction occurs in the mitochondria and involves the formation of ATP from NADH and $FADH_2$?

A. Glycolysis
B. Oxidative phosphorylation
C. Chemiosmosis
D. Fermentation

50. Which process couples the movement of electrons down the electron transport chain with the formation of ATP, using the driving force provided by the proton gradient?

A. Formation of acetyl CoA
B. Chemiosmosis
C. ATP synthase
D. Glycolysis

51. Which reaction occurs outside the mitochondria, whether oxygen is present or not, to produce 2 ATP, 2 NADH, and 2 pyruvate?

A. Glycolysis
B. Oxidative phosphorylation
C. Chemiosmosis
D. Fermentation

52. Cells must be able to produce usable energy regardless of oxygen being present. Which reaction is performed by cells in an effort to regenerate the NAD$^+$ required for glycolysis to continue when oxygen is not present?

    A. Glycolysis
    B. Oxidative phosphorylation
    C. Chemiosmosis
    D. Fermentation

53. What is the learning behavior exhibited by an organism as it reasons through a problem the first time with no prior experience?

    A. Associative learning
    B. Insight learning
    C. Imprinting
    D. Altruistic behavior

54. In interspecific interactions, organisms form relationships with other species in a community. When an organism helps another, even at its own expense, which is the learning behavior for the organisms?

    A. Associative learning
    B. Insight learning
    C. Imprinting
    D. Altruistic behavior

55. When an animal substitutes one stimulus for another in order to get the same result, the process is referred to as

    A. associative learning.
    B. insight learning.
    C. imprinting.
    D. altruistic behavior.

56. During the critical early life period for an organism, what innate behavior is learned?

    A. Associative learning
    B. Insight learning
    C. Imprinting
    D. Altruistic behavior

For questions 57–60, please use the information from the following laboratory experiment:

You are working as a summer intern at the local university laboratory, and a lab technician comes into your room, throws a few graphs and tables at you, and mutters, "Interpret this data for me . . . I need to go play golf. I'll be back this afternoon for your report."

Analyze the data this technician so kindly gave to you, and use it to answer questions 57–60. The reaction rates reported in the tables are relative to the original rate of the reaction in the absence of the enzymes. The three enzymes used are all being added to the same reactants to determine which should be used in the future.

Room Temperature (25°C), pH 7

ENZYME	REACTION RATE
1	1.24
2	1.51
3	1.33

Varying Temperature, Constant (pH 7)

ENZYME	0°C	5°C	10°C	15°C	20°C	25°C	30°C	35°C	40°C
1	1.00	1.02	1.04	1.19	1.20	1.24	1.29	1.27	1.22
2	1.01	1.12	1.35	1.39	1.65	1.51	1.40	1.12	1.01
3	1.06	1.21	1.55	1.44	1.35	1.33	1.15	1.10	1.06

Varying pH, Constant Temperature = 25°C

ENZYME	4	5	6	7	8	9	10
1	1.54	1.51	1.33	1.24	1.20	1.08	1.05
2	1.75	1.71	1.62	1.51	1.32	1.10	1.01
3	1.52	1.45	1.40	1.33	1.20	1.09	1.04

57. If you had also been given a graph that plotted the moles of product produced versus time, what would have been the best way to calculate the rate for the reaction?

- A. Calculate the average of the slope of the curve for the first and last minute of reaction.
- B. Calculate the slope of the curve for the portion of the curve that is constant.
- C. Calculate the slope of the curve for the portion where the slope begins to flatten out.
- D. Add up the total number of moles produced during each time interval and divide by the total number of time intervals measured.

58. Over the interval measured, at what temperature does enzyme 2 appear to have its optimal efficiency?

- A. 10°C
- B. 15°C
- C. 20°C
- D. 25°C

59. Which of the following statements about enzyme 3 is incorrect?

- A. At a pH of 6 and a temperature of 25°C, it is more efficient than enzyme 2 but less efficient than enzyme 1.
- B. It functions more efficiently in the acidic pH range than the basic pH range.
- C. At 30°C and a pH of 7, it is less efficient than both enzymes 1 and 2.
- D. Over the interval given, its optimal temperature at a pH of 7 is 10°C.

60. Which of the following statements can be made from review of these data?

- A. Enzyme 1 functions most efficiently in a basic environment and at a lower temperature.
- B. Enzyme 1 functions more efficiently than enzyme 2 at 10°C and a pH of 7.
- C. The pH does not affect the efficiency of enzyme 3.
- D. All three enzymes function more efficiently in an acidic environment than a basic environment.

AP Biology Diagnostic Exam: Section II

FREE-RESPONSE QUESTIONS

Time-1 hour and 30 minutes

(The first 10 minutes is a reading period. Do not begin writing until the 10-minute period has passed.)
Questions 1 and 2 are long free-response questions that should require about 20–25 minutes each.
Questions 3–6 are short-response questions that should require approximately 8–10 minutes each.
Outline form is not acceptable. Answers should be in essay form.

1. Huntington's disease is a genetic illness that leads to degeneration of the central nervous system. Symptoms typically do not present until between 30 and 40 years of age.

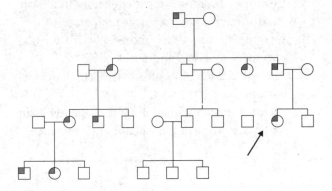

A. The pedigree on the left shows a family with Huntington's disease in its gene pool. The gray marks indicate the individuals that have Huntington's disease. **Describe** the pattern of inheritance shown and **explain** your reasoning.

B. The couple indicated by the arrow are planning to have a child. Assuming that the husband is healthy, **construct** a Punnett square to demonstrate the risk of inheritance for their offspring.

C. A randomized trial is conducted to examine whether the drug "Lauder" delays the emergence of symptoms among individuals who carry the genetic traits for inheritance. The age for the first emergence of symptoms is shown in the table provided. **Construct** an appropriately labeled graph of the average age of the onset of symptoms.

D. **Predict** what would happen if the family members in the pedigree were to all take the drug Lauder. **Justify** your prediction.

DRUG	PATIENT 1	PATIENT 2	PATIENT 3	PATIENT 4	PATIENT 5	PATIENT 6	MEAN	+2 SEM
Control	32	29	41				34	5.72
Lauder, 50 mg				47	46	42	45	2.42

2. Adequate nutrition intake, along with absorption of nutrients, is necessary for bodily functioning. Through aerobic respiration, eukaryotic organisms conduct cellular respiration in order to transfer organic molecules into usable energy in the form of adenosine triphosphate or ATP.

   A researcher is interested in the small and large intestines. Through intensive research, the scientist recognized a new syndrome that significantly reduces nutrient absorption. A new drug is then found and piloted to determine whether the newly developed drug is effective in treating patients with significantly reduced nutrient absorption. Nutrient absorption levels for each patient and the means are shown in the table.

PATIENT	CONTROL	DRUG
1	50	
2	43	
3	76	
4	34	
5		100
6		78
7		76
8		87
Mean	50.75	85.25
+2 SEM	15.64	9.48

   A. **Explain** how the ATP is produced in the mitochondria during aerobic respiration.
   B. **Identify** the independent and dependent variable in the experiment. Propose one limitation to the study.
   C. **Construct** an appropriately labeled graph of the drug's effect on nutrient absorption.
   D. **Identify** and **explain** the effectiveness of the new drug in treating patients with the syndrome.

3. Meiosis is a form of cell division in all sexually reproducing organisms during which the nucleus divides during the production of spores or gametes.
   A. **Describe** and **explain** TWO aspects of meiosis that contribute to genetic diversity.
   B. The mating of two individuals who are closely related is termed consanguineous. **Explain** how consanguinity would decrease the genetic diversity of offspring. **Justify** why this decreased diversity would be harmful to the offspring.

4. Scientists have recently discovered that the raccoon population in rural New York communicates using chemical signals via pheromones. The scientists consequently developed four pheromones in an attempt to replicate the natural pheromone. They measured the response time of five raccoons to the developed chemical compounds as an indication of chemical similarity between the developed and natural pheromones.
   A. Animals communicate through several mechanisms. **Describe** TWO methods of communication for animals.
   B. **Construct** an appropriately labeled graph to show the response time for the developed and natural pheromones for the raccoons.
   C. **Identify** which pheromones are most closely aligned to the racoon's natural producing pheromones.
   D. A follow-up study on raccoon pheromone response time is planned to determine whether response to pheromones is an innate or learned response. Response times will be compared between baby raccoons, young raccoons, and adult raccoons. **Predict** which data will show if the response to pheromones is an innate response.

5. A population of foxes and rabbits in Environment A exhibits the expected predator–prey population curve seen below.

   A. **Explain** the relationship represented by predator and prey in the graph.

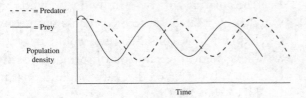

   B. A bacterial pathogen completely wipes out the population of foxes. Researchers closely watch the rabbit population and notice a new population fluctuation. **Identify** and **explain** this change in the population.

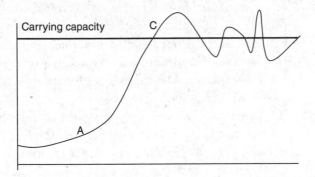

   C. **Predict** the state of the rabbit population in one year. **Justify** your prediction.

6. A population of wild cats lives in a temperate environment with four seasons. The cats have three main fur colors—white, light brown, and black.

   A scientist decides to transplant a random sample of these cats to an environment covered in snow throughout the full year. He notices that as time passes, the cats with one fur color tend to live longer and evade predators better than those with the other two fur colors.

   A. **Identify** the cats with the fur color that is expected to live longer in the new environment. **Justify** your reasoning.

   B. The scientist is also interested in better understanding the evolutionary relationships between the wild cats and several other wild species. Using the data collected on various traits by the scientist, **construct** a visual representation of the evolutionary relationships.

Species	TRAIT A	TRAIT B	TRAIT C
Animal 1	+	−	−
Animal 2	+	−	+
Animal 3	+	+	+
Animal 4	−	−	−

   C. A volcano erupts in the ecosystem that contains the wild cat population. **Predict** how this would impact the population. **Justify** your prediction.

› Answers and Explanations

MULTIPLE-CHOICE QUESTIONS

1. C—This question deals with the concept of pH: acids and bases. The pH scale is a logarithmic scale that measures how acidic or basic a solution is. A pH of 4 is 10 times more acidic than a pH of 5. A pH of 6 is 10^2 or 100 times more basic than a pH of 4, and so on. Therefore, a pH of 10 is 10^3, or 1,000 times more basic than a pH of 7.

2. D—This question deals with the cytoskeleton of cells. Cell division, cilia, and flagella would be compromised if the *microtubules* were damaged. Microfilaments, made from actin, are important to muscular contraction. Chitin is a polysaccharide found in fungi.

3. D—This is a prime example of disruptive selection. Take a look at the material from Chapter 11 on the various types of selection. The illustrations there are worth reviewing.

4. B—You have to know this fact. We don't want them to get you on this one if they ask it. ☺

5. D—C_4 photosynthesis is an adaptive photosynthetic process that attempts to counter the problems that hot and dry weather causes for plants. Be sure that you read about and understand the various forms of photosynthesis for the exam.

6. A—Retroviruses are RNA viruses that carry with them the reverse transcriptase enzyme. When they take over a host cell, they first use the enzyme to convert themselves into DNA. They next incorporate into the DNA of the host, and begin the process of viral replication. The HIV virus of AIDS is a well-known retrovirus.

7. C—Mutualism is the interaction in which both parties involved benefit.

8. A—Phototropism is a plant's growth in response to light. Auxin is the hormone involved in this process.

9. C—Thigmotropism is a plant's growth in response to touch.

10. A—This question deals with five types of reactions you should be familiar with for the AP Biology exam. A hydrolysis reaction is one in which water is added, causing the formation of a compound.

11. B—0.50

Let H^A = healthy and H^C = sickle cell trait

	H^A	H^C
H^A	$H^A H^A$	$H^A H^C$
H^C	$H^A H^C$	$H^C H^C$

The child will have a 25 percent chance of being healthy, a 50 percent chance of being a carrier, and a 25 percent chance of having sickle cell anemia.

12. A—0.25

First, determine the risk for one child of inheriting dwarfism. Since this is an autosomal dominant disease, the child needs to inherit only one dominant allele (Dd) to express the disease.

	D	d
d	Dd	dd
d	Dd	dd

The Punnett square demonstrates that each child has a 50 percent (or ½) chance of inheriting the dominant allele. The couple wants to know the probability that their two children BOTH will have dwarfism. To calculate the probability that both children inherit the dominant allele, multiply the probability of each individual event.

$$½ * ½ = ¼$$

Thus, the probability of both children being diagnosed with dwarfism is 25 percent, or ¼.

13. B—0.04

There are two main Hardy-Weinberg equations: $p + q = 1$ AND $p^2 + 2pq + q^2 = 1$.

p and q represent the frequency of the dominant and recessive alleles, respectively. p^2 and q^2 represent the frequency of the homozygous dominant and homozygous recessive phenotypes respectively. Lastly, $2pq$ represents the frequency of the heterozygous phenotype.

Hardy-Weinberg problems often start by providing information about the recessive phenotype.

In this case, we know that the recessive phenotype is in 1 out of every 2,500 mice; we can turn this into a frequency by creating a fraction: $1/2{,}500 = 0.0004$. This frequency is the homozygous recessive phenotype; thus we can equate $q^2 = 0.0004$.

The question asks for the frequency of the heterozygous phenotype (represented by $2pq$ above). Using our finding $q^2 = 0.0004$, we can determine the value of $2pq$.

$$q^2 = 0.0004$$

So, $q = 0.02$.

To calculate p, we can use the equation: $p + q = 1$. Plugging in $q = 0.02 \rightarrow p + 0.02 = 1 \rightarrow p = 0.98$.

Now to calculate $2pq$ (frequency of the heterozygous phenotype), plug in the known values: $2(0.98)(0.02) = 0.04$. In other words, 4 percent of the population is heterozygous.

14. **C**—Turner syndrome (XO) is an example of aneuploidy—conditions in which individuals have an abnormal number of chromosomes. These conditions can be monosomies, as is the case with Turner, or they can be trisomies, as is the case with Down, Klinefelter, and other syndromes.

15. **A**—The selectively permeable membrane is a lipid bilayer composed of phospholipids, proteins, and other macromolecules. Small, uncharged polar molecules and lipids are able to pass through these membranes without difficulty.

16. **D**—Glycogen is a carbohydrate. The three major types of lipids you should know are fats, phospholipids, and steroids. Cholesterol is a type of steroid.

17. **B**—This hormone, which is involved in controlling the function of the kidney, is released from the posterior pituitary.

18. **A**—The stupid phrase we use to remember this classification hierarchy is "Karaoke players can order free grape soda"—kingdom, phylum, class, order, family, genus, and species. This question is sneaky because it requires you to know that a division is the plant kingdom's version of

the phylum. The kingdom is the least specific subdivision, and the species the most specific. Therefore, A is the correct answer.

19. **A**—Guard cells are the cells responsible for controlling the opening and closing of the stomata of a plant.

20. **D**—If 9 percent of the population is recessive (ss), then $q^2 = 0.09$. Taking the square root of 0.09 gives us $q = 0.30$. Knowing as we do that $p + q = 1$, $p + 0.30 = 1$, and $p = 0.70$. The frequency of the heterozygous condition $= 2pq = 2(0.30)(0.70) = 42$ percent.

21. **D**—Epistasis exists when a gene at one locus affects a gene at another locus.

22. **A**—The inputs to the light reactions include light and water. During these reactions, photolysis occurs, which is the splitting of H_2O into hydrogen ions and oxygen atoms. These oxygen atoms from the water pair together immediately to form the oxygen we breathe.

23. **A**—0.40

Much of the logic from the previous problem will apply here. To reiterate, there are two main Hardy-Weinberg equations: $p + q = 1$ AND $p^2 + 2pq + q^2 = 1$. p and q represent the frequency of the dominant and recessive alleles, respectively. p^2 and q^2 represent the frequency of the homozygous dominant and homozygous recessive phenotypes, respectively. Lastly, $2pq$ represents the frequency of the heterozygous phenotype.

If 36 percent of the population is the recessive phenotype, $q^2 = 0.36$; thus, $q = 0.6$.

We want the value of p, the dominant allele. We can use: $p + q = 1$.

With $q = 0.6 \rightarrow p + 0.6 = 1 \rightarrow p = 0.4$.

The frequency of the dominant allele is thus 40 percent.

24. **C**—Prokaryotes are known for their simplicity. They do not contain a nucleus, nor do they contain membrane-bound organelles. They do have a few structures to remember: cell wall, plasma membrane, ribosomes, and a nucleoid. Lysosomes are found in eukaryotes, not prokaryotes.

25. **B**—Traits are said to be homologous if they are similar because their host organisms arose from a common ancestor. For example, the bone structure in bird wings is homologous in all bird species.

26. **C**—Polymerase chain reaction is the high-speed cloning machine of molecular genetics. It occurs at a much faster rate than does cloning.

27. **B**—Functional groups are a pain in the neck. But you need to be able to recognize them on the exam. Most often, the test asks students to identify functional groups by structure.

28. **D**—Active transport requires energy. The major types of cell transport you need to know for the exam are diffusion, osmosis, facilitated diffusion, endocytosis, exocytosis, and active transport.

29. **D**—Homologous chromosomes resemble one another in shape, size, and function. They pair up during meiosis and separate from each other during meiosis I.

30. **C**—DNA polymerase is the superstar enzyme of the replication process, which occurs during the S phase of the cell cycle in the nucleus of a cell. The process does occur in semiconservative fashion. You should learn the basic concepts behind replication as they are explained in Chapter 10.

31. **C**—Learn the defense mechanisms well from predator–prey relationships in Chapter 12. They will be represented on the exam.

32. **B**—A bottleneck is a specific example of genetic drift: the sudden change in allele frequencies due to random events.

33. **D**—You should learn the list of structures derived from endoderm, mesoderm, and ectoderm. (This could be an easy multiple-choice question for you if you do.)

34. **C**—12

We are given the observed values in the question prompt. Now you need to calculate the expected phenotypes utilizing a Punnett square. The question stem has provided that the cross is between a heterozygous red-tongued dog (Tt) and a purple-tongued dog (tt).

	T	t
t	Tt	tt
t	Tt	tt

The Punnett square suggests that this cross would lead to 50 percent red tongue, 50 percent white tongue. Out of 48 dogs, 24 would have a red tongue, and 24 would have a purple tongue.

For two options, the degree of freedom is 1. Since the chi-squared value of 12 is larger than the 5 percent probability value of 3.84, the data does not follow predicted values and is statistically significant. Discard the null hypothesis.

Phenotype	# Observed (o)	# Expected (e)	o − e	$\dfrac{(o-e)^2}{e}$
Red tongue	36	24	12	$\dfrac{(12)^2}{24}=6$
Purple tongue	12	24	−12	$\dfrac{(-12)^2}{24}=6$
TOTAL	48	48		SUM = 12

35. **A**—The Calvin cycle uses a disproportionate amount of ATP relative to NADPH. The cyclic light reactions exist to make up for this disparity. The cyclic reactions do not produce NADPH, nor do they produce oxygen.

36. **A**—Tay-Sachs disease, cystic fibrosis, and sickle cell anemia are all autosomal recessive conditions. It will serve you well to learn the most common autosomal recessive conditions, X-linked conditions, and autosomal dominant conditions.

37. **D**—It will serve you well for this exam to be reasonably familiar with biotechnology laboratory techniques. Lab procedures show up often on free-response questions and the later multiple-choice sections of the exam.

38. **C**—The small intestine hosts the most digestion of the digestive tract.

39. **D**—This is known as *cambium*.

40. **A**—The inner cell mass gives rise to the embryo, which eventually gives rise to the epiblast and hypoblast. The morula is an early stage of development.

41. **C**—Biomes are annoying and tough to memorize. Learn as much as you can about them without taking up too much time. More often than not there will be two to three multiple-choice questions about them. But you want to make sure you learn enough to work your way through a free-response question if you were to be so unfortunate as to have one on your test.

42. **B**—Incomplete dominance is the situation in which the heterozygous genotype produces an "intermediate" phenotype rather than the dominant phenotype; neither allele dominates the other.

43. **C**—The light-dependent reactions occur in the thylakoid membrane. The dark reactions, known as the *Calvin cycle*, occur in the stroma.

44. **D**—A J-shaped growth curve is characteristic of exponentially growing populations. That is a characteristic of R-selected strategists.

45. **C**—Mitosis makes up 10 percent of the cell cycle; the correct order of the stages is prophase, metaphase, anaphase, and telophase; mitosis is not performed by prokaryotic cells; and cell plates are formed in plant cells.

46. **B**—Thigmotropism, phototropism, and gravitropism are the major tropisms you need to know for plants. Thigmotropism, the growth response of a plant to touch, is the least understood of the bunch.

47. **A**—There are five plant hormones you should know for the exam. Auxin seems to come up the most, but it would serve you well to know the basic functions of all five of them.

48. **A**—An antigen is a molecule that is foreign to our bodies and acts as a signal molecule that cause an immune response.

49. **B**—Each NADH is able to produce up to 3 ATP. Each FADH2 can produce up to 2 ATP.

50. **B**—You have to know the concept of chemiosmosis for the AP exam. Make sure you study it well.

51. **A**—Glycolysis is the conversion of glucose into pyruvate that occurs in the cytoplasm and is the first step of both aerobic and anaerobic respiration.

52. **D**—Fermentation is anaerobic respiration, and it is the process that begins with glycolysis and ends with the regeneration of NAD^+.

53. **B**

54. **D**

55. **A**

56. **C**

57. **B**—The rate of reaction for an enzyme-aided reaction is best estimated by taking the slope of the constant portion of the moles–time plot.

58. **C**—They will test your ability to interpret data on this exam. You should make sure that you are able to look at a chart and interpret information given to you. This enzyme does indeed function most efficiently at 20°C. Above and below that temperature, the reaction rate is lower.

59. **A**—At a pH of 6 and a temperature of 25°C, enzyme 3 is actually LESS efficient than enzyme 2 and MORE efficient than enzyme 1.

60. **D**—This question requires you to know that a pH below 7 (pH < 7) is acidic and a pH above 7 (pH > 7) is basic. It is true that all three enzymes increase the rate of reaction more when in acidic environments than basic environments.

› Free-Response Grading Outline

1.

A. The pedigree shows a family with Huntington's disease in its gene pool. The grey marks indicate the individuals that has Huntington's disease. **Describe** the pattern of inheritance shown and **explain** your reasoning.

2 Points – Autosomal dominance inheritance is suspected. Looking at the pedigree, each generation is affected by the illness, which supports dominant as opposed to recessive inheritance. Recessive inheritance would instead show frequent skipping of generations in the pedigree. Autosomal as opposed to sex-linked inheritance is suspected, since males and females are equally affected.

B. The couple indicated by the arrow are planning to have a child. Assuming that the husband is healthy, **construct** a Punnett square to demonstrate the risk of inheritance for their offspring.

2 Points – To create the Punnett square, we need to determine whether the individual in row 5 is homozygous or heterozygous for the trait. Since one of her parents is unaffected, we can assume she is heterozygous. We are also told that her husband is healthy and, thus, homozygous recessive.

	H	h
h	Hh	hh
h	Hh	hh

The Punnett square above suggests that each offspring maintains a 50 percent chance of inheriting the disease.

C. A randomized trial is conducted to examine whether the drug "Lauder" delays the emergence of symptoms among individuals who carried the genetic traits for inheritance. The age for first emergence of symptoms is shown in the table provided. **Construct** an appropriately labeled graph of the average age of the onset of symptoms.

1 Point – Independent and dependent variable correctly plotted
1 Point – Correctly labeled

1 Point – Correctly scaled axis

First, calculate the average age of symptom onset for each of the two conditions:

$$\text{Control} = \frac{32 + 29 + 41}{3} = 34 \text{ yrs old}$$

$$\text{Drug} = \frac{47 + 46 + 42}{3} = 45 \text{ yrs old}$$

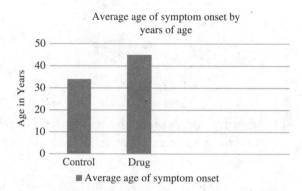

Average age of symptom onset by years of age

D. **Predict** what would happen if the family members in the pedigree were to all take the drug Lauder. **Justify** your prediction.

2 Points – By taking the drug "Lauder," the Huntington's condition would still be passed onto the next generation since the condition is genetic and would be passed onto the offspring regardless of the effects of the drug.

2.

A. **Explain** how the ATP is produced in the mitochondria during aerobic respiration.

2 Points – The electron transport chain creates a proton gradient which sends protons (H^+) out of the mitochondrial matrix using the energy carrying NADH and $FADH_2$. This proton is then allowed to flow back down through the ATP synthase and create the ATP necessary for bodily function.

B. **Identify** the independent and dependent variable in the experiment. Propose one limitation to the study.

1 Point – Independent variable – Exposure to new drug
1 Point – Dependent variable – Nutrient absorption

C. **Construct** an appropriately labeled graph of the drug's effect on nutrient absorption.

1 Point – Independent and dependent variable correctly plotted
1 Point – Correctly labeled
1 Point – Correctly scaled axis

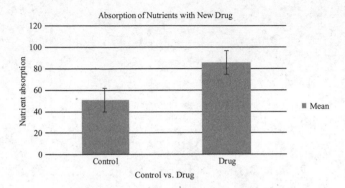

D. **Identify** and **explain** the effectiveness of the new drug in treating patients with the syndrome.

1 Point – The study suggests that the new drug has high levels of absorption than the control.
1 Point – There is a statistically significant difference between absorption of nutrients in the control and the new drug.

3.

A. **Describe** and **explain** TWO aspects of meiosis that contributes to genetic diversity.

2 Points – Two processes in meiosis that contribute to genetic diversity:
1. Crossing over between homologous chromosomes during prophase I. Complementary DNA strands are exchanged between the chromosomes.
2. *Random assortment* of homologous chromosomes at the metaphase plate. Homologous chromosomes are divided in half to become haploid cells. It is by chance on which side each pair of chromosomes from the mother and father align.

B. The mating of two individuals who are closely related is termed consanguineous. **Explain** how consanguinity would decrease the genetic diversity of offspring. **Justify** why this decreased diversity would be harmful to the offspring.

2 Points – Impact of consanguinity:
1. Genetic diversity would decrease since the mother and father maintain a more similar genetic makeup than a nonconsanguineous pairing.
2. Decreased diversity in this case could prove harmful in the case of recessive traits. For example, a trait could be rare, but since the mother and father are related, they could be more likely to both be carriers. If both parents are carriers, the probability that the child inherits one or two recessive alleles is increased.

4.

A. Animals communicate through several mechanisms. **Describe** TWO methods of communication for animals.
2 Points – Communication types include:
• Visual: the use of visual cues to relay meaning. Examples include peacock feather coloring, bared teeth, rolling over on back.
• Tactile: the use of touch to relay meaning. For example, monkeys will groom each other as a sign of affection.
• Auditory: the use of various sounds to relay meaning. For example, the frog chirps to attract a mate.
• Chemical: the use of chemical signals via pheromones. Pheromones play a significant role in animal mating.

B. **Construct** an appropriately labeled graph to show the response time for the developed and natural pheromones for the raccoons.

PHEROMONE	RACCOON 1	RACCOON 2	RACCOON 3	RACCOON 4	RACCOON 5	MEAN RESPONSE TIME	STANDARD ERROR OF THE MEAN (SEM)
I	15	13	16	7	8	11.8	1.8
II	10	8	7	11	15	10.2	1.4
III	3	6	5	9	4	5.4	1.0

C. **Identify** which pheromones are most closely aligned to the racoon's natural producing pheromones.

1 Point – Pheromone III demonstrated the fastest mean of the three pheromones tested and thus would be more likely to resemble the natural raccoon pheromones.

D. A follow-up study on raccoon pheromone response time is planned to determine whether response to pheromones is an innate or learned response. Response times will be compared between baby raccoons, young raccoons, and adult raccoons. **Predict** which data will show if the response to pheromones is an innate response.

1 Point – An innate response is a behavior that does not need to be taught. Thus, if the response to pheromones is innate, the response time of the young raccoons to the pheromones will be similar to the response time of the older raccoons.

5.

A. **Explain** the relationship represented by predator and prey in the graph.

1 Point – The curve demonstrates that the population concentrations are correlated. The foxes rely on the rabbits for food. As the foxes consume more rabbits, the fox population will grow due to higher supply levels. At some point, the rabbit population will have a higher death rate than birth rate, and thus the population will diminish. Consequently, the fox population will too decrease. Then with decreased predation by the foxes, the rabbit population will be able to rejuvenate.

B. A bacterial pathogen completely wipes out the population of foxes. Researches closely watch the rabbit population and notice a new population fluctuation. **Identify** and **explain** this change in the population.

2 Points – With the fox population and predation removed, the rabbits will be able to sustain exponential population growth. At some point, the rabbit population will reach a new carrying capacity, the maximum population size that the environment can support, and thus will level off.

C. **Predict** the state of the rabbit population in one year. **Justify** your prediction.

1 Point – The rabbit population will increase over the year, followed by the fox population as there are more rabbits (prey) available.

6.

A. **Identify** the cats with the fur color that is expected to live longer in the new environment. **Justify** your reasoning.

2 Points – This is a type of directional selection, where one extreme of the phenotype is "safer" or more adaptive in the environment. In this situation, the environment has snow year around. Thus the cats that have white fur are able to blend into their environment better than the cats with black or brown fur and evade predation more successfully.

B. The scientist is also interested in better understanding the evolutionary relationships between the wild cats and several other wild species. Using the data collected on various traits by the scientist, **construct** a visual representation of the evolutionary relationships.

1 Point – To create a cladogram, it is often easier to determine outliers for each trait. Beginning with Trait A, Animals 1–3 all have the trait, but Animal 4 does not. Animal 4 also does not have Traits B and C. Next with Trait C, Animals 2 and 3 share the trait, but Animal 1 does not. Lastly with Trait B, only Animal 3 has the trait.

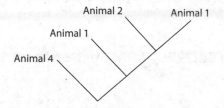

C. A volcano erupts in the ecosystem that contains the wild cat population. **Predict** how this would impact the population. **Justify** your prediction.

1 Point – The wild cat population would show an increase in the number of black cats due to their ability to blend into the lava rocks that came from the volcano eruption, increasing their ability to survive.

Scoring and Interpretation
AP BIOLOGY DIAGNOSTIC EXAM

SECTION I: Multiple-Choice Questions:

NUMBER CORRECT [ ] x 1.0000 = [ ]

WEIGHTED SECTION I SCORE

SECTION II: Free Response:

QUESTION 1 [ ] x 1.7647 [ ]
(out of 9)   (do not round)

QUESTION 2 [ ] x 1.7647 [ ]
(out of 9)   (do not round)

QUESTION 3 [ ] x 1.7647 [ ]
(out of 4)   (do not round)

QUESTION 4 [ ] x 1.7647 [ ]
(out of 4)   (do not round)

QUESTION 5 [ ] x 1.7647 [ ]
(out of 4)   (do not round)

QUESTION 6 [ ] x 1.7647 [ ]
(out of 4)   (do not round)

SECTION SCORE: (add 6 question totals together) [ ]
WEIGHTED SECTION II SCORE

TOTAL SCORE: (add Section I and Section II together) [ ]
OVERALL SCORE

AP BIOLOGY
SCORE CONVERSION CHART

COMPOSITE SCORE RANGE	AP EXAM SCORE
94 – 120	5
76 – 93	4
54 – 75	3
30 – 53	2
0 – 29	1

STEP 3

Develop Strategies for Success

CHAPTER 4   How to Approach Each Question Type

CHAPTER 4

How to Approach Each Question Type

IN THIS CHAPTER

Summary: Become familiar with the types of questions on the exam: multiple choice and free-response. Pace yourself and know when to skip a question that you can come back to later.

Key Ideas

✪ On multiple-choice questions, you no longer lose any points for wrong answers. So you should bubble in an answer for *every* question.

✪ On multiple-choice questions, don't "out-think" the test. Use common sense because that will usually get you to the right answer.

✪ Free-response answers must be in essay form. Outline form is not acceptable.

✪ Free-response questions tend to be multipart questions—be SURE to answer each part of the question or you will not be able to get the maximum possible number of points for that question.

✪ Make a quick outline before you begin writing your answer.

✪ The free-response questions are graded using a positive-scoring system, so wrong information is ignored.

Multiple-Choice Questions

You have approximately 90 seconds per question on the multiple-choice section of this exam. Remember that to be on pace for a great score on this exam, you need to correctly answer approximately 42 multiple-choice questions or more. Here are a few rules of thumb:

1. *Don't out-think the test.* It is indeed possible to be too smart for these tests. Frequently during these standardized tests we have found ourselves overanalyzing every single problem. If you encounter a question such as, "During what phase of meiosis does crossover (also referred to as *crossing over*) occur?" and you happen to know the answer immediately, this does not mean that the question is too easy. First, give yourself credit for knowing a fact. They asked you something, you knew it, and *wham*, you fill in the bubble. Do not overanalyze the question and assume that your answer is too obvious for that question. Just because you get it doesn't mean that it was too easy.

2. *Don't leave questions blank.* The AP Biology exam used to take off one-fourth point for each wrong answer. This is no longer the case. You should bubble in an answer for each multiple-choice question.

3. *Be on the lookout for trick wording!* Always pay attention to words or phrases such as "least," "most," "not," "incorrectly," and "does not belong." Do not answer the wrong question. There are few things as annoying as getting a question wrong on this test simply because you didn't read the question carefully enough, especially if you know the right answer.

4. *Use your time carefully.* Some of these questions require a lot of careful reading before you can answer them. If you find yourself struggling on a question, try not to waste too much time on it. Circle it in the booklet and come back to it later if time permits. Remember—you are looking to answer approximately 42 multiple-choice questions correctly to be on pace for a great score—this test should be an exercise in window shopping.

It does not matter *which* questions you get correct. What is important is that you answer enough questions correctly. Find the subjects that you know the best, answer those questions, and save the others for review later on.

5. *Be careful about changing answers!* If you have answered a question already, come back to it later on, and get the urge to change it . . . make sure that you have a real *reason* to change it. Often an urge to change an answer is the work of exam "elves" in the room who want to trick you into picking a wrong answer. Change your answer only if you can justify your reasons for making the switch.

6. *Check your calculations!* The math required in the grid-in section isn't overly complicated. That said, it would be unfortunate to lose points because of a silly calculation error. Make sure to work carefully and check your math. Happily, any equations you need will be provided for you.

Free-Response Questions

The free-response section consists of six broad questions. It is important that your answers to these questions display solid reasoning and analytical skills. The two long essays together carry approximately the same weight as the four short-response questions combined. Expect to often use data or information from your laboratory exercises as you answer some of the questions.

The free-response part of the exam includes two long free-response questions and four short free-response questions. The format for the questions is included below.

6 Questions | 1 Hour 30 Minutes | 50% of Exam Score

There are two long questions and four short-answer questions. Long questions are worth 8–10 points each; short-answer questions are worth 4 points each.

Free-Response Question #1 relates to interpreting and evaluating experimental results. This question is worth between 8 and 10 points and presents students with an authentic scenario accompanied by data in a table or graph. This question tests a student's ability to do the following in four question parts:

Part 1: (1-2 points) Describe and explain biological concepts, processes, or models.
Part 2: (3-4 points) Identify experimental design procedures.
Part 3: (1-3 points) Analyze the data.
Part 4: (2-4 points) Make predictions and then justify those predictions.

Free-Response Question #2 relates to interpreting and evaluating experimental results with graphing. This question is also worth between 8 and 10 points and presents students with an authentic scenario accompanied by data in a table or graph. This question tests a student's ability to do the following in four question parts:

Part 1: (1-2 points) Describe and explain biological concepts, processes, or models.
Part 2: (4 points) Create a graph, plot, or chart and use confidence intervals or error bars.
Part 3: (1-3 points) Analyze the data.
Part 4: (1-3 points) Make predictions and then justify those predictions.

Free-Response Question #3 relates to a lab experiment scenario. This question is worth 4 points. This question tests a student's ability to do the following in four question parts:

Part 1: (1 point) Describe and explain biological concepts, processes, or models.
Part 2: (1 point) Identify experimental design procedures.
Part 3: (1 point) Predict Results
Part 4: (1 point) Justify those predictions.

Free-Response Question #4 describes a biological phenomenon with a disruption. This question is worth 4 points. This question tests a student's ability to do the following in four question parts:

Part 1: (1 point) Describe biological concepts, processes, or models.
Part 2: (1 point) Explain biological concepts, processes, or models.
Part 3: (1 point) Predict Results
Part 4: (1 point) Justify those predictions.

Free-Response Question #5 presents students with an authentic scenario along with a visual model or representation. This question is worth 4 points. This question tests a student's ability to do the following in four question parts:

Part 1: (1 point) Describe biological concepts, processes, or models represented visually.
Part 2: (1 point) Explain these concepts processes or models visually.

Part 3: (1 point) Represent relationships with a biological model.
Part 4: (1 point) Explain properly how this visual representation relates to a larger biological concept, theory, or principle.

Free-Response Question #6 provides students with data represented in a graph, table or other form of visual representation. This question is worth 4 points. This question tests a student's ability to do the following in four question parts:

Part 1: (1 point) Describe data.
Part 2: (1 point) Describe data.
Part 3: (1 point) Use data to evaluate a hypothesis.
Part 4: (1 point) Explain properly how experimental results relate to a larger biological concept, theory, or principle.

Answers for the free-response questions must be in essay form. Outline form is not acceptable. Labeled diagrams may be used to supplement discussion, but in no case will a diagram alone suffice. It is important that you read each question completely before you begin to write. Write all of your answers on the pages following the questions in the booklet.

Free-Response Tips

Do not repeat the prompt. You do not earn any credit by doing so and is a waste of time since the reader already knows what the prompt is.

When formulating your response, do not use "it" to refer to anything you are speaking about. The reader does not know what "it" means. Make sure to explain what "it" means.

Answer each question using complete sentences. Do not use bullet points or list to answer a question.

When asked to make comparisons, make sure to compare or explain the differences between both groups not just one.

When discussing quantitative data, make sure you use units to help describe the data. Numbers alone will not get you credit.

Be sure to address whether trends are increasing, decreasing or remaining constant when asked to describe a trend.

When answering questions, make sure to:

Attempt and address all the parts of every question. Do not leave anything blank.
Identify the task verb and be familiar with what you are being asked to do.
Make necessary connections. The majority of questions are constructed to have you make connections between multiple concepts.

When deconstructing a question, keep in mind the following steps:

1. Locate any models, graphs, or data that are in the prompt. Examine them and ask the following questions: What do you see? What does it mean?
2. Read the prompt looking for boldface terms, which include the task verbs. These will ask: "What are you supposed to be doing?"
3. Re-read the prompt and look for any biology concepts that are present. These concepts will give you the background and context needed to answer the question.

Some important tips to keep in mind as you write your essays:

- The free-response questions tend to be multipart questions. You can't be expected to know everything about every topic, and the test preparers sometimes throw you a bone by writing questions that ask you to answer *two* of three parts or *three* of four parts. This gives you an opportunity to focus in on the material that you are most comfortable with. It is very important that you read the question carefully to make sure you understand exactly what the examiners are asking you to do.

- You are given 90 minutes to complete six free-response questions. The two long free-response questions should take 25 minutes each and the four short questions should take about 10 minutes each. This may not seem like a lot of time, but if you write a bunch of practice essays before you take the exam and budget your time wisely during the exam, you will not have to struggle with your timing. Below are suggestions for budgeting your time:

  - Read the question carefully and make sure you know what it is asking you to do.
  - Construct an outline that will help you organize your answer. Don't write the world's most elaborate outline. You won't get points for having the prettiest outline in the country—so there is no reason to spend an excessive amount of time putting it together. Just develop enough of an outline so that you have a basic idea of how you will construct your essay. Your essay is not graded based on how well it is put together, but it certainly will not hurt your score to write a well-organized and grammatically correct response.

- The free-response section is graded using a "positive scoring" system. This means that wrong information in an essay is ignored. You do not lose points for saying things that are incorrect. (Unfortunately, you do not *get* points for saying things that are incorrect either . . . if only!) The importance of this fact is basically that if you are unsure about something and think you may be right, give it a shot and include it in your essay. It's worth the risk.

STEP 4

Review the Knowledge You Need to Score High

CHAPTER **5**   Chemistry of Life

CHAPTER **6**   Cell Structure and Function

CHAPTER **7**   Cellular Energetics

CHAPTER **8**   Cell Communication and Cell Cycle

CHAPTER **9**   Heredity

CHAPTER **10** Molecular Genetics

CHAPTER **11** Evolution

CHAPTER **12** Ecology

CHAPTER **13** Laboratory Review

CHAPTER 5

Chemistry of Life
Exam Weight: 8–11%

IN THIS CHAPTER

Summary: This chapter introduces the chemical principles that are related to understanding the AP Biology topics covered throughout the course.

Key Ideas

✪ Organic compounds contain essential elements, including carbon, oxygen, hydrogen, nitrogen, and phosphorus.

✪ The structure and function of macromolecules (proteins, carbohydrates, lipids, and nucleic acids) are key to the organization of living systems.

✪ Water and its properties are instrumental in the organization and survival of all living organisms and systems.

✪ Hydrolysis and dehydration reactions are vital in the formation and cleavage of bonds between monomer units.

Introduction

What is the name of the test you are studying for? The AP Biology exam. Then why in tarnation are we starting your review with a chapter titled *Chemistry of Life*?!?!? Because it is important that you have an understanding of the key chemical principles before we dive into the deeper biological material. We will keep it short, don't worry. ☺

Elements, Compounds, Atoms, and Ions

By definition, **matter** is anything that has mass and takes up space; an **element** is defined as matter in its simplest form; an **atom** is the smallest form of an element that still displays its particular properties. (Terms boldfaced in text are listed in the Glossary at the end of the book.) For example, sodium (Na) is an element mentioned often in this book. The element sodium can exist as an atom of sodium, in which it is a neutral particle containing an equal number of protons and electrons. It can also exist as an ion, which is an atom that has a positive or negative charge. Ions such as sodium that take on a positive charge are called **cations,** and are composed of more protons than electrons. Ions with a negative charge are called **anions,** and are composed of more electrons than protons.

Elements can be combined to form **molecules,** for example, an oxygen molecule (O_2) or a hydrogen molecule (H_2). Molecules that are composed of more than one type of element are called **compounds,** for example H_2O. The two major types of compounds you need to be familiar with are **organic** and **inorganic** compounds. Organic compounds contain carbon and usually hydrogen; inorganic compounds do not. Some of you are probably skeptical, at this point, as to whether any of what we have said thus far matters for this exam. Bear with me because it does. You will deal with many important organic compounds later on in this book, including **carbohydrates, proteins, lipids,** and **nucleic acids**.

Before moving onto the next section, where we discuss these particular organic compounds in more detail, we would like to cover a topic that many find confusing and therefore ignore in preparing for this exam. This is the subject of **functional groups.** These poorly understood groups are responsible for the chemical properties of organic compounds. They should not intimidate you, nor should you spend a million hours trying to memorize them in full detail.

The following is a list of the functional groups you should study for this exam:

John (11th grade): "My teacher wanted me to know these structures . . . she was right!"

SYI-1
Living systems are organized in a hierarchy of structural levels that interact.

1. *Amino group.* An amino group has the following formula:

$$R-N\underset{H}{\overset{H}{<}}$$

The symbol R stands for "rest of the compound" to which this NH_2 group is attached. One example of a compound containing an amino group is an **amino acid.** Compounds containing amino groups are generally referred to as **amines.** Amino groups act as bases and can pick up protons from acids.

2. *Carbonyl group.* This group contains two structures:

$$\underset{R}{\overset{R}{\underset{|}{\overset{|}{C}}}}=O \qquad R-C\underset{H}{\overset{\diagup O}{\diagdown}}$$

ketone **aldehyde**

If the C=O is at the end of a chain, it is an **aldehyde.** Otherwise, it is a **ketone.** (*Note:* in *aldehydes,* there is an H at the end; there is no H in the word *ketone.*) A carbonyl group makes a compound **hydrophilic** and **polar.** *Hydrophilic* means water-loving, reacting well with water. A *polar* molecule is one that has an unequal distribution of charge, which creates a positive side and a negative side to the molecule.

3. **Carboxyl group**. This group has the following formula:

$$\underset{C}{\overset{R\quad O}{\diagup\diagdown}}$$
$$OH$$

A *carboxyl group* is a carbonyl group that has a hydroxide in one of the R spots and a carbon chain in the other. This functional group shows up along with amino groups in amino acids. Carboxyl groups act as acids because they are able to donate protons to basic compounds. Compounds containing carboxyl groups are known as *carboxylic acids*.

4. *Hydroxyl group*. This group has the simplest formula of the bunch:

$$R — OH$$

A hydroxyl group is present in compounds known as **alcohols.** Like carbonyl groups, hydroxyl groups are polar and hydrophilic.

5. *Phosphate group*. This group has the following formula:

$$R—O—\underset{\underset{O^-}{|}}{\overset{\overset{O}{|}}{P}}=O$$

Phosphate groups are vital components of compounds that serve as cellular energy sources: ATP, ADP, and GTP. Like carboxyl groups, phosphate groups are acidic molecules.

6. *Sulfhydryl group*. This group also has a simple formula:

$$R — SH$$

This functional group does not show up much on the exam, but you should recognize it when it does. This group is present in the amino acids methionine and cysteine and assists in structure stabilization in many proteins.

Water

Water is an inorganic compound consisting of one oxygen molecule covalently bonded to two hydrogen bonds. The electrons shared between the hydrogen and oxygen molecules are closer to the oxygen molecule due to its electronegativity, resulting in the oxygen molecule being negatively charged and the hydrogen molecule being positively charged. Water molecules are **polar** because they have a positive and a negative side. **Nonpolar** molecules have a neutral charge due to equal sharing of electrons.

Hydrogen bonding is the attraction between a positively charged hydrogen atom and any other electronegative atom, such as oxygen. These bonds may form between atoms within the same molecule or between two separate molecules. Water is a molecule that contains slightly positive charged hydrogens and slightly negative oxygen molecules. This allows water molecules to form up to two hydrogen bonds with other water molecules, leading to a variety of properties unique to water (Figure 5.1).

Properties of Water

Cohesion	• Water molecules linking together due to hydrogen bonds • Surface tension: The surface of water is difficult to break or stretch.
Adhesion	• A water molecule is attracted to another substance due to hydrogen bonds. • The adhesion of water to plant cell walls by hydrogen bonds help counter the pull of gravity in plants.
Evaporative cooling	• The surface of an object becomes cooler during evaporation as a result of water absorbing energy in the form of heat. • Evaporation of sweat from the skin of humans lowers body temperature.
Surface tension	• Surface tension allows water to be resistant to external forces, due to the cohesive nature of the water molecules to one another instead of to the surrounding molecules in the air.
Universal solvent	• Water dissolves more substances than any other liquid on Earth. • In life, wherever water moves, it takes with it the substances dissolved in it.

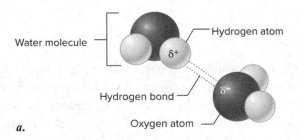

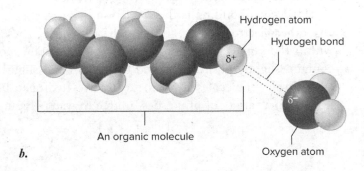

Figure 5.1   Structure of a hydrogen bond. *a.* Hydrogen bond between two water molecules. ***b.*** Hydrogen bond between an organic molecule (n-butanol) and water. H in *n*-butanol forms a hydrogen bond with oxygen in water. This kind of hydrogen bond is possible any time H is bound to a more electronegative atom. (*Reproduced with permission from Raven P, Johnson G, Mason K, Losos J, Duncan T;* Biology, *12th ed. New York: McGraw Hill; 2020*)

Macromolecules

Monomers and Polymers

Macromolecules are made up of single units called monomers that are joined together via covalent bonds to form large polymers, such as carbohydrates, nucleic acids, and proteins. Due to their large size, lipids are also classified as macromolecules even though they lack the repeating monomer subunits seen in the other molecules.

Macromolecules are assembled via **dehydration synthesis**, a reaction that forms a covalent bond between two monomer units while releasing a water molecule in the process.

Hydrolysis is the process by which the covalent bonds between monomer units are broken by the addition of water (Figure 5.2).

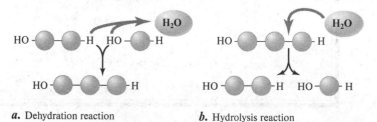

a. Dehydration reaction   *b.* Hydrolysis reaction

Figure 5.2   Making and breaking macromolecules. *a.* Biological macromolecules are polymers formed by linking monomers together through dehydration reactions. This process releases a water molecule for every bond formed. ***b.*** Breaking the bond between subunits involves hydrolysis, which reverses the loss of a water molecule by dehydration. (*Reproduced with permission from Raven P, Johnson G, Mason K, Losos J, Duncan T; Biology, 12th ed. New York: McGraw Hill; 2020*)

ENE-1

The highly complex organization of living systems requires constant input of energy and the exchange of macromolecules

Lipids

Lipids are organic compounds used by cells as long-term energy stores or building blocks. Lipids are hydrophobic and insoluble in water because they contain a hydrocarbon tail of CH_2S that is nonpolar and repellant to water. The most important lipids are **fats, oils, steroids,** and **phospholipids.**

Fats, which are lipids made by combining **glycerol** and three **fatty acids** (Figure 5.3), are used as long-term energy stores in cells. They are not as easily metabolized as carbohydrates, yet

SYI-1

Living systems are organized in a hierarchy of structural levels that interact

IST-1

Heritable information provides for the continuity of life

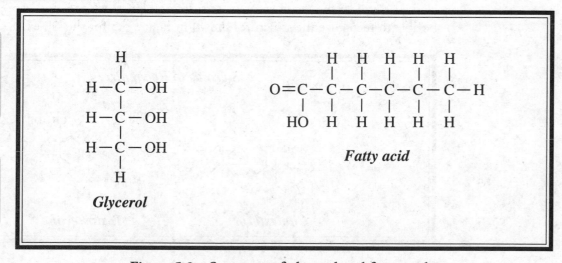

Figure 5.3   Structure of glycerol and fatty acids.

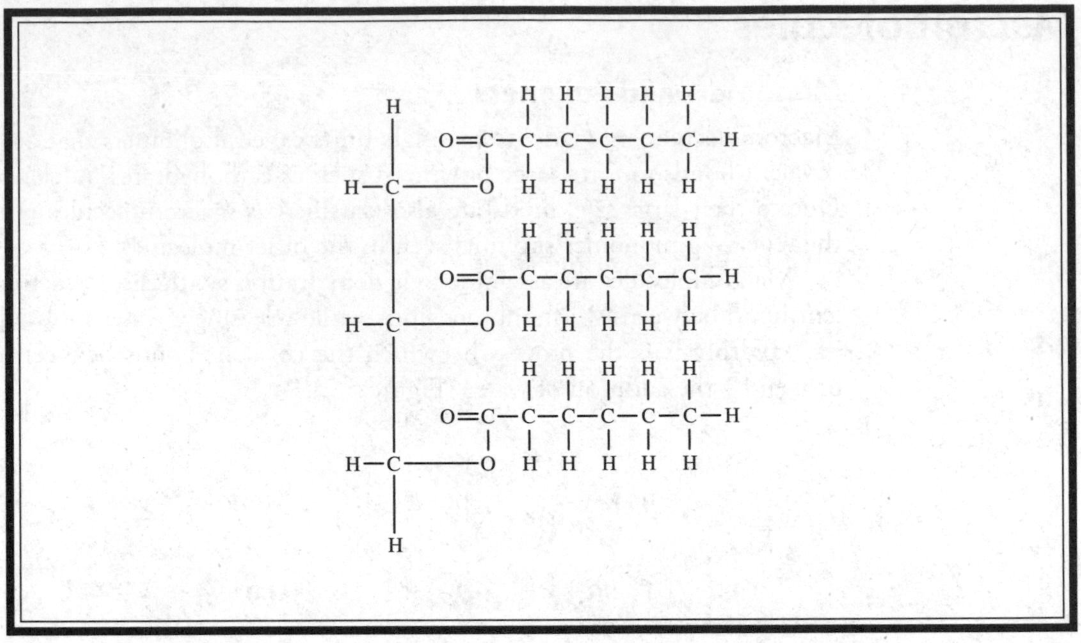

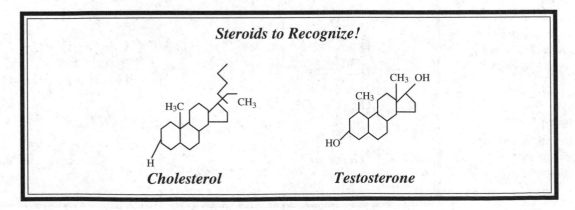

Figure 5.4   Fat structure (glycerol plus three fatty acids).

they are a more effective means of storage; for instance, one gram of fat provides two times the energy of one gram of carbohydrate. Fats can be **saturated** or **unsaturated**. Saturated fat molecules contain no double bonds. Unsaturated fats contain one (mono-) or more (poly-) double bonds, which means that they contain fewer hydrogen molecules per carbon than do saturated fats. Saturated fats are the bad guys and are associated with heart disease and atherosclerosis. Most of the fat found in animals is saturated, whereas plants tend to contain unsaturated fats. Fat is formed when three fatty-acid molecules connect to the OH groups of the glycerol molecule. These connecting bonds are formed by dehydration synthesis reaction (Figure 5.4).

   Steroids are lipids composed of four carbon rings that look like chicken-wire fencing in pictorial representations. One example of a steroid is cholesterol, an important structural component of cell membranes that serves as a precursor molecule for another important class of steroids: the sex hormones (testosterone, progesterone, and estrogen). You should be able to recognize the structures shown in Figure 5.5 for the AP exam.

Steroids to Recognize!

Cholesterol   *Testosterone*

Figure 5.5   Steroid structures.

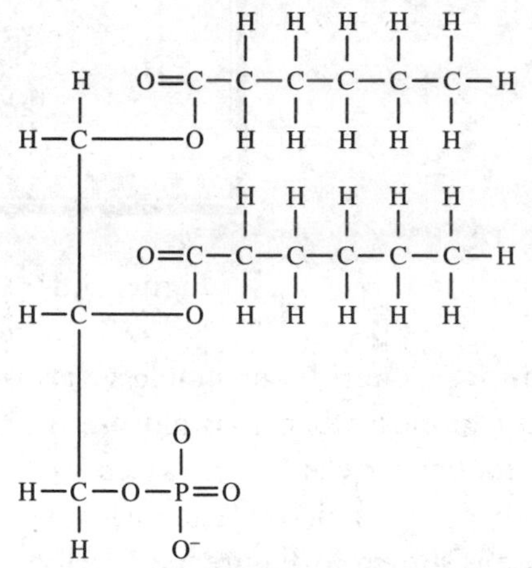

Figure 5.6   **Structure of phospholipid.**

A **phospholipid** is a lipid formed by combining a glycerol molecule with two fatty acids and a phosphate group (Figure 5.6). Phospholipids are **amphipathic** structures; they have both a hydrophobic tail (a hydrocarbon chain) and a hydrophilic head (the phosphate group) (Figure 5.7). They are the major component of cell membranes; the hydrophilic phosphate group forms the outside portion, and the hydrophobic tail forms the interior of the wall.

Carbohydrates

Carbohydrates can be simple sugars or complex molecules containing multiple sugars. Carbohydrates are used by the cells of the body in energy-producing reactions and as structural materials. Carbohydrates have the elements C, H, and O. Hydrogen and oxygen are present in a 2:1 ratio. The three main types of carbohydrates you need to know are monosaccharides, disaccharides, and polysaccharides.

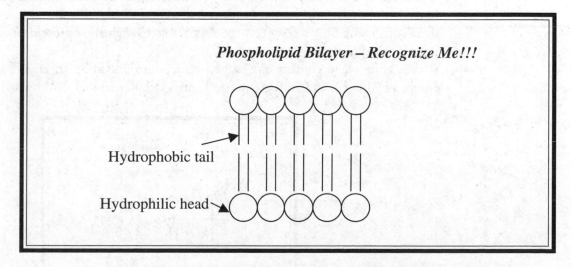

Figure 5.7   **Bilayered structure of phospholipids.**

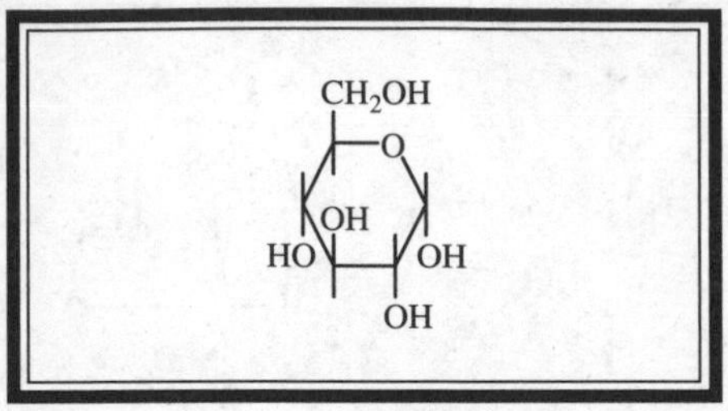

Figure 5.8 Glucose structure.

A **monosaccharide,** or simple sugar, is the simplest form of a carbohydrate. The most important monosaccharide is glucose ($C_6H_{12}O_6$), which is used in cellular respiration to provide energy for cells. Monosaccharides with five carbons ($C_5H_{10}O_5$) are used in compounds such as genetic molecules (RNA) and high-energy molecules (ATP). The structure of glucose is shown in Figure 5.8.

A **disaccharide** is a sugar consisting of two monosaccharides bound together. Common disaccharides include sucrose, maltose, and lactose. Sucrose, a major energy carbohydrate in plants, is a combination of fructose and glucose; maltose, a carbohydrate used in the creation of beer, is a combination of two glucose molecules; and lactose, found in dairy products, is a combination of galactose and glucose.

A **polysaccharide** is a carbohydrate containing three or more monosaccharide molecules. Polysaccharides, usually composed of hundreds or thousands of monosaccharides, act as a storage form of energy and as structural material in and around cells. The most important carbohydrates for storing energy are **starch** and **glycogen**. Starch, made solely of glucose molecules linked together, is the storage form of choice for plants. Animals store much of their carbohydrate energy in the form of glycogen, which is most often found in liver and muscle cells. Glycogen is formed by linking many glucose molecules together.

Julie (11th grade): "Remembering these four came in handy on the test!"

Two important structural polysaccharides are **cellulose** and **chitin**. Cellulose, a compound composed of many glucose molecules, is used by plants in the formation of their cell walls. Chitin is an important part of the exoskeletons of arthropods such as insects, spiders, and shellfish.

Proteins

A **protein** is a compound composed of chains of amino acids. Proteins have many functions in the body—they serve as structural components, transport aids, enzymes, and cell signals, to name only a few. You should be able to identify a protein or an amino acid by sight if asked to do so on the test.

An amino acid consists of a carbon center surrounded by an amino group, a carboxyl group, a hydrogen, and an R group (see Figure 5.9). Remember that the R stands for "rest" of

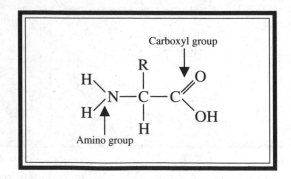

Figure 5.9 Structure of an amino acid.

$$H_2N - C - C - N - C - C - N - C - C = O$$

Figure 5.10   Amino acid structure exhibiting peptide linkage.

the compound, which provides an amino acid's unique personal characteristics. For instance, acidic amino acids have acidic R groups, basic amino acids have basic R groups, and so forth.

Many students preparing for the AP exam wonder if they need to memorize the 20 amino acids and their structures and whether they are polar, nonpolar, or charged. This is a lot of effort for perhaps one multiple-choice question that you might encounter on the exam. We think that this time would be better spent studying other potential exam questions. If this is of any comfort to you, we have yet to see an AP Biology question that asks something to the effect of "Which of these 5 amino acids is nonpolar?" (*Disclaimer:* This does not mean that it will never happen ☺.) It is more important for you to identify the general structure of an amino acid and know the process of protein synthesis.

A protein consists of amino acids linked together, as shown in Figure 5.10. They are most often much larger than that depicted here. Figure 5.10 is included to enable you to identify a peptide linkage on the exam. Most proteins have many more amino acids in the chain.

The AP exam may expect you to know about the structure of proteins:

Primary structure. The order of the amino acids that make up the protein.

Secondary structure. Three-dimensional arrangement of a protein caused by hydrogen bonding at regular intervals along the polypeptide backbone.

Tertiary structure. Three-dimensional arrangement of a protein caused by interaction among the various R groups of the amino acids involved.

Quaternary structure. The arrangement of separate polypeptide "subunits" into a single protein. Not all proteins have quaternary structure; many consist of a single polypeptide chain.

Proteins with only primary and secondary structure are called *fibrous* proteins. Proteins with only primary, secondary, and tertiary structures are called *globular* proteins. Either fibrous or globular proteins may contain a quaternary structure if there is more than one polypeptide chain.

Nucleic Acids

DNA Structure and Function

Deoxyribonucleic acid, known to her peers as DNA, is composed of four **nitrogenous bases:** adenine, guanine, cytosine, and thymine. Adenine and guanine are a type of nitrogenous base called a **purine,** and contain a double-ring structure. Thymine and cytosine are a type of nitrogenous base called a **pyrimidine,** and contain a single-ring structure. Two scientists, James D. Watson and Francis H.C. Crick, spent a good amount of time devoted to determining the structure of DNA. Their efforts paid off, and they were the ones given credit for realizing that DNA was arranged in what they termed a **double helix** composed of two strands of nucleotides held together by hydrogen bonds. They noted that adenine always pairs with thymine (A=T) held together by two hydrogen bonds and that guanine always pairs with cytosine (C≡G) held together by three hydrogen bonds. Each strand of DNA consists of a sugar-phosphate backbone that keeps the nucleotides connected with the strand. The sugar is deoxyribose. (See Figure 5.11 for a rough sketch of what purine–pyrimidine bonds look like.)

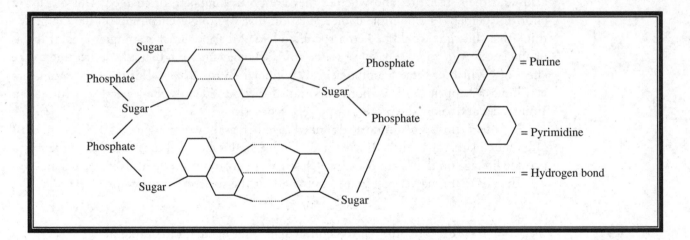

Figure 5.11   Purine–pyrimidine bonds.

One last structural note about DNA that can be confusing is that DNA has something called a 5′ end and a 3′ end (Figure 5.12). The two strands of a DNA molecule run antiparallel to each other; the 5′ end of one molecule is paired with the 3′ end of the other molecule, and vice versa.

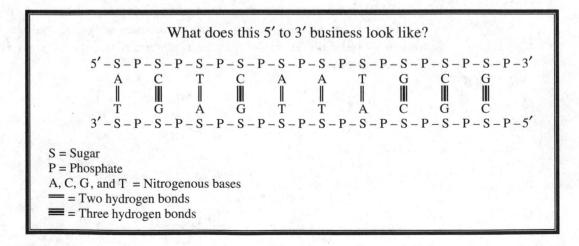

Figure 5.12   The 5′ and 3′ ends in DNA structure.

RNA Structure and Function

Ribonucleic acid is known to the world as RNA. There are some similarities between DNA and RNA. They both have a sugar-phosphate backbone. They both have four different nucleotides that make up the structure of the molecule. They both have three letters in their nickname—don't worry if you don't see that last similarity right away, . . . remember that we have been studying these things for years. These two molecules also have their share of differences. RNA's nitrogenous bases are adenine, guanine, cytosine, and **uracil.** There is no thymine in RNA; uracil beat out thymine for the job (probably had a better interview during the hiring process). Another difference between DNA and RNA is that the sugar for RNA is ribose instead of deoxyribose. While DNA exists as a double strand, RNA has a bit more of an independent personality and tends to roam the cells as a single-stranded entity.

There are three main types of RNA that you should know about, all of which are formed from DNA templates in the nucleus of eukaryotic cells: (1) messenger RNA (mRNA), (2) transfer RNA (tRNA), and (3) ribosomal RNA (rRNA).

pH: Acids and Bases

The pH scale is used to indicate how acidic or basic a solution is. It ranges from 0 to 14; 7 is neutral. Anything less than 7 is acidic; anything greater than 7 is basic. The pH scale is a logarithmic scale and as a result, a pH of 5 is 10 times more acidic than a pH of 6. Following the same logic, a pH of 4 is 100 times more acidic than a pH of 6. Remember that as the pH of a solution *decreases*, the concentration of hydrogen ions in the solution increases, and vice versa. For the most part, chemical reactions in humans function at or near a neutral pH. The exceptions to this rule are the chemical reactions involving some of the enzymes of the digestive system.

› Review Questions

For questions 1–4, please use the following answer choices:

(A)

(B)

(C)

(D)

1. Which of the structures shown above is a polypeptide?

2. Which of these structures is a disaccharide?

3. Which of these structures is a fat?

4. Which of these structures is an amino acid?

5. Which of the following has both a hydrophobic portion and a hydrophilic portion?

   A. Starch
   B. Phospholipids
   C. Proteins
   D. Steroids

6. A solution that has a pH of 2 is how many times more acidic than one with a pH of 5?

   A. 5
   B. 10
   C. 100
   D. 1,000

7. The structure below contains which functional group?

$$CH_3-CH_2-\overset{\displaystyle O}{\overset{\|}{C}}-CH_3$$

   A. Aldehyde
   B. Ketone
   C. Amino
   D. Hydroxyl

8. Which of the following will least affect the effectiveness of an enzyme?

   A. Temperature
   B. pH
   C. Concentration of enzyme
   D. Original activation energy of system

9. Which of the following is similar to the process of competitive inhibition?

   A. When you arrive at work in the morning, you are unable to park your car in your (assigned) parking spot because the car of the person who parks next to you has taken up just enough space that you cannot fit your own car in.
   B. When you arrive at work in the morning, you are unable to park your car in your parking spot because someone with a car exactly like yours has already taken your spot, leaving you nowhere to park your car.
   C. As you are about to park your car in your spot at work, a giant bulldozer comes along and smashes your car away from the spot, preventing you from parking your car in your spot.
   D. When you arrive at work in the morning, you are unable to park your car in your parking spot because someone has placed a giant cement block in front of your spot.

10. All the following are carbohydrates except

   A. starch.
   B. glycogen.
   C. chitin.
   D. glycerol.

11. An amino acid contains which of the following functional groups?

   A. Carboxyl group and amino group
   B. Carbonyl group and amino group
   C. Hydroxyl group and amino group
   D. Carboxyl group and hydroxyl group

› Answers and Explanations

1. **D**

2. **C**

3. **A**

4. **B**

5. **B**—A phospholipid has both a hydrophobic portion and a hydrophilic portion. The hydrocarbon portion, or tail, of the phospholipid dislikes water, and the phosphate portion, the head, is hydrophilic.

6. **D**—Because the pH scale is logarithmic, 2 is 1,000 times more acidic than 5.

7. **B**—This functional group is a carbonyl group. The two main types of carbonyl groups are ketones and aldehydes. In this case, it is a ketone because there are carbon chains on either side of the carbon double-bonded to the oxygen.

8. **D**—The four main factors that affect enzyme efficiency are pH, temperature, enzyme concentration, and substrate concentration.

9. **B**—Competitive inhibition is the inhibition of an enzyme–substrate reaction in which the inhibitor resembles the substrate and physically blocks the substrate from attaching to the active site. This parking spot represents the active site, your car is the substrate, and the other car already in the spot is the competitive inhibitor. Examples A and D more closely resemble noncompetitive inhibition.

10. **D**—Glycerol is not a carbohydrate. It is an alcohol. Starch is a carbohydrate stored in plant cells. Glycogen is a carbohydrate stored in animal cells. Chitin is a carbohydrate used by arthropods to construct their exoskeletons. Cellulose is a carbohydrate used by plants to construct their cell walls.

11. A

› Rapid Review

Try to rapidly review the following material:

Organic compounds: contain carbon; examples include lipids, proteins, and carbs (carbohydrates).

Functional groups: amino (NH_2), carbonyl (RCOR), carboxyl (COOH), hydroxyl (OH), phosphate (PO_4), sulfhydryl (SH).

Fat: glycerol + 3 fatty acids.

Saturated fat: bad for you; animals and some plants have it; solidifies at room temperature.

Unsaturated fat: better for you, plants have it; liquifies at room temperature.

Steroids: lipids whose structures resemble chicken-wire fence; include cholesterol and sex hormones.

Phospholipids: glycerol + 2 fatty acids + 1 phosphate group; make up membrane bilayers of cells; have hydrophobic interiors and hydrophilic exteriors.

Carbohydrates: used by cells for energy and structure; monosaccharides (glucose), disaccharides (sucrose, maltose, lactose), storage polysaccharides (starch [plants], glycogen [animals]), structural polysaccharides (chitin [fungi], cellulose [arthropods]).

Proteins: made with the help of ribosomes out of amino acids; serve many functions (e.g., transport, enzymes, cell signals, receptor molecules, structural components, and channels).

Enzymes: catalytic proteins that react in an induced-fit fashion with substrates to speed up the rate of reactions by lowering the activation energy; effectiveness is affected by changes in pH, temperature, and substrate and enzyme concentrations.

Competitive inhibition: inhibitor resembles substrate and binds to active site.

Noncompetitive inhibition: inhibitor binds elsewhere on enzyme; alters active site so that substrate cannot bind.

pH: logarithmic scale <7 acidic, 7 neutral, >7 basic (alkaline); pH 4 is 10 times more acidic than pH 5.

Reaction types:

  Hydrolysis reaction: breaks down compounds by adding water.

  Dehydration reaction: two components brought together, producing H_2O.

  Endergonic reaction: reaction that requires input of energy.

  Exergonic reaction: reaction that gives off energy.

  Redox reaction: electron transfer reactions.

Cell Structure and Function
Exam Weight: 10–13%

Summary: This chapter discusses the different types of cells (eukaryotic and pro-karyotic) and the important organelles, structures, and transport mechanisms that power these cells.

Key Ideas

✪ Prokaryotic cells are simple cells with no nuclei or organelles.

✪ Animal cells do not contain cell walls or chloroplasts and have small vacuoles.

✪ Plant cells do not have centrioles.

✪ The fluid mosaic model states that a cell membrane consists of a phospholipid bilayer with proteins of various lengths and sizes interspersed with cholesterol among the phospholipids.

✪ Passive transport is the movement of a particle across a selectively permeable membrane down its concentration gradient (e.g., diffusion, osmosis).

✪ Active transport is the movement of a particle across a selectively permeable membrane against its concentration gradient (e.g., sodium-potassium pump).

✪ A cell's size affects its ability to obtain the necessary resources and eliminate wastes.

✪ The endosymbiotic theory states that eukaryotic cells originated from a symbi-otic partnership of prokaryotic cells.

✪ Water potential is a force that drives water to move from areas of high water potential to areas of low water potential.

Introduction

A cell is defined as a small room, sometimes a prison room, usually designed for only one person (but usually housing two or more inmates, except for solitary-confinement cells). It is a place for rehabilitation—whoops! We're looking at the wrong notes here. Sorry, let's start again. A cell is the basic unit of life (that's more like it), discovered in the seventeenth century by Robert Hooke. There are two major divisions of cells: prokaryotic and eukaryotic. This chapter starts with a discussion of these two cell types, followed by an examination of the organelles found in cells. We conclude with a look at the fluid mosaic model of the cell membrane and a discussion of the different types of cell transport: diffusion, facilitated diffusion, osmosis, active transport, endocytosis, and exocytosis.

Types of Cells

The **prokaryotic** cell is a *simple* cell. It has no nucleus, and no membrane-bound organelles. The genetic material of a prokaryotic cell is found in a region of the cell known as the **nucleoid.** Bacteria are a fine example of prokaryotic cells and divide by a process known as *binary fission*; they duplicate their genetic material, divide in half, and produce two identical daughter cells. Prokaryotic cells are found only in the kingdom Monera (bacteria group).

Steve (12th grade): "Five questions on my test dealt with organelle function—know them."

The **eukaryotic** cell is much more complex. It contains a nucleus, which functions as the control center of the cell, directing DNA replication, transcription, and cell growth. Eukaryotic organisms may be unicellular or multicellular. One of the key features of eukaryotic cells is the presence of membrane-bound organelles, each with its own duties. Two prominent members of the "Eukaryote Club" are animal and plant cells; the differences between these types of cells are discussed in the next section.

Endosymbiotic Theory

SYI-1

Living systems are organized in a hierarchy of structural levels that interact.

The **endosymbiotic theory** states that eukaryotic cells originated from a symbiotic partnership of prokaryotic cells. This theory focuses on the origin of mitochondria and chloroplasts from aerobic heterotrophic and photosynthetic prokaryotes, respectively.

We can see why scientists examining these two organelles would think that they may have originated from prokaryotes. They share many characteristics: (1) they are the same size as eubacteria, (2) they also reproduce in the same way as prokaryotes (binary fission), and (3), if their ribosomes are sliced open and studied, they are found to more closely resemble those of a prokaryote than those of a eukaryote. They are prokaryotic groupies living in a eukaryotic world.

Bill (11th grade): "Important concept to know."

The eukaryotic organism that scientists believe most closely resembles prokaryotes is the **archezoa,** which does not have mitochondria. One phylum grouped with the archezoa is the **diplomonads.** A good example of a diplomonad you should remember is *Giardia*—an infectious agent you would do well to avoid. *Giardia* is a parasitic organism that takes hold in your intestines and essentially denies your body the ability to absorb any fat. This infection makes for very uncomfortable and unpleasant GI (gastrointestinal) issues and usually results from the ingestion of contaminated water.

Organelles

You should familiarize yourselves with approximately a dozen organelles and cell structures before taking the AP Biology exam:

Prokaryotic Organelles

You should be familiar with the following structures:

Plasma membrane. This is a selective barrier around a cell composed of a double layer of phospholipids. Part of this selectivity is due to the many proteins that either rest on the exterior of the membrane or are embedded in the membrane of the cell. Each membrane has a different combination of lipids, proteins, and carbohydrates that provide it with its unique characteristics.

Cell wall. This is a wall or barrier that functions to shape and protect cells. This is present in all prokaryotes.

Ribosomes. These function as the host organelle for protein synthesis in the cell. They are found in the cytoplasm of cells and are composed of a large unit and a small subunit.

Eukaryotic Organelles

You should be familiar with the following structures:

Ribosomes. As in prokaryotes, eukaryotic ribosomes serve as the host organelles for protein synthesis. Eukaryotes have *bound* ribosomes, which are attached to endoplasmic reticula and form proteins that tend to be exported from the cell or sent to the membrane. There are also *free* ribosomes, which exist freely in the cytoplasm and produce proteins that remain in the cytoplasm of the cell. Eukaryotic ribosomes are built in a structure called the **nucleolus.**

Smooth endoplasmic reticulum. This is a membrane-bound organelle involved in lipid synthesis, detoxification, and carbohydrate metabolism. Liver cells contain a lot of **smooth endoplasmic reticulum** (SER) because they host a lot of carbohydrate metabolism (glycolysis). It is given the name "smooth" endoplasmic reticulum because there are no ribosomes on its cytoplasmic surface. The liver contains much SER for another reason—it is the site of alcohol detoxification.

Rough endoplasmic reticulum. This membrane-bound organelle is termed "rough" because of the presence of ribosomes on the cytoplasmic surface of the cell. The proteins produced by this organelle are often secreted by the cell and carried by vesicles to the **Golgi apparatus** for further modification.

Golgi apparatus. Proteins, lipids, and other macromolecules are sent to the Golgi to be modified by the addition of sugars and other molecules to form **glycoproteins.** The products are then sent in vesicles (escape pods that bud off the edge of the Golgi) to other parts of the cell, directed by the particular changes made by the Golgi. We think of the Golgi apparatus as the post office of the cell—packages are dropped off by customers, and the Golgi adds the appropriate postage and zip code to make sure that the packages reach proper destinations in the cell.

Mitochondria. These are double-membraned organelles that specialize in the production of ATP. The innermost portion of the mitochondrion is called the *matrix,* and the folds created by the inner of the two membranes are called *cristae.* The mitochondria are the host organelles for the Krebs cycle (matrix) and oxidative phosphorylation (cristae) of respiration, which we discuss in Chapter 7. We think of the mitochondria as the power plants of the cell.

Lysosome. This is a membrane-bound organelle that specializes in digestion. It contains enzymes that break down (hydrolyze) proteins, lipids, nucleic acids, and carbohydrates. This organelle is the stomach of the cell. Absence of a particular lysosomal hydrolytic enzyme can lead to a variety of diseases known as **storage diseases.** An example of this is **Tay-Sachs disease** (discussed in Chapter 9), in which an enzyme used to digest lipids is absent, leading to excessive accumulation of lipids in the brain. Lysosomes are often referred to as "suicide sacs" of the cell. Cells that are no longer needed are often destroyed in these sacs. An example of this process involves the cells of the tail of a tadpole, which are digested as a tadpole changes into a frog.

Nucleus. This is the control center of the cell. In eukaryotic cells, this is the storage site of genetic material (DNA). It is the site of replication, transcription, and posttranscriptional modification of RNA. It also contains the nucleolus, the site of ribosome synthesis.

Vacuole. This is a storage organelle that acts as a vault. Vacuoles are quite large in plant cells but small in animal cells.

Peroxisomes. These are organelles containing enzymes that produce hydrogen peroxide as a by-product while performing various functions, such as breakdown of fatty acids and detoxification of alcohol in the liver. Peroxisomes also contain an enzyme that converts the toxic hydrogen peroxide by-product of these reactions into cell-friendly water.

Chloroplast. This is the site of photosynthesis and energy production in plant cells. Chloroplasts contain many pigments, which provide leaves with their color. Chloroplasts are divided into an inner portion and an outer portion. The inner fluid portion is called the **stroma,** which is surrounded by two outer membranes. Winding through the stroma is an inner membrane called the **thylakoid membrane system,** where the light-dependent reactions of photosynthesis occur. The light-independent (dark) reactions occur in the stroma.

Cytoskeleton. The skeleton of cells consists of three types of fibers that provide support, shape, and mobility to cells: microtubules, microfilaments, and intermediate filaments. **Microtubules** are constructed from tubulin and have a lead role in the separation of cells during cell division. Microtubules are also important components of cilia and flagella, which are structures that aid the movement of particles. **Microfilaments,** constructed from actin, play a big part in muscular contraction. **Intermediate filaments** are constructed from a class of proteins called *keratins* and are thought to function as reinforcement for the shape and position of organelles in the cell.

TIP

Remember me!
Of the structures listed above, animal cells contain **all *except*** cell walls and chloroplasts, and their vacuoles are small. Plant cells contain **all** the structures listed above, and their vacuoles are large. Animal cells have centrioles (cell division structure); plant cells **do not.**

As a cell grows in size, its internal volume increases, and its cell membrane (surface area) expands to respond to the growth of the cell. However, as the volume of the cell increases, the cell membrane (surface area) does *not* keep up. This results in the cell not having enough surface area to pass materials produced by the increasing volume of the cell. So the cell must stop growing in order to survive (See Figure 6.1).

Cell Size

ENE-1
The highly complex organization of living systems requires constant input of energy and the exchange of macromolecules.

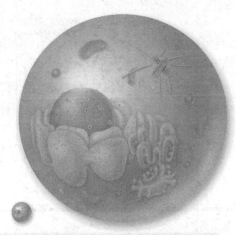

Cell radius (*r*)	1 unit	10 unit
Surface area ($4\pi r^2$)	12.57 unit^2	1,257 unit^2
Volume ($\frac{4}{3}\pi r^3$)	4.189 unit^3	4,189 unit^3
Surface Area / Volume	3	0.3

Figure 6.1   Surface area-to-volume ratio. As a cell gets larger, its volume increases at a faster rate than its surface area. If the cell radius increases by 10 times, the surface area increases by 100 times, but the volume increases by 1000 times. A cell's surface area must be large enough to meet the metabolic needs of its volume. (*Reproduced with permission from Raven P, Johnson G, Mason K, Losos J, Duncan T;* Biology, *12th ed. New York: McGraw Hill; 2020*)

- As the surface-area-to-volume ratio of a cell increases, the exchange efficiency of materials with the environment increases as well.
- The surface-area-to-volume ratio affects the ability of a cell to maintain homeostasis between its internal environment and external environment.

<u>**Volume equations to know**</u>
Volume of a sphere $V = 4/3\pi r^3$
Volume of a rectangle solid $V = lwh$
Volume of a cylinder $V = \pi r^2 h$
Volume of a cube $V = s^3$
<u>**Surface area equations to know**</u>
Surface area of a sphere $SA = 4\pi r^2$
Surface area of a rectangle solid $SA = 2lh + 2lw + 2wh$
Surface area of a cylinder $SA = 2\pi rh + 2\pi r^2$
Surface area of a cube $SA = 6s^2$

Cell Membranes: Fluid Mosaic Model

As discussed above, a cell membrane is a selective barrier surrounding a cell that has a phospholipid bilayer as its major structural component. Remember that the outer portion of the bilayer contains the hydrophilic (water-loving) head of the phospholipid, while the inner portion is composed of the hydrophobic (water-fearing) tail of the phospholipid (Figure 6.2).

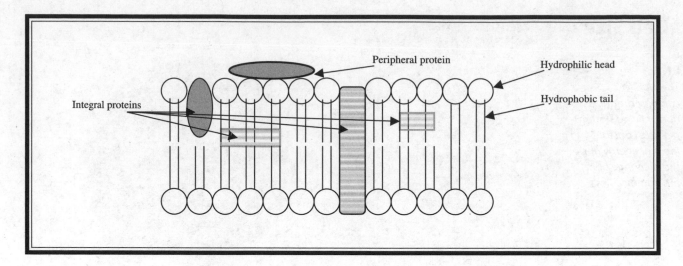

Figure 6.2   Cross-section of a cell membrane showing phospholipid bilayer.

The **fluid mosaic model** is the most accepted model for the arrangement of membranes. It states that the membrane consists of a phospholipid bilayer with proteins of various lengths and sizes interspersed with cholesterol among the phospholipids. These proteins perform various functions depending on their location within the membrane.

The fluid mosaic model consists of **integral proteins,** which are implanted within the bilayer and can extend partway or all the way across the membrane, and **peripheral proteins,** such as receptor proteins, which are not implanted in the bilayer and are often attached to integral proteins of the membrane. These proteins have various functions in cells. A protein that stretches across the membrane can function as a channel to assist the passage of desired molecules into the cell. Proteins on the exterior of a membrane with binding sites can act as receptors that allow the cell to respond to external signals such as hormones. Proteins embedded in the membrane can also function as enzymes, increasing the rate of cellular reactions.

The cell membrane is "selectively" permeable, meaning that it allows some molecules and other substances through, while others are not permitted to pass. The membrane is like a bouncer at a popular nightclub. What determines the selectivity of the membrane? One factor is the size of the substance, and the other is the charge. The bouncer lets small, uncharged polar substances and hydrophobic substances such as lipids through the membrane, but larger uncharged polar substances (such as glucose) and charged ions (such as sodium) cannot pass through. The other factor determining what is allowed to pass through the membrane is the particular arrangement of proteins in the lipid bilayer. Different proteins in different arrangements allow different molecules to pass through.

Cells are so small that you need a microscope to view them. Why is that? Cells must interact with their surrounding environment in order to survive and they must also bring in nutrients and remove waste across their membranes 24/7.

Types of Cell Transport

There are six basic types of cell transport:

1. **Diffusion:** the movement of molecules down their concentration gradient without the use of energy. It is a *passive* process during which substances move from a region of higher concentration to a region of lower concentration. The rate of diffusion of substances varies from membrane to membrane because of different selective permeabilities.

ENE-2

Cells have membranes that allow them to establish and maintain internal environments that are different from their external environments.

2. **Osmosis:** the *passive* diffusion of water down its concentration gradient across selectively permeable membranes. Water moves from a region of *high* water concentration to a region of *low* water concentration. Thinking about osmosis another way, water will flow from a region with a *lower* solute concentration (hypotonic) to a region with a *higher* solute concentration (hypertonic) (See Figure 6.4). **Isotonic** indicates there is no net movement of water across the membrane. This process does not require the input of energy. For example, visualize two regions—one with 10 particles of sodium per liter of water; the other with 15. Osmosis would drive water from the region with 10 particles of sodium toward the region with 15 particles of sodium (See Figure 6.3).

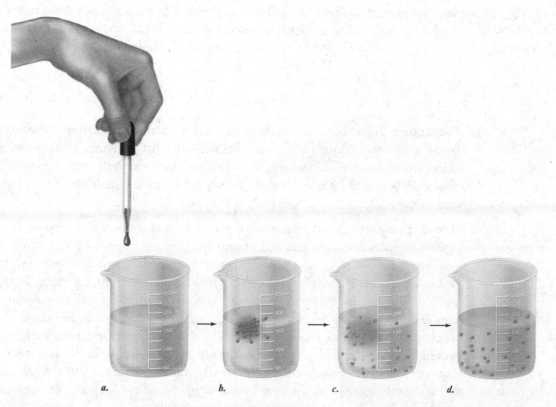

Figure 6.3   Diffusion. If a drop of colored ink is dropped into a beaker of water *(a)* its molecules dissolve *(b)* and diffuse *(c)*. Eventually, diffusion results in an even distribution of ink molecules throughout the water *(d)*. (*Reproduced with permission from Raven P, Johnson G, Mason K, Losos J, Duncan T; Biology, 12th ed. New York: McGraw Hill; 2020*)

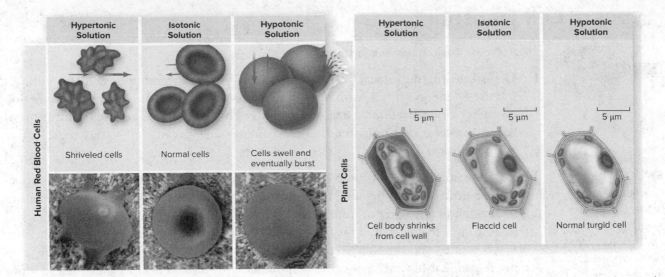

Figure 6.4   How solutes create osmotic pressure. In a hypertonic solution, water moves out of the cell, causing the cell to shrivel. In an isotonic solution, water diffuses into and out of the cell at the same rate, with no change in cell size. In a hypotonic solution, water moves into the cell. Direction and amount of water movement is shown with blue arrows *(top)*. As water enters the cell from a hypotonic solution, pressure is applied to the plasma membrane until the cell ruptures. Water enters the cell due to osmotic pressure from the higher solute concentration in the cell. Osmotic pressure is measured as the force needed to stop osmosis. The strong cell wall of plant cells can withstand the hydrostatic pressure to keep the cell from rupturing. This is not the case with animal cells. (left, middle, right): ©David M. Phillips/Science Source (*Reproduced with permission from Raven P, Johnson G, Mason K, Losos J, Duncan T; Biology, 12th ed. New York: McGraw Hill; 2020*)

3. **Facilitated diffusion:** the diffusion of particles across a selectively permeable membrane with the assistance of the membrane's transport proteins. These proteins will not bring any old molecule looking for a free pass into the cell; they are specific in what they will carry and have binding sites designed for molecules of interest. Like diffusion and osmosis, this process does not require the input of energy.

4. **Active transport:** the movement of a particle across a selectively permeable membrane *against* its concentration gradient (from low concentration to high). This movement requires the input of energy, which is why it is termed "active" transport. As is often the case in cells, adenosine triphosphate (ATP) is called on to provide the energy for this reactive process. These active-transport systems are vital to the ability of cells to maintain particular concentrations of substances despite environmental concentrations. For example, cells have a very high concentration of potassium and a very low concentration of sodium. Diffusion would like to move sodium in and potassium out to equalize the concentrations. The all-important **sodium-potassium pump** actively moves potassium *into* the cell and sodium *out of* the cell against their respective concentration gradients to maintain appropriate levels inside the cell. This is the major pump in animal cells.

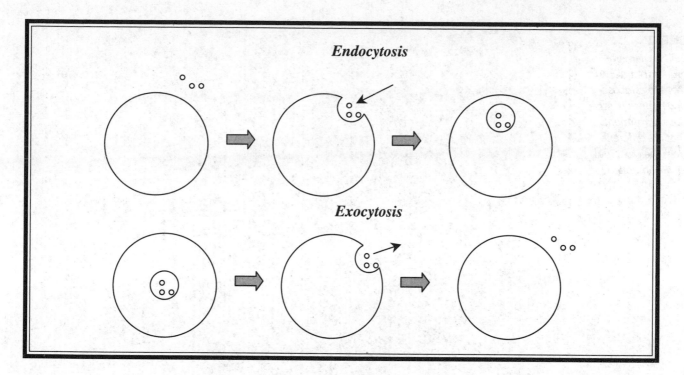

Figure 6.5   Endocytosis and exocytosis.

5. **Endocytosis:** a process in which substances are brought into cells by the enclosure of the substance into a membrane-created vesicle that surrounds the substance and escorts it into the cell (Figure 6.5). This process is used by immune cells called **phagocytes** to engulf and eliminate foreign invaders.

6. **Exocytosis:** a process in which substances are exported out of the cell (the reverse of endocytosis). A vesicle again escorts the substance to the plasma membrane, causes it to fuse with the membrane, and ejects the contents of the substance outside the cell (Figure 6.5). In exocytosis, the vesicle functions like the trash chute of the cell.

7. **Pinocytosis:** a process of bringing in droplets of extracellular fluid via tiny vesicles.

8. **Receptor-mediated endocytosis:** a specialized type of pinocytosis that moves specific molecules into a cell due to the budding of specific molecules with receptor sites on the cell membrane.

Water Potential

How does a plant defy gravity and stand up? How do fish survive in saltwater? Well, it has to do with water potential. Water potential ($\Psi = \Psi_p + \Psi_s$) indicates how freely water molecules can move in a particular environment or system. It is determined by the solute potential and pressure potential of each environment. Solute potential (Ψ_s), also called osmotic potential, depends on the amount of solute in a solution and *decreases* as the concentration of solute

ENE-2

Cells have membranes that allow them to establish and maintain internal environments that are different from their external environments.

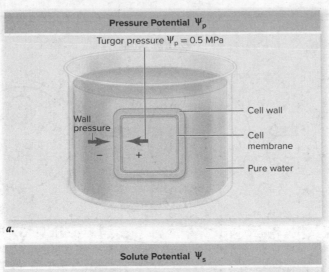

a.

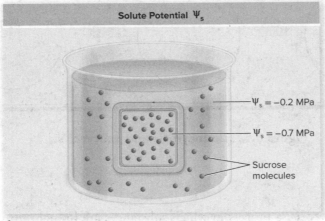

b.

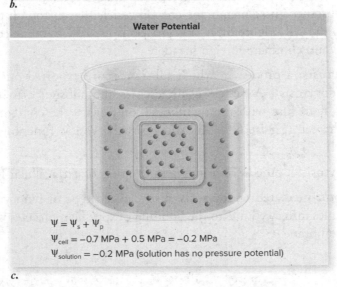

c.

Figure 6.6 Determining water potential. *a.* Cell walls exert pressure in the opposite direction of cell turgor pressure. *b.* Using the given solute potentials, predict the direction of water movement based only on solute potential. *c.* Total water potential is the sum of ψs and ψp. Because the water potential inside the cell equals that of the solution, there is no net movement of water. (*Reproduced with permission from Raven P, Johnson G, Mason K, Losos J, Duncan T; Biology, 12th ed. New York: McGraw Hill; 2020*)

increases. It is negative in a plant cell and zero in distilled water. Pressure potential (Ψ_p), also called turgor potential, refers to the physical pressure exerted by objects or cell membranes on water molecules and *increases* with increasing pressure. Plant cells maintain a positive pressure to hold their shape, allowing them to stay rigid (See Figure 6.6).

$$\Psi = \Psi_p + \Psi_s$$
Ψ_p = pressure potential
Ψ_s = solute potential

In an open container, water potential is equal to the solute potential due to the pressure potential being zero in an open container.

$$\Psi_s = -iCRT$$
i = ionization constant (Sucrose = 1)
C = molar concentration
R = pressure constant (R = 0.0831 liter bars/mole K)
T = temperature in Kelvin (°C + 273)

Osmoregulation is the ability to maintain water balance and allows organisms to control their internal environments by maintaining the right concentrations of solutes and the amount of water in their body fluids. The solute potential of a solution ($\Psi_s = -iCRT$) depends on the ionization constant (i), molar concentration (C), pressure constant (R), and temperature (T).

› Review Questions

For questions 1–4, please use the following answer choices:

A. Cell wall
B. Mitochondrion
C. Ribosome
D. Lysosome

1. This organelle is present in plant cells, but not animal cells.

2. Absence of enzymes from this organelle can lead to storage diseases such as Tay-Sachs disease.

3. This organelle is the host for the Krebs cycle and oxidative phosphorylation of respiration.

4. This organelle is synthesized in the nucleolus of the cell.

5. Which of the following best describes the fluid mosaic model of membranes?

   A. The membrane consists of a phospholipid bilayer with proteins of various lengths and sizes located on the exterior portions of the membrane.
   B. The membrane consists of a phospholipid bilayer with proteins of various lengths and sizes located in the interior of the membrane.
   C. The membrane is composed of a phospholipid bilayer with proteins of uniform lengths and sizes located in the interior of the membrane.
   D. The membrane contains a phospholipid bilayer with proteins of various lengths and sizes interspersed among the phospholipids.

6. Which of the following types of cell transport requires energy?

   A. The movement of a particle across a selectively permeable membrane down its concentration gradient
   B. The movement of a particle across a selectively permeable membrane against its concentration gradient
   C. The movement of water down its concentration gradient across selectively permeable membranes
   D. The movement of a sodium ion from an area of higher concentration to an area of lower concentration

7. Which of the following structures is present in prokaryotic cells?

   A. Nucleus
   B. Mitochondria
   C. Cell wall
   D. Golgi apparatus

8. Which of the following represents an *incorrect* description of an organelle's function?

   A. *Chloroplast:* the site of photosynthesis and energy production in plant cells
   B. *Peroxisome:* organelle that produces hydrogen peroxide as a by-product of reactions involved in the breakdown of fatty acids, and detoxification of alcohol in the liver
   C. *Golgi apparatus:* structure to which proteins, lipids, and other macromolecules are sent to be modified by the addition of sugars and other molecules to form glycoproteins
   D. *Rough endoplasmic reticulum:* membrane-bound organelle lacking ribosomes on its cytoplasmic surface, involved in lipid synthesis, detoxification, and carbohydrate metabolism

9. The destruction of which of the following would most cripple a cell's ability to undergo cell division?

   A. Microfilaments
   B. Intermediate filaments
   C. Microtubules
   D. Actin fibers

10. Which of the following can easily diffuse across a selectively permeable membrane?

    A. Na^+
    B. Glucose
    C. Large uncharged polar molecules
    D. Lipids

› **Answers and Explanations**

1. **A**—Cell walls exist in plant cells and prokaryotic cells, but not animal cells. They function to shape and protect cells.

2. **D**—The lysosome acts like the stomach of the cell. It contains enzymes that break down proteins, lipids, nucleic acids, and carbohydrates. Absence of these enzymes can lead to storage disorders such as Tay-Sachs disease.

3. **B**—The mitochondrion is the power plant of the cell. This organelle specializes in the production of ATP and hosts the Krebs cycle and oxidative phosphorylation.

4. **C**—The ribosome is an organelle made in the nucleolus that serves as the host for protein synthesis in the cell. It is found in both prokaryotes and eukaryotes.

5. **D**—The fluid mosaic model says that proteins can extend all the way through the phospholipid bilayer of the membrane, and that these proteins are of various sizes and lengths.

6. **B**—Answer choice B is the definition of active transport, which requires the input of energy. Simple diffusion (answer choices A and D) and osmosis (answer choice C) are all passive processes that do not require energy input.

7. **C**—Prokaryotes do not contain many organelles, but they do contain cell walls.

8. **D**—This is the description of the *smooth* endoplasmic reticulum. We know that this is a tricky question, but we wanted you to review the distinction between the two types of endoplasmic reticulum.

9. **C**—Microtubules play an enormous role in cell division. They make up the spindle apparatus that works to pull apart the cells during mitosis (Chapter 9). A loss of microtubules would cripple the cell division process. Actin fibers (answer choice D) are the building blocks of microfilaments (answer choice A), which are involved in muscular contraction. Keratin fibers are the building blocks of intermediate filaments (answer choice B), which function as reinforcement for the shape and position of organelles in the cell.

10. **D**—Lipids are the only substances listed that are able to freely diffuse across selectively permeable membranes.

❯ Rapid Review

Try to rapidly review the materials presented in the following table and list:

ORGANELLE	PROKARYOTES	ANIMAL CELLS EUKARYOTES	PLANT CELLS EUKARYOTES	FUNCTION
Cell wall	+	–	+	Protects and shapes the cell
Plasma membrane	+	+	+	Regulates what substances enter and leave a cell
Ribosome	+	+	+	Host for protein synthesis; formed in nucleolus
Smooth ER*	–	+	+	Lipid synthesis, detoxification, carbohydrate metabolism; no ribosomes on cytoplasmic surface
Rough ER*	–	+	+	Synthesizes proteins to secrete or send to plasma membrane; contains ribosomes on cytoplasmic surface
Golgi	–	+	+	Modifies lipids, proteins, etc., and sends them to other sites in the cell
Mitochondrion	–	+	+	Power plant of cell; hosts major energy-producing steps of respiration
Lysosome	–	+	–	Contains enzymes that digest organic compounds; serves as cell's stomach
Nucleus	–	+	+	Control center of cell; host for transcription, replication, and DNA
Peroxisome	–	+	+	Breaks down fatty acids, detoxification of alcohol
Chloroplast	–	–	+	Site of photosynthesis in plants
Cytoskeleton	–	+	+	Skeleton of cell; consists of microtubules (cell division, cilia, flagella), microfilaments (muscles), and intermediate filaments (reinforcing position of organelles)
Vacuole	–	+, small	+, large	Storage vault of cells
Centriole	–	+	–	Part of microtubule separation apparatus that assists cell division in animal cells

*Endoplasmic reticulum

Fluid mosaic model: plasma membrane is a selectively permeable phospholipid bilayer with proteins of various lengths and sizes interspersed with cholesterol among the phospholipids.

Integral proteins: proteins implanted within lipid bilayer of plasma membrane.

Peripheral proteins: proteins attached to exterior of membrane.

Diffusion: passive movement of substances down their concentration gradient (from high to low concentrations).

Osmosis: passive movement of water from the side of low solute concentration to the side of high solute concentration (hypotonic to hypertonic).

Facilitated diffusion: assisted transport of particles across membrane (no energy input needed).

Active transport: movement of substances against concentration gradient (low to high concentrations; requires energy input).

Endocytosis: phagocytosis of particles into a cell through the use of vesicles.

Exocytosis: process by which particles are ejected from the cell, similar to movement in a trash chute.

Water potential: ($\Psi = \Psi_p + \Psi_s$) indicates how freely water molecules can move in a particular environment or system. It is determined by the solute potential and pressure potential of each environment.

Hypertonic: a solution that contains a higher solute concentration when compared to inside the cell.

Hypotonic: a solution that contains a lower solute concentration when compared to inside the cell.

Isotonic: indicates there is no net movement of water across the membrane due to an equal concentration of solutes on both sides.

Pinocytosis: a process of bringing in droplets of extracellular fluid via tiny vesicles.

Phagocytosis: a process in which substances are brought into cells by the enclosure of the substance into a membrane-created vesicle that surrounds the substance and escorts it into the cell.

CHAPTER 7

Cellular Energetics
Exam Weight: 12–16%

IN THIS CHAPTER

Summary: This chapter covers the basics behind the energy-creation processes known as respiration and photosynthesis. This chapter will teach you the difference between aerobic and anaerobic respiration and take you through the steps that convert a glucose molecule into ATP. It will also teach you how plants generate their energy from light in two distinct stages—the light-dependent and the light-independent reactions.

Key Ideas

- ✪ Aerobic respiration: glycolysis → Krebs cycle → oxidative phosphorylation → 36 ATP.
- ✪ Anaerobic respiration: glycolysis → regenerate NAD^+ → much less ATP.
- ✪ Oxidative phosphorylation results in the production of large amounts of ATP from NADH and $FADH_2$.
- ✪ Chemiosmosis is the coupling of the movement of electrons down the electron transport chain with the formation of ATP using the driving force provided by the proton gradient.
- ✪ Overall photosynthesis reaction: $H_2O + CO_2 + light → O_2 + glucose + H_2O$.
- ✪ Light-dependent reactions: inputs are water and light; products are ATP, NADPH, and O_2.
- ✪ The oxygen produced in photosynthesis comes from the water.
- ✪ The carbon in the glucose produced in photosynthesis comes from the CO_2.
- ✪ Light-independent reactions (dark reactions): inputs are NADPH, ATP, and CO_2; products are ADP, $NADP^+$, and sugar.

Introduction

In this chapter, we explore how cells obtain energy. It is important that you do not get lost or buried in the details. You should finish this chapter with an understanding of the basic processes.

The AP Biology exam will not ask you to identify by name the enzyme that catalyzes the third step of glycolysis, nor will it require you to name the fourth molecule in the Krebs cycle. But it *will* ask you questions that require an understanding of the respiration process.

The AP Biology exam will not ask you to draw a picture of the thylakoid membrane system. But it will want you to know that photosynthesis is the process by which plants generate their energy from light or that most of plant photosynthesis occurs in the plant's leaves or that the majority of the chloroplasts of a plant are found in mesophyll cells.

It's important to remember that there are two stages to photosynthesis: the light-dependent reactions and the light-independent reactions, commonly called the dark reactions. The simplified equation of photosynthesis is:

$$H_2O + CO_2 + light \rightarrow O_2 + glucose + H_2O$$

Enzymes

> **ENE-1**
>
> *The highly complex organization of living systems requires constant input of energy and the exchange of macromolecules.*

Enzymes are proteins that act as organic catalysts and will be encountered often in your review for this exam. **Catalysts** speed up reactions by lowering the energy (activation energy) needed for the reaction to take place, but are not used up in the reaction. The substances that enzymes act on are known as **substrates**.

Enzymes are selective; they interact only with particular substrates. It is the shape of the enzyme that provides the specificity. The part of the enzyme that interacts with the substrate is called the **active site.** The lock and key model describes a substrate's interaction with the enzyme's active sight and suggests that the enzyme and the substrate possess specific complementary geometric shapes that fit perfectly just like a key fighting into a lock. The **induced-fit model** of enzyme-substrate interaction describes the active site of an enzyme as specific for a particular substrate that fits its shape.

When the enzyme and substrate bind together, the enzyme is *induced* to alter its shape for a tighter active site–substrate attachment. This tight fit places the substrate in a favorable position to react, speeding up (accelerating) the rate of reaction. After an enzyme interacts with a substrate, converting it into a product, it is free to find and react with another substrate; thus, a small concentration of enzyme can have a major effect on a reaction.

Each enzyme functions best at an optimal temperature, pH, and salt concentration. If those values stray too far from "optimal," the effectiveness of the enzyme will suffer and the enzyme could **denature**. The weak chemical bonds and interactions within a protein may be destroyed, causing the protein to unravel and lose its shape. The effectiveness of an enzyme can be affected by four things:

1. The temperature
2. The pH
3. The concentration of the substrate involved
4. The concentration of the enzyme involved

You should be able to identify the basic components of an activation energy diagram if you encounter one on the AP exam. The important parts are identified in Figure 7.1.

The last enzyme topic to cover is the difference between competitive and noncompetitive inhibition. In **competitive inhibition** (Figure 7.2), an inhibitor molecule resembling the substrate binds to the active site and physically blocks the substrate from attaching.

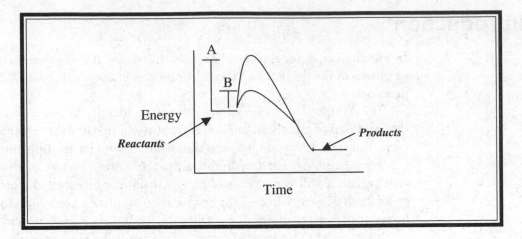

Figure 7.1   Plot showing energy versus time. Height A represents original activation energy; height B represents the lowered activation energy due to the addition of enzyme.

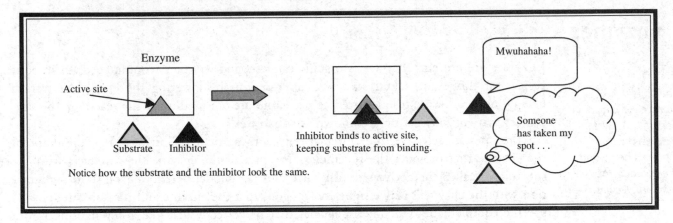

Figure 7.2   Competitive inhibition.

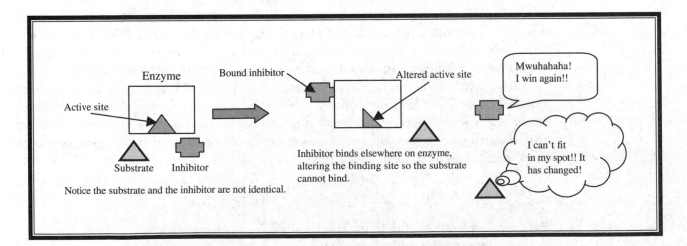

Figure 7.3   Noncompetitive inhibition.

Competitive inhibition can sometimes be overcome by adding a high concentration of substrate to outcompete the inhibitor. In **noncompetitive inhibition** (Figure 7.3), an inhibitor molecule binds to a different part of the enzyme, causing a change in the shape of the active site so that it can no longer interact with the substrate.

Cellular Energy

All living organisms rely on a constant input of energy in different forms to survive and thrive. This flow of energy follows the laws of thermodynamics that govern all forms of energy. The first law of thermodynamics states that energy cannot be created or destroyed; it can only change form, and it must be obtained through its environment. The second law of thermody- namics states that life is in a constant movement toward entropy or a "gradual decline of order" in a system and requires a constant input of energy from its environment that can be used to overcome this decline of order. Without the constant input of energy, an organism will die!!!

The constant input of energy to overcome energy and the idea that energy cannot be created or destroyed is the foundation upon which trophic or energy dynamics on Earth rest. The movement energy comes from the coupling of endergonic and exergonic reac- tions. **Endergonic reactions** are reactions in which energy is absorbed from the surround- ings. **Exergonic reactions** are reactions in which free energy is released (See Figure 7.4).

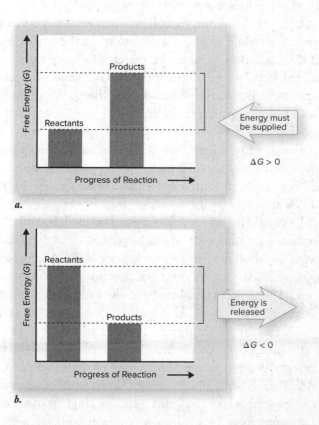

Figure 7.4   Energy in chemical reactions. *a.* In an endergonic reaction, the products of the reaction con- tain more energy than the reactants, and the extra energy must be supplied for the reaction to proceed. ***b.*** In an exergonic reaction, the products contain less energy than the reactants, and the excess energy is released. (*Reproduced with permission from Raven P, Johnson G, Mason K, Losos J, Duncan T;* Biology, *12th ed. New York: McGraw Hill; 2020*)

This constant exchange of free energy is maintained in living systems through con- trolled and efficient transfer of energy during the metabolic pathway. The products of one reaction in a metabolic pathway become the reactants for the next step in the pathway. One such reaction is the production of adenosine triphosphate (ATP) in cells. ATP is the energy currency of life. It is the high-energy molecule that stores the energy that life needs to do just about everything. ATP is constructed from an adenosine diphosphate (ADP) and an inorganic phosphate group (Pi) through phosphorylation, a chemical process in which a phosphate group is added using free energy.

Aerobic Respiration

Glycolysis

Glycolysis occurs in the cytoplasm of cells and is the beginning pathway for both aerobic and anaerobic respiration. During glycolysis, a glucose molecule is broken down through a series of reactions into two molecules of pyruvate. It is important to remember that oxygen plays no role in glycolysis. This reaction can occur in oxygen-rich and oxygen-poor environments. However, when in an environment lacking oxygen, glycolysis slows because the cells run out (become depleted) of NAD^+. For reasons we will discuss later, a lack of oxygen prevents oxidative phosphorylation from occurring, causing a buildup of NADH in the cells. This buildup causes a shortage of NAD^+. This is bad for glycolysis because it requires NAD^+ to function. Fermentation is the solution to this problem—it takes the excess NADH that builds up and converts it back to NAD^+ so that glycolysis can continue. More to come on fermentation later . . . be patient. ☺

To reiterate, the AP Biology exam will not require you to memorize the various steps of respiration. Your time is better spent studying the broad explanation of respiration, to understand the basic process, and become comfortable with respiration as a whole. Major concepts are the key. We will explain the specific steps of glycolysis because they will help you understand the big picture—but do not memorize them all. Save the space for other facts you have to know from other chapters of this book.

Examine Figure 7.5, which illustrates the general layout of glycolysis. The beginning steps of glycolysis require energy input. The first step adds a phosphate to a molecule of glucose with the assistance of an ATP molecule to produce *glucose-6-phosphate* (G6P). The newly formed G6P rearranges to form a molecule named *fructose-6-phosphate* (F6P). Another molecule of ATP is required for the next step, which adds another phosphate group to produce fructose 1,6-biphosphate. Already, glycolysis has used two of the ATP molecules that it is trying to produce—seems stupid . . . but be patient . . . the genius has yet to show its face. F6P splits into two 3-carbon-long fragments known as **PGAL** (glyceraldehyde phosphate). With the formation of PGAL, the energy-producing portion of glycolysis begins. Each PGAL molecule takes on an inorganic phosphate from the cytoplasm to produce 1,3-diphosphoglycerate. During this reaction, each PGAL gives up two electrons and a hydrogen to molecules of NAD^+ to form the all-important NADH molecules. The next step is a big one, as it leads to the production of the first ATP molecule in the process of respiration—the 1,3-diphosphoglycerate molecules donate one of their two phosphates to molecules of ADP to produce ATP and 3-phosphoglycerate (3PG). You'll notice that there are *two* ATP molecules formed here because before this step, the single molecule of glucose divided into *two* 3-carbon fragments. After 3PG rearranges to form 2-phosphoglycerate, phosphoenolpyruvate (PEP) is formed, which donates a phosphate group to molecules of ADP to form another pair of ATP molecules and pyruvate. This is the final step of glycolysis. In total, two molecules each of ATP, NADH, and pyruvate are formed during this process. Glycolysis produces the same result under anaerobic conditions as it does under aerobic conditions: two ATP molecules. If oxygen is present, more ATP is later made by oxidative phosphorylation.

If you are going to memorize one fact about glycolysis, remember that one glucose molecule produces two pyruvate, two NADH, and two ATP molecules.

One glucose → 2 pyruvate, 2 ATP, 2 NADH

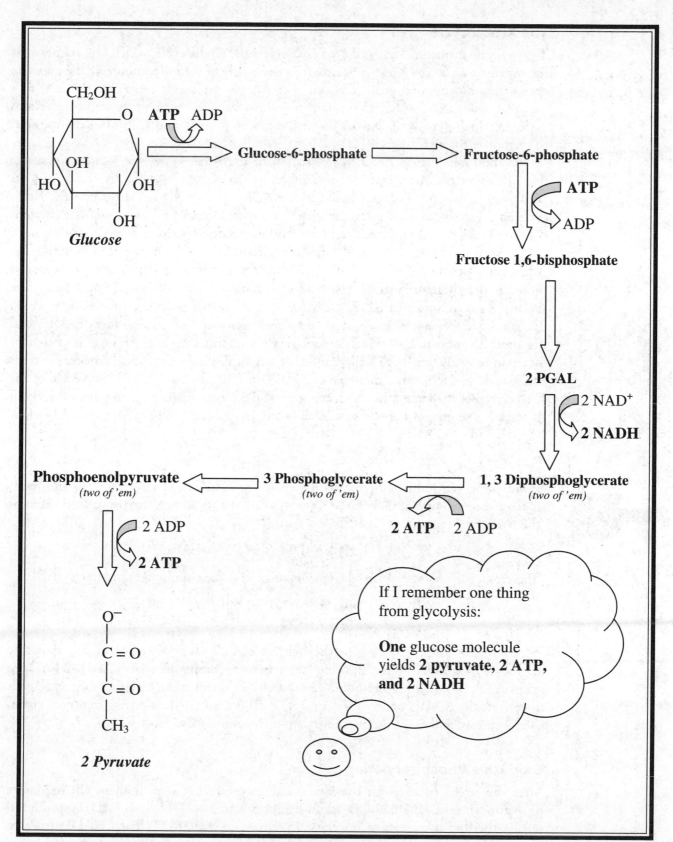

Figure 7.5   Glycolysis.

The Krebs Cycle

The pyruvate formed during glycolysis next enters the **Krebs cycle,** which is also known as the *citric acid cycle.* The Krebs cycle occurs in the matrix of the **mitochondria.** The pyruvate enters the mitochondria of the cell and is converted into acetyl coenzyme A (CoA) in a step that produces an NADH. This compound is now ready to enter the eight-step Krebs cycle, in which pyruvate is broken down completely to H_2O and CO_2. You do not need to memorize the eight steps.

As shown in Figure 7.6, a representation of the Krebs cycle, the 3-carbon pyruvate does not enter the Krebs cycle per se. Rather, it is converted, with the assistance of CoA and NAD^+, into 2-carbon acetyl CoA and NADH. The acetyl CoA dives into the Krebs cycle and reacts with oxaloacetate to form a 6-carbon molecule called *citrate.* The citrate is converted to a molecule named isocitrate, which then donates electrons and a hydrogen to NAD^+ to form 5-carbon α-ketoglutarate, carbon dioxide, and a molecule of NADH. The α-ketoglutarate undergoes a reaction very similar to the one leading to its formation and produces 4-carbon succinyl CoA and another molecule each of NADH and CO_2. The succinyl CoA is converted into succinate in a reaction that produces a molecule of ATP. The succinate then transfers electrons and a hydrogen atom to FAD to form $FADH_2$ and fumarate. The next-to-last step in the Krebs cycle takes fumarate and rearranges it to another 4-carbon molecule: malate. Finally, in the last step of the cycle, the malate donates electrons and a hydrogen atom to a molecule of NAD^+ to form the final NADH molecule of the Krebs cycle, at the same time regenerating the molecule of oxaloacetate that helped kick off the cycle. One turn of the Krebs cycle takes a single pyruvate and produces one ATP, four NADH, and one $FADH_2$.

If you are going to memorize one thing about the Krebs cycle, remember that for each glucose dropped into glycolysis, the Krebs cycle occurs twice. Each pyruvate dropped into the Krebs cycle produces

$$4 \text{ NADH, } 1 \text{ FADH}_2, 1 \text{ ATP, and } 2 \text{ CO}_2$$

Therefore, the *pyruvate* obtained from the original glucose molecule produces:

$$8 \text{ NADH, } 2 \text{ FADH}_2, \text{ and } 2 \text{ ATP}$$

Up to this point, having gone through glycolysis and the Krebs cycle, one molecule of glucose has produced the following energy-related compounds: 10 NADH, 2 $FADH_2$, and 4 ATP. Not bad for an honest day's work . . . but the body wants more and needs to convert the NADH and $FADH_2$ into ATP. This is where the electron transport chain, chemiosmosis, and oxidative phosphorylation come into play.

Oxidative Phosphorylation

After the Krebs cycle comes the largest energy-producing step of them all: **oxidative phosphorylation.** During this aerobic process, the NADH and $FADH_2$ produced during the first two stages of respiration are used to create ATP. Each NADH leads to the production of up to three ATP, and each $FADH_2$ will lead to the production of up to two ATP molecules. This is an inexact measurement—those numbers represent the

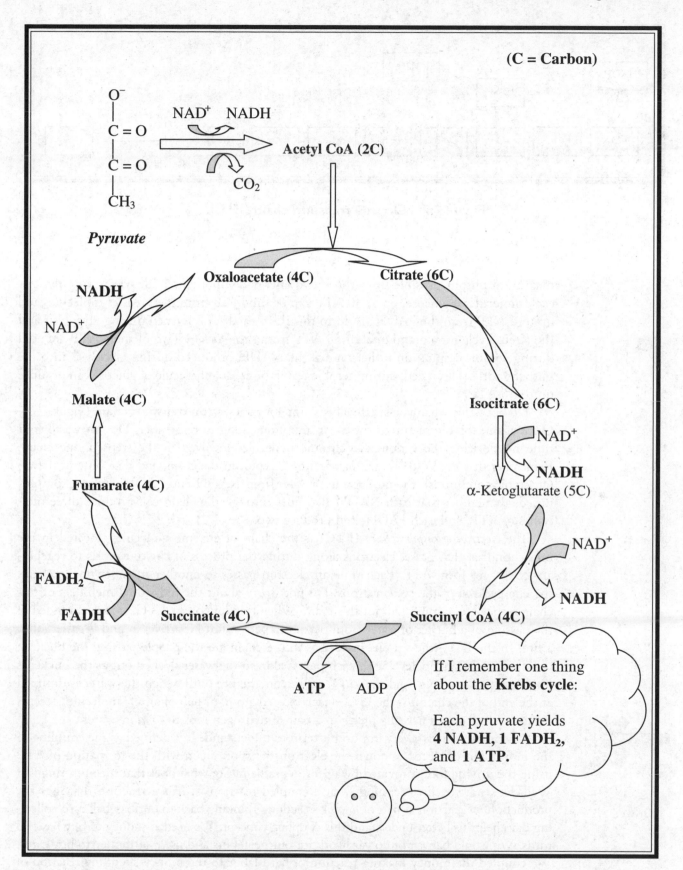

Figure 7.6   The Krebs cycle.

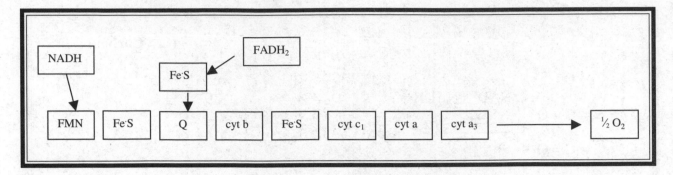

Figure 7.7   Electron transport chain (ETC).

maximum output possible from those two energy components if all goes smoothly. For each molecule of glucose, up to 30 ATP can be produced from the NADH molecules and up to 4 ATP from the $FADH_2$. Add to this the 4 total ATP formed during glycolysis and the Krebs cycle for a grand total of 38 ATP from *each glucose*. Two of these ATP are used during aerobic respiration to help move the NADH produced during glycolysis into the mitochondria. All totaled, during aerobic respiration, each molecule of glucose can produce up to 36 ATP.

Do not panic when you see the illustration for the **electron transport chain** (Figure 7.7). Once again, the big picture is the most important thing to remember. Do not waste your time memorizing the various cytochrome molecules involved in the steps of the chain. Remember that the ½ O_2 is the final electron acceptor in the chain, and that without the O_2 (anaerobic conditions), the production of ATP from NADH and $FADH_2$ will be compromised. Remember that each NADH that goes through the chain can produce three molecules of ATP, and each $FADH_2$ can produce two.

The *electron transport chain* (ETC) is the chain of enzyme molecules, located in the mitochondria, that passes electrons along during the process of chemiosmosis to regenerate NAD^+ to form ATP. Each time an electron passes to another member of the chain, the energy level of the system drops. Do not worry about the individual members of this chain—they are unimportant for this exam. When thinking of the ETC, we are reminded of the passing of a bucket of water from person to person until it arrives at and is tossed onto a fire. In the ETC, the various molecules in the chain are the people passing the buckets; the drop in the energy level with each pass is akin to the water sloshed out as the bucket is hurriedly passed along, and the ½ O_2 represents the fire onto which the water is dumped at the end of the chain. As the ½ O_2 (each oxygen atom, or half of an O_2 molecule) accepts a pair of electrons, it actually picks up a pair of hydrogen ions to *produce* water.

Chemiosmosis is a very important term to understand. It is defined as the coupling of the movement of electrons down the electron transport chain with the formation of ATP using the driving force provided by a proton gradient. So, what does that mean in English? Well, let's start by first defining what a coupled reaction is. It is a reaction that uses the product of *one* reaction as part of *another* reaction. Thinking back to our baseball card collecting days helps us better understand this coupling concept. We needed money to buy baseball cards. We would babysit or do yardwork for our neighbors and use that money to buy cards. We coupled the money-making reaction of hard labor to the money-spending reaction of buying baseball cards.

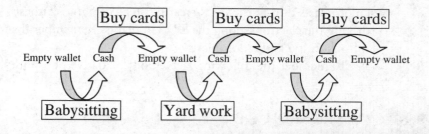

Let's look more closely at the reactions that are coupled in chemiosmosis. If you look at Figure 7.8a, a crude representation of a mitochondrion, you will find the ETC embedded within the inner mitochondrial membrane. As some of the molecules in the chain accept and then pass on electrons, they pump hydrogen ions into the space between the inner and outer membranes of the mitochondria (Figure 7.8b). This creates a proton gradient that drives the production of ATP. The difference in hydrogen concentration on the two sides of the membrane causes the protons to flow back into the matrix of the mitochondria through ATP synthase channels (Figure 7.8c). **ATP synthase** is an enzyme that uses the flow of hydrogens to drive the phosphorylation of an ADP molecule to produce ATP. This reaction completes the process of oxidative phosphorylation and chemiosmosis. The proton gradient created by the movement of electrons from molecule to molecule has been used to form the ATP that this process is designed to produce. In other words, the formation of ATP has been coupled to the movement of electrons and protons.

Chemiosmosis is not oxidative phosphorylation per se; rather, it is a major *part* of oxidative phosphorylation. An important fact we want you to take out of this chapter is that chemiosmosis is not unique to the mitochondria. It is the same process that occurs in the

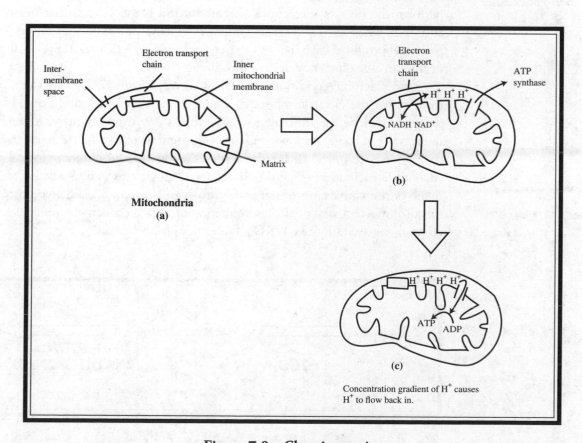

Figure 7.8   Chemiosmosis.

chloroplasts during the ATP-creating steps of photosynthesis. The difference is that light is driving the electrons along the ETC in plants. Remember that chemiosmosis occurs in both mitochondria and chloroplasts.

Remember the following facts about oxidative phosphorylation (Ox-phos):

1. Each NADH → 3 ATP.
2. Each $FADH_2$ → 2 ATP.
3. ½ O_2 is the final electron acceptor of the electron transport chain, and the chain will not function in the absence of oxygen.
4. Ox-phos serves the important function of regenerating NAD^+ so that glycolysis and the Krebs cycle can continue.
5. Chemiosmosis occurs in photosynthesis as well as respiration.

Anaerobic Respiration

ENE-1

The highly complex organization of living systems requires constant input of energy and the exchange of macromolecules.

Anaerobic respiration, or *fermentation,* occurs when oxygen is unavailable or cannot be used by the organism. As in aerobic respiration, glycolysis occurs and pyruvate is produced. The pyruvate enters the Krebs cycle, producing NADH, $FADH_2$, and some ATP. The problem arises in the ETC—because there is no oxygen available, the electrons do not pass down the chain to the final electron acceptor, causing a buildup of NADH in the system. This buildup of NADH means that the NAD^+ normally regenerated during oxidative phosphorylation is not produced, and this creates an NAD^+ shortage. This is a problem, because in order for glycolysis to proceed to the pyruvate stage, it needs NAD^+ to help perform the necessary reactions. **Fermentation** is the process that begins with glycolysis and ends when NAD^+ is regenerated. A glucose molecule that enters the fermentation pathway produces two net ATP per molecule of glucose, representing a tremendous decline in the efficiency of ATP production.

Under aerobic conditions, NAD^+ is recycled from NADH by the movement of electrons down the electron transport chain. Under anaerobic conditions, NAD^+ is recycled from NADH by the movement of electrons to pyruvate, namely, fermentation. The two main types of fermentation are **alcohol fermentation** and **lactic acid fermentation.** Refer to Figures 7.9 and 7.10 for the representations of the different forms of fermentation. Alcohol fermentation (Figure 7.9) occurs in fungi, yeast, and some bacteria. The first step involves the conversion of pyruvate into two 2-carbon acetaldehyde molecules. Then, in the all-important step of alcohol fermentation, the acetaldehyde molecules are converted to ethanol, regenerating two NAD^+ molecules in the process.

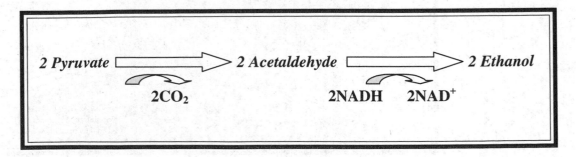

Figure 7.9 Alcohol fermentation.

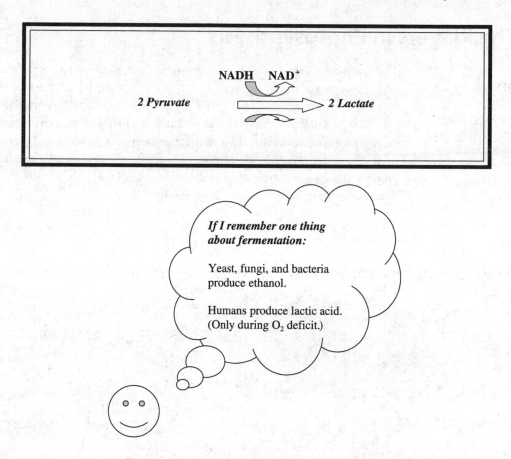

Figure 7.10   Lactic acid fermentation.

Lactic acid fermentation (Figure 7.10) occurs in human and animal muscle cells when oxygen is not available. This is a simpler process than alcoholic fermentation—the pyruvate is directly reduced to lactate (also known as lactic acid) by NADH to regenerate the NAD^+ needed for the resumption of glycolysis. Have you ever had a cramp during exercise? The pain you felt was the result of lactic acid fermentation. Your muscle was deprived of the necessary amount of oxygen to continue glycolysis, and it switched over to fermentation. The pain from the cramp came from the acidity in the muscle.

The Players in Photosynthesis

The host organelle for photosynthesis is the **chloroplast,** which is divided into an inner and outer portion. The inner fluid portion is called the **stroma,** which is surrounded by two outer membranes. In Figure 7.11, you can see that winding through the stroma is an inner membrane called the **thylakoid membrane system.** This is where the first stage of photosynthesis occurs. This membrane consists of flattened channels and disks arranged in stacks called **grana.** We always remember the thylakoid system as resembling stacks of poker chips, where each chip is a single thylakoid. It is within these poker chips that the light-dependent reactions of photosynthesis occur.

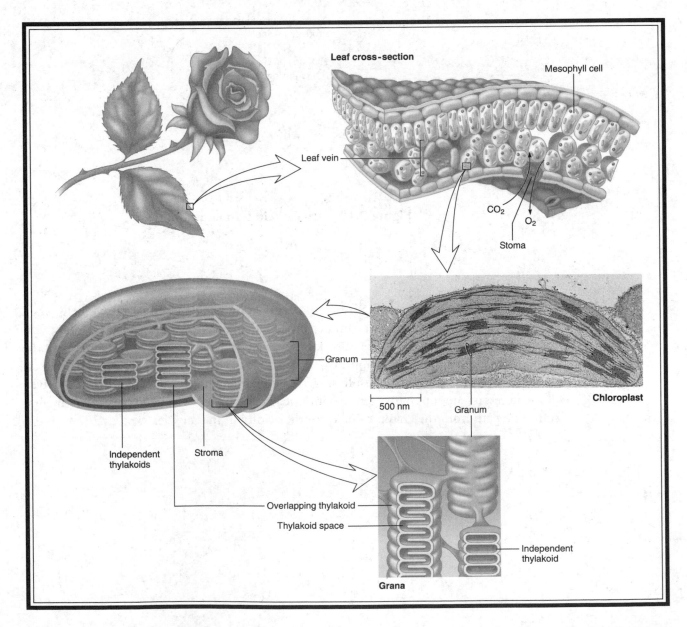

Figure 7.11   An overall view of photosynthesis. (*From* Biology, *8th ed., by Sylvia S. Mader, © 1985, 1987, 1990, 1993, 1996, 1998, 2001, 2004 by the McGraw Hill Companies, Inc. Reproduced with permission of The McGraw Hill Companies.*)

Before we examine the process of photosynthesis, here are some definitions that will make things a bit easier as you read this chapter.

Autotroph: an organism that is self-nourishing. It obtains carbon and energy without ingesting other organisms. Plants and algae are good examples of autotrophic organisms—they obtain their energy from carbon dioxide, water, and light. They are the producers of the world.

Bundle sheath cells: cells that are tightly wrapped around the veins of a leaf. They are the site for the **Calvin cycle** in C_4 plants.

C_4 plant: plant that has adapted its photosynthetic process to more efficiently handle hot and dry conditions.

Heterotroph: organisms that must consume other organisms to obtain nourishment. They are the consumers of the world.

Mesophyll: interior tissue of a leaf.

Mesophyll cells: cells that contain many chloroplasts and host the majority of photosynthesis.

Photolysis: process by which water is broken up by an enzyme into hydrogen ions and oxygen atoms; occurs during the light-dependent reactions of photosynthesis.

Photophosphorylation: process by which ATP is produced during the light-dependent reactions of photosynthesis. It is the chloroplast equivalent of oxidative phosphorylation.

Photorespiration: process by which oxygen competes with carbon dioxide and attaches to RuBP. Plants that experience photorespiration have a lowered capacity for growth.

Photosystem: a cluster of light-trapping pigments involved in the process of photosynthesis. Photosystems vary tremendously in their organization and can possess hundreds of pigments. The two most important are photosystems I and II of the light reactions.

Pigment: a molecule that absorbs light of a particular wavelength. Pigments are vital to the process of photosynthesis and include **chlorophyll, carotenoids,** and **phycobilins.**

Rubisco: an enzyme that catalyzes the first step of the Calvin cycle in C_3 plants.

Stomata: structure through which CO_2 enters a plant and water vapor and O_2 leave.

Transpiration: natural process by which plants lose H_2O via evaporation through their leaves.

The Reactions of Photosynthesis

The process of photosynthesis can be neatly divided into two sets of reactions: the light-dependent reactions and the light-independent reactions. The light-dependent reactions occur first and require an input of water and light. They produce three things: the oxygen we breathe, NADPH, and ATP. These last two products of the light reactions are then consumed during the second stage of photosynthesis: the dark reactions. These reactions, which need CO_2, NADPH, and ATP as inputs, produce sugar and recycle the $NADP^+$ and ADP to be used by the next set of light-dependent reactions.

Now, we would be too kind The process of photosynthesis can be neatly divided into two sets of reactions: the light-dependent reactions and the light-independent reactions. The light-dependent reactions occur first and require an input of water and light. They produce three things: the oxygen we breathe, NADPH, and ATP. These last two products of the light reactions are then consumed during the second stage of photosynthesis: the dark reactions. These reactions, which need CO_2, NADPH, and ATP as inputs, produce sugar and recycle the $NADP^+$ and ADP to be used by the next set of light-dependent reactions. Now, we would be too kind if we left the discussion there. Let's look at the reactions in more detail. Stop groaning . . . you know we have to go there.

Light-Dependent Reactions

Light-dependent reactions occur in the thylakoid membrane system. The thylakoid system is composed of the various stacks of poker chip look-alikes located within the stroma of the chloroplast. Within the thylakoid membrane is a photosynthetic participant termed **chlorophyll**. There are two main types of chlorophyll that you should remember: chlorophyll *a* and chlorophyll *b*. Chlorophyll *a* is the major pigment of photosynthesis, while chlorophyll *b* is considered to be an accessory pigment. The pigments are very similar structurally, but the minor differences are what account for the variance in their absorption of light. Chlorophyll absorbs light of a particular wavelength, and when it does, one of its electrons is elevated to a higher energy level (it is "excited"). Almost immediately, the excited electron drops back down to the ground state, giving off heat in the process. This energy is passed along until it finds chlorophyll *a*, which, when excited, passes its electron to the primary electron acceptor; then, the light-dependent reactions are under way.

The pigments of the thylakoid space organize themselves into groups called *photosystems*. These photosystems consist of varying combinations of chlorophylls *a*, *b*, and others; pigments called **phycobilins;** and another type of pigment called **carotenoids.** The accessory pigments help pick up light when chlorophyll *a* cannot do it as effectively. An example is red algae on the ocean bottom. When light is picked up by the accessory pigments, it is fluoresced and altered so that chlorophyll *a* can use it.

Imagine that the plant represented in Figure 7.12 is struck by light from the sun. This light excites the **photosystem** of the thylakoid space, which absorbs the photon and transmits the energy from one pigment molecule to another. As this energy is passed along, it loses a bit of energy with each step and eventually reaches chlorophyll *a*, which proceeds to kick off the process of photosynthesis. It initiates the first step of photosynthesis by passing the electron to the primary electron acceptor.

Before we continue, there are two major photosystems we want to tell you about—you might want to get out a pen or pencil here to jot this down, because the names for these photosystems may seem confusing. They are photosystem I and photosystem II. The only difference between these two **reaction centers** is that the main chlorophyll of photosystem I absorbs light with a wavelength of 700 nm, while the main chlorophyll of photosystem II absorbs light with a wavelength of 680 nm. By interacting with different thylakoid membrane proteins, they are able to absorb light of slightly different wavelengths.

Now let's get back to the reactions. Let's go through the rest of Figure 7.12 and talk about the light-dependent reactions. For the sole purpose of confusing you, plants start photosynthesis by using photosystem II before photosystem I. As light strikes photosystem II, the energy is absorbed and passed along until it reaches the P680 chlorophyll. When this chlorophyll is excited, it passes its electrons to the primary electron acceptor. This is where the water molecule comes into play. **Photolysis** in the thylakoid space takes electrons from H_2O and passes them to P680 to replace the electrons given to the primary acceptor. With this reaction, a lone oxygen atom and a pair of hydrogen ions are formed from the water. The oxygen atom quickly finds another oxygen atom buddy, pairs up with it, and generates the O_2 that the plants so graciously put out for us every day. This is the first product of the light reactions.

The light reactions do not stop here, however. We need to consider what happens to the electron that has been passed to the primary electron acceptor. The electron is passed to photosystem I, P700, in a manner reminiscent of the electron transport chain. As the

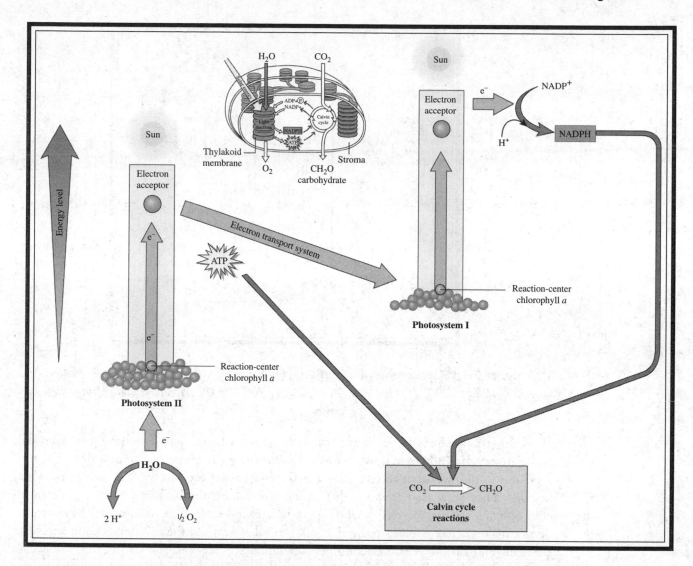

Figure 7.12 **Light-dependent reactions.** (*From* Biology, *8th ed., by Sylvia S. Mader,* © *1985, 1987, 1990, 1993, 1996, 1998, 2001, 2004 by the McGraw Hill Companies, Inc. Reproduced with permission of The McGraw Hill Companies.*)

electrons are passed from P680 to P700, the lost energy is used to produce ATP (remember chemiosmosis). This ATP is the second product of the light reactions and is produced in a manner mechanistically similar to the way ATP is produced during oxidative phosphorylation of respiration. In plants, this process of ATP formation is called **photophosphorylation.**

After the photosystem I electrons are excited, photosystem I passes the energy to its own primary electron acceptor. These electrons are sent down another chain to **ferredoxin,** which then donates the electrons to $NADP^+$ to produce NADPH, the third and final product of the light reactions. (Notice how in photosynthesis, there is NADPH instead of NADH. The symbol P can help you remember that it relates to photosynthesis. ☺)

Remember the following about the light reactions:

1. The light reactions occur in the thylakoid membrane.
2. The inputs to the light reactions are water and light.
3. The light reactions produce three products: ATP, NADPH, and O_2.
4. The oxygen produced in the light reactions comes from H_2O, not CO_2.

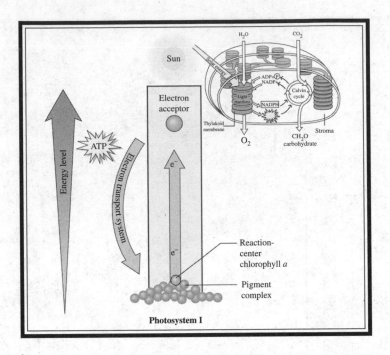

Figure 7.13 Cyclic phosphorylation. (*From* Biology, *8th ed., by Sylvia S. Mader,* © *1985, 1987, 1990, 1993, 1996, 1998, 2001, 2004 by the McGraw Hill Companies, Inc. Reproduced with permission of The McGraw Hill Companies.*)

Two separate light-dependent pathways occur in plants. What we have just discussed is the **noncyclic light reaction** pathway. Considering the name of the first one, it is not shocking to discover that there is also a **cyclic light reaction** pathway (Figure 7.13). One key difference between the two is that in the noncyclic pathway, the electrons taken from chlorophyll *a* are not recycled back down to the ground state. This means that the electrons do not make their way back to the chlorophyll molecule when the reaction is complete. The electrons end up on NADPH. Another key difference between the two is that the cyclic pathway uses only photosystem I; photosystem II is not involved. In the cyclic pathway, sunlight hits P700, thus exciting the electrons and passing them from P700 to its primary electron acceptor. It is called the *cyclic pathway* because these electrons pass down the electron chain and eventually back to P700 to complete the cycle. The energy given off during the passage down the chain is harnessed to produce ATP—the only product of this pathway. Neither oxygen nor NADPH is produced from these reactions.

A question that might be forming as you read this is: "Why does this pathway continue to exist?" or perhaps you are wondering "Why do they insist on torturing me by writing about all of this photosynthesis stuff?" We will answer the first question and ignore the second one. The cyclic pathway exists because the Calvin cycle, which we discuss next, uses more ATP than it does NADPH. This eventually causes a problem because the light reactions produce equal amounts of ATP and NADPH. The plant compensates for this disparity by dropping into the cyclic phase when needed to produce the ATP necessary to keep the light-independent reactions from grinding to a halt.

Before moving on to the Calvin cycle, it is important to understand how ATP is formed. We know, we know . . . you thought we were finished . . . but we want you to be an expert in the field of photosynthesis. You never know when these facts might come in handy. For example, just the other day one of us was offered $10,000 by a random person on the street to recount the similarities between photosynthesis and respiration. So, this stuff *is* useful in everyday life. As the electrons are passing from the primary electron acceptor to the next photosystem, hydrogen ions are picked up from outside the membrane and brought back into the thylakoid compartment, creating an H$^+$ gradient similar to what we saw in oxidative phosphorylation. During the light-dependent reactions, when hydrogen ions are taken from water during photolysis, the proton gradient grows larger, causing some protons to leave, leading to the formation of ATP.

You'll notice that this process in plants is a bit different from oxidative phosphorylation of the mitochondria, where the proton gradient is created by pumping protons from the matrix *out* to the intermembrane space. In the mitochondria, the ATP is produced when the protons move back *in*. But in plants, photophosphorylation creates the gradient by pumping protons in from the stroma to the thylakoid compartment, and the ATP is produced as the protons move back *out*. The opposing reactions produce the same happy result—more ATP for the cells.

Light-Independent Reactions (Calvin Cycle)

After the light reactions have produced the necessary ATP and NADPH, the synthesis phase of photosynthesis is ready to proceed. The inputs into the Calvin cycle are NADPH (which provides hydrogen and electrons), ATP (which provides energy), and CO_2. From here on, just so we don't drive you *insane* switching from term to term, we are going to call the dark reactions of photosynthesis the *Calvin cycle* (Figure 7.14). The Calvin cycle occurs

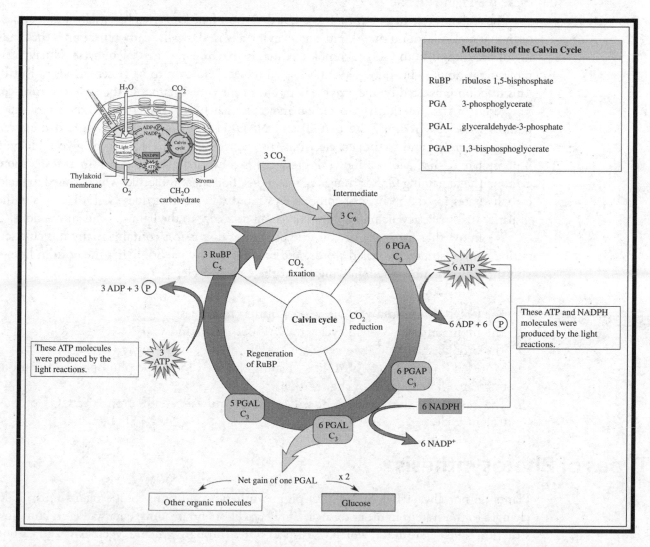

Figure 7.14 The Calvin cycle. (*From* Biology, *8th ed., by Sylvia S. Mader, © 1985, 1987, 1990, 1993, 1996, 1998, 2001, 2004 by the McGraw Hill Companies, Inc. Reproduced with permission of The McGraw Hill Companies.*)

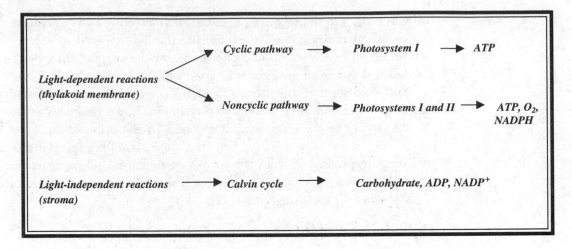

Figure 7.15 Summary of photosynthesis.

in the stroma of the chloroplast, which is the fluid surrounding the thylakoid "poker chips." (For further distinctions among the cyclic pathway, the noncyclic pathway, and the Calvin cycle, see Figure 7.15.)

The Calvin cycle begins with a step called **carbon fixation.** This is a tricky and complex term that makes it sound more confusing than it really is. Basically, carbon fixation is the binding of the carbon from CO_2 to a molecule that is able to enter the Calvin cycle. Usually this molecule is ribulose bis-phosphate, a 5-carbon molecule known to its closer friends as RuBP. This reaction is assisted by the enzyme with one of the cooler names in the business: **rubisco.** The result of this reaction is a 6-carbon molecule that breaks into two 3-carbon molecules named *3-phosphoglycerate* (3PG). ATP and NADPH step up at this point and donate a phosphate group and hydrogen electrons, respectively, to (3PG) to form glyceraldehyde 3-phosphate (G3P). Most of the G3P produced is converted back to RuBP so as to fix more carbon. The remaining G3P is converted into a 6-carbon sugar molecule, which is used to build carbohydrates for the plant. This process uses more ATP than it does NADPH. This is the disparity that makes cyclic photophosphorylation necessary in the light-dependent reactions.

We know that for some of you, the preceding discussion contains many difficult scientific names, strangely spelled words, and esoteric acronyms. So, here's the bottom line—you should remember the following about the Calvin cycle:

1. The Calvin cycle occurs in the stroma of the chloroplast.
2. The inputs into the Calvin cycle are NADPH, ATP, and CO_2.
3. The products of the Calvin cycle are $NADP^+$, ADP, and a sugar.
4. More ATP is used than NADPH, creating the need for cyclic photophosphorylation to create enough ATP for the reactions.
5. The carbon of the sugar produced in photosynthesis comes from the CO_2 of the Calvin cycle.

Types of Photosynthesis

Plants do not always live under ideal photosynthetic conditions. Some plants must make changes to the system in order to successfully use light and produce energy. Plants contain a structure called a **stomata,** which consists of pores through which oxygen exits and carbon dioxide enters the leaf to be used in photosynthesis. **Transpiration** is the natural process by which plants lose water by evaporation from their leaves. When the temperature is very high, plants have to worry about excess transpiration. This is a potential problem for plants because they need the water to continue the process of photosynthesis. To combat this evaporation problem, plants must close their stomata to conserve water. But this solution leads to two different problems: (1) how will they bring in the CO_2 required for photosynthesis? and (2) what will the plants do with the excess O_2 that builds up when the stomata are closed?

When plants close their stomata to protect against water loss, they experience a shortage of CO_2, and the oxygen produced from the light reactions is unable to leave the plant. This excess oxygen competes with the carbon dioxide and attaches to RuBP in a reaction called **photorespiration.** This results in the formation of one molecule of PGA and one molecule of phosphoglycolate. This is not an ideal reaction because the sugar formed in photosynthesis comes from the PGA, not phosphoglycolate. As a result, plants that experience photorespiration have a lowered capacity for growth. Photorespiration tends to occur on hot, dry days when the stomata of the plant are closed.

A group of plants called **C_4 plants** combat photorespiration by altering the first step of their Calvin cycle. Normally, carbon fixation produces two 3-carbon molecules. In C_4 plants, the carbon fixation step produces a 4-carbon molecule called **oxaloacetate.** This molecule is converted into malate and sent from the mesophyll cells to the bundle sheath cells, where the CO_2 is used to build sugar. The **mesophyll** is the tissue of the interior of the leaf, and **mesophyll cells** are cells that contain bunches of chloroplasts. **Bundle sheath cells** are cells that are tightly wrapped around the veins of a leaf. They are the site for the Calvin cycle in C_4 plants.

What is the difference between C_3 plants and C_4 plants? One difference is that C_4 plants have two different types of photosynthetic cells: (1) tightly packed bundle sheath cells, which surround the vein of the leaf, and (2) mesophyll cells. Another difference involves the first product of carbon fixation. For C_3 plants, it is PGA, for C_4 plants, it is oxaloacetate. C_4 plants are able to successfully perform photosynthesis in these hot areas because of the presence of an enzyme called PEP (*phosphoenolpyruvate*) *carboxylase*. This enzyme really wants to bind to CO_2 and is not tricked by the devious oxygen into using it instead of the necessary CO_2. PEP carboxylase prefers to pair up with CO_2 rather than O_2, and this cuts down on photorespiration for C_4 plants. The conversion of PEP to oxaloacetate occurs in the mesophyll cells; then, after being converted into malate, PEP is shipped to the bundle sheath cells. These cells contain the enzymes of photosynthesis, including our good pal rubisco. The malate releases the CO_2, which is then used by rubisco to perform the reactions of photosynthesis. This process counters the problem of photorespiration because the shuttling of CO_2 from the mesophyll cells to the bundle sheath cells keeps the CO_2 concentration high enough so that it is not beat out by oxygen for rubisco's love and attention.

One last variation of photosynthesis that we should look at is the function performed by **CAM** (Crassulacean acid metabolizing) plants—water-storing plants, such as cacti, that close their stomata by day and open them by night to avoid transpiration during the hot days, without depleting the plant's CO_2 reserves. The CO_2 taken in during the night is stored as organic acids in the vacuoles of mesophyll cells until daybreak when the stomata close. The Calvin cycle is able to proceed during the day because the stored CO_2 is released, as needed, from the organic acids to be incorporated into the sugar product of the Calvin cycle.

KEY IDEA

To sum up these two variations of photosynthesis:

C₄ photosynthesis: photosynthetic process that first converts CO_2 into a 4-carbon molecule in the mesophyll cells, converts that product to malate, and then shuttles the malate into the bundle sheath cells. There, malate releases CO_2, which reacts with rubisco to produce the carbohydrate product of photosynthesis.

CAM photosynthesis: plants close their stomata during the day, collect CO_2 at night, and store the CO_2 in the form of acids until it is needed during the day for photosynthesis.

› Review Questions

1. Most of the ATP creation during respiration occurs as a result of what driving force?

   A. Electrons moving down a concentration gradient
   B. Electrons moving down the electron transport chain
   C. Protons moving down a concentration gradient
   D. Sodium ions moving down a concentration gradient

2. Which of the following processes occurs in both respiration and photosynthesis?

   A. Calvin cycle
   B. Chemiosmosis
   C. Citric acid cycle
   D. Krebs cycle

3. What is the cause of the cramps you feel in your muscles during strenuous exercise?

   A. Lactic acid fermentation
   B. Alcohol fermentation
   C. Chemiosmotic coupling
   D. Too much oxygen delivery to the muscles

4. Which of the following statements is *incorrect*?

   A. Glycolysis can occur with or without oxygen.
   B. Glycolysis occurs in the mitochondria.
   C. Glycolysis is the first step of both anaerobic and aerobic respiration.
   D. Glycolysis of one molecule of glucose leads to the production of 2 ATP, 2 NADH, and 2 pyruvate.

For questions 5–8, use the following answer choices:

   A. Krebs cycle
   B. Oxidative phosphorylation
   C. Lactic acid fermentation
   D. Chemiosmosis

5. This reaction occurs in the matrix of the mitochondria and includes $FADH_2$ among its products.

6. This reaction is performed to recycle NAD^+ needed for efficient respiration.

7. This process uses the proton gradient created by the movement of electrons to form ATP.

8. This process includes the reactions that use NADH and $FADH_2$ to produce ATP.

9. Which of the following molecules can give rise to the most ATP?

   A. NADH
   B. $FADH_2$
   C. Pyruvate
   D. Glucose

10. Which of the following is a proper representation of the products of a single glucose molecule after it has completed the Krebs cycle?

   A. 10 ATP, 4 NADH, 2 $FADH_2$
   B. 10 NADH, 4 $FADH_2$, 2 ATP
   C. 10 ATP, 4 $FADH_2$, 2 NADH
   D. 10 NADH, 4 ATP, 2 $FADH_2$

Questions 11–14 refer to the following answer choices—use each answer only once.

A. Transpiration
B. Calvin cycle
C. CAM photosynthesis
D. Cyclic photophosphorylation

11. Plants use this process so that they can open their stomata at night and close their stomata during the day to avoid water loss during the hot days, without depleting the plant's CO_2 reserves.

12. Uses NADPH, ATP, and CO_2 as the inputs to its reactions.

13. Photosynthetic process that has ATP as its sole product. There is no oxygen and no NADPH produced from these reactions.

14. The process by which plants lose water via evaporation through their leaves.

15. The photosynthetic process performed by some plants in an effort to survive the hot and dry conditions of climates such as the desert is called

A. carbon fixation.
B. C_3 photosynthesis.
C. C_4 photosynthesis.
D. cyclic photophosphorylation.

16. Which of the following is the photosynthetic stage that produces oxygen?

A. The light-dependent reactions
B. Chemiosmosis
C. The Calvin cycle
D. Carbon fixation

17. Which of the following reactions occur in both cellular respiration and photosynthesis?

A. Carbon fixation
B. Fermentation
C. Reduction of $NADP^+$
D. Chemiosmosis

18. Which of the following is *not* a product of the light-dependent reactions of photosynthesis?

A. O_2
B. ATP
C. NADPH
D. Sugar

19. Which of the following is an advantage held by a C_4 plant?

A. More efficient light absorption
B. More efficient photolysis
C. More efficient carbon fixation
D. More efficient uptake of carbon dioxide into the stomata

20. Carbon dioxide enters the plant through the

A. Stomata
B. Stroma
C. Thylakoid membrane
D. Bundle sheath cell

21. Which of the following is the source of the oxygen released during photosynthesis?

A. CO_2
B. H_2O
C. Rubisco
D. PEP carboxylase

22. Which of the following is an *incorrect* statement about the Calvin cycle?

A. The main inputs to the reactions are NADPH, ATP, and CO_2.
B. The main outputs of the reactions are $NADP^+$, ADP, and sugar.
C. More NADPH is used than ATP during the Calvin cycle.
D. Carbon fixation is the first step of the process.

23. Which of the following is the source of the carbon in sugar produced during photosynthesis?

A. CO_2
B. H_2O
C. Rubisco
D. PEP carboxylase

24. The light-dependent reactions of photosynthesis occur in the

A. stroma.
B. mitochondrial matrix.
C. thylakoid membrane.
D. cytoplasm.

› Answers and Explanations

1. **C**—This is the concept of chemiosmosis: the coupling of the movement of electrons down the electron transport chain and the formation of ATP via the creation of a proton gradient. The protons are pushed out of the matrix during the passage of electrons down the chain. They soon build up on the other side of the membrane, and are driven back inside because of the difference in concentration. ATP synthase uses the movement of protons to produce ATP.

2. **B**—This is an important concept to understand. The AP examiners love this topic!

3. **A**—Lactic acid fermentation occurs in human muscle cells when oxygen is not available. Answer choice B would be incorrect because alcohol fermentation occurs in yeast, fungi, and some bacteria. During exercise, if your muscle becomes starved for oxygen, glycolysis will switch over to fermentation. The pain from the cramp is due to the acidity in the muscle caused by the increased concentration of lactate.

4. **B**—Glycolysis occurs in the cytoplasm. All the other statements are correct.

5. **A**

6. **C**

7. **D**

8. **B**

9. **D**—A glucose molecule can net 36 ATP, an NADH molecule can net 3, an $FADH_2$ molecule can net 2, and a pyruvate molecule can net 15.

10. **D**—During glycolysis, a glucose molecule produces 2 ATP, 2 NADH, and 2 pyruvate. The 2 pyruvate then go on to produce 8 NADH, 2 $FADH_2$, and 2 ATP during the Krebs cycle to give the total listed in answer choice D.

11. **C**—CAM plants open their stomata at night and close their stomata during the day to avoid water loss due to heat. The carbon dioxide taken in during the night is incorporated into organic acids and stored in vacuoles until the next day, when the stomata close and CO_2 is needed for the Calvin cycle.

12. **B**—The Calvin cycle uses ATP, NADPH, and CO_2 to produce the desired sugar output of photosynthesis.

13. **D**—Cyclic photophosphorylation occurs because the Calvin cycle uses more ATP than it does NADPH. This is a problem because the light reactions produce an equal amount of ATP and NADPH. The plant compensates for this disparity by dropping into the cyclic phase when needed to produce the ATP necessary to keep the light-independent reactions from grinding to a halt.

14. **A**—Transpiration is the process by which plants lose water through their leaves. Not much else to be said about that. ☺

15. **C**—One of the major problems encountered by plants in hot and dry conditions is of photo-respiration. In hot conditions, plants close their stomata to avoid losing water to transpiration. The problem with this is that the plants run low on CO_2 and fill with O_2. The oxygen competes with the carbon dioxide and attaches to RuBP, leaving the plant with a lowered capacity for growth. C_4 plants cycle CO_2 from mesophyll cells to bundle sheath cells, creating a higher concentration of CO_2 in that region, thus allowing rubisco to carry out the Calvin cycle without being distracted by the O_2 competitor.

16. **A**—The light-dependent reactions are the source of the oxygen given off by plants.

17. **D**—Chemiosmosis occurs in both photosynthesis and cellular respiration. This is the process by which the formation of ATP is driven by electrochemical gradients in the cell. Hydrogen ions accumulate on one side of a membrane, creating a proton gradient that causes them to move through channels to the other side of that membrane, thus leading, with the assistance of ATP synthase, to the production of ATP.

18. **D**—Sugar is a product not of the light-dependent reactions of photosynthesis but of the Calvin cycle (the dark reactions). The outputs of the light-dependent reactions are ATP, NADPH, and O_2.

19. **C**—C_4 plants fix carbon more efficiently than do C_3 plants. Please see answer 15 for a more detailed explanation of this answer.

20. **A**—The stomata is the structure through which the CO_2 enters a plant and the oxygen produced in the light-dependent reactions leaves the plant.

21. **B**—The source of the oxygen produced during photosynthesis is the water that is split by the process of photolysis during the light-dependent reactions of photosynthesis. In this reaction, two hydrogen ions and an oxygen atom are formed from the water. The oxygen atom immediately finds and pairs up with another oxygen atom to form the oxygen product of the light-dependent reactions.

22. **C**—This is a trick question. We reversed the two compounds (NADPH and ATP) in this one. More ATP than NADPH is used in the Calvin cycle. It is for this reason that cyclic photophosphorylation exists—to produce ATP to make up for this disparity.

23. **A**—The carbon of CO_2 is used to produce the sugar created during the Calvin cycle.

24. **C**—The light-dependent reactions occur in the thylakoid membrane of the chloroplast. Remember, the thylakoid system resembles the various stacks of poker chips located within the stroma of the chloroplast. The light-independent reactions occur in the stroma of the chloroplast.

› Rapid Review

Try to rapidly review the material presented below.

There are two main categories of respiration: aerobic and anaerobic.

Aerobic respiration: glycolysis → Krebs cycle → oxidative phosphorylation → 36 ATP per glucose molecule

Anaerobic respiration (*fermentation*): glycolysis → regenerate NAD^+ → 2 ATP per glucose molecule

Glycolysis: conversion of 1 glucose molecule into 2 pyruvate, 2 ATP, and 2 NADH; occurs in the cytoplasm, and in both aerobic *and* anaerobic respiration; *must* have NAD^+ to proceed.

Total energy production to this point → 2 ATP + 2 NADH

Krebs cycle: conversion of 1 pyruvate molecule into 4 NADH, 1 $FADH_2$, 1 ATP, H_2O, and CO_2; occurs *twice* for each glucose to yield 8 NADH, 2 $FADH_2$, and 2 ATP; occurs in mitochondria.

Total energy production per glucose molecule to this point → 4 ATP + 10 NADH + 2 $FADH_2$

Oxidative phosphorylation: production of large amounts of ATP from NADH and $FADH_2$.

- Occurs in the mitochondria; requires presence of oxygen to proceed.

- NADH and $FADH_2$ pass their electrons down the electron transport chain to produce ATP.

- Each NADH can produce up to 3 ATP; each $FADH_2$ up to 2 ATP.

- ½ O_2 is the final acceptor in the electron transport chain.

- Movement of electrons down the chain leads to movement of H^+ out of matrix.

- Ox-phos *regenerates* NAD^+ so that glycolysis and the Krebs cycle can continue!

Chemiosmosis: coupling of the movement of electrons down the ETC with the formation of ATP using the driving force provided by the proton gradient; occurs in *both* cell respiration *and* photosynthesis to produce ATP.

ATP synthase: enzyme responsible for using protons to actually produce ATP from ADP.

Total energy production per glucose molecule to this point → 38 ATP (use 2 in process) → 36 ATP total

Fermentation (*general*): process that regenerates NAD^+ so glycolysis can begin again.

- Occurs in the absence of oxygen.

- Begins with glycolysis: 2 ATP, 2 pyruvate, and 2 NADH are produced from 1 glucose molecule.

- Because there is no oxygen to accept the electron energy on the chain, there is a shortage of NAD^+, which prevents glycolysis from continuing.

Fermentation (*alcohol*): occurs in fungi, yeast, and bacteria; causes conversion of pyruvate to ethanol.

Fermentation (*lactic acid*): occurs in human and animal muscle cells; causes conversion of pyruvate → lactate; causes cramping sensation when oxygen runs low in muscle cells.

The following terms should be thoroughly familiar to you:

Photosynthesis: process by which plants use the energy from light to generate sugar.

- Occurs in chloroplasts

- Light reactions (thylakoid)

- Calvin cycle (stroma)

Autotroph: self-nourishing organism that is also known as a *producer* (plants).

Heterotroph: organisms that must consume other organisms to obtain energy—*consumers* (humans).

Transpiration: loss of water via evaporation through the stomata (natural process).

Photophosphorylation: process by which ATP is made during light reactions.

Photolysis: process by which water is split into hydrogen ions and oxygen atoms (light reactions).

Stomata: structure through which CO_2 enters a plant, and water vapor and oxygen leave a plant.

Pigment: molecule that absorbs light of a particular wavelength (chlorophyll, carotenoid, phycobilins).

There are three types of photosynthesis reactions:

(*Noncyclic*) *light-dependent reactions*

- Occur in thylakoid membrane of chloroplast.

- Inputs are light and water.

- Light strikes photosystem II (P680).

- Electrons pass along until they reach primary electron acceptor.

- Photolysis occurs—H_2O is split to H^+ and O_2.

- Electrons pass down an ETC to P700 (photosystem I), forming ATP by chemiosmosis.

- Electrons of P700 pass down another ETC to produce NADPH.

- Three products of light reactions are NADPH, ATP, and O_2.

- Oxygen produced comes from H_2O.

(Cyclic) light-dependent reactions

- Occur in thylakoid membrane.

- Only involves photosystem I; no photosystem II.

- ATP is the only product of these reactions.

- No NADPH or oxygen are produced.

- These reactions exist because the Calvin cycle uses more ATP than NADPH; this is how the difference is made up.

Light-independent reactions (Calvin cycle)

- Occurs in stroma of chloroplast.

- Inputs are NADPH, ATP, and CO_2.

- First step is carbon fixation, which is catalyzed by an enzyme named rubisco.

- A series of reactions leads to the production of $NADP^+$, ADP, and sugar.

- More ATP is used than NADPH, which creates the need for the cyclic light reactions.

- The carbon of the sugar product comes from CO_2.

Also:

C_4 plants—plants that have adapted their photosynthetic process to more efficiently handle hot and dry conditions.

C_4 photosynthesis—process that first converts CO_2 into a 4-carbon molecule in the mesophyll cells, converts *that* product to malate, and then shuttles it to the bundle sheath cells, where the malate releases CO_2 and rubisco picks it up as if all were normal.

CAM plants—plants that close their stomata during the day, collect CO_2 at night, and store the CO_2 in the form of acids until it is needed during the day for photosynthesis.

CHAPTER 8

Cell Communication and Cell Cycle
Exam Weight: 10–15%

IN THIS CHAPTER

Summary: This chapter teaches you what you need to know about cell communication, signal transduction pathway, feedback mechanisms, the cell cycle, mitosis, and cell cycle regulation.

Key Ideas

- ✪ Cells communicate by cell-to-cell contact or via chemical signals over distance in an organism.
- ✪ Signal transduction pathway starts with a signal followed by a transduction of the signal resulting in a cellular response.
- ✪ Feedback mechanisms are used to maintain homeostasis.
- ✪ There are four main stages in the cell cycle: G_1, S, G_2, and M.
- ✪ The stages of mitosis are prophase, metaphase, anaphase, telophase, and cytokinesis.
- ✪ Examples of cell division control mechanisms are growth factors, checkpoints, density-dependent inhibition, and cyclins/protein kinases.

Introduction

Cells use energy in many ways: for maintenance of homeostasis through feedback mechanisms, for communication with other cells, and for replication. In this chapter, we will discuss how cells communicate with one another via cell-to-cell contact or chemical signals with signal transduction pathways. Next, we will discuss how cells respond to their changing environments via negative and positive feedback pathways. After dissecting the cell cycle and the phases of mitosis, we will touch on cell cycle regulation.

Cell Communication

IST-3

Cells communicate by generating, transmitting, receiving, and responding to chemical signals.

The ability of a cell to communicate with its environment and with itself is key to maintaining homeostasis and surviving. This survival depends on receiving and processing information from outside the cell—information about changing environmental conditionals, availability of nutrients, or any other information vital to surviving. Cells have developed a variety of signaling mechanisms to accomplish the transmission of important biological information. For example, the presence of receptors that allow ion currents to flow in response to photons, which translate light into chemical messengers inside the retina of the eye.

Cell signaling involves a ligand, a signaling molecule, and a receptor protein to which the ligand binds. The receptor can be located on the cell membrane for hydrophilic ligands that can't cross the membrane, or it can be located *inside* the cell for hydrophobic ligands that are small enough to cross the membrane.

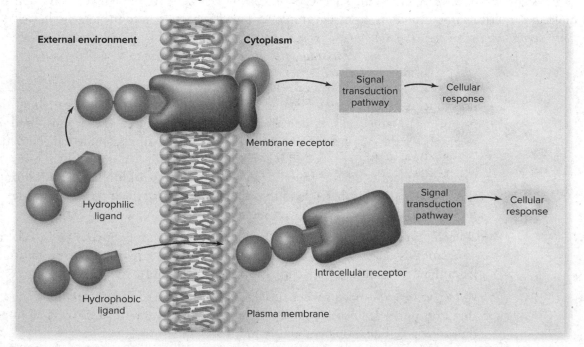

Figure 8.1   Overview of cell signaling. Cell signaling involves a signal molecule called a ligand, a receptor, and a signal transduction pathway that produces a cellular response. The location of the receptor can either be intracellular, for hydrophobic ligands that can cross the membrane, or in the plasma membrane, for hydrophilic ligands that cannot cross the membrane. (*Reproduced with permission from Raven P, Johnson G, Mason K, Losos J, Duncan T;* Biology, *12th ed. New York: McGraw Hill; 2020*)

Signaling

Cells communicate in a variety of ways, depending on the distance between the cells communicating.

1. *Direct cell-to-cell signaling* involves the direct physical contact between cells during communication. Gap junctions in animals and plasmodesmata in plants are tiny channels that directly connect to neighboring cells, which allow the cells to transfer signaling molecules that transmit their current state of homeostasis with one another.

2. *Paracrine signaling* involves cells close to one another but not in direct contact. A cell releases a short-lived signal into a localized area that will induce changes in a nearby cell. Paracrine signals can diffuse only over relatively short distances.

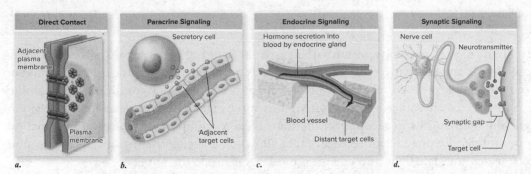

Figure 8.2 Four kinds of cell signaling. Cells communicate in several ways. **_a._** Two cells in direct contact with each other may send signals across gap junctions. **_b._** In paracrine signaling, secretions from one cell have an effect only on cells in the immediate area. **_c._** In endocrine signaling, hormones are released into the organism's circulatory system, which carries them to the target cells. **_d._** Chemical synapse signaling involves transmission of signal molecules, called neurotransmitters, from a neuron over a small synaptic gap to the target cell. (_Reproduced with permission from Raven P, Johnson G, Mason K, Losos J, Duncan T;_ Biology, _12th ed. New York: McGraw Hill; 2020_)

3. _Endocrine signaling_ involves cells far apart in which a longer-lasting signal, called a hormone, is released into the extracellular fluid and travels widely throughout the organisms to target cells. Protein hormones are large molecules that must bind to receptors on the cell membrane. Steroid hormones are lipid-soluble molecules that are able to pass through the cell membrane and attach to an intracellular receptor. One example of endocrine signaling involves the release of human growth hormone (HGH) from the pituitary gland into the bloodstream, which targets bone and muscle cells to trigger growth (See Figure 8.2 _a-d_).

4. _Synaptic signaling_ involves a specialized nerve cell, a neuron, and its target cell. This association is called a chemical synapse and involves the release of neurotransmitters from the neuron into the synaptic gap to target the target cell.

5. _Autocrine signaling_ occurs when a cell sends a signal to itself by secreting something that in turn binds to specific receptors on its own membrane. This plays an important role in cell development and immune system.

Signal Transduction Pathway

When a ligand binds to a receptor on a cell, the work has just begun for the cell. The cell relays the message through a series of reactions to elicit a cellular response known as the signal transduction pathway (Figure 8.1). The binding of the ligand to the receptor generally causes the receptor to change shape, resulting in an activation of an enzyme or binding of other molecules. This starts a signaling cascade that can amplify the signal through a series of reactions that leads to a cellular response, resulting in a change to a cell's behavior or characteristics.

Phosphorylation

The signal transduction pathway may require activating or inactivating proteins via the addition of a phosphate group in a process called phosphorylation.

The phosphorylation of proteins (addition of phosphate groups) is catalyzed by enzymes called **kinases**. There are many different types of kinases that target different proteins in the cell. The dephosphorylation of proteins (removal of phosphate groups) is catalyzed by enzymes called **phosphatases**. Many proteins are activated when phosphorylated and deactivated when dephosphorylated, which creates a pretty nifty way for cells to turn on and off various important cellular pathways (See Figure 8.3).

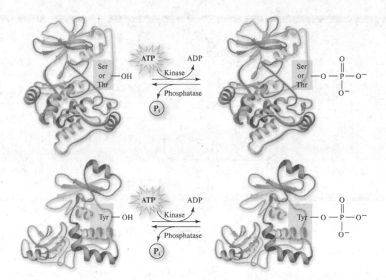

Figure 8.3   Phosphorylation of proteins. Many proteins are controlled by their phosphorylation state—that is, they are activated by phosphorylation and deactivated by dephosphorylation or the reverse. The enzymes that add phosphate groups are called kinases. These form two classes depending on the amino acid the phosphate is added to, either serine– threonine kinases or tyrosine kinases. The action of kinases is reversed by protein phosphatase enzymes. (*Reproduced with permission from Raven P, Johnson G, Mason K, Losos J, Duncan T;* Biology, *12th ed. New York: McGraw Hill; 2020*)

Secondary Messengers

While proteins are a main component of most signal transduction pathways, many other molecules play important roles in the process as secondary messengers, which are small, nonprotein molecules that pass messages along.

1. Calcium (Ca^{2+}): Calcium is widely used by cells as a secondary messenger. Some proteins have binding sites for Ca^{2+} and when calcium binds to the protein, the shape changes, leading to a change in function. One such example is the use of Ca^{2+} in muscle to start muscle contraction after receiving a signal from a neuron.
2. Cyclic AMP (cAMP): Cyclic adenosine monophosphate (cAMP) is involved in many signal cascade pathways. Protein hormones activate cAMP though a multistep process that begins with protein-hormone activation of relay proteins such as G-proteins. These proteins are able to directly activate a compound known as adenyl cyclase, which in turn produces cAMP (See Figure 8.4).

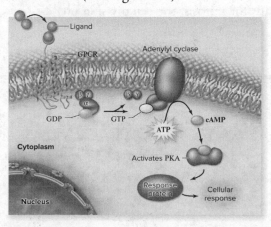

Figure 8.4   cAMP signaling pathway. Extracellular signal binds to a GPCR, activating a G protein. The G protein then activates the effector protein adenylyl cyclase, which catalyzes the conversion of ATP to cAMP. The cAMP then activates protein kinase A (PKA), which phosphorylates target proteins to cause a cellular response. (*Reproduced with permission from Raven P, Johnson G, Mason K, Losos J, Duncan T;* Biology, *12th ed. New York: McGraw Hill; 2020*)

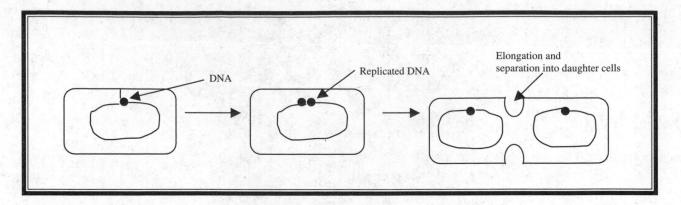

Figure 8.5   Binary fission.

Cell Division in Prokaryotes

Prokaryotes are simple single-celled organisms without a nucleus. Their genetic material is arranged in a single circular chromosome of DNA, which is anchored to the cell membrane. As in eukaryotes, the genetic material of prokaryotes is duplicated before division. However, instead of entering into a complex cycle for cell division, prokaryotes simply elongate until they are double their original size. At this point, the cell pinches in and separates into two identical daughter cells in a process known as **binary fission** (Figure 8.5).

The Cell Cycle

IST-1

Heritable information provides for continuity.

Eukaryotic cell reproduction is a bit more complicated. The cell cycle functions as the daily planner of growth and development for the eukaryotic cell. It tells the cell when and in what order it is going to do things, and consists of all the necessary steps required for the reproduction of a cell. It begins after the creation of the cell and concludes with the formation of two daughter cells through cell division. It then begins again for the two daughter cells that have just been formed. There are four main stages to the cell cycle, and they occur in the following sequence: **phases G_1, S, G_2, and M** (Figure 8.6). Phases G_1 and G_2 are growth stages; S is the part of the cell cycle during which the DNA is duplicated; and the M phase stands for mitosis, the cell division phase.

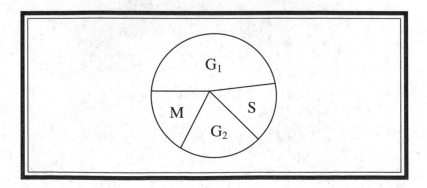

Figure 8.6   Pie chart showing the four main stages of the cell cycle.

Stages of the Cell Cycle

G₁ phase. During the first growth phase of the cell cycle, the cell prepares itself for the synthesis stage of the cycle, making sure that it has all the necessary raw materials for DNA synthesis.

S phase. The DNA is copied so that each daughter cell has a complete set of chromosomes at the conclusion of the cell cycle.

G₂ phase. During the second growth phase of the cycle, the cell prepares itself for mitosis (for producing body cells) and/or meiosis (for producing gametes), making sure that it has the raw materials necessary for the physical separation and formation of daughter cells.

M phase. Mitosis is the stage during which the cell separates into two new cells.

The first three stages of the cycle (G_1, S, and G_2) make up the portion of the cell cycle known as **interphase.** A cell spends approximately 90 percent of its cycle in this phase. The other 10 percent is spent in the final stage, mitosis.

The amount of time that a cell requires to complete a cycle varies by cell type. Some cells complete a full cycle in hours, while others can take days to finish. The rapidity with which cells replicate also varies. Skin cells are continually zipping along through the cell cycle, whereas nerve cells do not replicate—once they are damaged, they are lost for good. This is one reason why the death of nerve cells is such a problem—these cells cannot be repaired or regenerated through mitotic replication.

Mitosis

During mitosis, the fourth stage of the cell cycle, the cell actually takes the second copy of DNA made during the S phase and divides it equally between two cells. Single-cell eukaryotes undergo mitosis for the purpose of asexual reproduction. More complex multicellular eukaryotes use mitosis for other processes as well, such as growth and repair.

Mitosis consists of four major stages: prophase, metaphase, anaphase, and telophase. These stages are immediately followed by **cytokinesis**—the physical separation of the newly formed daughter cells. During interphase, chromosomes are invisible. The **chromatin**—the raw material that gives rise to the chromosomes—is long and thin during this phase. When the chromatin condenses to the point where the chromosome becomes visible through a microscope, the cell is said to have begun mitosis. The AP Biology exam is not going to ask you detailed questions about the different stages of mitosis; just have a *general* understanding of what happens during each step.

Mitosis

Prophase. Nucleus and nucleolus disappear; chromosomes appear as two identical, connected sister chromatids; mitotic spindle (made of microtubules) begins to form; centrioles move to opposite poles of the cell (plant cells do not have centrioles).

Metaphase. For metaphase, think middle. The sister chromatids line up along the middle of the cell, ready to split apart.

Anaphase. For anaphase, think apart. The split sister chromatids move via the microtubules to the opposing poles of the cell—the chromosomes are pulled to opposite poles by the spindle apparatus. After anaphase, each pole of the cell has a complete set of chromosomes.

Telophase. The nuclei for the newly split cells form; the nucleoli reappear, and the chromatin uncoils.

Cytokinesis. Newly formed daughter cells split apart. Animal cells are split by the formation of a cleavage furrow, and plant cells split by the formation of a cell plate (See Figure 8.7).

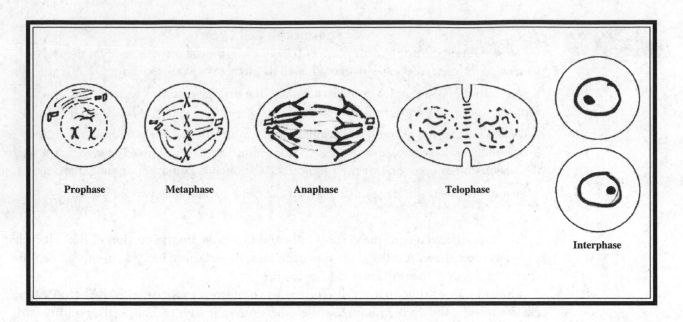

Figure 8.7 Pictorial representation of the stages of mitosis.

Here are the definitions for words you may need to know:

Cell plate: plant cell structure, constructed in the Golgi apparatus, composed of vesicles that fuse together along the middle of the cell, completing the separation process.

Cleavage furrow: groove formed (in animal cells) between the two daughter cells that pinches together to complete the separation of the two cells after mitosis.

Cytokinesis: the actual splitting of the newly formed daughter cells that completes each trip around the cell cycle—some consider it part of mitosis; others regard it as the step immediately following mitosis.

Mitotic spindle: apparatus constructed from microtubules that assists the cell in the physical separation of the chromosomes during mitosis.

Control of Cell Division

Sam (12th grader): "Control mechanisms are an important theme for this test. Be able to write about them."

Control of the cell cycle is important to normal cell growth. There are various ways in which the cell controls the process of cell division:

1. *Checkpoints.* There are checkpoints throughout the cell cycle where the cell verifies that there are enough nutrients and raw materials to progress to the next stage of the cycle. The G_1 checkpoint, for example, makes sure that the cell has enough raw materials to progress to and successfully complete the S phase.

2. *Density-dependent inhibition.* When a certain density of cells is reached, growth of the cells will slow or stop because there are not enough raw materials for the growth and survival of more cells. Cells that are halted by this inhibition enter a quiescent phase of the cell cycle known as G_0. Cancer cells can lose this inhibition and grow out of control.

3. *Growth factors.* Some cells will not divide if certain factors are absent. Growth factors, as their name indicates, assist in the growth of structures.

4. *Cyclins and protein kinases.* **Cyclin** is a protein that accumulates during G_1, S, and G_2 of the cell cycle. A **protein kinase** is a protein that controls other proteins through the addition of phosphate groups. Cyclin-dependent kinase (CDK) is present at all times throughout the cell cycle and binds with cyclin to form a complex known as MPF (maturation or mitosis promoting factor). Early in the cell cycle, because the cyclin concentration is low, the concentration of MPF is also low. As the concentration of cyclin reaches a certain threshold level, enough MPF is formed to push the cell into mitosis. As mitosis proceeds, the level of cyclin declines, decreasing the amount of MPF present and pulling the cell out of mitosis.

Apoptosis

Cells have the ability to undergo programmed cell death known as apoptosis, which is key to maintaining a proper balance of cells in the human body. Apoptosis removes cells during development, which is vital to the elimination of cancerous and virus-infected cells. If a cancerous cell is able to escape apoptosis, it will continue to divide and eventually create a tumor.

Feedback

ENE-3

Timing and coordination of biological mechanisms involved in growth, reproduction, and homeostasis depend on organisms responding to environmental cues.

How is the hormone secretion process of the body regulated? The two main types of regulation with which you should be familiar are negative feedback and positive feedback. **Negative feedback** occurs when a hormone acts to directly or indirectly inhibit further secretion of the hormone of interest. A good example of negative feedback involves insulin, which is secreted by the pancreas. When the blood glucose gets too high, the pancreas is stimulated to produce insulin, which causes cells to use more glucose. As a result of this activity, the blood glucose level declines, halting the production of insulin by the pancreas. **Positive feedback** occurs when a hormone acts to directly or indirectly cause increased secretion of the hormone. An example of this feedback mechanism is the LH surge that occurs prior to ovulation in females. Estrogen is released as a result of the action of FSH, and travels to the anterior pituitary to stimulate the release of LH, which acts on the ovaries to stimulate further secretion of estrogen.

Homeostasis

NYC teacher: "This could make a nice subquestion to an essay. Understand these relationships."

Homeostasis is the maintenance of balance. Hormones can work antagonistically to maintain homeostasis in the body. Two examples we will talk about are insulin/glucagon and calcitonin/PTH:

1. *Insulin/glucagon.* Both are hormones of the pancreas and have opposing effects on blood glucose. Let's say that you eat a nice sugary snack that pushes the blood glucose above its desired level. This results in the release of insulin from the pancreas to stimulate the uptake of glucose from the blood to the liver to be stored as glycogen. It also causes other cells of the body to take up glucose to be used for energy. Sometimes if you go a long time between meals, your blood glucose can dip *below* the desired level. This sets glucagon into action and causes its release from the pancreas. Glucagon acts on the liver to stimulate the removal of glycogen from storage to produce glucose to pump into the bloodstream. When the glucose level gets back to the appropriate level, glucagon

release ceases. This back-and-forth dance works to keep the glucose concentration in our bodies relatively stable over time.

2. *Calcitonin/PTH.* Like glucose, the body has a desired blood calcium (Ca^{2+}) level it tries to maintain. If it drops below this level, PTH is released by the parathyroid gland and works to increase the amount of Ca^{2+} in circulation in three major ways: it (a) releases Ca^{2+} from bones, (b) increases absorption of Ca^{2+} by the intestines, and (c) increases reabsorption of Ca^{2+} by the kidneys. If the blood Ca^{2+} level gets too high, the thyroid gland releases calcitonin, which pretty much performs the three *opposite* responses to PTH's work: it (a) puts Ca^{2+} *into* bone, (b) decreases absorption of Ca^{2+} by the intestines, and (c) decreases reabsorption of Ca^{2+} by the kidneys.

› Review Questions

1. Which of the following plant types has the gametophyte as its prominent generation?

    A. Angiosperms
    B. Bryophytes
    C. Conifers
    D. Gymnosperms

2. During which phase of the cell cycle does crossing over occur?

    A. Metaphase of mitosis
    B. Metaphase I of meiosis
    C. Prophase I of meiosis
    D. Prophase of mitosis

For questions 3–6, please use the following answer choices:

    A. Prophase
    B. Metaphase
    C. Anaphase
    D. Cytokinesis

3. During this phase, the split sister chromatids, now considered to be chromosomes, are moved to the opposite poles of the cell.

4. During this phase, the nucleus deteriorates, and the mitotic spindle begins to form.

5. During this phase, the two daughter cells are actually split apart.

6. During this phase, the sister chromatids line up along the equator of the cell, preparing to split.

7. Which of the following organisms is diploid ($2n$) only as a zygote and is haploid for every other part of its life cycle?

    A. Humans
    B. Bryophytes
    C. Fungi
    D. Bacteria

8. Which of the following statements is true about a human meiotic cell after it has completed meiosis I?

    A. It is diploid ($2n$).
    B. It is haploid (n).
    C. It has divided into four daughter cells.
    D. It proceeds directly to meiosis II without an intervening intermission.

9. Which of the following is *not* true about cyclin-dependent kinase (CDK)?

    A. It is present only during the M phase of the cell cycle.
    B. When enough of it is combined with cyclin, the MPF (mitosis promoting factor) formed initiates mitosis.
    C. It is a protein that controls other proteins using phosphate groups.
    D. It is present at all times during the cell cycle.

10. Which of the following statements about meiosis and/or mitosis is incorrect?

    A. Mitosis results in two diploid daughter cells.
    B. Meiosis in humans occurs only in gonad cells.
    C. Homologous chromosomes line up along the metaphase plate during mitosis.
    D. Crossover occurs during prophase I of meiosis.

› Answers and Explanations

1. **B**—Bryophytes, or mosses, are the plant type that has the gametophyte (haploid) as its dominant generation. The others in this question have the sporophyte (diploid) as their dominant generation.

2. **C**—Crossover occurs in humans only in prophase I. Prophase I is a major source of variation in the production of offspring.

3. **C**

4. **A**

5. **D**

6. **B**

7. **C**—The life cycle for fungi is different from that of humans. Fungi exist as haploid organisms, and the only time they exist in diploid form is as a zygote. Like humans, the gametes for fungi are haploid (n) and combine to form a diploid zygote. Unlike in humans, the fungus zygote divides by meiosis to form a haploid organism.

8. **B**—Human cells start with 46 chromosomes arranged in 23 pairs of homologous chromosomes. At this time, they are $2n$ because they have two copies of each chromosome. After the S phase of the cell cycle, the DNA has been doubled in preparation for cell division. The first stage of meiosis pulls apart the homologous pairs of chromosomes. This means that after meiosis I, the cells are n, or haploid—they no longer consist of *two* full sets of chromosomes.

9. **A**—CDK is present at all times during the cell cycle. It combines with a protein called *cyclin,* which accumulates during interphase of the cell cycle, to form MPF. When enough MPF is formed, the cell is pushed to begin mitosis. As mitosis continues, cyclin is degraded, and when the concentration of MPF drops below a level sufficient to maintain mitotic division, mitosis grinds to a halt until the threshold is reached again next time around the cycle.

10. **C**—Answer choices A, B, and D, are all correct. C is incorrect because homologous pairs of chromosomes pair together only during meiosis. During mitosis, the sister chromatid pairs align along the metaphase plate, separate from the homologous counterpart.

› Rapid Review

You should be familiar with the following terms:

Binary fission: prokaryotic cell division; double the DNA, double the size, then split apart.

Cell cycle: $G_1 \rightarrow S \rightarrow G_2 \rightarrow M$ should be familiar with the following growth$_1$ → synthesis → growth$_2$ → mitosis → etc.

Interphase: $G_1 + S + G_2 = 90$ percent of the cell cycle.

Cytokinesis: physical separation of newly formed daughter cells of cell division.

STAGE	MITOSIS	MEIOSIS
Prophase	Nucleus, nucleolus disappear; mitotic spindle forms	—
Metaphase	Sister chromatids line up at middle	—
Anaphase	Sister chromatids are split apart	—
Telophase	Nuclei of new cells re-form; chromatin uncoils	—
Prophase I	—	Each chromosome pairs with its homolog; there is crossover
Metaphase I	—	Chromosome pairs align along middle of cell, ready to split apart
Anaphase I	—	Homologous chromosomes split apart
Telophase I	—	Nuclear membrane reforms; daughter cells are now haploid (n)
Prophase II	—	Nucleus disappears, spindle apparatus forms
Metaphase II	—	Sister chromatids line up at middle
Anaphase II	—	Sister chromatids are split apart
Telophase II	—	Nuclei of new cells reform; chromatin uncoils

Cell division control mechanisms:

1. *Growth factors*: factors that when present, promote growth, and when absent, impede growth.
2. *Checkpoints*: a cell stops growing to make sure it has the nutrients and raw materials to proceed.
3. *Density-dependent inhibition*: cell stops growing when certain density is reached—runs out of food!!!
4. *Cyclins and protein kinases*: cyclin combines with CDK to form a structure known as MPF that pushes cell into mitosis when enough is present.

Haploid (n): one copy of each chromosome.

Diploid ($2n$): two copies of each chromosome.

Homologous chromosomes: chromosomes that are similar in shape, size, and function.

Spermatogenesis: the process of male gamete formation (four sperm from one cell).

Oogenesis: the process of female gamete formation (one ovum from each cell).

Life cycles: Sequence of events that make up the reproductive cycle of an organism.

- *Human*: zygote $(2n)$ → multicellular organism $(2n)$ → gametes (n) → zygote $(2n)$

- *Fungi*: zygote $(2n)$ → multicellular organism (n) → gametes (n) → zygote $(2n)$

- *Plants*: zygote $(2n)$ → sporophyte $(2n)$ → spores (n) → gametophyte (n) → gametes (n) → zygote $(2n)$

Sources of variation: crossover, 2^n possible gametes that can be formed, random pairing of gametes.

CHAPTER 9

Heredity
Exam Weight: 8–11%

IN THIS CHAPTER

Summary: This chapter examines Mendel's fundamental laws (law of segregation, law of independent assortment, and law of dominance) as well as some classic exceptions to these laws (intermediate inheritance, multiple alleles, polygenic traits, epistasis, and pleiotropy). This chapter also covers linkage (sex linkage, gene linkage, and linkage maps), and chromosomal errors such as nondisjunction, deletions, duplications, translocations, and inversion.

Key Ideas

- ✪ Crossing over occurs during prophase I of meiosis.
- ✪ Sources of cell variation: crossover, 2n possible gametes, and random pairing of gametes.
- ✪ Law of segregation: the two alleles for a trait separate during the formation of gametes—one to each gamete.
- ✪ Law of independent assortment: inheritance of one trait does not interfere with the inheritance of another trait.
- ✪ Law of dominance: if two opposite pure-breeding varieties are crossed (BB × bb), all offspring resemble the BB parent.
- ✪ Linked genes that lie along the same chromosome do not follow the law of independent assortment.
- ✪ Autosomal recessive disorders: Tay-Sachs, cystic fibrosis, sickle cell anemia, phenylketonuria.
- ✪ Autosomal dominant disorders: Huntington, achondroplasia.
- ✪ Nondisjunction errors: Down, Klinefelter, Turner syndromes.

Introduction

How many times have you heard someone say as they look at a baby, "Awwww, he looks like his daddy" or "She has her mother's eyes"? What exactly is it that causes an infant to look like his or her parents? This question is the basis of the study of heredity—the study of the passing of traits from generation to generation. Its basic premise is that offspring are more like their parents than less closely related individuals.

In this chapter, we will begin by discussing meiosis. We will then discuss some terms that will prove important to your study of heredity. This is followed by an examination of Mendel's *law of segregation* and the *law of independent assortment*, including how they were discovered and how they can be applied. We will examine the *law of dominance*, which arose from Mendel's work, and we will also discuss some exceptions to Mendel's fundamental laws such as intermediate inheritance (incomplete dominance and codominance), multiple alleles, polygenic traits, epistasis, and pleiotropy.

In the next section, we will examine Thomas Morgan's work on fruit flies, which paved the way for the discovery of linked genes, genetic recombination, and sex-linked inheritance. This discussion concludes with a look at gene linkage and linkage maps.

Finally, since chromosomes carry the vital genes necessary for proper development and passage of hereditary material from one generation to the next, it is important to discuss the types of chromosomal errors that can occur during reproduction. This includes the various forms of nondisjunction, or the improper separation of chromosomes during meiosis (which leads to an abnormal number of chromosomes in offspring). The chapter concludes with an examination of the other major types of chromosomal errors: deletions, duplications, translocations, and inversions.

Haploid Versus Diploid Organisms

One thing that is often a major source of confusion for some of my students is the distinction between being haploid and being diploid. Let's start with a definition of the terms:

A *haploid* (*n*) organism is one that has only one copy of each type of chromosome. In humans, this refers to a cell that has one copy of each type of homologous chromosome.

A *diploid* (2*n*) organism is one that has two copies of each type of chromosome. In humans, this refers to the pairs of homologous chromosomes.

During the discussion of meiosis below, the terms *haploid* and *diploid* will be used often. Whenever we say "2*n*," or diploid, we are referring to an organism that contains two full *sets* of chromosomes. The letter *n* is used to represent the number of sets of chromosomes. So if an organism is said to have 4*n* chromosomes, this means that it has four complete sets of chromosomes. Humans are diploid, and consist of 2*n* chromosomes at all times except as gametes, when they are *n*. Humans have 23 *different* chromosomes; there are two full *sets* of these 23 chromosomes, one from each parent, for a total of 46 chromosomes. Human sex cells have 23 chromosomes each.

Meiosis

IST-1

Heritable information provides for continuity of life.

Now that we have armed you with the knowledge of the distinction between haploid and diploid, it is time to dive into the topic of meiosis, which occurs during the process of sexual reproduction. A cell destined to undergo meiosis goes through the cell cycle, synthesizing a second copy of DNA just like mitotic cells. But after G_2, the cell instead enters meiosis, which consists of *two* cell divisions, not one. The second cell division exists because the gametes to be formed from meiosis must be haploid. This is because they are going to join with another haploid gamete at conception to produce the diploid zygote. Meiosis is like a two-part made-for-TV miniseries. It has two acts: meiosis I and meiosis II. Each of these two acts is divided into four steps, reminiscent of mitosis: prophase, metaphase, anaphase, and telophase.

Homologous chromosomes resemble one another in shape, size, function, and the genetic information they contain. In humans, the 46 chromosomes are divided into 23 homologous pairs. One member of each pair comes from an individual's mother, and the other member comes from the father. Meiosis I is the separation of the homologous pairs into two separate cells. Meiosis II is the separation of the duplicated sister chromatids into chromosomes. As a result, a single meiotic cycle produces *four* cells from a single cell. The cells produced during meiosis in the human life cycle are called **gametes.**

Again, the AP Biology exam is not going to test your mastery of the minute details of the meiotic process. However, a general understanding of the various steps is important:

Meiosis I

Prophase I. Each chromosome pairs with its homolog. Crossover (synapsis) occurs in this phase. The nuclear envelope breaks apart, and spindle apparatus begins to form.

Metaphase I. Chromosomes align along the metaphase plate matched with their homologous partner. This stage ends with the separation of the homologous pairs.

Anaphase I. Separated homologous pairs move to opposite poles of the cell.

Telophase I. Nuclear membrane reforms; the process of cytoplasmic division begins.

Cytokinesis. After the daughter cells split, the two newly formed cells are haploid (*n*).

As discussed earlier, meiosis consists of a single synthesis period during which the DNA is replicated, followed by two acts of cell division. With the completion of the first cell division, meiosis I, the cells are haploid because they no longer consist of two full *sets* of chromosomes. Each cell has one of the duplicated chromatid pairs from each homologous pair. The cell then enters meiosis II.

Meiosis II

Prophase II. The nuclear envelope breaks apart, and spindle apparatus begins to form.

Metaphase II. Sister chromatids line up along the equator of the cell.

Anaphase II. Sister chromatids split apart and are called *chromosomes* as they are pulled to the poles.

Telophase II. The nuclei and the nucleoli for the newly split cells return.

Cytokinesis. Newly formed daughter cells physically divide (See Figure 9.1).

In humans, the process of gamete formation is different in women and men. In men, **spermatogenesis** leads to the production of four haploid sperm during each meiotic cycle. In women, the process is called **oogenesis.** It is a trickier process than spermatogenesis, and each complete meiotic cycle leads to the production of a single ovum, or egg.

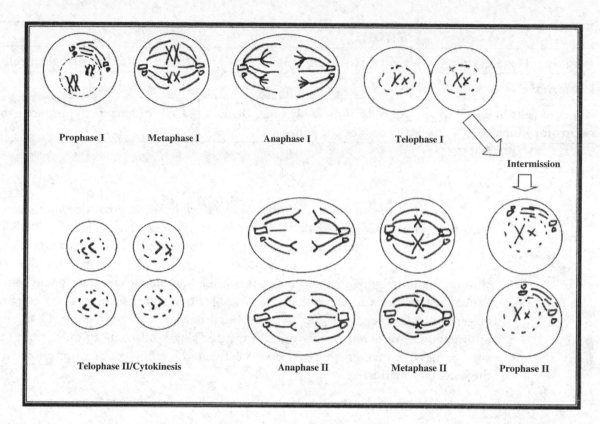

Figure 9.1 The stages of meiosis. Pictorial representation of the stages of meiosis I and II.

After meiosis I in females, one cell receives half the genetic information and the majority of the cytoplasm of the parent cell. The other cell, the **polar body,** simply receives half of the genetic information and is cast away. During meiosis II, the remaining cell divides a second time, and forms a polar body that is cast away, and a single haploid ovum that contains half the genetic information and nearly all the cytoplasm of the original parent cell. The excess cytoplasm is required for proper growth of the embryo after fertilization. Thus, the process of oogenesis produces two polar bodies and a single haploid ovum.

To review, why is it important to produce haploid gametes during meiosis? During fertilization, a sperm (n) will meet up with an egg (n), to produce a diploid zygote ($2n$). If either the sperm or the egg were diploid, then the offspring produced during sexual reproduction would contain more chromosomes than the parent organism. Meiosis circumvents this problem by producing gametes that are haploid and consist of one copy of each type of chromosome. During fertilization between two gametes, each copy will match up with another copy of each type of chromosome to form the diploid zygote.

Before moving on, there are a few important distinctions between meiosis and mitosis that should be emphasized. In meiosis during prophase I, the homologous pairs join together. This matching of chromosomes into homologous pairs does not occur in mitosis. In mitosis, the 46 chromosomes simply align along the metaphase plate alone.

KEY IDEA

	MITOSIS	MEIOSIS
Resulting daughter cells	Two diploid (2n) daughter cells	Four haploid (n) daughter cells
Crossover?	No	Yes—prophase I
Types of cells in which it occurs for humans	All cells of the body other than the cells of the gonads	Cells of gonads to produce gametes

An event of major importance that occurs during meiosis that does not occur during mitosis is known as **crossover** (also known as *crossing over*) (Figure 9.2). When the homologous pairs match up during prophase I of meiosis, complementary pieces from the two homologous chromosomes wrap around each other and are exchanged between the chromosomes. Imagine that chromosome A is the homologous partner for chromosome B. When they pair up during prophase I, a piece of chromosome A containing a certain stretch of genes can be exchanged for the piece of chromosome B containing the same genetic information. This is one of the mechanisms that allows offspring to differ from their parents. Remember that crossing over occurs between the homologous chromosome pairs, *not* the sister chromatids.

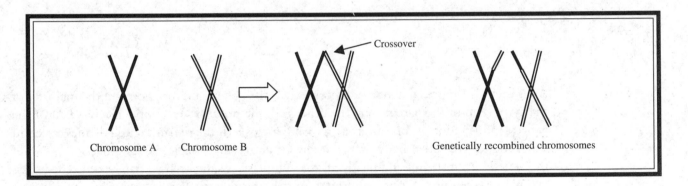

Figure 9.2   Crossover.

Some Important Terms to Know

The following is a list of terms that will help in your understanding of heredity:

Allele: a variant of a gene for a particular character. For example, two alleles for fur color could be B (dominant) and b (recessive).

F_1: the first generation of offspring, or the first "filial" generation in a genetic cross.

F_2: the second generation of offspring, or the second "filial" generation in a genetic cross.

Genotype: an organism's genetic makeup for a given trait. A simple example of this could involve fur color where B represents the allele for brown and b represents the allele for black. The possible genotypes include homozygous brown (BB), heterozygous brown (Bb), and homozygous black (bb).

Heterozygous (hybrid): an individual is heterozygous (or a hybrid) for a gene if the two alleles are different (Bb).

Homozygous (pure): an individual is homozygous for a gene if both of the given alleles are the same (BB or bb).

Karyotype: a chart that organizes chromosomes in relation to number, size, and type.

Nondisjunction: the improper separation of chromosomes during meiosis, which leads to an abnormal number of chromosomes in offspring. A few classic examples of non-disjunction-related syndromes are Down, Turner, and Klinefelter syndromes.

P_1: the parent generation in a genetic cross.

Phenotype: the physical expression of the trait associated with a particular genotype. Some examples of the phenotypes for Mendel's peas were round or wrinkled, green or yellow, purple flower or white flower.

Sources of Cell Variation

NYC teacher: "Knowing the sources of variation is important."

What makes us different from our parents? Why do some people look amazingly like their parents while others do not? The process of cell division provides ample opportunity for variation. Remember that during meiosis, homologous chromosome pairs align together along the metaphase plate. This alignment is a completely random process, and there is a 50 percent chance that the chromosome in the pair from the individual's mother will go to one side, and a 50 percent chance that the chromosome in the pair from the individual's father will go to that side. This is true for all the homologous pairs in an organism. This means that 2^n possible gametes can form from any given set of n chromosomes. For example, in a 3-chromosome organism, there are $2^3 = 8$ possible gametes. In humans, there are 23 homologous pairs. This comes out to 2^{23} (8,388,608) different ways the gametes can separate during gametogenesis.

Another source of variation during sexual reproduction is the random determination of which sperm meets up with which ovum. In humans, the sperm represents one of 2^{23} possibilities from the male gamete factory; the ovum, one of 2^{23} possibilities from the female gamete factory. All these factors combine to explain why siblings may look nothing like each other.

A third major source of variation during gamete formation is the **crossover** (or *crossing over*) that occurs during prophase I of meiosis. It is very important for you to remember that this process happens *only* during that stage of cell division. It does not occur in mitosis.

Mendel and His Peas

EVO-2

Organisms are linked by lines of descent from common ancestry.

The person whose name is most often associated with heredity is Gregor Mendel. Mendel spent many years working with peas. It was a very strange hobby, indeed, but it proved quite useful to the world of science. He mated peas to produce offspring and recorded the phenotype results in order to determine how certain characters are inherited. A **character** is a genetically inherited characteristic that differs from person to person.

Before he began his work in the 1850s, the accepted theory of inheritance was the **"blending" hypothesis,** which stated that the genes contributed by two parents mix as colors do. For example, a blue flower mixed with a yellow flower would produce a green flower. The exact genetic makeup of each parent could never be recovered; the genes would be as inseparable as the blended colors. Mendel used plant experiments to test this hypothesis and developed his two fundamental theories: the law of segregation and the law of independent assortment.

When Mendel was observing a single character during a mating, he was doing something called a **monohybrid cross**—a cross that involves a single character in which both parents are heterozygous (Bb × Bb). A monohybrid cross between heterozygous gametes gives a 3 : 1 phenotype ratio in the offspring (Figure 9.3). As you can see in Figure 9.3, an offspring is three times more likely to express the dominant B trait than the recessive b trait.

	B	b
B	BB	Bb
b	Bb	bb

Figure 9.3   Monohybrid cross.

Mendel also experimented with multiple characters simultaneously. The crossing of two different hybrid characters is termed a **dihybrid cross** (BbRr × BbRr). A dihybrid cross between heterozygous gametes gives a 9 : 3 : 3 : 1 phenotype ratio in the offspring (Figure 9.4).

	BR	**Br**	**bR**	**br**
BR	BBRR	BBRr	BbRR	BbRr
Br	BBRr	BBrr	BbRr	Bbrr
bR	BbRR	BbRr	bbRR	bbRr
br	BbRr	Bbrr	bbRr	bbrr

Figure 9.4 Dihybrid cross.

From his experiments, Mendel developed two major hereditary laws: the law of segregation and the law of independent assortment.

The law of segregation. Every organism carries pairs of factors, called *alleles,* for each trait, and the members of the pair segregate (separate) during the formation of gametes. For example, if an individual is Bb for eye color, during gamete formation, one gamete would receive a B, and the other made from that cell would receive a b.

The law of independent assortment. Members of each pair of factors are distributed independently when the gametes are formed. Quite simply, inheritance of one trait or characteristic does not interfere with inheritance of another trait. For example, if an individual is BbRr for two genes, gametes formed during meiosis could contain BR, Br, bR, or br. The B and b alleles assort *independently* of the R and r alleles.

The law of dominance. Also based on Mendel's work, this states that when two opposite pure-breeding varieties (homozygous dominant vs. homozygous recessive) of an organism are crossed, all the offspring resemble one parent. This is referred to as the *dominant* trait. The variety that is hidden is referred to as the *recessive* trait.

It is time for you to answer a question for us (of course, we have no way of knowing whether or how you will answer this question): Can the phenotype of an organism be determined from simple observation? Yes—just look at the organism and determine whether it is tall or short, has blue eyes or brown eyes, and so on. However, the genotype of an organism *cannot* always be determined from simple observation. In the case of a recessive trait, the genotype is known. If a person has blue eyes (recessive to brown), the genotype is bb. But if that person has brown eyes, you cannot be sure if the genotype is Bb or BB—the individual can be either homozygous dominant or heterozygous dominant. To determine the exact genotype, you must run an experiment called a **test cross.** Geneticists breed the organism whose genotype is unknown with an organism that is homozygous recessive for the trait. This results in offspring with observable phenotypes. If the unknown genotype is heterozygous, probability indicates one-half of the offspring *should* express the recessive phenotype. If the unknown genotype is homozygous dominant, *all* the organism's offspring *should* express the dominant trait. Of course, such experiments are not done on humans.

Remember me!

Mendel discovered many statistical laws of heredity. He learned that a monohybrid cross such as Yy × Yy will result in a phenotype ratio of 3:1 in favor of the dominant trait. He learned that a dihybrid cross, such as YyRr × YyRr, will result in a phenotype ratio of 9:3:3:1 (9 RY, 3 rY, 3 Ry, 1 ry). These two ratios, when they appear in genetic analysis problems, imply mono- and dihybrid crosses.

Non-Mendelian Genetics

SYI-3

Naturally occurring diversity among and between components within biological systems affects interactions with the environment.

Gregor Mendel's work with pea plants and their genes was not able to account for many patterns of inheritance that occur in life (sex-linked traits, incomplete dominance, and codominance, to name a few). The observed phenotypes of these traits differ from the predicted ratios.

Non-nuclear inheritance, in which offspring get DNA only from the male or female parent, does not follow the Mendelian pattern of inheritance. For example, in humans, children get mitochondrial DNA from only the mother and not the father.

Intermediate Inheritance

Marcy (college freshman): "Understanding this concept is worth 2 points on the exam."

The inheritance of traits is not always as simple as Mendel's pea experiments seem to indicate. Traits are not always dominant or recessive, and phenotype ratios are not always 9:3:3:1 or 3:1. Mendel's experiments did not account for something called **intermediate inheritance,** in which an individual heterozygous for a trait (Yy) shows characteristics not exactly like *either* parent. The phenotype is a "mixture" of both of the parents' genetic input. There are two major types of intermediate inheritance:

1. Incomplete dominance or "blending inheritance"
2. Codominance

Incomplete Dominance ("Blending Inheritance")

In **incomplete dominance** ("blending inheritance"), the heterozygous genotype produces an "intermediate" phenotype rather than the dominant phenotype; neither allele dominates the other. A classic example of incomplete dominance is flower color in snapdragons—crossing a snapdragon plant that has red flowers with one that has white flowers yields offspring with pink flowers.

One genetic condition in humans that exhibits incomplete dominance is **hypercholesterolemia**—a recessive disorder (hh) that causes cholesterol levels to be many times higher than normal and can lead to heart attacks in children as young as 2 years old. Those who are HH tend to have normal cholesterol levels, and those who are Hh have cholesterol levels somewhere in between the two extremes. As with many conditions, the environment plays a major role in how genetic conditions express themselves. Thus, people who are HH do not necessarily have normal cholesterol levels if, for example, they have poor diet or exercise habits.

One important side note—try not to confuse the terms blending "hypothesis" and blending "inheritance." The latter is another name for incomplete dominance, whereas the former was the theory on heredity before Mendel worked his magic. The blending "hypothesis" says that the HH and hh extremes can never be retrieved. In reality, and according to blending inheritance, if you were to cross two Hh individuals, the offspring could still be HH or hh, which the blending "hypothesis" says cannot happen once the blending has occurred.

Codominance

Codominance is the situation in which both alleles express themselves fully in a heterozygous organism. A good example of codominance involves the human blood groups: M, N, and MN. Individuals with group M blood have the M glycoprotein on the surface of the blood cell; individuals with group N blood have N glycoproteins on the blood cell; and those with group MN blood have *both*. This is not incomplete dominance because both alleles are fully expressed in the phenotype—they are codominant.

Other Forms of Inheritance

Polygenic Traits

Another interesting form of inheritance involves **polygenic traits,** or traits that are affected by more than one gene. Eye color is an example of a polygenic trait. The *tone* (color), *amount* (blue eyes have less than brown eyes), and *position* (how evenly distributed the pigment is) of pigment *all* play a role in determining eye color. Each of these characteristics is determined by separate genes. Another example of this phenomenon is skin color, which is determined by at least three different genes working together to produce a wide range of possible skin tones.

Multiple Alleles

Many monogenic traits (traits expressed via a single gene) correspond to two alleles, one dominant and one recessive. Other traits, however, involve more than two alleles. A classic example of such a trait is the human blood type. On the most simplistic level, there are four major blood types: A, B, AB, and O. They are named based on the presence or absence of certain antigens on the surface of the red blood cells. The gene for blood type has three possible alleles (multiple alleles): I^A, which causes antigens A to be produced on the surface of the red blood cell; I^B, which causes antigens B to be produced; and i, which causes *no* antigens to be produced. The following are the possible genotypes for human blood type: $I^A i$ (type A), $I^A I^A$ (type A), $I^B i$ (type B), $I^B I^B$ (type B), $I^A I^B$ (type AB), ii (type O). Type AB blood displays the *codominance* of blood type. As we saw in MN blood groups, both the A and the B alleles succeed in their mission—their antigens appear on the surface of the red blood cell (Figure 9.5). Analyzing blood type can be really complex because human blood types involve not only multiple alleles (I^A, I^B, and i) and codominance (type AB blood), but classic dominance of I^A and I^B over i as well.

Blood Type	Antigens on surface of RBC	Antibodies produced by the body	Can be transfused with which types of blood?	Can be donated to individuals of which type?
A	Antigen A	Anti B	Type A, O	Type A, AB
B	Antigen B	Anti A	Type B, O	Type B, AB
AB	Antigens A & B	None	All Types	Type AB
O	No Antigens	Anti A and Anti B	Only O	All Types

Figure 9.5   Several human blood type characteristics.

If you have ever watched an episode of *ER* on television, you have heard one of the doctors frantically scream, "We need to type her and bring some O blood down here *stat*!" Why is it important for the physician to determine what type of blood the patient has, and why is it okay to give the patient O blood in the meantime? People with type A blood produce anti-B antibodies because the B antigen that is present on type B and type AB blood is a foreign molecule to someone with type A blood. This is simply the body's defense mechanism doing its job. Following the same logic, those with type B blood make anti-A antibodies, and those with type O blood make anti-A *and* anti-B antibodies. People who are type AB make none, and are therefore the universal acceptor of blood. It is important to find out what kind of blood a person has because if you give type B blood to a person with type A blood, the recipient will have an immune response to the transfused blood. Why is O blood given while they wait to see what blood type the patient is? This is because type O blood has neither antigen on the surface of red blood cells. People with type O blood are universal donors because few people will have an adverse reaction to type O blood.

Epistasis

In **epistasis** the expression of one gene affects the expression of another gene. A classic example of epistasis involves the coat color of mice. Black is dominant over brown, and brown fur has the genotype bb. There is also another gene locus independent of the coat color gene that controls the deposition of pigment in the fur. If a mouse has a dominant allele of this pigment gene (Cc or CC), it leads to pigment deposition and the coloring of the fur according to the coat color gene's instructions. If a mouse is double recessive for this trait (cc), it will have white fur no matter what the coat color gene wants because it will not put any pigment into the fur. It is almost as if the pigment gene were overruling the coat color gene. If you mate two black mice that are BbCc, the ratio of phenotypes in the offspring would not be the 9 : 3 : 3 : 1 ratio that Mendel predicts, but rather 9 : 4 : 3 black : white : brown because the epistatic gene alters the phenotype.

Pleiotropy

In **pleiotropy**, a single gene has multiple effects on an organism. A good example of pleiotropy is the mutation that causes sickle cell anemia. This single gene mutation "sickles" the blood cells, leading to systemic symptoms such as heart, lung, and kidney damage; muscle pain; weakness; and generalized fatigue. The problems do not stop there; these symptoms can lead to disastrous side effects such as kidney failure. The mutation of a single gene wreaks havoc on the system as a whole.

Sex Determination and Sex Linkage

Mendel was not the only one to make progress in the field of heredity. In the early 1900s, Thomas Morgan made key discoveries regarding sex linkage and linked genes.

In human cells, all chromosomes occur in structurally identical pairs except for two very important ones: the sex chromosomes, X and Y. Women have two structurally identical X chromosomes. Men have one X and one Y.

Sex-Linked Traits

Morgan experimented with a quick-breeding fruit fly species. The fruit flies had four pairs of chromosomes: three autosomal pairs and one sex chromosome pair. An **autosomal chromosome** is one that is not directly involved in determining gender. In fruit flies, the more common phenotype for a trait is called the **wild-type phenotype** (e.g., red eyes). Traits that are different from the normal are called **mutant phenotypes** (e.g., white eyes). Morgan crossed a white-eyed male with a red-eyed female, and all the F_1 offspring had red eyes. When he bred the F_1 together, he obtained Mendel's 3:1 ratio. But, there was a slight difference from what Mendel's theories would predict—the white trait was restricted to the males. Morgan's conclusion was that the gene for eye color is on the X chromosome. This means that the poor male flies get only a single copy, and if it is abnormal, they are abnormal. But, the lucky ladies have two copies and are normal even if one copy is not.

IST-1

Heritable information provides for continuity of life.

It is this male–female sex chromosomes difference that allows for sex-linked conditions. If a gene for a recessive disease is present on the X chromosome, then a female must have two defective versions of the gene to show the disease while a male needs only one. This is so because males have no corresponding gene on the Y chromosome to help counter the negative effect of a recessive allele on the X chromosome. Thus, more males than females show recessive X-linked phenotypes. In a pedigree (see Figure 9.8 later in this chapter), a pattern of sex-linked disease will show the sons of carrier mothers with the disease.

The father plays no part in the passage of an X-linked gene to the male children of a couple. Fathers pass X-linked alleles to their daughters, but not to their sons. Do you understand why this is so? The father does not give an X chromosome to the male offspring because he is the one who provides the Y chromosome that makes his son a male. A mother can pass a sex-linked allele to both her daughters *and* sons because she can pass only X chromosomes to her offspring.

Emily (12th grader):
"Be able to categorize diseases for this exam!"

Three common sex-linked disorders are Duchenne's muscular dystrophy, hemophilia, and red-green colorblindness. **Duchenne's muscular dystrophy** is a sex-linked disorder that is caused by the absence of an essential muscle protein. Its symptoms include a progressive loss of muscle strength and coordination. **Hemophilia** is caused by the absence of a protein vital to the clotting process. Individuals with this condition have difficulty clotting blood after even the smallest of wounds. Those most severely affected by the disease can bleed to death after the tiniest of injuries. Females with this condition rarely survive. People afflicted with **red-green colorblindness** are unable to distinguish between red and green colors. This condition is found primarily in males.

X Inactivation

Here is an important question for you to ponder while preparing for this exam: "Are all the cells in a female identical?"

The answer to this question is "No." Females undergo a process called **X inactivation.** During the development of a female embryo, one of the two X chromosomes in each cell remains coiled as a **Barr body** whose genes are not expressed. A cell expresses the alleles only of the active X chromosome. X inactivation occurs separately in each cell and involves random inactivation of one of a female's X chromosomes. But not all cells inactivate the same X. As a result, different cells will have different active X chromosomes.

Why don't females always express X-linked diseases when this X inactivation occurs? Sometimes they do, but usually they have enough cells with a "good" copy of the allele to compensate for the presence of the recessive allele.

One last sex-related inheritance pattern that needs to be mentioned is **holandric traits,** which are traits inherited via the Y chromosome. An example of a holandric trait in humans is ear hair distribution.

Linkage and Gene Mapping

Each chromosome has hundreds of genes that tend to be inherited together because the chromosome is passed along as a unit. These are called **linked genes.** Linked genes lie on the same chromosome and do not follow Mendel's law of independent assortment.

Morgan performed an experiment in which he looked at body color and wing size on his beloved fruit flies. The dominant alleles were G (gray) and V (normal wings); the recessive alleles were g (black) and v (vestigial wings). GgVv females were crossed with ggvv males. Mendel's law of independent assortment predicts offspring of four different phenotypes in a 1:1:1:1 ratio. But that is not what Morgan found. Because the genes are linked, the gray/normal flies produce only GV or gv gametes. Thus, Morgan expected the ratio of offspring to be 1:1, half GgVv and half ggvv. Morgan found that there were more wild-type and double-mutant flies than independent assortment would predict, but surprisingly, some Gv and gV were also produced.

How did those other combinations result from the cross if the genes are linked? **Crossover** (also known as *crossing over*), a form of genetic recombination that occurs during prophase I of meiosis, led to their production. The less often this recombination occurs, the closer the genes must be on the chromosome. The farther apart two genes are on a chromosome, the more often crossover will occur. Recombination frequency can be used to determine how close two genes are on a chromosome through the creation of linkage maps, which we will look at next.

Linkage Maps

A **linkage map** is a genetic map put together using crossover frequencies. Another unit of measurement, the **map unit** (also known as *centigram*), is used to geographically relate the genes on the basis of these frequencies. One map unit is equal to a 1 percent crossover frequency. A linkage map does not provide the *exact* location of genes; it gives only the relative location. Imagine that you want to determine the relative locations of four genes: A, B, C, and D. You know that A crosses over with C 20 percent of the time, B crosses over with C 15 percent of the time, A crosses over with D 10 percent of the time, and D crosses over with B 5 percent of the time. From this information you can determine the sequence (Figure 9.6). Gene A must be 20 units from gene C. Gene B must be 15 units from C, but B could be 5 or 35 units from A. But, because you also know that A is 10 units from D and that D is 5 units from B, you can determine that B must be 5 units from A as well, if A is also to be 10 units from D. This gives you the sequence of genes as ABDC.

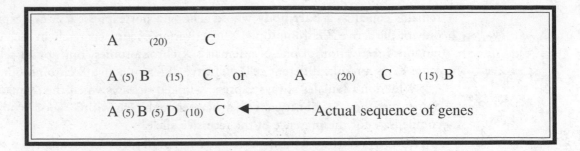

Figure 9.6   A genetic linkage map.

Heads or Tails?

Probability is a concept important to a full understanding of heredity and inheritance. What is the probability that a flipped coin will come up heads? You can answer that easily: ½. What is the probability that two coins flipped simultaneously will *both* be heads? This is a little harder—it is ½ × ½ = ¼. Take a look at Figure 9.7. The first time you toss the coin, there is a probability of ½ that it will land heads and ½ that it will land tails. When you toss it again, it again has a probability of ½ that it will land heads, and ½ that it will land tails. So in the figure, just concentrate on the ½ of the tosses that land heads. Of those, ½ of them will land heads the second time—or ½ of ½. Multiplied together, this results in the ¼ chance of getting heads twice with two coin tosses. This example illustrates the **law of multiplication** with probabilities. This law states that to determine the probability that two random events will occur in succession, you simply multiply the probability of the first event by the probability of the second event.

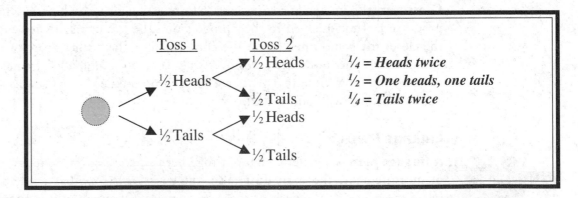

Figure 9.7   Probability in the law of multiplication.

This is the same thought process that we follow to understand Mendel's law of segregation. If you are Aa for a trait, what is your chance of passing on the A? That's right—½. If you are AaBb, what is the chance you pass on both A and B? Clever you are—you multiply ½ × ½ to get ¼.

Pedigrees

Pedigrees are family trees used to describe the genetic relationships within a family. Comprehension of the probability concept is important for a full understanding of pedigree analysis. Squares represent males, and circles are used for females. A horizontal line from

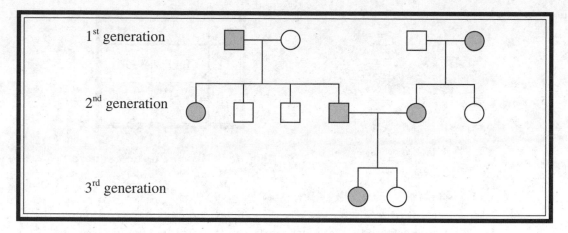

Figure 9.8 Schematic of a pedigree.

*CT teacher:
"Test almost
always has two
to three questions
about this topic."*

male to female represents mates that have produced offspring. The offspring are listed below their parents from oldest to youngest. A fully shaded individual possesses the trait being studied. If the condition being studied is a monogenic recessive condition (rr), then those shaded gray have the genotype rr. If the condition being studied is a dominant condition (Rr or RR), then those that are *un*shaded have the genotype rr. A line through a symbol indicates that the person is deceased. A sample pedigree is shown in Figure 9.8.

Pedigrees can be used in many ways. One use is to determine the risk of parents passing certain conditions to their offspring. Imagine that two people want to have a child, and they both have a family history of a certain autosomal recessive condition (dd). Neither has the particular condition, but the man has a brother who died of the disease and the woman's mother died of the disease at an older age. They want to know the probability of having a child with the condition. You must first determine the probability that each parent is a carrier, and then determine the probability of the parents having a child with the disease, given that they are carriers. See the pedigree in Figure 9.9.

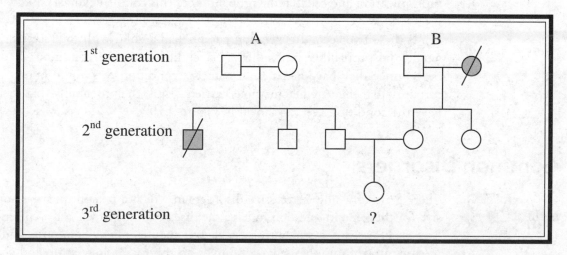

Figure 9.9 Three-generation pedigree indicating probability of inheriting a particular disease.

First, we can determine the father's (second-generation) probability of being a carrier. We know that both of his parents must be carriers with a genotype of Dd. Why is this the case? Although neither parent has the condition, they must both be carriers for his brother

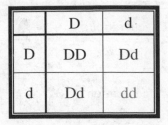

	D	d
D	DD	Dd
d	Dd	dd

Figure 9.10   A Punnett square.

to have received two recessive alleles and thus have contracted the disease. How can we calculate the potential probability of the father being a carrier? We construct a Punnett square for a monohybrid cross of the father's parents (first generation) (Figure 9.10).

We know with certainty that he is not dd, otherwise, he would have the condition. This leaves three equally likely possible genotypes for the father, two of which are "carrier" genotypes (Dd). Thus, the probability of his being a carrier is ⅔.

What is the probability that the mother (second generation) is a carrier? We don't even need a Punnett square to determine this one. Her mother (first generation) died of the condition, which means that she must have been dd, and thus must have passed along a d to each of her children. The mother in question does not have the condition, so she must have a D as well. Therefore her genotype *must* be Dd.

To determine the probability that *both* parents are carriers, apply the law of multiplication with probabilities (similar to tossing a coin) and use the following formula:

$$\text{PF} \times \text{PM} = \tfrac{2}{3} \times 1 = \tfrac{2}{3}$$

(where PF, PM = probabilities of father, mother being carriers).

Now that we have determined the probability that they are both carriers, we need to determine the probability that one of their offspring will have the condition. Their Punnett square would be the same as that shown in Figure 9.10, and we can see that the probability of having a child with the recessive condition is ¼. Again, we use the law of multiplication and see that the probability of this couple having a child with the condition is ⅔ × ¼ = ⅙.

If these two second-generation parents had a child with the recessive condition, what would the probability be of their next child having the condition? It would no longer be ⅙; once they have had a child with the condition, we would know with 100 percent certainty that they are heterozygous carriers. Thus, the probability that their next child will have the condition is ¼, as shown in Figure 9.10.

Common Disorders

There are many simple recessive disorders in which a person must be homozygous recessive for the gene in question to have the disease. Some of the most common examples are Tay-Sachs disease, cystic fibrosis, sickle cell anemia, phenylketonuria, and albinism. These diseases are commonly used as examples on the AP Biology exam and could also aid you in constructing a well-supported essay answer to a question about heredity and inherited disorders.

Tay-Sachs disease is a fatal genetic disorder that renders the body unable to break down a particular type of lipid that accumulates in the brain and eventually causes blindness and brain damage. Individuals with this disease typically do not survive more than a few years. Carriers of this disease do not show any of the effects of the disease, and thus the allele is preserved in the population because carriers usually live to reproduce and potentially pass on the recessive copy of the allele. This disease is found in a higher-than-normal percentage of people of eastern European Jewish descent.

Cystic fibrosis (CF), a recessive disorder, is the most common fatal genetic disease in this country. The gene for this disease is located on chromosome 7. The normal allele for this gene is involved in cellular chloride ion transport. A defective version of this gene results in the excessive secretion of a thick mucus, which accumulates in the lungs and digestive tract. Left untreated, children with CF die at a very young age. Statistically, 1 in 25 Caucasians is a carrier for this disease.

Sickle cell anemia is a common recessive disease that occurs as a result of an improper amino acid substitution during translation of an important red blood cell protein called *hemoglobin*. It results in the formation of a hemoglobin protein that is less efficient at carrying oxygen. It also causes hemoglobin to deform to a sickle shape when the oxygen content of the blood is low, causing pain, muscle weakness, and fatigue.

Sickle cell anemia is the most common inherited disease among African Americans. It affects 1 out of every 400 African Americans, and 1 out of 10 African Americans is a carrier of the disease. The recessive trait is so prevalent because carriers (who are said to have sickle cell "trait") have increased resistance to malaria. In tropical regions, where malaria occurs, the sickle cell trait actually increases an individual's probability of survival, and thus the trait's presence in the population increases (heterozygote advantage).

Phenylketonuria (PKU) is another autosomal recessive disease caused by a single gene defect. Children with PKU are unable to successfully digest phenylalanine (an amino acid). This leads to the accumulation of a by-product in the blood that can cause mental retardation. If the disease is caught early, retardation can be prevented by avoiding phenylalanine in the diet.

Dominant disorders are less common in humans. One example of a dominant disorder is **Huntington disease,** a fatal disease that causes the breakdown of the nervous system. It does not show itself until a person is in their 30s or 40s, and individuals afflicted with this condition have a 50 percent chance of passing it to their offspring.

Why are lethal dominant alleles less common than lethal recessive alleles? Think about how recessive alleles often are passed on from generation to generation. An individual can be a carrier of a recessive condition and pass it along without even knowing it. On the other hand, it is impossible to be an unaffected carrier of a dominant condition, and many lethal conditions have unfortunately killed the individual before reproductive maturity has been achieved. This makes it more difficult for the dominant gene to be passed along. To remain prevalent in the population, a dominant disorder must not kill the individual until reproduction has occurred.

Chromosomal Complications

We have spent a lot of time discussing how genes are inherited and passed from generation to generation. It is also important to discuss the situations in which something goes wrong with the chromosomes themselves that affects the inheritance of genes by the offspring. **Nondisjunction** is an error in homologous chromosome separation. It can occur during meiosis I or II. The result is that one gamete receives too many of one kind of chromosome, and another gamete receives none of a particular chromosome. The fusing of an abnormal gamete with a normal one can lead to the production of offspring with an abnormal number of chromosomes (**aneuploidy**).

Down syndrome is a classic aneuploid example, affecting 1 out of every 700 children born in this country. It most often involves a trisomy of chromosome 21, and leads to mental retardation, heart defects, short stature, and characteristic facial features. Most people with trisomy 21 are sterile.

Trisomy 21 is not the only form of nondisjunction caused by error in the chromosome separation process. Trisomy 13, also known as **Patau syndrome,** causes serious brain and circulatory defects. Trisomy 18, also known as **Edwards syndrome,** can affect all organs. It is rare for a baby to survive for more than a year with either of these two conditions. There are also syndromes involving aneuploidy of the sex chromosomes. Males can receive an extra Y chromosome (XYY). Although this nondisjunction does not seem to produce a major syndrome, XYY males tend to be taller than average, and some geneticists believe they display a higher degree of aggressive behavior. A male can receive an extra X chromosome, as in **Klinefelter syndrome** (XXY). These infertile individuals have male sex organs but show several feminine body characteristics. Nondisjunction occurs in females as well. Females who are XXX have no real syndrome. Females who are missing an X chromosome (XO) have a condition called **Turner syndrome.** XO individuals are sterile females who possess sex organs that fail to mature at puberty.

Trisomies are not the only kind of chromosomal abnormalities that lead to inherited diseases. A **deletion** occurs when a piece of the chromosome is lost in the developmental process. Deletions, such as **cri-du-chat syndrome,** can lead to problems. This syndrome occurs with a deletion in chromosome 5 that leads to mental retardation, abnormal facial features, and a small head. Most affected individuals die very young.

Chromosomal translocations, in which a piece of one chromosome is attached to another, nonhomologous chromosome, can cause major problems. **Chronic myelogenous leukemia** is a cancer affecting white blood cell precursor cells. In this disease, a portion of chromosome 22 has been swapped with a piece of chromosome 9.

A **chromosome inversion** occurs when a portion of a chromosome separates and reattaches in the opposite direction. This can have no effect at all, or it can render a gene nonfunctional if it occurs in the middle of a sequence. A **chromosome duplication** results in the repetition of a genetic segment. A **chromosome duplication** results in the repetition of a genetic segment . . . whoops . . . sorry. . . . Duplications often have serious effects on an organism.

These are the major concepts of heredity with which the AP Biology exam writers would like you to be familiar. Try the practice problems that follow and be sure you are able to construct, read, and analyze both Punnett squares and pedigrees, keeping in mind the laws of probability.

› Review Questions

1. The following crossover frequencies were noted via experimentation for a set of five genes on a single chromosome:

   A and B → 35%
   B and C → 15%
   A and C → 20%
   A and D → 10%
   D and B → 25%
   A and E → 5%
   B and E → 40%

Pick the answer that most likely represents the relative positions of the five genes.

A. |------|------------|------------|------------------|
 E   A   D   C   B

B. |------|------------|------------|------------------|
 A   E   C   D   B

C. |------|------------|------------|------------------|
 E   A   C   D   B

D. |------------|------------|------|------|
 B   C   D E   A

2. Imagine that in squirrels, gray color (G) is dominant over black color (g). A black squirrel has the genotype gg. Crossing a gray squirrel with which of the following would let you know with the most certainty the genotype of the gray squirrel?

   A. GG
   B. Gg
   C. gg
   D. Cannot be determined from the information given

3. From a cross of AABbCC with AaBbCc, what is the probability that the offspring will display a genotype of AaBbCc?

   A. ½
   B. ⅓
   C. ¼
   D. ⅛

Use the following pedigree of an autosomal recessive condition for questions 4–6.

4. What is the genotype of person A?

   A. Bb
   B. BB
   C. bb
   D. Cannot be determined from the given information

5. What is the most likely genotype of person B?

   A. Bb
   B. BB
   C. bb
   D. Cannot be determined from the information given

6. What is the probability that persons C and D would have a child with the condition?

   A. ½
   B. ¼
   C. ⅙
   D. ⅛

7. Which of the following disorders is X-linked?

   A. Tay-Sachs disease
   B. Cystic fibrosis
   C. Hemophilia
   D. Albinism

8. A court case is trying to determine the father of a particular baby. The mother has type O blood, and the baby has type B blood. Which of the following blood types would mean that the man was definitely *not* the father of the baby?

   A. B and A
   B. AB and A
   C. O and B
   D. O and A

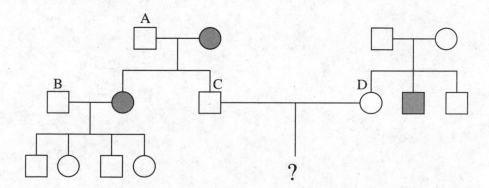

9. Assume that gray squirrel color results from a dominant allele G. The father squirrel is black, the mother squirrel is gray, and their first baby is black. What is the probability that their second baby is also black?

   A. 1.00
   B. 0.75
   C. 0.50
   D. 0.25

10. Imagine that tulips are either yellow or white. You start growing tulips and find out that if you want to get yellow tulips, then at least one of the parents must be yellow. Which color is dominant?

    A. White
    B. Yellow
    C. Neither; it is some form of intermediate inheritance
    D. Cannot be determined from the given information

11. Suppose that 200 red snapdragons were mated with 200 white snapdragons and they produced only pink snapdragons. The mating of two pink snapdragons would most likely result in off-spring that are

    A. 50 percent pink, 25 percent red, 25 percent white
    B. 100 percent pink
    C. 25 percent pink, 50 percent red, 25 percent white
    D. 75 percent red, 25 percent white

12. Which of the following represents the number of possible gametes produced from a genotype of RrBBCcDDEe?

    A. 2
    B. 4
    C. 8
    D. 16

13. Which of the following diseases is *not* caused by trisomy nondisjunction?

    A. Down syndrome
    B. Klinefelter syndrome
    C. Turner syndrome
    D. Patau syndrome

14. The pedigree below is most likely a pedigree of a condition of which type of inheritance?

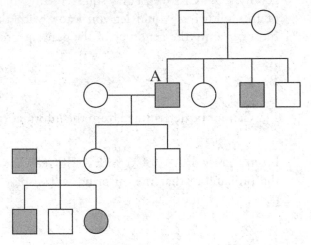

    A. Autosomal dominant
    B. Autosomal recessive
    C. Sex-linked dominant
    D. Sex-linked recessive

› Answers and Explanations

1. **A**—The crossover frequencies are an indication of the distance between the different genes on a chromosome. The farther apart they are, the greater chance there is that they will cross over during prophase I of meiosis. You are first told that A and B cross over with a frequency of 35 percent, so imagine that they are 35 units apart on a chromosome map.

   A (35) B   B (15) C   A (20) C

   We can then tell you that B and C have a frequency of 15 percent. They are 15 units apart on the map,

   but you cannot yet be sure what side of gene A that C is on. Gene A and C cross with 20 percent frequency. This means that gene C must be in between A and B.

   A (20) C (15) B   A (10) D   D (25) B

   Gene A crosses over with D 10 percent of the time, and D crosses with B 25 percent of the time; therefore, D must also be in between A and B. It is closer to A than it is to B. You can use this knowledge to eliminate answer choices B and C.

   A (10) D (10) C (15) B

   Gene A crosses over with E with a frequency of 5 percent. You do not know which side of A gene E is on until you know its crossover frequency with B. Because the question tells you that it has a 40 percent frequency with B, you know that it must be on the *left* of A. This completes your map, leaving A as the correct answer.

2. **C**—This is a test cross. To determine the genotype of an individual showing the dominant phenotype, you cross that individual with a homozygous recessive individual for the same trait. If they have no offspring with the recessive phenotype, then the individual displaying the dominant phenotype is most likely GG. If approximately one-half of the offspring have the recessive phenotype, you know the individual has the genotype Gg.

3. **D**—The Punnett square shown below shows all the possible gamete combinations from this cross. Two-sixteenths or one-eighth of the possible gametes will be AaBbCc. A quick way to determine the number of possible gametes that an individual can produce given a certain genotype is to use the formula 2^n. For example, an individual who is AABbCc can have $2^2 = 4$ possible gametes because Bb and Cc are heterozygous.

	ABC	**AbC**	**ABc**	**Abc**	**aBC**	**abC**	**aBc**	**abc**
ABC	AABBCC	AABbCC	AABBCc	AABbCc	AaBBCC	AaBbCC	AaBBCc	AaBbCc
AbC	AABbCC	AAbbCC	AABbCc	AAbbCc	AaBbCC	AabbCC	AaBbCc	AabbCc

4. **A**—Person A must have genotype Bb because he has some children that have the recessive condition and some that do not. Because his wife is pure recessive, she can contribute only a b. The father must therefore be the one who contributes the B to the child who does not have the condition, and the second b to the one with the condition.

5. **B**—Person B most likely has a genotype of BB. Because he does not have the condition, we know that his genotype is either BB or Bb. If it were Bb, then when crossed with his wife who has a genotype of bb, 50 percent of his children would be expected to have the recessive condition. None of the children have the condition, which leads you to believe that he is most likely BB. (This test is, of course, not 100 percent accurate. Answer choice B is not certain, but is the most probable conclusion.)

6. **C**—We know that neither parent in the question has the recessive condition. We therefore need to calculate the probability that each of them is Bb. The probability that person C is Bb is 1. Because his mother has the condition, she *must* pass a b to him during gamete formation. So the only possible genotypes he can have are Bb and bb. Since he does not have the condition, he must be Bb with a probability of 1. The probability that person D is Bb is 0.67. Neither of her parents has the

condition, but she has a brother who is bb. This means that each of her parents must be a carrier for the condition (Bb). You know that this woman is not bb, because she does not have the condition. As a result, there are only *three* possible genotypes from the cross remaining. Two of these three are Bb, giving her a probability of ⅔, or 0.67, of being Bb. The probability that *both* person C and person D are Bb is (1) × (0.67) = (0.67). Now it is necessary to calculate the probability that two Bb parents will produce a kid who is bb. The Punnett square says that there is a 0.25 chance of this result. To calculate the probability that they will have a child with the recessive condition, you multiply the probability that they are both Bb (0.67) times the probability that two individuals Bb will produce a bb child (0.25). Thus, the probability of an affected child being produced from these two parents is ⅙.

7. **C**—Hemophilia is an X-linked condition. An XY male with hemophilia gets his Y chromosome from his father, and his X chromosome from his mother. All that is needed for the hemophilia condition to occur is a copy of the defective recessive allele from his mother.

8. **D**—Types O and A would prove that he was not the father of this particular child. If the mother has type O blood, this means that her genotype is ii and she *must* pass along an i allele to her child. The baby has type B blood, and her genotype could be $I^B i$ or $I^B I^B$. Since the mother must give an i, then the baby's genotype must be $I^B i$. It follows that the father must provide the I^B allele to the baby to complete the known genotype. If he is type O, he won't have an I^B to pass along since his genotype would be ii. This would also be the case if he were type A, because his genotype would be either $I^A I^A$ or $I^A i$. Therefore, those two blood types would prove that he is not the father of this child.

9. **C**—To figure out this problem, you need to know the genotype of the mother. The father is black, meaning that his genotype is gg. The two of them produced a squirrel that is also black, which means that the gray mother gave a g to the baby. The mother's genotype is Gg. A cross of Gg × gg produces a phenotype ratio of 1:1 gray:black. They have a 0.5 chance of producing another black baby.

10. **B**—According to this scenario, yellow and white are the only colors possible. If white were dominant, and both parents were Ww, you *could* produce a yellow offspring if the two recessive w's combined. If it were intermediate inheritance, you probably would not produce a straight yellow tulip in the offspring because they would either meet halfway (incomplete dominance), or both express fully (codominance). If yellow were dominant, then you could produce a yellow offspring only if there were a Y allele in one of the parents. A cross of yy × yy would produce only white tulips if white were recessive.

11. **A**—This problem involves incomplete dominance. The genotype of the pink offspring from the first generation is RW. When the two RW snapdragons are mated together, they produce the following results:

	R	W
R	RR	RW
W	RW	WW

The offspring will be 25 percent red (RR), 50 percent pink (RW), and 25 percent white (WW).

12. **C**—In a problem like this, you will save time by thinking about the laws of probability. The genotype is RrBBCcDDEe. How many possible combinations of the R gene are there? There are two: R and r. How many for B? Only one: B. Following the same logic, C has two and D has one. Now you multiply the possibilities: (2 × 1 × 2 × 1 × 2) = 8. There are 8 possible gametes from this genotype. Another way to arrive at this answer is by use of the expression 2^n, where *n* is the number of hybrid traits being examined. In this case, it would be 2^3 or 8 possible gametes.

13. **C**—Down syndrome is most often due to a trisomy of chromosome 21. Klinefelter syndrome is a trisomy of the sex chromosomes (XXY). Patau syndrome is a trisomy of chromosome 15. Edwards syndrome is a trisomy of chromosome 18. Turner syndrome, the only nontrisomy listed in this problem, is a *monosomy* of the sex chromosomes (XO).

14. **D**—This is most likely a sex-linked recessive disease. The father in the first generation does not have the condition, so his genotype would be $X^N Y$. The original couple has four children, two boys with the condition, and one girl and one boy without the condition. The genotype of the boys with the condition would be $X^n Y$. This means that the original mother's genotype would be $X^N X^n$—thus she is a carrier. One of the children who inherited the condition has children with a woman from a different family, and neither of their two children displays the condition. However, the daughter of son A has three children with a man who is $X^n Y$, and she has a daughter and a son who show the recessive condition and one normal son. This means that the daughter of son A is most likely $X^N X^n$—another carrier of the condition. This disease is a condition that is, according to the pedigree, more often seen in men, and passed along to men by the X chromosome from the mother. However, it is important to note that if a father who has the X-linked condition has a child with a female carrier for the condition, that couple can indeed produce a female with the condition.

› Rapid Review

You should be familiar with the following terms:

Character: heritable feature, such as flower color.

Monohybrid cross: cross involving one character (Bb × Bb) → (3:1 phenotype ratio).

Dihybrid cross: cross involving two different characters (BbRr × BbRr) → (9:3:3:1 phenotype ratio).

Law of segregation: the two alleles for a trait separate during the formation of gametes—one to each gamete.

Law of independent assortment: inheritance of one trait does not interfere with the inheritance of another trait.

Law of dominance: if two opposite pure-breeding varieties (BB × bb) are crossed, all offspring resemble BB parent.

Intermediate inheritance: heterozygous (Yy) individual shows characteristics unlike *either* parent.

- *Incomplete dominance*: Yy produces an intermediate phenotype between YY and yy (snapdragons).

- *Codominance*: both alleles express themselves fully in a Yy individual—(MN blood groups).

Polygenic traits: traits that are affected by more than one gene (eye color, skin color).

Multiple alleles: traits that correspond to more than two alleles (ABO blood type: I^A, I^B, i).

Epistasis: a gene at one locus alters the phenotypic expression of a gene at another locus (coat color in mice).

Pleiotropy: a single gene has multiple effects on an organism (sickle cell anemia).

Sex determination: males are XY, females are XX.

Autosomal chromosome: not involved in gender.

Fruit flies: wild-type traits are the normal phenotype; mutant traits are those that are different from normal.

Sex-linked traits: passed along the X chromosome; more common in males than females (males have only one X) (e.g., hemophilia [can't clot blood], Duchenne's muscular dystrophy [muscle weakness], colorblindness).

X inactivation: one of two X chromosomes is randomly inactivated and remains coiled as a Barr body.

Holandric trait: one that is inherited via the Y chromosome.

Linked genes: genes that lie along the same chromosome and do not follow the law of independent assortment.

- *Crossover*: a form of genetic recombination that occurs during prophase I of meiosis.
- The further apart two genes are along a chromosome, the more often they will cross over.

Linkage map: genetic map put together using crossover frequencies.

- Can determine the relative location of a set of genes according to how often they cross over.
- If two genes cross over in 20 percent of the crosses, they are 20 map units apart, etc.

Law of multiplication: To determine the probability that two random events will occur in succession, multiply the probability of the first event by the probability of the second event. (Useful in pedigree analysis!)

Pedigree: family tree used to describe genetic relationships (use pedigree diagram in review question 14 for clearer understanding). To calculate the risk a couple faces of having a child that has a recessive (bb) condition, first determine the probability that *both* parents are Bb (if neither have the condition), or the probability that one is Bb (if one *has* the condition). Once determined, multiply this probability times the probability that a Bb × Bb cross will produce a bb (¼) or that a bb × Bb will produce a bb (½).

Autosomal Recessive Disorders

Tay-Sachs: fatal, storage disease, lipid builds up in brain, mental retardation, increased incidence in eastern European Jews.

Cystic fibrosis: increased mucus buildup in lungs; untreated children die at young age; 1 in 25 Caucasians is a carrier.

Sickle cell anemia: caused by error of single amino acid; hemoglobin is less able to carry O_2, and sickles when O_2 content of blood is low; 1 in 10 African Americans is a carrier. Heterozygous condition protects against malaria.

Phenylketonuria: inability to digest phenylalanine, which can cause mental retardation if not avoided in diet.

Autosomal dominant disorders: Huntington disease (nervous system disease) and achondroplasia (dwarfism).

Nondisjunction: error in which homologous chromosomes do not separate properly.

- *Monosomy*: (one copy): Turner syndrome.

- *Trisomy*: (three copies): Down syndrome (21), Patau syndrome (13), Edwards syndrome (18).

Klinefelter syndrome: XXY; XYY males, XXX females.

Chromosome disorders: deletion (cri-du-chat), inversions, duplications, and translocations (leukemia).

CHAPTER 10

Molecular Genetics
Exam Weight: 12–16%

IN THIS CHAPTER

Summary: This chapter describes the various processes in cells that take DNA from gene to protein: replication, transcription, posttranscriptional modification, and translation. It also discusses the regulation of these processes before concluding with a discussion about viruses, bacteria, and genetic engineering.

Key Ideas

KEY IDEA

○ DNA: adenine-thymine, cytosine-guanine—arranged in a double helix.
○ RNA: adenine-uracil, cytosine-guanine—single stranded.
○ DNA replication occurs during the S-phase in a semi-conservative fashion and in a 5′ to 3′ direction.
○ Types of DNA replication mutations: frameshift, missense, nonsense.
○ Transcription: mRNA is formed from a DNA template.
○ Translation: process by which mRNA specified sequence of amino acids is lined up on a ribosome for protein synthesis.
○ Operons act as on-off switches for transcription—allow for production of genes only when needed.
○ Types of genetic recombination: transformation, transduction, and conjugation.

Introduction

Genetics has implications for all of biology. We begin our study of this subject with an introduction to DNA and RNA, followed by a description of the various processes in cells that take DNA from gene to protein: replication, transcription, posttranscriptional modification, translation, and the regulation of all these processes. The genetics of viruses and bacteria follows, and the chapter concludes with a discussion of genetic engineering.

The Central Dogma

The central dogma (Figure 10.1) is a phrase coined by Francis Crick in 1957 to describe the flow of genetic information through a biological system. It consists of DNA → RNA → Proteins and the processes involved in making this flow of information possible. Those processes are replication, transcription, and translation.

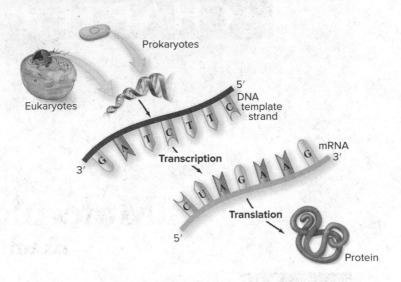

Figure 10.1   The Central Dogma. (*Reproduced with permission from Raven P, Johnson G, Mason K, Losos J, Duncan T; Biology, 12th ed. New York: McGraw Hill; 2020*)

First, take a second to review the structure of DNA and RNA that is located in Chapter 5. Remember DNA is a double helix that is made up of two strands of nucleotides held together by hydrogen bonds while RNA is a single strand of nucleotides. Take a look at the following table:

	DNA	RNA
Shape	Double helix – double strand of nucleotides	Single strand of nucleotides
Sugar	Deoxyribose	Ribose
Bases	Adenine (A), guanine (G), cytosine (C), thymine (T)	Adenine (A), guanine (G), cytosine (C), uracil (U)

Replication of DNA

Human cells do not have copy machines to do the dirty work for them. Instead, they use a system called **DNA replication** to copy DNA molecules from cell to cell. As we discussed in Chapter 8, this process occurs during the S-phase of the cell cycle to ensure that every cell produced during mitosis or meiosis receives the proper amount of DNA.

The mechanism for DNA replication was the source of much debate in the mid-1900s. Some argued that it occurred in what was called a "conservative" (**conservative DNA replication**) fashion. In this model, the original double helix of DNA does not change at all; it is as if the DNA is placed on a copy machine and an exact duplicate is made. DNA from the parent appears in only one of the two daughter cells. A different model called the **semiconservative DNA replication** model agrees that the original DNA molecule serves as the template but proposes that before it is copied, the DNA unzips, with each single strand

(Figure 10.2) serving as a template for the creation of a new double strand. One strand of DNA from the parent goes to one daughter cell, and the second parent strand to the second daughter cell. A third model, the **dispersive DNA replication model,** suggested that every daughter strand contains *some* parental DNA, but it is dispersed among pieces of DNA not of parental origin. Figure 10.2 is a simplistic sketch showing these three main theories. Watson and Crick would not be pleased to see that we did not draw the DNA as a double helix . . . but as long as you realize this is not how the DNA truly looks, the figure serves its purpose.

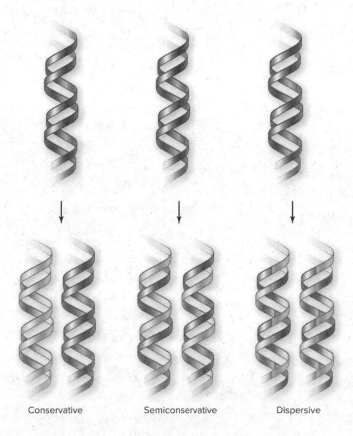

Conservative   Semiconservative   Dispersive

Figure 10.2   Three DNA replication models. The conservative model produces one entirely new molecule and conserves the old. The semiconservative model produces two hybrid molecules of old and new strands. The dispersive model produces hybrid molecules with each strand a mixture of old and new. (*Reproduced with permission from Raven P, Johnson G, Mason K, Losos J, Duncan T;* Biology, *12th ed. New York: McGraw Hill; 2020*)

An experiment performed in the 1950s by Meselson and Stahl (Figure 10.3) helped select a winner in the debate about replication mechanisms. The experimenters grew bacteria in a medium containing ^{15}N (a heavier-than-normal form of nitrogen) to create DNA that was denser than normal. The DNA was denser because the bacteria picked up the ^{15}N and incorporated it into their DNA. The bacteria were then transferred to a medium containing normal ^{14}N nitrogen. The DNA was allowed to replicate and produced DNA that was half ^{15}N and half ^{14}N. When the first generation of offspring replicated to form the second generation of offspring, the new DNA produced was of two types—one type that had half ^{15}N and half ^{14}N, and another type that was completely ^{14}N DNA. This gave a hands-down victory to the semi-conservative theory of DNA replication. Let's take a look at the mechanism of semi-conservative DNA replication.

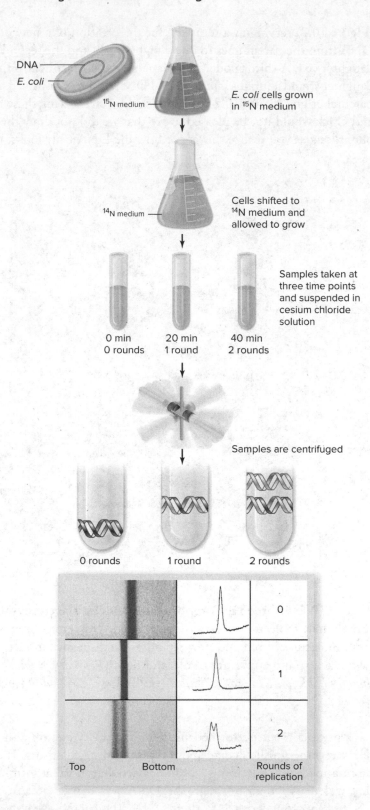

Figure 10.3   The Meselson–Stahl experiment. Bacteria grown in heavy 15N medium are shifted to light 14N medium and grown for two rounds of replication. Samples are taken at time points corresponding to zero, one, and two rounds of replication and centrifuged in cesium chloride to form a gradient. The actual data are shown at the bottom with the interpretation of semiconservative replication shown schematically (*Reproduced with permission from Raven P, Johnson G, Mason K, Losos J, Duncan T;* Biology, *12th ed. New York: McGraw Hill; 2020*)

During the S-phase of the cell cycle, the double-stranded DNA unzips and pre-pares to replicate. An enzyme called **helicase** unzips the DNA just like a jacket, break-ing the hydrogen bonds between the nucleotides and producing the **replication fork** (Figure 10.4). Each strand then functions as a template for production of a new double-stranded DNA molecule. Specific regions along each DNA strand serve as **primer sites** that signal where replication should originate. Primase binds to the primer, and **DNA poly-merase,** the superstar enzyme of this process, attaches to the primer region and adds nucle-otides to the growing DNA chain in a 5′-to-3′ direction. DNA polymerase is restricted in that it can only add nucleotides to the 3′ end of a parent strand. This creates a problem because this means that only one of the strands can be produced in a continuous fashion.

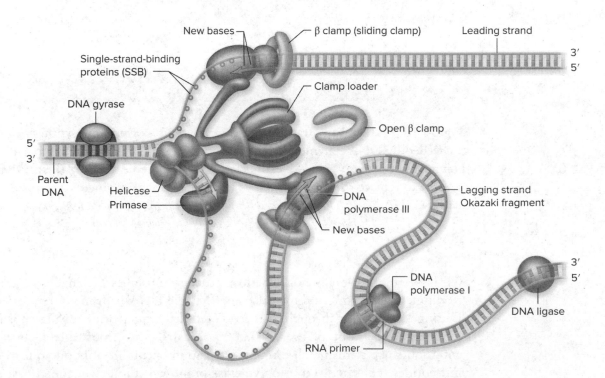

Figure 10.4   The replication fork. A model for the structure of the replication fork with two polymerase III enzymes held together by a large complex of accessory proteins. These include the "clamp loader," which loads the β subunit sliding clamp periodically on the lagging strand. The polymerase III on the lagging strand periodically releases its template and reassociates along with the β clamp. The loop in the lagging-strand template allows both polymerases to move in the same direction despite DNA being antiparallel. Primase, which makes primers for the lagging-strand fragments, and helicase are also associated with the central complex. Polymerase I removes primers and ligase joins the fragments together. (*Reproduced with permission from Raven P, Johnson G, Mason K, Losos J, Duncan T;* Biology, *12th ed. New York: McGraw Hill; 2020*)

This continuous strand is known as the **leading strand.** The other strand is affection-ately known as the **lagging strand.** You will notice that in the third step of the process in Figure 10.5, the lagging strand consists of tiny pieces called **Okazaki fragments,** which are later connected by an enzyme called DNA ligase to produce the completed double-stranded daughter DNA molecule. This is the semi-conservative model of DNA replication.

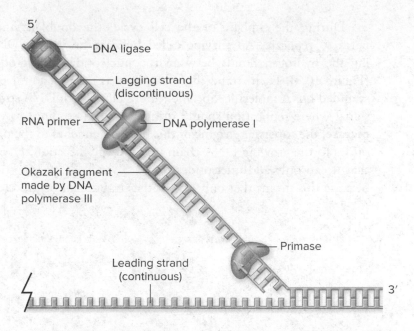

Figure 10.5   Lagging-strand synthesis. The action of primase synthesizes the primers needed by DNA polymerase III (not shown). These primers are removed by DNA polymerase I using its 5′-to-3′ exonuclease activity, then extending the previous Okazaki fragment to replace the RNA. The nick between Okazaki fragments after primer removal is sealed by DNA ligase. (*Reproduced with permission from Raven P, Johnson G, Mason K, Losos J, Duncan T;* Biology, *12th ed. New York: McGraw Hill; 2020*)

DNA replication is not a perfect process—mistakes are made. A series of proof-reading enzymes function to make sure that the DNA is properly replicated each time. During the first run-through, it is estimated that a nucleotide mismatch is made during replication in 1 out of every 10,000 basepairs. The proofreaders must do a pretty good job since a mismatch error in replication occurs in only one out of every *billion* nucleotides replicated. DNA polymerase proofreads the newly added base right after it is added on to make sure that it is the correct match. Repair is easy—the polymerase simply removes the incorrect nucleotide, and adds the proper one in its place. This process is known as **mismatch repair.** Another repair mechanism is **excision repair,** in which a *section* of DNA containing an error is cut out and the gap is filled in by DNA polymerase. There are other proteins that assist in the repair process, but their identities are not of major importance. Just be aware that DNA repair exists and is a very efficient process.

Key Enzymes to Know for DNA Replication

Helicase: enzyme that unzips DNA, breaking the hydrogen bonds between the nucleotides and producing the replication fork for replication

Topoisomerase: enzyme that helps in the unwinding or rewinding of DNA.

DNA polymerase: the main enzyme in DNA replication that attaches to primer proteins and adds nucleotides to the growing DNA chain in a 5′-to-3′ chain.

Ligase: enzyme that connects two strands of DNA together by forming a bond between the phosphate group of one strand and the deoxyribose group of another.

RNA polymerase: enzyme that runs transcription and adds the appropriate nucleotides to the 3' end of the growing strand.

Telomeres

In eukaryotic chromosomes, DNA replication (Figure 10.6) creates an issue for the structure of the chromosome. The leading strand is completely replicated, but the lagging strand is not able to be completed all the way to the end. This occurs because the primer used to start DNA replication on the lagging strand is not replaced. As a result, during each round of replication, the lagging strand template would produce a shorter chromosome (Figure 10.7). This is where telomeres come into play. Telomeres are specialized structures composed of short repeated sequences of DNA that are made by telomerase. They are found on the ends of eukaryotic chromosomes that protect the integrity and length of the chromosomes after each replication.

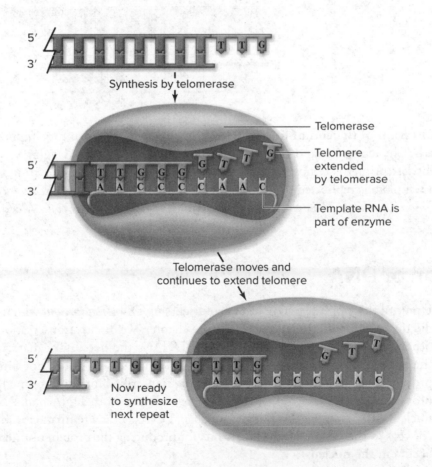

Figure 10.6   Action of telomerase. Telomerase contains an internal RNA that the enzyme uses as a template to extend the DNA of the chromosome end. Multiple rounds of synthesis by telomerase produce repeated sequences. This single strand is completed by normal synthesis using it as a template (not shown). (*Reproduced with permission from Raven P, Johnson G, Mason K, Losos J, Duncan T;* Biology, *12th ed. New York: McGraw Hill; 2020*)

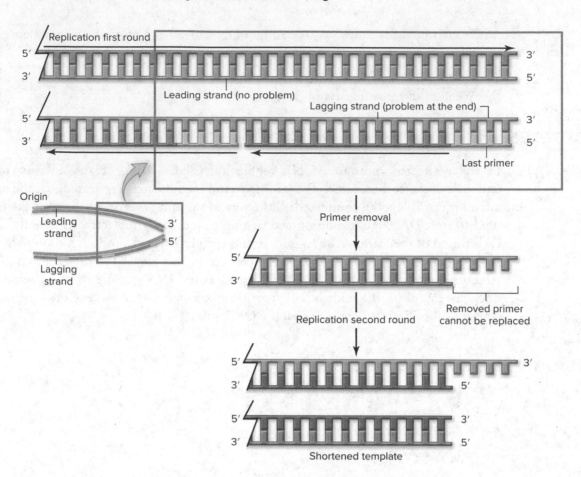

Figure 10.7   Replication of the end of linear DNA. Only one end is shown for simplicity; the problem exists at both ends. The leading strand can be completely replicated, but the lagging strand cannot be finished. When the last primer is removed, it cannot be replaced. During the next round of replication, when this shortened template is replicated, it will produce a shorter chromosome. (*Reproduced with permission from Raven P, Johnson G, Mason K, Losos J, Duncan T; Biology, 12th ed. New York: McGraw Hill; 2020*)

Transcription of DNA

NY teacher: "Know the basic principles. They'll ask you about this process."

Up until this point, we have just been discussing DNA *replication,* which is simply the production of more DNA. In the rest of the chapter, we discuss transcription, translation, and other processes involving DNA. While DNA is the hereditary material responsible for the passage of traits from generation to generation, DNA does not directly produce the proteins that it encodes. DNA must first be transcribed into an intermediary: mRNA. This process is called *transcription* (Figure 10.8) because both DNA and RNA are built from nucleotides—they speak a similar language. DNA acts as a template for mRNA, which then conveys to the ribosomes the blueprints for producing the protein of interest. Transcription occurs in the nucleus.

Transcription consists of three steps: initiation, elongation, and termination. The process begins when **RNA polymerase** attaches to the promoter region of a DNA strand (initiation). A **promoter region** is simply a recognition site that shows the polymerase where transcription should begin. The promoter region contains a group of nucleotides known as the **TATA box,** which is important to the binding of RNA polymerase. As in DNA replication, the polymerase of transcription needs the assistance of helper proteins to find and attach

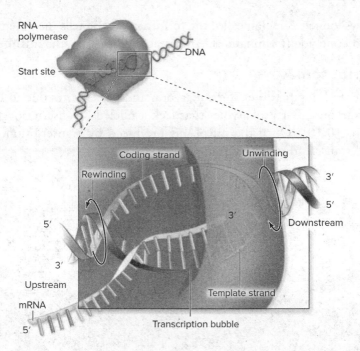

Figure 10.8   Model of a transcription bubble. The DNA duplex is unwound by the RNA polymerase complex, rewinding at the end of the bubble. One of the strands of DNA functions as a template, and nucleotide building blocks are added to the 3′ end of the growing RNA. There is a short region of RNA–DNA hybrid within the bubble. (*Reproduced with permission from Raven P, Johnson G, Mason K, Losos J, Duncan T; Biology, 12th ed. New York: McGraw Hill; 2020*)

to the promoter region. These helpers are called transcription factors (Figure 10.9). Once bound, the RNA polymerase works its magic by adding the appropriate RNA nucleotide to the 3′ end of the growing strand (elongation). Like DNA polymerase of replication, RNA polymerase adds nucleotides 5′ to 3′. The growing mRNA strand separates from the DNA as

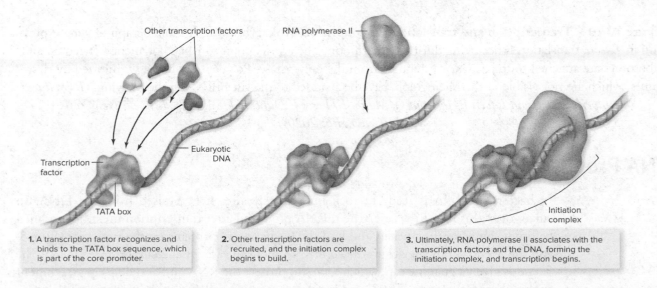

1. A transcription factor recognizes and binds to the TATA box sequence, which is part of the core promoter.

2. Other transcription factors are recruited, and the initiation complex begins to build.

3. Ultimately, RNA polymerase II associates with the transcription factors and the DNA, forming the initiation complex, and transcription begins.

Figure 10.9   Eukaryotic initiation complex. Unlike transcription in prokaryotic cells, in which the RNA polymerase recognizes and binds to the promoter, eukaryotic transcription requires the binding of transcription factors to the promoter before RNA polymerase II binds to the DNA. The association of transcription factors and RNA polymerase II at the promoter is called the initiation complex. (*Reproduced with permission from Raven P, Johnson G, Mason K, Losos J, Duncan T; Biology, 12th ed. New York: McGraw Hill; 2020*)

it grows longer. A region called the **termination site** tells the polymerase when transcription should conclude (termination). After reaching this site, the mRNA is released and set free.

Polyribosomes

The central dogma differs for eukaryotes and prokaryotes due to the presence of a nucleus in eukaryotes. For prokaryotes that lack a nucleus, transcription is coupled to translation (Figure 10.10). Once the mRNA is produced by transcription, then translation begins before transcription is finished.

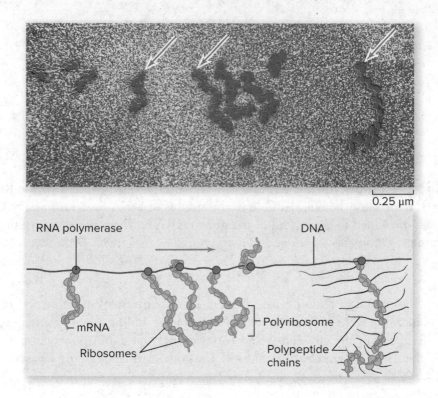

Figure 10.10   Transcription and translation are coupled in prokaryotes. In this micrograph of gene expression in *E. coli*, translation is occurring during transcription. The arrows point to RNA polymerase enzymes, and ribosomes are attached to the mRNAs extending from the polymerase. Polypeptides being synthesized by ribosomes, which are not visible in the micrograph, have been added to the last mRNA in the drawing. (*Reproduced with permission from Raven P, Johnson G, Mason K, Losos J, Duncan T; Biology, 12th ed. New York: McGraw Hill; 2020*)

RNA Processing

In bacteria, mRNA is ready to rock immediately after it is released from the DNA. In eukaryotes, this is not the case. The mRNA produced after transcription must be modified before it can leave the nucleus and lead the formation of proteins on the ribosomes. The 5′ and the 3′ ends of the newly produced mRNA molecule are touched up (Figure 10.11). The 5′ end is given a guanine cap, which serves to protect the RNA and also helps in attachment to the ribosome later on. The 3′ end is given something called a *polyadenine tail,* which may help ease the movement from the nucleus to the cytoplasm.

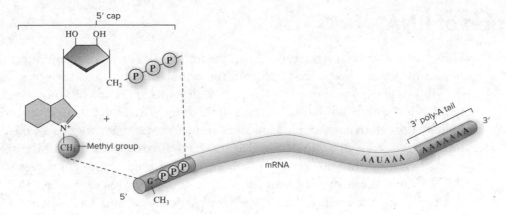

Figure 10.11   Posttranscriptional modifications to 5′ and 3′ ends. Eukaryotic mRNA molecules are modified in the nucleus with the addition of a methylated GTP to the 5′ end of the transcript, called the 5′ cap, and a long chain of adenine residues to the 3′ end of the transcript, called the 3′ poly-A tail. (*Reproduced with permission from Raven P, Johnson G, Mason K, Losos J, Duncan T; Biology, 12th ed. New York: McGraw Hill; 2020*)

Along with these changes, the **introns** (noncoding regions produced during transcription) are cut out of the mRNA, and the remaining **exons** (coding regions) are glued back together to produce the mRNA that is translated into a protein (Figure 10.12). This is called **RNA splicing.** We admit that it does seem strange and inefficient that the DNA would contain so many regions that are not used in the production of the gene, but perhaps there is a method to the madness. It is hypothesized that introns exist to provide flexibility to the genome. They could allow an organism to make different proteins from the same gene; the only difference is which introns get spliced out from one to the other. It is also possible that this whole splicing process plays a role in allowing the movement of mRNA from the nucleus to the cytoplasm.

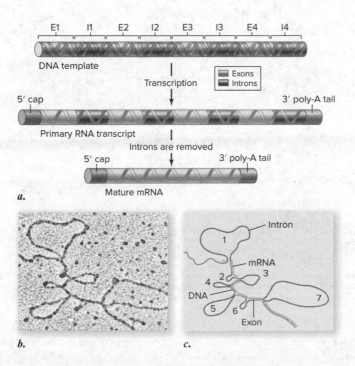

Figure 10.12   Eukaryotic genes contain introns and exons. *a.* Eukaryotic genes contain sequences that form the coding sequence called exons and intervening sequences called introns. ***b.*** An electron micrograph showing hybrids formed with the mRNA and the DNA of the ovalbumin gene, which has seven introns. Introns within the DNA sequence have no corresponding sequence in the mRNA and thus appear as seven loops. c. A schematic drawing of the micrograph. (*Reproduced with permission from Raven P, Johnson G, Mason K, Losos J, Duncan T; Biology, 12th ed. New York: McGraw Hill; 2020*)

Translation of RNA

Now that the mRNA has escaped from the nucleus, it is ready to help direct the construction of proteins. This process occurs in the cytoplasm, and the site of protein synthesis is the ribosome. As mentioned in Chapter 5, proteins are made of amino acids. Each protein has a distinct and particular amino acid order. Therefore, there must be some system used by the cell to convert the sequences of nucleotides that make up an mRNA molecule into the sequence of amino acids that make up a particular protein. The cell carries out this conversion from nucleotides to amino acids through the use of the **genetic code.** An mRNA molecule is divided into a series of codons that make up the code. Each **codon** is a triplet of nucleotides that codes for a particular amino acid. There are 20 different amino acids, and 64 different combinations of codons. This means that some amino acids are coded for by more than one codon. For example, the codons GCU, GCC, GCA, and GCG all call for the addition of the amino acid alanine during protein creation. Of these 64 possibilities, one is a **start codon,** AUG, which establishes the reading frame for protein formation. Also among these 64 codons (Table 10.1) are three **stop codons:** UGA, UAA, and UAG. When the protein formation machinery hits these codons, the production of a protein stops.

| TABLE 10.1 | The Genetic Code | | | | |

First Letter	SECOND LETTER				Third Letter
	U	**C**	**A**	**G**	
U	UUU Phe Phenylalanine	UCU Ser Serine	UAU Tyr Tyrosine	UGU Cys Cysteine	U
	UUC	UCC	UAC	UGC	C
	UUA Leu Leucine	UCA	UAA "Stop"	UGA "Stop"	A
	UUG	UCG	UAG "Stop"	UGG Trp Tryptophan	G
C	CUU Leu Leucine	CCU Pro Proline	CAU His Histidine	CGU Arg Arginine	U
	CUC	CCC	CAC	CGC	C
	CUA	CCA	CAA Gln Glutamine	CGA	A
	CUG	CCG	CAG	CGG	G
A	AUU Ile Isoleucine	ACU Thr Threonine	AAU Asn Asparagine	AGU Ser Serine	U
	AUC	ACC	AAC	AGC	C
	AUA	ACA	AAA Lys Lysine	AGA Arg Arginine	A
	AUG Met Methionine; "Start"	ACG	AAG	AGG	G
G	GUU Val Valine	GCU Ala Alanine	GAU Asp Aspartate	GGU Gly Glycine	U
	GUC	GCC	GAC	GGC	C
	GUA	GCA	GAA Glu Glutamate	GGA	A
	GUG	GCG	GAG	GGG	G

A codon consists of three nucleotides read in the sequence shown. For example, ACU codes for threonine. The first letter, A, is in the First Letter column; the second letter, C, is in the Second Letter column; and the third letter, U, is in the Third Letter column. Each of the mRNA codons is recognized by a corresponding anticodon sequence on a tRNA molecule. Many amino acids are specified by more than one codon. For example, threonine is specified by four codons, which differ only in the third nucleotide (ACU, ACC, ACA, and ACG).

Before we go through the steps of protein synthesis, we would like to introduce to you the other players involved in the process. We have already spoken about mRNA, but we should meet the host of the entire shindig, the **ribosomes,** which are made up of a large and a small subunit. A huge percentage of a ribosome is built out of the second type of RNA mentioned earlier, rRNA. Two other important parts of a ribosome that we will discuss in more detail later are the **A site** and the **P site,** which are tRNA attachment sites. The job of tRNA is to carry amino acids to the ribosomes. The mRNA molecule that is involved in the formation of a protein consists of a series of codons. Each tRNA has, at its attachment site, a region called the **anticodon,** which is a three-nucleotide sequence that is perfectly complementary to a particular codon. For example, a codon that is AUU has an **anticodon** that reads UAA in the same direction. Each tRNA molecule carries an amino acid that is coded for by the codon that its **anticodon** matches up with. Once the tRNA's amino acid has been incorporated into the growing protein, the tRNA leaves the site to pick up another amino acid just in case its services are needed again at the ribosome. An enzyme known as **aminoacyl tRNA synthetase** (Figure 10.13) makes sure that each tRNA molecule picks up the appropriate amino acid for its anticodon.

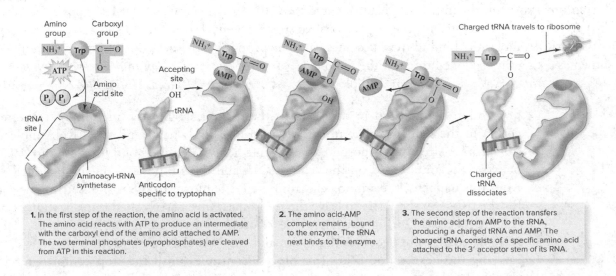

1. In the first step of the reaction, the amino acid is activated. The amino acid reacts with ATP to produce an intermediate with the carboxyl end of the amino acid attached to AMP. The two terminal phosphates (pyrophosphates) are cleaved from ATP in this reaction.

2. The amino acid-AMP complex remains bound to the enzyme. The tRNA next binds to the enzyme.

3. The second step of the reaction transfers the amino acid from AMP to the tRNA, producing a charged tRNA and AMP. The charged tRNA consists of a specific amino acid attached to the 3′ acceptor stem of its RNA.

Figure 10.13   The Binding of amino acids to specific tRNA molecules. (*Reproduced with permission from Raven P, Johnson G, Mason K, Losos J, Duncan T; Biology, 12th ed. New York: McGraw Hill; 2020*)

Uh-oh . . . there is a potential problem here. There are fewer than 50 different types of tRNA molecules. But there are more codons than that. Oh, dear . . . but wait! This is not a problem because some tRNA are able to match with more than one codon. How can this be? This works thanks to a phenomenon known as **wobble,** where a uracil in the third position of an anticodon can pair with A or G instead of just A. There are some tRNA molecules that have an altered form of adenine, called inosine (I), in the third position of the anticodon. This nitrogenous base is able to bind with U, C, *or* A. Wobble allows the 45 tRNA molecules to service all the different types of codons seen in mRNA molecules.

We have met all the important players in the translation process (see also Figure 10.14), which begins when an mRNA attaches to a small ribosomal subunit. The first codon for this process is always AUG. This attracts a tRNA molecule carrying methionine to attach to the AUG codon. When this occurs, the large subunit of the ribosome, containing the A site and the P site, binds to the complex. The elongation of the protein is ready to begin. The P site is the host for the tRNA carrying the growing protein, while the A site is where the tRNA carrying the next amino acid sits. Think of the A site as the on-deck circle of a baseball field, and the p site as the batter's box. So, AUG is the

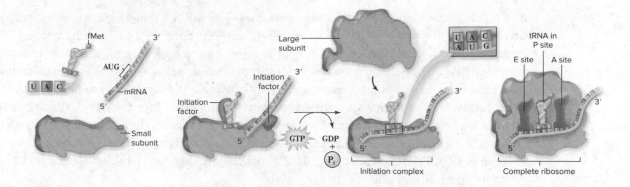

Figure 10.14 Initiation of translation. In prokaryotes, initiation factors play key roles in positioning the small ribosomal subunit, the initiator tRNAfMet, and the mRNA. When the tRNAfMet is positioned over the first AUG codon of the mRNA, the large ribosomal subunit binds, forming the E, P, and A sites where successive tRNA molecules bind to the ribosomes, and polypeptide synthesis begins. Ribosomal subunits are shown as a cutaway sectioned through the middle. (*Reproduced with permission from Raven P, Johnson G, Mason K, Losos J, Duncan T; Biology, 12th ed. New York: McGraw Hill; 2020*)

first codon bound, and in the P site is the tRNA carrying the methionine. The next codon in the sequence determines which tRNA binds next, and that tRNA molecule sits in the A site of the ribosome. An enzyme helps a peptide bond form (Figure 10.15) between the amino acid on the A site tRNA and the amino acid on the P site tRNA. After this happens, the amino acid from the P site moves to the A site, setting the stage for the tRNA in the P site to leave the ribosome. Now a step called translocation occurs (Figure 10.16). During this step, the ribosome moves along the mRNA in such a way that the A site becomes the P site and the next tRNA comes into the new A site carrying the next amino acid. This process continues until the stop codon is reached (Figure 10.17), causing the completed protein to leave the ribosome.

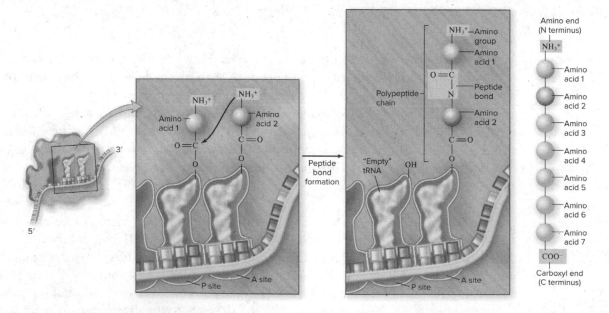

Figure 10.15 Peptide bond formation. Peptide bonds are formed between a "new" charged tRNA in the A site and the growing chain attached to the tRNA in the P site. The bond forms between the amino group of the new amino acid and the carboxyl group of the growing chain. This breaks the bond between the growing chain and its tRNA, transferring it to the A site as the new amino acid remains attached to its tRNA. (*Reproduced with permission from Raven P, Johnson G, Mason K, Losos J, Duncan T; Biology, 12th ed. New York: McGraw Hill; 2020*)

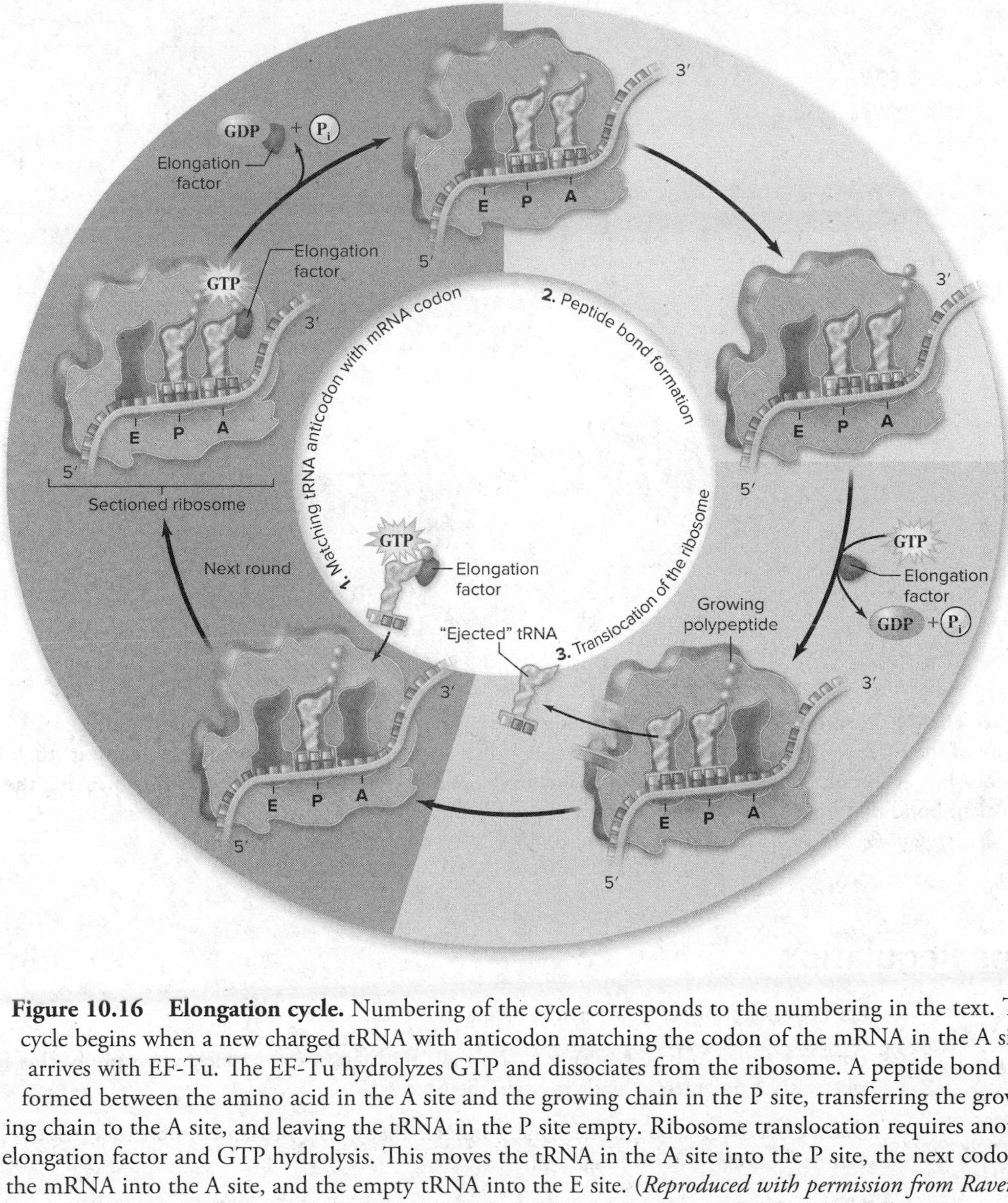

Figure 10.16 Elongation cycle. Numbering of the cycle corresponds to the numbering in the text. The cycle begins when a new charged tRNA with anticodon matching the codon of the mRNA in the A site arrives with EF-Tu. The EF-Tu hydrolyzes GTP and dissociates from the ribosome. A peptide bond is formed between the amino acid in the A site and the growing chain in the P site, transferring the growing chain to the A site, and leaving the tRNA in the P site empty. Ribosome translocation requires another elongation factor and GTP hydrolysis. This moves the tRNA in the A site into the P site, the next codon in the mRNA into the A site, and the empty tRNA into the E site. (*Reproduced with permission from Raven P, Johnson G, Mason K, Losos J, Duncan T; Biology, 12th ed. New York: McGraw Hill; 2020*)

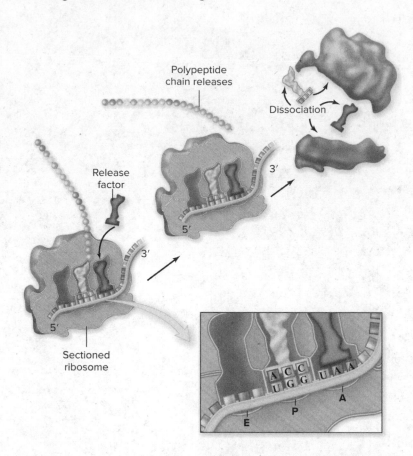

Figure 10.17 Termination of protein synthesis. There is no tRNA with an anticodon complementary to any of the three termination signal codons. When a ribosome encounters a termination codon, it stops translocating. A specific protein release factor facilitates the release of the polypeptide chain by breaking the covalent bond that links the polypeptide to the P site tRNA. (*Reproduced with permission from Raven P, Johnson G, Mason K, Losos J, Duncan T; Biology, 12th ed. New York: McGraw Hill; 2020*)

Gene Regulation

IST-2

Differences in the expression of genes account for some of the phenotypic differences between organisms.

Let's cover some vocabulary before diving into this section:

Promoter region: a base sequence that signals the start site for gene transcription; this is where RNA polymerase binds to begin the process.

Operator: a short sequence near the promoter that assists in transcription by interacting with regulatory proteins (transcription factors).

Operon: a promoter/operator pair that services multiple genes; the **lac operon** is a well-known example (Figure 10.18).

Repressor: protein that prevents the binding of RNA polymerase to the promoter site.

CT teacher: "Be able to write about operons."

Enhancer: DNA region, also known as a "regulator," that is located thousands of bases away from the promoter; it influences transcription by interacting with specific transcription factors.

Inducer: a molecule that binds to and inactivates a repressor (e.g., lactose for the *lac* operon).

Prokaryotic Gene Regulation

The control of gene expression is vital to the proper and efficient functioning of an organism. In bacteria, operons are a major method of gene expression control. The lactose operon services a series of three genes involved in the process of lactose metabolism. This contains the genes that help the bacteria digest lactose. It makes sense for bacteria to produce these genes only if lactose is present. Otherwise, why waste the energy on unneeded enzymes? This is where operons come into play—in the absence of lactose, a repressor binds to the promoter region and prevents transcription from occurring. When lactose is present, there is a binding site on the repressor where lactose attaches, causing the repressor to let go of the promoter region. RNA polymerase is then free to bind to that site and initiate transcription of the genes. When the lactose is gone, the repressor again becomes free to bind to the promoter, halting the process.

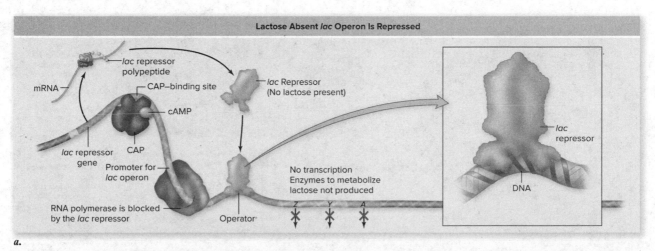

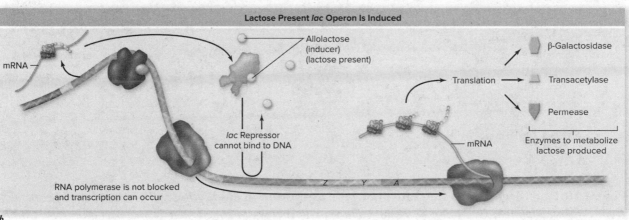

Figure 10.18   Induction of the *lac* operon. a. In the absence of lactose the lac repressor binds to DNA at the operator site, thus preventing transcription of the operon. When the repressor protein is bound to the operator site, the *lac* operon is shut down (repressed). **b.** The *lac* operon is transcribed (induced) when CAP is bound and when the repressor is not bound. Allolactose binding to the repressor alters the repressor's shape so it cannot bind to the operator site and block RNA polymerase activity. (*Reproduced with permission from Raven P, Johnson G, Mason K, Losos J, Duncan T; Biology, 12th ed. New York: McGraw Hill; 2020*)

Eukaryotic Gene Regulation

Because gene expression in eukaryotes involves more steps, there are more places where gene control can occur. Here are the different ways that gene expression occurs in eukaryotes (Figures 10.19–10.21):

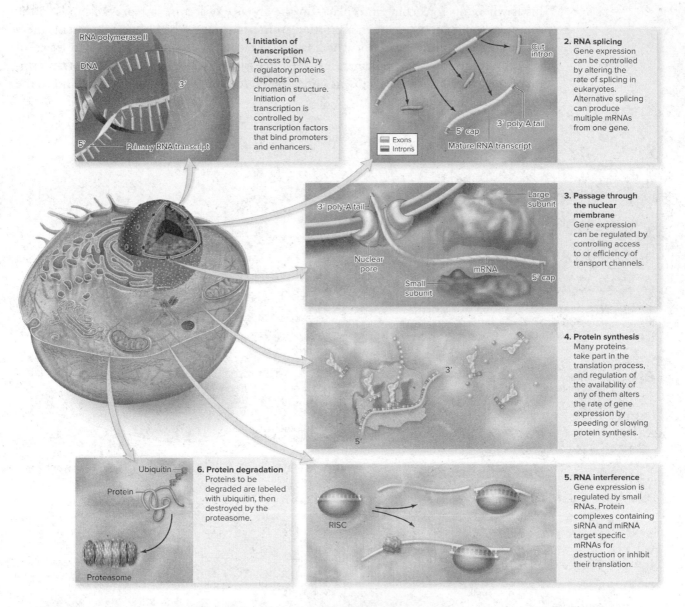

Figure 10.19 Mechanisms for control of gene expression in eukaryotes. (*Reproduced with permission from Raven P, Johnson G, Mason K, Losos J, Duncan T; Biology, 12th ed. New York: McGraw Hill; 2020*)

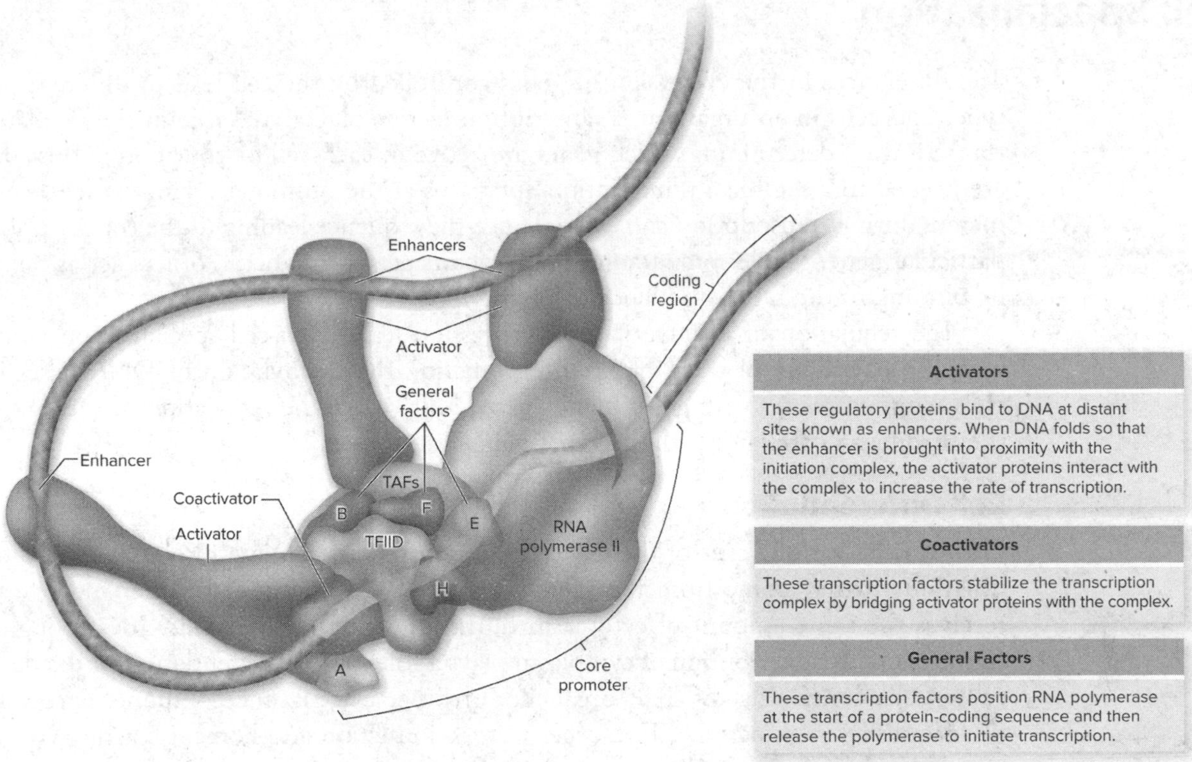

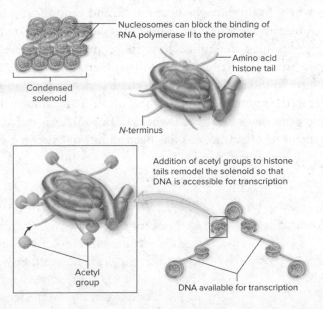

Figure 10.20   Interactions of various factors within the transcription complex. All specific transcription factors bind to enhancer sequences that may be distant from the promoter. These proteins can then interact with the initiation complex by DNA looping to bring the factors into proximity with the initiation complex. As detailed in the text, some transcription factors, called activators, can directly interact with the RNA polymerase II or the initiation complex, whereas others require additional coactivators. (*Reproduced with permission from Raven P, Johnson G, Mason K, Losos J, Duncan T;* Biology, *12th ed. New York: McGraw Hill; 2020*)

Figure 10.21   Histone modification affects chromatin structure. DNA in eukaryotes is organized first into nucleosomes and then into higher-order chromatin structures. The histones that make up the nucleosome core have amino tails that protrude. These amino tails can be modified by the addition of acetyl groups. The acetylation alters the structure of chromatin, making it accessible to the transcription apparatus. (*Reproduced with permission from Raven P, Johnson G, Mason K, Losos J, Duncan T;* Biology, *12th ed. New York: McGraw Hill; 2020*)

Cell Specialization

The differences in the expression of genes controlled by the cell lead to different phenotypes and cells in an organism. Transcription factors play a vital role in the regulation of transcription, determining which genes are active in each cell of your body. These factors are needed to assemble a transcription apparatus at the promoter region with RNA polymerase during transcription and can enhance the sequence leading to the transcription of a particular gene. While some transcription factors act as enhancers, others act as repressors by binding to the DNA and blocking transcription.

The regulation of eukaryotic gene expression leading to cell specialization continues with the packaging of the DNA into chromatin. The methylation of DNA bases in the chromatin correlates with genes being "turned off" while the acetylation of DNA bases in the chromatin correlates with the genes being "turned on."

Cell Differentiation

How do the various cells of the developing embryo differentiate into cells with different functions if they come from the same parent cell? As mentioned earlier, not every cell receives the same amount of cytoplasm during the cleavage divisions. It is thought that this asymmetric distribution of cytoplasm plays a role in the differentiation of the daughter cells. Cells containing different organelles or other cytoplasmic components are able to perform different functions. Two other factors, induction and homeotic genes, contribute to cellular differentiation.

Induction is the influence of one group of cells on the development of another through physical contact or chemical signaling. Just in case you are asked to write an essay on induction, it is good to know a bit about the experiments of the German embryologist Hans Spemann. His experiments revealed that the notochord induces cells of the dorsal ectoderm to develop into the neural plate. When cells from the notochord of an embryo are transplanted to a different place near the ectoderm, the neural plate will develop in the new location. The cells from the notochord region act as "project directors," telling the ectoderm where to produce the neural tube and central nervous system.

Homeotic genes regulate or "direct" the body plan of organisms. For example, a fly's homeotic genes help determine how its segments will develop and which appendages should grow from each segment. Scientists interfering with the development of these poor creatures have found that mutations in these genes can lead to the production of too many wings, legs in the wrong place, and other unfortunate abnormalities. The DNA sequence of a homeotic gene that tells the cell where to put things is called the homeobox. It is similar from organism to organism and has been found to exist in a variety of organisms—birds, humans, fish, and frogs.

KEY IDEA

Factors in Cellular Differentiation	
Cytoplasmic distribution	Asymmetry contributes to differentiation, since different areas have different amounts of cytoplasm, and thus perhaps different organelles and cytoplasmic structures.
Induction	One group of cells influences another group of cells through physical contact or chemical signaling.
Homeotic genes	Regulatory genes that determine how segments of an organism will develop.

Mutations

A mutation is a heritable change in the genes of an organism. These heritable changes can result in changes to the phenotype of an organism or be silent and not affect the phenotype of an organism. These alterations of the DNA sequences in organisms contribute to variation in a population and can be subject to natural selection.

Point mutations, which alter a single base, can be a substitution of another base, a deletion of a base(s) or an addition of a base(s). It is important that you can identify the different types of mutations. The table and figure below show each type of mutation.

Here is a short list of mutation types (Figure 10.22) that you should know:

> **IST-2**
>
> *Differences in the expression of genes account for some of the phenotypic differences between organisms.*

1. *Frameshift mutations.* Deletion or addition of DNA nucleotides that does not add or remove a multiple of three nucleotides. mRNA is produced on a DNA template and is read in bunches of three called **codons,** which tell the protein synthesis machinery which amino acid to add to the growing protein chain. If the mRNA reads: THE FAT CAT ATE HER HAT, and the F is removed because of an error somewhere, the frame has now *shifted* to read THE ATC ATA THE ERH AT . . . (gibberish). This kind of mutation usually produces a nonfunctional protein unless it occurs late in protein production.

> **IST-4**
>
> *The processing of genetic information is imperfect and is a source of genetic variation.*

2. *Missense mutation.* Substitution of the wrong nucleotides into the DNA sequence. These substitutions still result in the addition of amino acids to the growing protein chain during translation, but they can sometimes lead to the addition of *incorrect* amino acids to the chain. It could cause no problem at all, or it could cause a big problem as in sickle cell anemia, in which a single amino acid error caused by a substitution mutation leads to a disease that wreaks havoc on the body as a whole.

3. *Nonsense mutation.* Substitution of the wrong nucleotides into the DNA sequence. These substitutions lead to premature stoppage of protein synthesis by the early placement of a **stop codon,** which tells the protein synthesis machinery to grind to a halt. The stop codons are UAA, UAG, and UGA. This type of mutation usually leads to a nonfunctional protein.

4. *Thymine dimers.* Result of too much exposure to UV (ultraviolet) light. Thymine nucleotides located adjacent to one another on the DNA strand bind together when this exposure occurs. This can negatively affect replication of DNA and help cause further mutations.

Sickle cell anemia represents a prime example of a point mutation leading to a phenotypic change in humans. Sickle cell is caused by a mutation of the fourth codon in the gene for hemoglobin. The substitution of glycine (a polar amino acid) to valine (a nonpolar amino acid) causes the shape of the hemoglobin protein to change, distorting the shape of the red blood cells. Figure 10.23 shows the mutation leading to the altered protein.

Chromosomal mutations can change the structure of chromosomes and lead to many different disorders found in humans. The following figure shows the four types of chromosomal mutations: deletion, duplication, inversion, and reciprocal translocation (Figure 10.24).

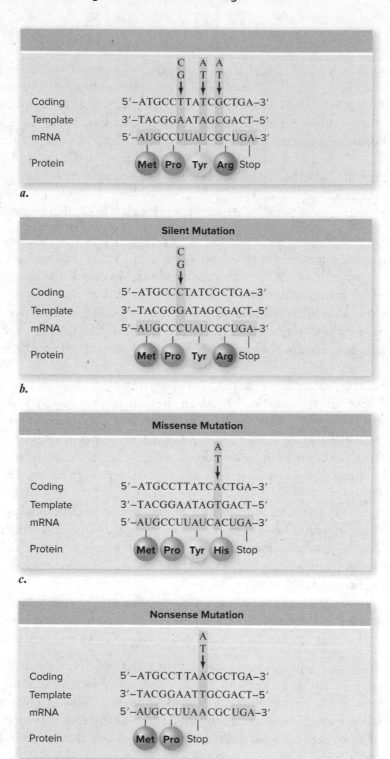

Figure 10.22 Types of point mutations. *a*. A hypothetical gene is shown with encoded mRNA and protein. Arrows above the gene indicate sites of mutations described in the rest of the figure. ***b*.** Silent mutation. Due to degeneracy in the genetic code, base substitution does not always change an amino acid. This usually involves the third position of a codon, in this case a T/A to C/G mutation. ***c*.** Missense mutation. The G/C to A/T mutation changes the amino acid encoded from arginine to histidine. ***d*.** Nonsense mutation. The T/A to A/T mutation produces a UAA stop codon in the mRNA. (*Reproduced with permission from Raven P, Johnson G, Mason K, Losos J, Duncan T; Biology, 12th ed. New York: McGraw Hill; 2020*)

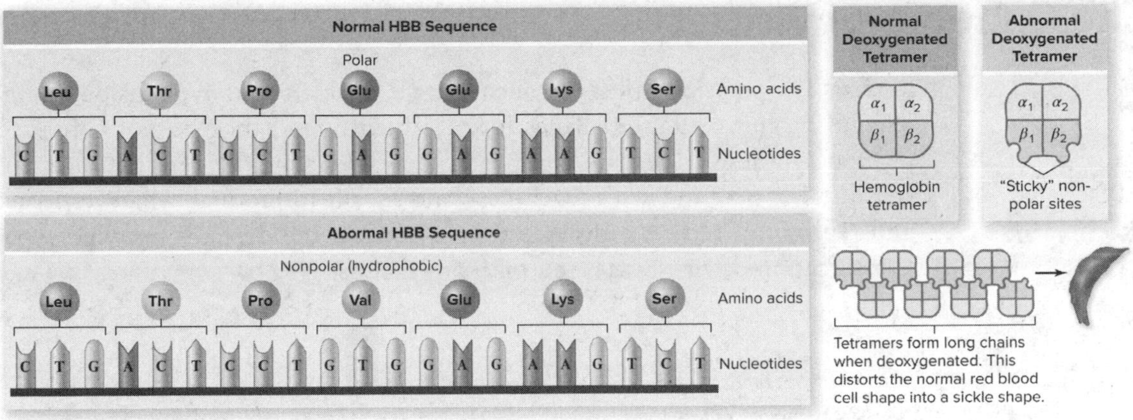

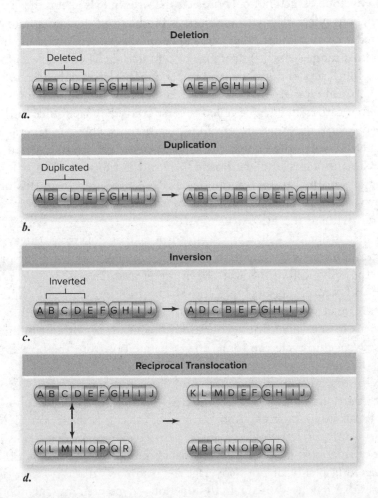

Figure 10.23 Sickle cell anemia is caused by an altered protein. Hemoglobin is composed of a tetramer of two α-globin and two β-globin chains. The sickle cell allele of the β-globin gene contains a single base change resulting in the substitution of Val for Glu. This creates a hydrophobic region on the surface of the protein that is "sticky," leading to their association into long chains that distort the shape of the red blood cells. (*Reproduced with permission from Raven P, Johnson G, Mason K, Losos J, Duncan T;* Biology, *12th ed. New York: McGraw Hill; 2020*)

Figure 10.24 Chromosomal mutations. Larger-scale changes in chromosomes are also possible. Material can be deleted **(a)**, duplicated **(b)**, and inverted **(c)**. Translocations occur when one chromosome is broken and becomes part of another chromosome. This often occurs where both chromosomes are broken and exchange material, an event called a reciprocal translocation **(d)**. (*Reproduced with permission from Raven P, Johnson G, Mason K, Losos J, Duncan T;* Biology, *12th ed. New York: McGraw Hill; 2020*)

The Genetics of Viruses

A **virus** is a parasitic infectious agent that is unable to survive outside of a host organism. Viruses do not contain enzymes for metabolism, and they do not contain ribosomes for protein synthesis. They are completely dependent on their host. Once a virus infects a cell, it takes over the cell's machinery and uses it to produce whatever it needs to survive and reproduce. How a virus acts after it enters a cell depends on what type of virus it is. Classification of viruses is based on many factors:

Genetic material: DNA, RNA, protein, etc.?

Capsid: type of capsid?

Viral envelope: present or absent?

Host range: what type of cells does it affect?

All viruses have a genome (DNA or RNA) and a protein coat (capsid). A **capsid** is a protein shell that surrounds the genetic material. Some viruses are surrounded by a structure called a **viral envelope,** which not only protects the virus but also helps the virus attach to the cells that it prefers to infect. The viral envelope is produced in the endoplasmic reticulum (ER) of the infected cell and contains some elements from the host cell and some from the virus. Each virus has a **host range,** which is the range of cells that the virus is able to infect. For example, HIV infects the T cells of our body, and bacteriophages infect only bacteria.

A special type of virus that merits discussion is one called a retrovirus. This is an RNA virus that carries an enzyme called **reverse transcriptase.** Once in the cytoplasm of the cell, the RNA virus uses this enzyme and "reverse transcribes" its genetic information from RNA into DNA, which then enters the nucleus of the cell. In the nucleus, the newly transcribed DNA incorporates into the host DNA and is transcribed into RNA when the host cell undergoes normal transcription. The mRNA produced from this process gives rise to new retrovirus offspring, which can then leave the cell in a lytic pathway. A well-known example of a retrovirus is the HIV virus of AIDS.

Once inside the cell, a DNA virus can take one of two pathways—a lytic or a lysogenic pathway. In a **lytic cycle,** the cell actually produces many viral offspring, which are released from the cell—killing the host cell in the process. In a **lysogenic cycle,** the virus falls dormant and incorporates its DNA into the host DNA as an entity called a **provirus.** The viral DNA is quietly reproduced by the cell every time the cell reproduces itself, and this allows the virus to stay alive from generation to generation without killing the host cell. Viruses in the lysogenic cycle can sometimes separate out from the host DNA and enter the lytic cycle (like a bear awaking from hibernation).

Viruses come in many shapes and sizes. Although many viruses are large, **viroids** are plant viruses that are only a few hundred nucleotides in length, showing that size is not the only factor in viral success. Another type of infectious agent you should be familiar with is a **prion**—an incorrectly folded form of a brain cell protein that works its magic by converting other normal host proteins into misshapen proteins. An example of a prion disease that has been getting plenty of press coverage is "mad cow" disease. Prion diseases are degenerative diseases that tend to cause brain dysfunction—dementia, muscular control problems, and loss of balance.

The Genetics of Bacteria

Bacteria are prokaryotic cells that consist of one double-stranded circular DNA molecule. Present in the cells of many bacteria are extra circles of DNA called **plasmids,** which contain just a few genes and have been useful in genetic engineering. Plasmids replicate independently of the main chromosome. Bacterial cells reproduce in an asexual fashion, undergoing **binary fission.** Quite simply, the cell replicates its DNA and then physically pinches in half, producing a daughter cell that is identical to the parent cell. From this description of binary fission, it seems unlikely that there could be variation among bacterial cells. This is not the case, thanks to mutation and genetic recombination. As in humans, DNA mutation in bacteria occurs very rarely, but some bacteria replicate so quickly that these mutations can have a pronounced effect on their variability.

Transformation

An experiment performed by Griffith in 1928 provides a fantastic example of **transformation**— the uptake of foreign DNA from the surrounding environment. Transformation occurs through the use of proteins on the surface of cells that snag pieces of DNA from around the cell that are from closely related species. This particular experiment involved a bacteria known as *Streptococcus pneumoniae,* which existed as either a rough strain (R), which is nonvirulent, or as a smooth strain (S), which is virulent. A virulent strain is one that can lead to contraction of an illness. The experimenters exposed mice to different forms of the bacteria. Mice given live S bacteria died. Mice given live R bacteria survived. Mice given heat-killed S bacteria survived. Mice given heat-killed S bacteria combined with live R bacteria died. This was the kicker . . . all the other results to this point were expected. Those exposed to heat-killed S combined with live R bacteria contracted the disease because the live R bacteria underwent transformation. Some of the R bacteria picked up the portion of the heat-killed S bacteria's DNA, which contained the instructions on how to make the vital component necessary for successful disease transmission. These R bacteria became virulent.

Transduction

To understand transduction, you first need to be introduced to something called a **phage** a virus that infects bacteria. The mechanism by which a phage (otherwise known as bacterio-phage) infects a cell reminds me of a syringe. A phage contains within its capsid the DNA that it is attempting to deliver. A phage latches onto the surface of a cell and, like a syringe, fires its DNA through the membrane and into the cell. **Transduction** is the movement of genes from one cell to another by phages. The two main forms of transduction you should be familiar with are generalized and specialized transduction.

Generalized Transduction   Imagine that a phage virus infects and takes over a bacterial cell that contains a functional gene for resistance to penicillin. Occasionally during the creation of new phage viruses, pieces of host DNA instead of viral DNA are accidentally put into a phage. When the cell lyses, expelling the newly formed viral particles, the phage containing the host DNA may latch onto another cell, injecting the host DNA from one cell into another bacterial cell. If the phage attaches to a cell that contains a nonfunctional gene for resistance to penicillin, the effects of this transduction process can be observed. After injecting the host DNA containing the functional penicillin resistance gene, crossover could occur between the comparable gene regions, switching the nonfunctional gene with the functional gene. This would create a new cell that is resistant to penicillin.

Specialized Transduction This type of transduction involves a virus that is in the lysogenic cycle, resting quietly along with the other DNA of the host cell. Occasionally when a lysogenic virus switches cycles and becomes lytic, it may bring with it a piece of the host DNA as it pulls out of the host chromosome. Imagine that the host DNA it brought with it contains a functional gene for resistance to penicillin. This virus, now in the lytic cycle, will produce numerous copies of new viral offspring that contain this resistance gene from the host cell. If the new phage offspring attaches to a cell that is not penicillin resistant and injects its DNA and crossover occurs, specialized transduction will have occurred.

Conjugation

This is the raciest of the genetic recombinations that we will cover . . . the bacterial version of sex. It is the transfer of DNA between two bacterial cells connected by appendages called **sex pili**. Movement of DNA between two cells occurs across a cytoplasmic connection between the two cells and requires the presence of an **F-plasmid**, which contains the genes necessary for the production of a sex pilus.

Biotechnology

> **IST-1**
>
> *Heritable information provides for continuity of life.*

DNA technology is advancing at a rapid rate, and you need to have a basic understanding of the most common laboratory techniques for the AP Biology exam.

Restriction enzymes are enzymes that cut DNA at specific nucleotide sequences. When added to a solution containing DNA, the enzymes cut the DNA wherever the enzyme's particular sequence appears. This creates DNA fragments with single-stranded ends called "**sticky-ends,**" which find and reconnect with other DNA fragments containing the same ends (with the assistance of DNA ligase). Sticky ends allow DNA pieces from different sources to be connected, creating **recombinant DNA**. Another concept important to genetic engineering is the **vector**, which moves DNA from one source to another. Plasmids can be removed from bacterial cells and used as vectors by cutting the DNA of interest and the DNA of the plasmid with the same restriction enzyme to create DNA with similar sticky ends. The DNA can be attached to the plasmid, creating a vector that can be used to transport DNA.

Gel Electrophoresis

This technique is used to separate and examine DNA fragments (Figure 10.25). The DNA is cut with our new friends, the restriction enzymes, and then separated by electrophoresis. The pieces of DNA are separated on the basis of size with the help of an electric charge. DNA is added to the wells at the negative end of the gel. When the electric current is turned on, the migration begins. Smaller pieces travel farther along the gel, and larger pieces do not travel as far. The bigger you are, the harder it is to move. This technique can be used to sequence DNA and determine the order in which the nucleotides appear. It can be used in a procedure known as **Southern blotting** (after Edwin M. Southern, a British biologist) to determine if a particular sequence of nucleotides is present in a sample of DNA. Electrophoresis is used in forensics to match DNA found at the crime scene with DNA of suspects. This requires the use of pieces of DNA called *restriction fragment length polymorphisms* (RFLPs). DNA is specific to each individual, and when it is mixed with restriction enzymes, different combinations of RFLPs will be obtained from person to person. Electrophoresis separates DNA samples from the suspect and whatever sample is found at the scene of the crime. The two are compared, and if the RFLPs match, there is a high degree of certainty that the DNA sample came from the suspect.

Cloning

Sometimes it is desirable to obtain large quantities of a gene of interest, such as insulin for the treatment of diabetes. The process of cloning involves many of the steps we just

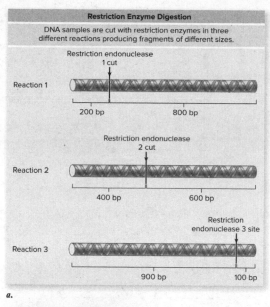

Restriction Enzyme Digestion

DNA samples are cut with restriction enzymes in three different reactions producing fragments of different sizes.

Restriction endonuclease 1 cut

Reaction 1

200 bp   800 bp

Restriction endonuclease 2 cut

Reaction 2

400 bp   600 bp

Restriction endonuclease 3 site

Reaction 3

900 bp   100 bp

a.

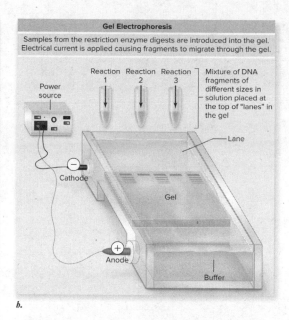

Gel Electrophoresis

Samples from the restriction enzyme digests are introduced into the gel. Electrical current is applied causing fragments to migrate through the gel.

Reaction 1   Reaction 2   Reaction 3

Power source

Mixture of DNA fragments of different sizes in solution placed at the top of "lanes" in the gel

Lane

Cathode

Gel

Anode

Buffer

b.

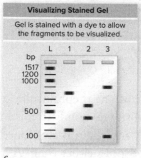

Visualizing Stained Gel

Gel is stained with a dye to allow the fragments to be visualized.

bp   L   1   2   3
1517
1200
1000

500

100

c.

Figure 10.25   Gel electrophoresis separates DNA fragments based on size. *a.* Three restriction enzymes are used to cut DNA into specific pieces, depending on each enzyme's recognition sequence. *b.* The fragments are loaded into a gel (agarose or polyacrylamide), and an electrical current is applied. The DNA fragments migrate through the gel based on size, with larger fragments moving more slowly. *c.* This results in a pattern of fragments separated based on size, with the smaller fragments migrating farther than larger ones. A series of fragments of known sizes produces a ladder so that sizes of fragments of unkown size can be estimated (bp = base-pairs; L = ladder; 1, 2, 3 = fragments from piece of DNA cut with restriction endonucleases 1, 2, and 3, respectively). (*Reproduced with permission from Raven P, Johnson G, Mason K, Losos J, Duncan T; Biology, 12th ed. New York: McGraw Hill; 2020*)

mentioned. Plasmids used for cloning often contain two important genes—one that provides resistance to an antibiotic, and one that gives the bacteria the ability to metabolize some sugar. In this case, we will use a galactose hydrolyzing gene and a gene for ampicillin resistance. The plasmid and DNA of interest are both cut with the same restriction enzyme. The restriction site for this enzyme is right in the middle of the galactose gene of the plasmid. When the sticky ends are created, the DNA of interest and the plasmid molecules are mixed and join together. Not every combination made here is what the scientist is looking for. The recombinant plasmids produced are transformed into bacterial cells. This is where the two specific genes for the plasmid come into play. The transformed cells are allowed to reproduce and are placed on a medium containing ampicillin. Cells that have taken in the ampicillin resistance gene will survive, while those that have not will perish. The medium also contains a special sugar that is broken down by the galactose enzyme present in the vector to form a colored product. The cells containing the gene of interest will remain white since the galactose gene has been interrupted and rendered nonfunctional. This allows the experimenter to isolate cells that contain the desired product. Now, it is time for us to quit cloning around and move onto another genetic engineering technique.

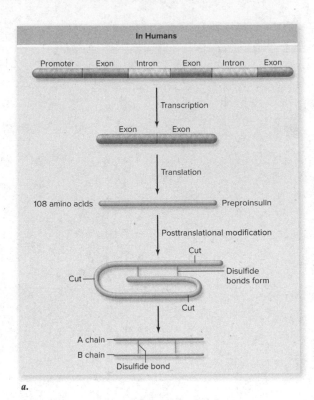

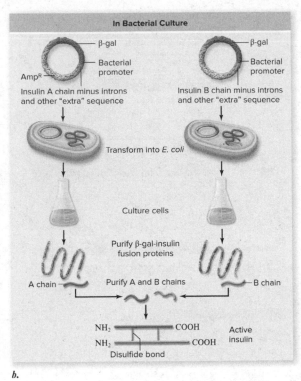

Figure 10.26 Making insulin in genetically engineered *E. coli*. *a.* In human cells one preproinsulin polypeptide is processed posttranslationally into insulin chains A and B that associate via disulfide bonds to form mature insulin. ***b.*** Two cDNAs corresponding to the gene sequences for insulin chain A and chain B are cloned into plasmids and introduced into different *E. coli*. Cultures of the two types of *E. coli* express either chain A or chain B. Chains A and B are purified from the different *E. coli* and, when mixed, associate into active mature insulin. (*Reproduced with permission from Raven P, Johnson G, Mason K, Losos J, Duncan T;* Biology, *12th ed. New York: McGraw Hill; 2020*)

Polymerase Chain Reaction

Think of this technique as a high-speed copy machine. It is used to produce large quantities of a particular sequence of DNA in a very short amount of time. If the cloning reaction is the 747 of copying DNA, then polymerase chain reaction (PCR) is the Concorde. This process begins with double-stranded DNA containing the gene of interest. DNA polymerase, the superstar enzyme of DNA replication, is added to the mixture along with a huge number of nucleotides and primers specific for the sequence of interest, which help initiate the synthesis of DNA. PCR begins by heating the DNA to split the strands, followed by the cooling of the strands to allow the primers to bind to the sequence of interest. DNA polymerase then steps up to the plate and produces the rest of the DNA molecule by adding the nucleotides to the growing DNA strand. Each cycle concludes having doubled the amount of DNA present at the beginning of the cycle. The cycle is repeated over and over, every few minutes, until a huge amount of DNA has been created. PCR is used in many ways, such as to detect the presence of viruses like HIV in cells, diagnose genetic disorders, and amplify trace amounts of DNA found at crime scenes (Figure 10.26*a* and *b*).

DNA Sequencing

In 2003, the international science community completed sequencing of the human genome. Using cutting edge techniques, scientists were able to determine the sequence of nucleotide bases for a human's DNA. This discovery has led to new techniques and technologies that allow for the sequencing of small pieces of DNA to entire genomes of organisms.

› Review Questions

1. Which of the following statements is *incorrect*?

   A. Messenger RNA must be processed before it can leave the nucleus of a eukaryotic cell.

   B. A virus in the lysogenic cycle does not kill its host cell, whereas a virus in the lytic cycle destroys its host cell.

   C. DNA polymerase is restricted in that it can add nucleotides only in a 5′-to-3′ direction.

   D. During translation, the A site holds the tRNA carrying the growing protein, while the P site holds the tRNA carrying the next amino acid.

2. The process of transcription results in the formation of

   A. DNA.
   B. proteins.
   C. lipids.
   D. RNA.

3. Which of the following codons signals the beginning of the translation process?

   A. AGU
   B. UGA
   C. AUG
   D. AGG

4. Which of the following is an improper pairing of DNA or RNA nucleotides?

   A. Thymine-adenine
   B. Guanine-thymine
   C. Uracil-adenine
   D. Guanine-cytosine

5. Which of the following is responsible for the type of diseases that includes "mad cow" disease?

   A. Viroids
   B. Plasmids
   C. Prions
   D. Provirus

6. Which of the following is the correct sequence of events that must occur for translation to begin?

   A. Transfer RNA binds to the small ribosomal subunit, which leads to the attachment of the large ribosomal subunit. This signals to the mRNA molecule that it should now bind, with its first codon in the correct site, to the protein synthesis machinery, and translation begins.

   B. Messenger RNA attaches to the small ribosomal subunit, with its first codon in the correct site, thus attracting a tRNA molecule to attach to the codon. This signals to the large subunit that it should now bind to the protein synthesis machinery, and translation can begin.

   C. Messenger RNA attaches to the large ribosomal subunit with its first codon in the correct site, attracting a tRNA molecule to attach to the codon. This signals to the small subunit that it should now bind to the protein synthesis machinery, and translation can begin.

   D. Transfer RNA binds to the large ribosomal subunit, which leads to the attachment of the small ribosomal subunit. This signals to the mRNA molecule that it should now bind with its first codon in the correct site to the protein synthesis machinery, and translation begins.

7. All the following are players involved in the control of gene expression *except*

   A. episomes.
   B. repressors.
   C. operons.
   D. methylation.

8. Which of the following does *not* occur during RNA processing in the nucleus of eukaryotes?

   A. The removal of introns from the RNA molecule

   B. The addition of a string of adenine nucleotides to the 3′ end of the RNA molecule

   C. The addition of a guanine cap to the 5′ end of the RNA molecule

   D. The addition of methyl groups to certain nucleotides of the RNA molecules

9. Which of the following statements is *not* true of a tRNA molecule?

   A. The job of transfer RNA is to carry amino acids to the ribosomes.

   B. At the attachment site of each tRNA, there is a region called the *anticodon*, which is a three-nucleotide sequence that is perfectly complementary to a particular codon.

   C. Each tRNA molecule has a short lifespan and is used only once during translation.

   D. The enzyme responsible for ensuring that a tRNA molecule is carrying the appropriate amino acid is aminoacyl tRNA synthase.

For questions 10 and 11, please use the following gel:

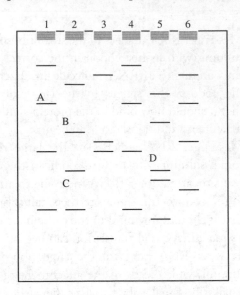

10. Which of the DNA pieces in the gel is smallest in size?

A. A
B. B
C. C
D. D

11. If well 1 is DNA from a crime scene, which individual should contact a lawyer?

A. Person 2
B. Person 3
C. Person 4
D. Person 5

› Answers and Explanations

1. **D**—During translation, the **P site** holds the tRNA carrying the growing protein, while the **A site** holds the tRNA carrying the next amino acid. When translation begins, the first codon bound is the AUG codon, and in the P site is the tRNA with the methionine. The next codon in the sequence determines which tRNA binds next, and the appropriate tRNA molecule sits in the A site of the ribosome. A peptide bond forms between the amino acid on the A site tRNA and the amino acid on the P site tRNA. The amino acid from the P site then moves to the A site, allowing the tRNA in the P site to leave the ribosome. Next, the ribosome moves along the mRNA in such a way that the A site is now the P site and the next tRNA comes into the A site carrying the next amino acid. Answer choices A, B, and C are all true.

2. **D**—The process of transcription leads to the production of RNA. RNA is not immediately ready to leave the nucleus after it is produced. It must first be processed, during which a 3′ poly-A tail and a 5′ cap are added and the introns are spliced from the RNA molecule. After this process, the RNA is free to leave the nucleus and lead the production of proteins.

3. **C**—AGG codes for the amino acid arginine. AGU codes for the amino acid serine. UGA and UAG are stop codons, which signal the end of the translation process. AUG is the start codon, which also codes for methionine.

4. **B**—Guanine does not pair with thymine in DNA or RNA. Watson and Crick discovered that adenine pairs with thymine (A=T) held together by two hydrogen bonds and guanine pairs with cytosine (C≡G) held together by three hydrogen bonds. One way that RNA differs from DNA is that it contains uracil instead of thymine. But in RNA, guanine still pairs with cytosine and adenine instead pairs with uracil. Watson and Crick also discovered that for the structure of DNA they discovered to be true, a purine must always be paired with a pyrimidine. Adenine and guanine are the purines, and thymine and cytosine are the pyrimidines.

5. **C**—Prions are the culprit for mad cow disease. *Viroids* are tiny viruses that infect plants. *Plasmids* are small circles of DNA in bacteria that are separate from the main chromosome. They are self-replicating and are vital to the process of genetic engineering. A *provirus* is that which is formed during the lysogenic cycle of a virus when it falls dormant and incorporates its DNA into the host DNA. A *retrovirus* is an RNA virus that carries an enzyme called reverse transcriptase. A classic example of a retrovirus is HIV.

6. **B**—Translation begins when the mRNA attaches to the small ribosomal subunit. The first codon for this process is always AUG. This attracts a tRNA molecule carrying methionine to attach to the AUG codon. When this occurs, the large subunit of the ribosome, containing the A site and the P site, binds to the complex. The elongation of the protein is ready to begin after the complex has been properly constructed. Answers A, C, and D are all in the incorrect order.

7. **A**—Episomes are not involved in gene expression regulation. *Episomes* are plasmids that can be incorporated into a bacterial chromosome. *Repressors* are regulatory proteins involved in gene regulation. They work by preventing transcription by binding to the promoter region. *Operons* are a promoter-operator pair that controls a group of genes, such as the lac operon. Methylation is involved in gene regulation. Barr bodies, discussed in Chapter 9, are found to contain a very high level of methylated DNA. Methyl groups have been associated with inactive DNA that does not undergo transcription. Hormones can affect transcription by acting directly on the transcription machinery in the nucleus of cells.

8. **D**—The mRNA produced after transcription must be modified before it can leave the nucleus and lead the translation of proteins in the ribosomes. Introns are cut out of the mRNA, and the remaining exons are ligated back together to produce the mRNA ready to be translated into a protein. Also, the 5′ end is given a guanine cap, which serves to protect the RNA and also helps the mRNA attach to the ribosome. The 3′ end is given the poly-A tail, which may help ease the movement from the nucleus to the cytoplasm. Methylation does not occur during posttranscriptional modification—it is a means of gene expression control.

9. **C**—tRNA does not have a short lifespan. Each tRNA molecule is released and recycled to bring more amino acids to the ribosomes to aid in translation. It is like a taxicab constantly picking up new passengers to deliver from place to place. Answer choices A, B, and D are all true.

10. **A**—Gel electrophoresis separates DNA fragments on the basis of size—the smaller you are, the farther you go. Because C went the farthest in this gel, this must be the smallest of the four selected DNA pieces. Of the four labeled, piece A must be the largest because it moved the least.

11. **C**—Person 4 should contact a lawyer. The DNA from the crime scene seems to match the DNA fingerprint from person 4. Electrophoresis is a very useful tool in forensics and can very accurately match DNA found at crime scenes with potential suspects.

› Rapid Review

Briefly review the following terms:

DNA: contains A and G (purines), C and T (pyrimidines), arranged in a double helix of two strands held together by hydrogen bonds (A with T, and C with G).

RNA: contains A and G (purines), C and U (pyrimidines), single stranded. There are three types: mRNA (blueprints for proteins), tRNA (brings acids to ribosomes), and rRNA (make up ribosomes).

DNA replication: occurs during S-phase, semi-conservative, built in 5′-to-3′ direction. Helicase unzips the double strand, DNA polymerase comes in and adds on the nucleotides. Proofreading enzymes minimize errors of process.

Frameshift mutation: deletion or addition of nucleotides (not a multiple of 3); shifts reading frame.

Missense mutation: substitution of wrong nucleotide into DNA (e.g., sickle cell anemia); still produces a protein.

Nonsense mutation: substitution of wrong nucleotide into DNA that produces an early stop codon.

Transcription: process by which mRNA is synthesized on a DNA template.

RNA processing: introns (noncoding) are spliced out, exons (coding) glued together: 3′ poly-A tail, 5′ G cap.

Translation: process by which the mRNA specified sequence of amino acids is lined up on a ribosome for protein synthesis.

Codon: triplet of nucleotides that codes for a particular amino acid: **start codon** = AUG; **stop codon** = UGA, UAA, UAG. (For specifics on translation, please flip to text for a good description.)

Promoter: base sequence that signals start site for transcription.

Repressor: protein that prevents the binding of RNA polymerase to promoter site.

Inducer: molecule that binds to and inactivates a repressor.

Operator: short sequence near the promoter that assists in transcription by interacting with transcription factors.

Operon: on/off switch for transcription. Allows for production of genes only when needed. Remember the *lac* operon—lactose is the inducer, when present, transcription on; when absent, it is off.

Viruses: parasitic infectious agent unable to survive outside the host; can contain DNA or RNA, or have a viral envelope (protective coat).

- *Lytic cycle*: one in which the virus is actively reproducing and kills the host cell.
- *Lysogenic cycle*: one in which the virus lies dormant within the DNA of the host cell.

Retrovirus: RNA virus that carries with it reverse transcriptase (HIV).

Prion: virus that converts host brain proteins into misshapen proteins (mad cow disease).

Viroids: tiny plant viruses.

Phage: virus that infects bacteria.

Bacteria: prokaryotic cells; consist of one double-stranded circular DNA molecule; reproduce by binary fission (e.g., **plasmid**—extra circle of DNA present in bacteria that replicate independently of main chromosome).

Genetic Recombination

Transformation: uptake of foreign DNA from the surrounding environment (smooth vs. rough pneumococcus).

Transduction: movement of genes from one cell to another by phages, which are incorporated by crossover.

- *Generalized*: lytic cycle accidently places host DNA into a phage, which is brought to another cell.
- *Specialized*: virus leaving lysogenic cycle brings host DNA with it into phage.

Conjugation: transfer of DNA between two bacterial cells connected by sex pili.

Genetic Engineering

Restriction enzymes: enzymes that cut DNA at particular sequences, creating sticky ends.

Vector: mover of DNA from one source to another (plasmids are good vectors).

Cloning: somewhat slow process by which a desired sequence of DNA is copied numerous times.

Gel electrophoresis: technique used to separate DNA according to size (small = faster). DNA moves from: − to +.

Polymerase chain reaction (PCR): produces large quantities of sequence in short amount of time.

CHAPTER 11

Evolution
Exam Weight: 13–20%

IN THIS CHAPTER

Summary: This chapter discusses evolution and the four major modes in which it occurs. It introduces you to the various forms of selection: natural, directional, stabilizing, disruptive, sexual, and artificial. It discusses the two main forms of speciation (allopatric and sympatric) and briefly touches on the theory behind how life on this planet emerged many years ago.

Key Ideas

- ✪ The four major modes of evolution are genetic drift, gene flow, mutation, and natural selection.
- ✪ Natural selection is based on three conditions: variation, heritability, and differential reproductive success.
- ✪ There are four basic patterns of evolution: co-evolution, convergent evolution, divergent evolution, and parallel evolution.
- ✪ Sources of variation within populations: mutation, sexual reproduction, and balanced polymorphism.
- ✪ Hardy-Weinberg conditions: no mutations, no gene flow, no genetic drift, no natural selection, and random mating.
- ✪ Hardy-Weinberg equations: $p + q = 1$ and $p^2 + 2pq + q^2 = 1$.
- ✪ Evidence for evolution: homologous characters, embryology, and vestigial structures.
- ✪ Evolutionary relationships are shown with phylogenetic trees and/or cladograms using fossils, molecular clocks, and/or molecular data.

Introduction

This chapter begins with an introduction to the concept of evolution and the four major modes in which it occurs. From there we focus more closely on natural selection and the work of Lamarck and Darwin. We then briefly touch on adaptations before looking at the various types of selection: directional, stabilizing, disruptive, sexual, and artificial selection. This is followed by a quick look at the sources of variation within populations followed by a look at the two main types of speciation: allopatric and sympatric. Next, will come the yucky math portion of the chapter: the Hardy-Weinberg equation and the conditions necessary for its existence. The chapter concludes with a look at the existing evidence in support of the theory of evolution and a discussion of how life on this planet emerged so many years ago.

Definition of Evolution

How often have you heard executives report that "the idea evolved into a successful project" or popular science show narrators describe how a star "has been evolving for millions of years"? *Evolution* is no longer strictly a biological term since every academic field and nonacademic industry uses it. Such uses of the verb *evolve* reveal its meaning in its simplest form—to evolve means to change. For the AP Biology exam, however, you should remember the biological definition of evolution: *descent with modification.* Don't let the general uses of the word mislead you; a key part of this definition is *descent,* which can happen only when one group of organisms gives rise to another. When you see the word *evolution*, think of something that happens in populations, not in individuals.

More specifically, evolution describes change in allele frequencies in populations over time. When one generation of organisms (whether algae or giraffes or ferns) reproduces and creates the next, the frequencies of the alleles for the various genes represented in the population may be different from what they were in the parent generation. Frequencies can change so much that certain alleles are lost or others become fixed—all individuals have the same allele for that character. Over many generations, the species can change so much that it becomes quite different from the ancestral species, or a part of the population can branch off and become a new species (**speciation**). Why do we see this change in allele frequencies with time?

Allele frequencies may change because of random factors or by natural selection. Let's consider chance events first. Imagine a population of fish in a large pond that exhibits two alleles for fin length (short and long) and is isolated from other populations of the same species. One day, a tornado kills 50 percent of the fish population. Completely by chance, most of the fish killed possess the long-fin allele, and very few of these individuals are left in the population. In the next generation, there are many fewer fish with long fins because fewer long-finned fish were left to reproduce; that allele is much more poorly represented in the pond than it was in the original parent generation before the catastrophe. This is an example of **genetic drift** (Figure 11.1): a change in allele frequencies that is due to chance events. When drift dramatically reduces population size, we call it a **bottleneck.**

EVO-1

Evolution is characterized by a change in the genetic makeup of a population over time and is supported by multiple lines of evidence.

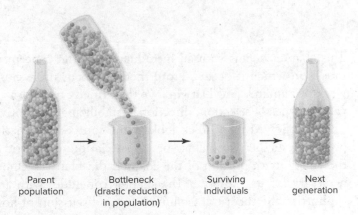

Parent population · Bottleneck (drastic reduction in population) · Surviving individuals · Next generation

Figure 11.1   Genetic drift: A bottleneck effect. The parent population contains roughly equal numbers of green and yellow individuals and a small number of red individuals. By chance, the few remaining individuals that contribute to the next generation are mostly green. The bottleneck occurs because so few individuals form the next generation, as might happen after an epidemic or a catastrophic storm. (*Reproduced with permission from Raven P, Johnson G, Mason K, Losos J, Duncan T; Biology, 12th ed. New York: McGraw Hill; 2020*)

Now imagine that the same pond becomes connected to another pond by a small stream. The two populations mix, and by chance, all the long-finned fish migrate to the other pond, and no long-finned fish migrate in. Again, which individuals migrated was random in this example; thus, there will be a change in the allele frequencies in the next generation. This is an example of **gene flow,** or the change in allele frequencies as genes from one population are incorporated into another.

Gene flow (also more loosely known as *migration* when the individuals are actively relocating) is random with respect to which organisms succeed, but keep in mind that we could think of situations in which migration is not random. For example, if only the short-finned fish could fit in the stream connecting the two ponds, the alleles represented in the subsequent generation would *not* be random with respect to that allele. We also have not stated that the short-finned fish have an advantage by swimming to the other pond—if they did, this would be an example of natural selection, which we'll discuss below.

Finally, let's consider **mutation,** the third random event that can cause changes in allele frequencies. Mutation is *always* random with respect to which genes are affected, although the changes in allele frequencies that occur as a result of the mutation may not be. Let's say that a mutation occurs in the offspring of a fish in our hypothetical pond. The mutation creates a new allele. As a result, the allele frequencies in the offspring generation has changed, simply because we have added a new allele (remember that allele frequencies for a given gene always add up to one). As you can imagine, one mutation on its own does not have the potential to dramatically alter the allele frequencies in a population, unless this is a *really* small pond! But mutation is extremely important because it is the basis of the variation we see in the first place and it is a very strong force when it is paired with natural selection.

KEY IDEA

The five major modes of evolution (Figure 11.2) are

1. Genetic drift
2. Gene flow (also called *migration*)
3. Mutation
4. Natural selection
5. Nonrandom mating

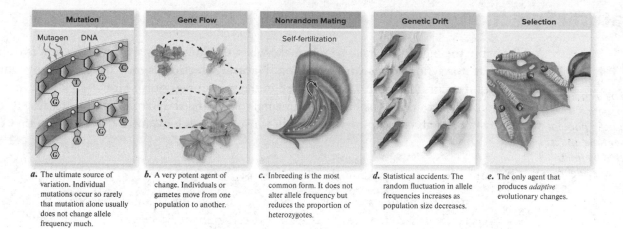

Mutation	Gene Flow	Nonrandom Mating	Genetic Drift	Selection

a. The ultimate source of variation. Individual mutations occur so rarely that mutation alone usually does not change allele frequency much.

b. A very potent agent of change. Individuals or gametes move from one population to another.

c. Inbreeding is the most common form. It does not alter allele frequency but reduces the proportion of heterozygotes.

d. Statistical accidents. The random fluctuation in allele frequencies increases as population size decreases.

e. The only agent that produces *adaptive* evolutionary changes.

Figure 11.2 Five agents of evolutionary change. (*Reproduced with permission from Raven P, Johnson G, Mason K, Losos J, Duncan T;* Biology, *12th ed. New York: McGraw Hill; 2020*)

Nonrandom mating or sexual selection is considered by some to be a subset of natural selection, while others believe that it is separate from natural selection. In random mating, organisms participate in intrasexual selection, which represent competitive interactions between the same sex (male-to-male or female-to-female) and intersexual selection, which represents the selection of reproductive partners of the opposite sex. This leads to the evolution of secondary sexual characteristics for organisms to persuade members of the opposite sex such as the female peahen preferring a male with the greatest number of eyespots on his feathers (Figure 11.3).

Figure 11.3 Products of sexual selection. In bird species such as the peacock, *Pavo cristatus*, males use their much longer tail feathers in courtship displays. (*Reproduced with permission from Raven P, Johnson G, Mason K, Losos J, Duncan T;* Biology, *12th ed. New York: McGraw Hill; 2020*)

Remember that the first three factors act randomly with respect to the alleles in the population—which alleles increase and which decrease in frequency are determined by chance events, not because some alleles are inherently better than others. We'll now turn to the fourth mode or process of evolution, natural selection, where the modification that occurs with descent is *nonrandom*.

Natural Selection

EVO-1

Evolution is characterized by a change in the genetic makeup of a population over time and is supported by multiple lines of evidence.

Probably the biggest mistake people make when thinking about natural selection is thinking that it is synonymous with evolution. **Natural selection** is only one process by which evolution occurs (the others are discussed in the previous section). However, it is an important process because it has been instrumental in shaping the natural world. Because of the theory of natural selection, we can explain why organisms look and behave the way they do.

Natural selection is based on three conditions:

1. *Variation:* for natural selection to occur, a population must exhibit phenotypic variance—in other words, differences must exist between individuals, even if they are slight.
2. *Heritability:* parents must be able to pass on the traits that are under natural selection. If a trait cannot be inherited, it cannot be selected for or against.
3. *Differential reproductive success:* this sounds complicated, but it's a simple concept. **Reproductive success** measures how many offspring you produce that survive relative to how many the other individuals in your population produce. The condition simply states that there must be variation between parents in how many offspring they produce as a result of the different traits that the parents have.

It is easiest to illustrate natural selection with an example. Let's revisit our pond before the tornado came, where short- and long-finned fish inhabit murky waters. A new predator invades the pond. Fin length determines swimming speed (longer fins allow a fish to swim faster), and only the fastest fish can escape the predator. How would you expect the allele frequencies to change under these conditions? Fish with what length fin would be eaten the most? Because the short-finned fish would be the slowest, they would be featured on the menu. But the long-finned fish, able to escape this new predator, would survive and reproduce, and the frequency of the long-fin allele would increase relative to the short-fin allele. We have created a situation in which allele frequencies change as a result of a nonrandom event; the predator's presence results in a predictable decrease in the short-fin allele and a consequent increase in the long-fin allele. Remember that allele frequencies always add up to 100 percent, so the long-finned fish don't have to do particularly well for the long-fin allele to increase—they only have to do well *relative* to the short-finned fish. The actual numbers of fish could decrease for both variants of this fish species.

Why aren't organisms perfectly adapted to their environments? Since natural selection increases the frequencies of advantageous alleles, why don't we get to a point where all individuals have all the best alleles? For one, different alleles confer different advantages in different environments. Furthermore, remember that the environment—which includes everything from habitat, to climate, to competitors, to predators, to food resources—is constantly changing. Species are therefore also constantly changing as the traits that give them an advantage also change. In cases where a trait becomes unconditionally advantageous, we do in fact see fixed alleles; for example, all spiders have eight legs because the alternatives just aren't as good under any circumstances. But where there are heritable characters that both vary and confer fitness advantages (or disadvantages) on their host organisms, natural selection can occur.

Lamarck and Darwin

The two key figures whose research you should know for the evolution section of the AP Biology exam are Jean-Baptiste Lamarck and Charles Darwin. Lamarck proposed the idea that evolution occurs by the inheritance of acquired characters. The classic example is giraffe necks: Lamarck proposed that giraffes evolved long necks because individuals were constantly reaching for the leaves at the tops of trees. A giraffe's neck lengthened during its lifetime, and then that giraffe's offspring had a long neck because of all that straining its parents did. The key here is that change happened within organisms during their lifetimes and then the change in the trait was passed on.

What's wrong with Lamarck's theory? Try explaining to yourself how the changed character could be passed on to the offspring. The answer is that it couldn't—the instructions in the sex chromosomes that direct the production of offspring cannot be changed after they are created at the birth of an organism. Lamarck confused genetic and environmental (postconceptive) change, which is not surprising because no one had discovered genes yet.

Darwin had another idea, one that ended up being entirely consistent with Mendelian genetics (although Mendel had already written his thesis during Darwin's time, it is rumored that his book sat on Darwin's shelf, with the pages still uncut, until Darwin's death). Darwin suggested the idea of natural selection described above and coined the phrase "survival of the fittest." Although he didn't call them *genes,* he proposed a hypothetical unit of heredity that passed from parent to offspring. Incidentally, a man named Wallace also came up with the idea of natural selection during the same time, but Darwin got the publication out first and has become famous as a result.

Adaptations

An **adaptation** is a trait that if altered, affects the fitness of the organism. Adaptations are the result of natural selection and can include not only physical traits such as eyes, fingernails, and livers but also the intangible traits of organisms. For example, lifespan length is an adaptation, albeit a variable one. Mating behavior is also an adaptation—it has been selected by natural selection because it is an effective strategy. An individual with a different form of mating behavior may do better or worse than the average, but a change is likely to have some effect on reproductive success. For example, individuals whose mating strategy is to attempt to court women by running at them, arms flailing while screaming wildly, and salivating heavily, do worse than the average male.

Let's take a look at how such a behavioral adaptation can evolve. Reproductive maturity is a good example. Female chimpanzees become reproductively mature at around the age of 13. Females that mature at age 12 spend less time growing and may therefore be more susceptible to problems with pregnancy. Females that mature at 14 have lost valuable time—their earlier-maturing peers have gained a year on them. You can imagine that from generation to generation, females that matured at age 13 became better represented in the population compared to faster and slower maturers. Although there will always be individuals that differ from the mode, we can view age at reproductive maturation as an adaptation.

Types of Selection

Natural selection can change the frequencies of alleles in populations through various processes. The most commonly described are the following three (Figure 11.4):

a. **Directional selection.** This occurs when members of a population at one end of a spectrum are selected against, while those at the other end are selected for. For example, imagine a population of elephants with various-sized trunks. In this particular environment, much more food is available in the very tall trees than in the shorter trees.

Mike (fresh-man in college): "Learn these selection types . . . they make good multiple-choice questions."

Elephants with what length trunk will survive and reproduce the most successfully? Those with the longest trunks. Those with shorter trunks will be strongly selected against (and those in the middle will also be in the middle in terms of success). Over time we expect to see an increasing percentage of elephants with long trunks (how quickly this change occurs depends on the strength of selection—if all the short-trunked elephants die, we can imagine that the allele frequencies will change very quickly).

b. **Stabilizing selection.** This describes selection for the mean of a population for a given allele. A real example of this is human infant birth weight—it is a disadvantage to be really small *or* really big, and it is best to be somewhere in between. Stabilizing selection has the effect of reducing variation in a population.

c. **Disruptive selection.** Also known as *diversifying selection,* this process can be regarded as being the opposite of stabilizing selection. We say that selection is disruptive when individuals at the two extremes of a spectrum of variation do better than the more common forms in the middle. Snail shell color is an example of disruptive selection. Imagine an environment in which snails with very dark shells and those with very light shells are best able to hide from predators. Those with an in-between shell color are gulped up like escargot at a cocktail party, creating the double-hump curve.

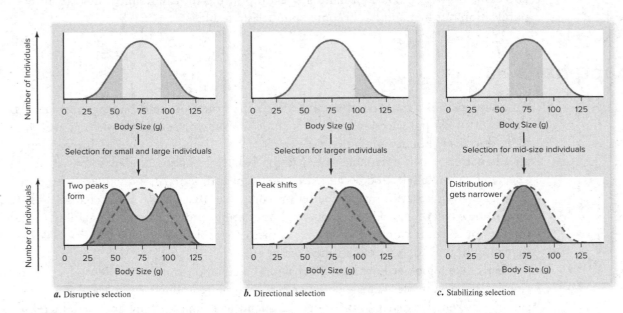

Figure 11.4 Three types of selection: (a) disruptive; (b) directional; (c) stabilizing. (*Reproduced with permission from Raven P, Johnson G, Mason K, Losos J, Duncan T; Biology, 12th ed. New York: McGraw Hill; 2020*)

EVO-3

Life continues to evolve within a changing environment.

These three processes describe the way in which allele frequencies can change as a result of the forces of natural selection. It is also important to remember two other types of selection that complement natural selection: sexual selection and artificial selection.

Sexual selection occurs because individuals differ in mating success. In other words, because not all individuals will have the maximum number of possible offspring, there must be some reason why some individuals have greater reproductive success than others. Think about how this is different from natural selection, which includes both reproduction and survival. Sexual selection is purely about access to mating opportunities.

Sexual selection occurs by two primary processes: **within-sex competition** and **choice.** In mammals and many nonmammalian species, females are limited in the number of offspring they can produce in their lifetimes (because of internal gestation), while males are not (because sperm are cheap to produce and few males participate in offspring care). Which sex do you think will compete, and which sex will be choosier? In most mammals for instance, males compete and females choose. It makes sense that males have to compete because females are a limiting resource, and it makes sense that females are choosy because they invest a lot in each reproductive effort. This leads to the evolution of characters that are designed for two main functions: (1) as weaponry or other tools for male competition (e.g., large testes for sperm competition) and (2) as traits that increase mating opportunities because females prefer to mate with males who have them (e.g., colorful feathers in many birds).

On what do females base their choices? While you need not become an expert on this matter, it is important to remember that female mate choice for certain characters is not random. One hypothesis for why females choose males with colorful feathers, for example, is that colorful feathers indicate good genes, which is important for a female's offspring. Bright colors are costly, so a male with brightly colored feathers is probably healthy (which may, in turn, indicate an ability to reduce parasite load, for example). We call such sexually selected traits that are the result of female choice **honest indicators.** Keep in mind that selecting a mate for particular features does not necessarily involve conscious thought, and in most animals never does; the female does not think, "Oh! What nice feathers. He must come from good genes." Rather, females who choose males that display honest indicators have more surviving offspring than do females who don't, and as a result, the "choosing males with colorful feathers" trait increases in the population.

When humans become the agents of natural selection, we describe the process as **artificial selection.** Instead of allowing individuals to survive and reproduce as they would without human intervention, we may specifically select certain individuals to breed while restraining others from doing so. Artificial selection has resulted in the domestication of a wide range of plant and animal species and the selection of certain traits (e.g., cattle with lean meat, flowers with particular color combinations, dogs with specific kinds of skill).

Evolution Patterns

There are four basic patterns of evolution:

EVO-3
Life continues to evolve within a changing environment.

Coevolution. The mutual evolution between two species, which is exemplified by predator–prey relationships. The prey evolves in such a way that those remaining are able to escape predator attack. Eventually, some of the predators survive that can overcome this evolutionary adaptation in the prey population. This goes back and forth, over and over.

Convergent evolution. Two unrelated species evolve in a way that makes them *more* similar (think of them as converging on a single point). They are both responding in the same way to some environmental challenge, and this brings them closer together. We call two *characters* **convergent characters** if they are similar in two species, even though the species do *not* share a common ancestor. For example, birds and insects both have wings in order to fly, despite the fact that insects are not directly related to birds.

Divergent evolution. Two related species evolve in a way that makes them *less* similar. Divergent evolution can lead to speciation (allopatric or sympatric).

Parallel evolution. Similar evolutionary changes occurring in two species that can be related or unrelated. They are simply responding in a similar manner to a similar environmental condition.

Sources of Variation

Remember that one of the conditions for natural selection is variation. Where does this variation within populations come from?

EVO-3

Life continues to evolve within a changing environment.

SYI-3

Naturally occurring diversity among and between components within biological systems affects interactions with the environment.

1. **Mutation.** We already discussed mutations as a mechanism by which evolution occurs. Random changes in the DNA of an individual can introduce new alleles into a population.
2. **Sexual reproduction.** The three main sources of variation in sexual reproduction are crossing over which occurs in prophase 1 of meiosis 1, random assortment during metaphase 1, and the random fertlization of gametes.
3. **Balanced polymorphism.** Some characters are fixed, meaning that all individuals in a species or population have them: for example, all tulips develop from bulbs. However, other characters are polymorphic, meaning that there are two or more phenotypic variants. For example, tulips come in a variety of colors. If one phenotypic variant leads to increased reproductive success, we expect directional selection to eventually eliminate all other varieties. However, we can find many examples in the natural world where variation is prominent and one allele is not uniformly better than the others. The various ways in which balanced polymorphism is maintained are presented in Figure 11.5.

Mechanism	Description	Example
Heterozygote advantage	The heterozygous condition has an advantage over either homozygote, so both alleles are maintained (AA is worse off than Aa).	Sickle cell trait, a heterozygous condition, gives people in malarial environments an advantage because they are resistant to this disease.
Hybrid vigor and outbreeding	Two unrelated individuals are less likely to have the same recessive, deleterious allele than are relatives; therefore, their offspring are less likely to be homozygous for that allele; in addition, outbreeding increases the number of heterozygous alleles, increasing heterozygote advantage.	Artificially selected plants are carefully outbred in order to increase hybrid vigor; mating two inbred strains of potato will increase the number of heterozygous loci and increase the species' resistance to disease.
Frequency-dependent selection	The least common phenotype is selected for, while common phenotypes have a disadvantage.	In some fruit flies, females choose to mate with males that have the rarer phenotype, resulting in selection against the more common variants.

Figure 11.5   How balanced polymorphism is maintained.

Speciation

EVO-3

Life continues to evolve within a changing environment.

A **species** is a group of interbreeding (or potentially interbreeding) organisms. **Speciation,** the process by which new species evolve, can take one of several forms. You should be familiar with the two main forms of speciation:

1. **Allopatric speciation.** Interbreeding ceases because some sort of barrier separates a single population into two (an area with no food, a mountain, etc.). The two populations evolve independently (by any of the four processes discussed earlier), and if they change enough, then even if the barrier is removed, they cannot interbreed.
2. **Sympatric speciation.** Interbreeding ceases even though no physical barrier prevents it. This may take several forms.

Two other important terms are **polyploidy** and **balanced polymorphism:**

Polyploidy. A condition in which an individual has more than the normal number of sets of chromosomes. Although the individual may be healthy, it cannot reproduce with nonpolyploidic members of its species. This is unusual, but in some plants, it has resulted in new species because polyploidic individuals are only able to mate with each other.

Balanced polymorphism. This condition (described above) can also lead to speciation if two variants diverge enough to no longer be able to interbreed (if, e.g., potential mates no longer recognize each other as possible partners).

One more term to mention before moving on is **adaptive radiation** (Figure 11.6), which is a rapid series of speciation events that occur when one or more ancestral species invades a new environment. This process was exemplified by Darwin's finches. If there are many ecological niches (see Chapter 12, Ecology in Further Detail), several species will evolve because each can fill a different niche.

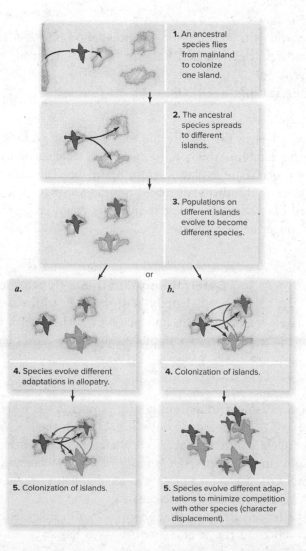

Figure 11.6 Classic model of adaptive radiation on island archipelagoes. *(1)* An ancestral species colonizes an island in an archipelago. Subsequently, the population colonizes other islands *(2)*, after which the populations on the different islands speciate in allopatry *(3)*. Then some of these new species colonize other islands, leading to local communities of two or more species. Adaptive differences can either evolve when species are in allopatry in response to different environmental conditions *(a)* or as the result of ecological interactions between species *(b)* by the process of character displacement. (*Reproduced with permission from Raven P, Johnson G, Mason K, Losos J, Duncan T; Biology, 12th ed. New York: McGraw Hill; 2020*)

When Evolution Is Not Occurring: Hardy-Weinberg Equilibrium

EVO-1

Evolution is characterized by a change in the genetic makeup of a population over time and is supported by multiple lines of evidence.

Evolutionary change is constantly happening in humans and other species; this seems sensible because evolution is the change in allele frequencies over time. It makes sense that these frequencies are highly variable and subject to change as the environment changes. However, biologists use a theoretical concept called the **Hardy-Weinberg equilibrium** to describe those special cases where a population is in stasis, or not evolving (Figure 11.7).

Only if the following conditions are met can a population be in Hardy-Weinberg equilibrium:

KEY IDEA

Hardy-Weinberg Conditions

1. No mutations
2. No gene flow
3. No genetic drift (and for this, the population must be large)
4. No natural selection (so that the traits are neutral; none gives an advantage or disadvantage)
5. Random mating

Notice items 1–4 in this list are the four modes of evolution, which makes sense—if we are trying to establish the conditions under which evolution does *not* occur, we must keep these processes of evolution from occurring! The fifth condition, random mating, is included because if individuals mated nonrandomly (e.g., if individuals mated with others that looked like them), the allele frequencies could change in a certain direction, and we would no longer be in equilibrium.

KEY IDEA

Determining Whether a Population Is in Hardy-Weinberg Equilibrium

Unfortunately for you, there is an equation associated with the Hardy-Weinberg equilibrium that the test writers love to put on the exam. Don't let it scare you!

$$p + q = 1$$

CT teacher: "Knowing how to do Hardy-Weinberg problems is worth 2 points to you . . . easy points."

This equation is used to determine if a population is in Hardy-Weinberg equilibrium. The symbol p is the frequency of allele 1 (often the *dominant allele*), and q is the frequency of allele 2 (often the recessive allele). Remember that the frequency of two alleles always adds up to 1 *if the population is in Hardy-Weinberg equilibrium*. For example, if 60 percent of the alleles for a given trait are dominant (p), then $p = 0.6$, and q (the recessive allele) $= 1 - 0.6$, or 0.4 (40 percent).

There is a second equation that goes along with this theory: $p^2 + 2pq + q^2 = 1$, where p^2 and q^2 represent the frequency of the two homozygous conditions (AA and aa). The frequency of the heterozygotes is pq plus qp or $2pq$ (Aa and aA). Since p represents the dominant allele, it makes sense that p^2 represents the homozygous dominant condition. By the same logic, q^2 represents the homozygous recessive condition.

Let's say that you are told that a population of acacia trees is 16 percent short (which is a, recessive) and 84 percent tall (which is A, dominant). What are the frequencies of the two alleles? Remember that it is not 0.16 and 0.84 because there are also the heterozygotes to consider!

In a problem like this, it is important to determine the value of q first because we know that all individuals with the recessive phenotype must be aa (q^2). You cannot begin by calculating the value of p because it is not true that all the individuals with the dominant phenotype can be lumped into p^2. Some folks displaying the dominant phenotype are heterozygous Aa (pq).

We know that $q^2 = 0.16$, so we find q by calculating $\sqrt{0.16} \rightarrow q = 0.400$. Now remember that they do not let you use a calculator. So these problems will give numbers that are fairly easy to work with. Do not despair.

What about p? Since $p + q$ is 1, and we know $q = 0.40$, then p must equal $1 - 0.40$ or 0.600.

You may also be asked to go a step further and give the percentages of the homozygous dominant and heterozygous conditions (remember, we know that the recessive condition is 16 percent—all these individuals must be aa in order to express the recessive trait). This is simple—just plug in what you know about p and q:

$$2pq = (2)\,(0.6)\,(0.4) = 0.48 \text{ or } 48\%$$
$$p^2 = (0.6)\,(0.6) = 0.36 \text{ or } 36\%$$

Now check your math: do the frequencies add up to 100 percent?

$$16 + 48 + 36 = 100$$

Why do we ever use the Hardy-Weinberg equation if it rarely applies to real populations? This can be an excellent tool to determine whether a population is evolving or not; if we find that the allele frequencies do not add up to one, then we need to look for the reasons for this (perhaps the population is too small and genetic drift is a factor, or perhaps one of the alleles is advantageous and is therefore being selected for and increasing in the population). Therefore, although the Hardy-Weinberg equilibrium is largely theoretical, it does have some important uses in evolutionary biology. Figure 11.7 shows an example of the Hardy-Weinberg equation in use!

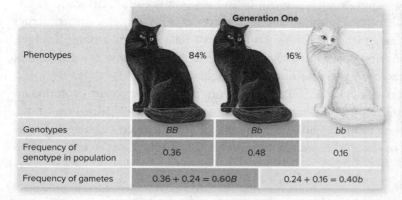
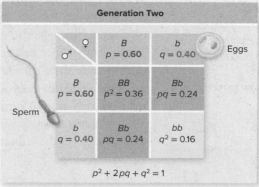

Figure 11.7 The Hardy–Weinberg equilibrium. In the absence of factors that alter them, the frequencies of gametes, genotypes, and phenotypes remain constant generation after generation. (*Reproduced with permission from Raven P, Johnson G, Mason K, Losos J, Duncan T; Biology, 12th ed. New York: McGraw Hill; 2020*)

The Evidence for Evolution

Support for the theory of evolution can be found in varied kinds of evidence:

> **EVO-1**
>
> *Evolution is characterized by a change in the genetic makeup of a population over time and is supported by multiple lines of evidence.*

1. **Homologous characters.** Traits are said to be homologous if they are similar because their host organisms arose from a common ancestor (which implies that they have evolved). For example, the bone structure in bird wings is homologous in all bird species.

2. **Embryology.** The study of embryos reveals remarkable similarities between organisms at the earliest stages of life, although as adults (or even at birth) the species look completely different. Human embryos, for example, actually have gills for a short time during early development, hinting at our aquatic ancestry. Darwin used embryology as an important piece of evidence for the process of evolution. In 1866, the scientist Ernst Haeckel uttered the phrase, "Ontogeny recapitulates phylogeny." **Ontogeny** is an *individual's* development; **phylogeny** is a **species'** evolutionary history. What Haeckel meant was that during an organism's embryonic development, it will at some point resemble the adult form of all its ancestors before it. For example, human embryos at some point look a lot like fish embryos. The important conclusion from this is that Haeckel and others thought that embryologic similarity between developing individuals could be used to deduce phylogenetic relationships. By the end of the nineteenth century, it was clear this law rarely holds. The real development of organisms differs in several important ways from Haeckel's schemes.

3. **Vestigial characters.** Most organisms carry characters that are no longer useful, although they once were. This should remind you of our short discussion about why organisms are not perfectly adapted to their environments (because the environment is constantly changing). Sometimes an environment changes so much that a trait is no longer needed, but is not deleterious enough to actually be selected against and eliminated. Darwin used vestigial characters as evidence in his original formulation of the process of evolution, listing the human appendix as an example.

Keep in mind that the kinds of evidence we've described are often found in the **fossil record**—the physical manifestation of species that have gone extinct (including things like bones as well as imprints). The most important thing to remember is that adaptations are the result of natural selection.

Phylogeny

> **EVO-3**
>
> *Life continues to evolve within a changing environment.*

Systematics is the study of evolutionary relationships and looks at the similarities and differences between species. With the similarities and differences established, you can construct phylogenetic trees and cladograms that show evolutionary relationships among lineages. While both show relationships between lineages, phylogenetic trees show the amount of change over time calibrated by fossils or a molecular clock.

Phylogenetic trees and cladograms (Figure 11.8) are used to represent evolutionary relationships among organisms as well as track traits that are either lost or gained over time. Shared characteristics will be found in multiple lineages. Shared, derived characteristics are shared only by the subset of the species and are not inherited from the most recent common ancestor.

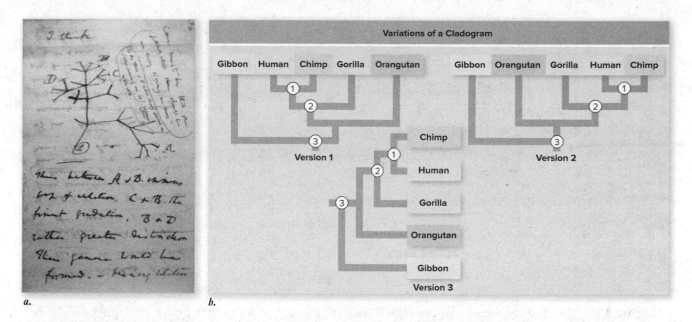

Figure 11.8 Phylogenies depict evolutionary relationships. *a.* A drawing from one of Darwin's notebooks, written in 1837 as he developed his ideas that led to *On the Origin of Species*. Darwin viewed life as a branching process akin to a tree, with species on the twigs, and evolutionary change represented by the branching pattern displayed by a tree as it grows. *b.* An example of a phylogeny. Note that these three versions convey the same information despite the differences in arrangement of species and orientation. Humans and chimpanzees are more closely related to each other than they are to any other living species. This is apparent because they share a common ancestor (the node labeled 1) that was not an ancestor of other species. Similarly, humans, chimpanzees, and gorillas are more closely related to one another than any of them is to orangutans because they share a common ancestor (node 2) that was not ancestral to orangutans. Node 3 represents the common ancestor of all apes. At each node, the two descendants can be rotated without changing the meaning. For example, one difference between versions 1 and 2 is that the descendants of node 2 have been rotated so that gorilla branches to the right in version 1 and to the left in version 2. However, this does not affect the interpretation that humans and chimps are more closely related to each other than either species is to gorillas. (*Reproduced with permission from Raven P, Johnson G, Mason K, Losos J, Duncan T;* Biology, *12th ed. New York: McGraw Hill; 2020*)

Key Ideas

The construction and/or analysis of phylogenetic trees and cladograms (Figure 11.9) is crucial on the AP exam. Keep the following in mind when constructing or analyzing them:

- Be able to read a derived characteristic chart.

- Nodes or branching points represent the most recent common ancestor of any two groups or lineage.

- Morphological similarities of living or fossil species can be used to construct phylogenetic trees or cladograms.

- Molecular data such as DNA or protein sequences can be used to construct phylogenetic trees or cladograms (Figure 11.10).

- Phylogenetic trees and cladograms are constantly being revised and revisited as new evidence is presented.

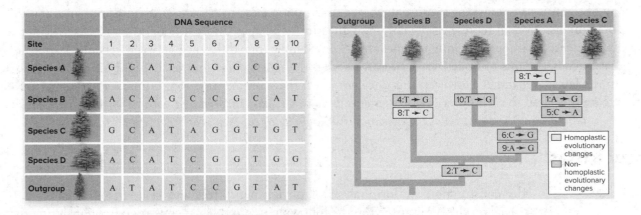

Traits: Organism	Jaws	Lungs	Amniotic Membrane	Hair	No Tail	Bipedal
Lamprey	0	0	0	0	0	0
Shark	1	0	0	0	0	0
Salamander	1	1	0	0	0	0
Lizard	1	1	1	0	0	0
Tiger	1	1	1	1	0	0
Gorilla	1	1	1	1	1	0
Human	1	1	1	1	1	1

a.

b.

Figure 11.9   A cladogram. *a.* Morphological data for a group of seven vertebrates are tabulated. A "1" indicates possession of the derived character state, and a "0" indicates possession of the ancestral character state (note that the derived state for character "no tail" is the absence of a tail; for all other traits, absence of the trait is the ancestral character state). *b.* A tree, or cladogram, diagrams the relationships among the organisms based on the presence of derived characters. The derived characters between the cladogram branch points are shared by all organisms above the branch points and are not present in any below them. The outgroup (in this case, the lamprey) does not possess any of the derived characters. (*Reproduced with permission from Raven P, Johnson G, Mason K, Losos J, Duncan T; Biology, 12th ed. New York: McGraw Hill; 2020*)

Site	1	2	3	4	5	6	7	8	9	10
Species A	G	C	A	T	A	G	G	C	G	T
Species B	A	C	A	G	C	C	G	C	A	T
Species C	G	C	A	T	A	G	G	T	G	T
Species D	A	C	A	T	C	G	G	T	G	G
Outgroup	A	T	A	T	C	C	G	T	A	T

Figure 11.10   Cladistic analysis of DNA sequence data. Sequence data are analyzed just like any other data. The most parsimonious interpretation of the DNA sequence data requires nine evolutionary changes. Each of these changes is indicated on the phylogeny. Change in site 8 is homoplastic: Species A and B independently evolved from thymine to cytosine at that site. Nonhomoplastic changes are those in which all species that possess the trait derived it from the same common ancestor. Such traits are referred to as homologous. (*Reproduced with permission from Raven P, Johnson G, Mason K, Losos J, Duncan T; Biology, 12th ed. New York: McGraw Hill; 2020*)

Molecular data is the most accurate and reliable evidence for constructing phylogenetic trees or cladograms. In the following figures, a classic analysis of DNA sequence data of five different tree species is used to establish evolutionary relationships.

Macroevolution

EVO-3
Life continues to evolve within a changing environment.

Biologists distinguish between microevolution and macroevolution. **Microevolution** includes all of what we have been discussing so far in this chapter—evolution at the level of species and populations. Think of **macroevolution** as the big picture, which includes the study of evolution of groups of species over very long periods of time.

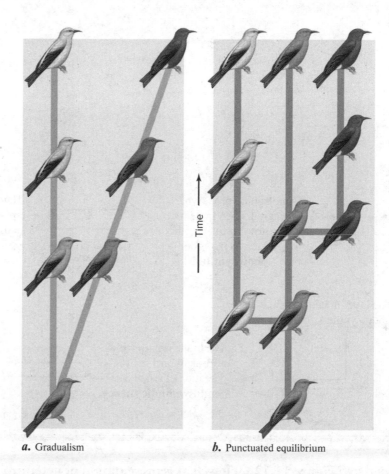

a. Gradualism *b.* Punctuated equilibrium

Figure 11.11 Gradualism versus punctuated equilibrium. (*Reproduced with permission from Raven P, Johnson G, Mason K, Losos J, Duncan T;* Biology, *12th ed. New York: McGraw Hill; 2020*)

There are disagreements in the field as to the typical pattern of macroevolution. Those who believe in **gradualism** assert that evolutionary change is a steady, slow process, while those who think that evolution is best described by the **punctuated equilibria model** believe that change occurs in rapid bursts separated by large periods of stasis (no change) (see comparison in Figure 11.11). Because the fossil record is incomplete, it is very hard to test the two theories—if we find no fossils for a species over a contested period, how can we determine whether change was occurring? The debate therefore continues.

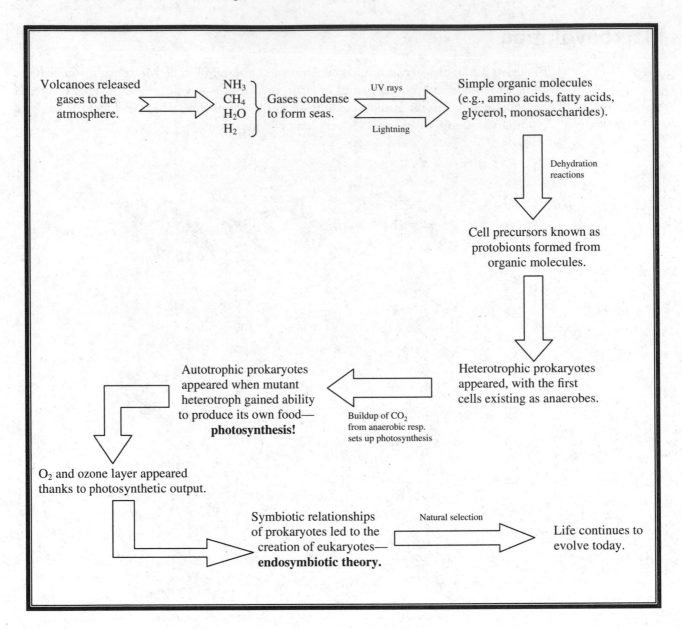

Figure 11.12 Flowchart representation of heterotroph theory.

Origins of Life on Earth

SYI-3

Naturally occurring diversity among and between components within biological systems affects interactions with the environment.

The AP Biology exam often includes questions on how life originated. It is therefore wise to learn the steps of the **heterotroph theory** (Figure 11.12), so named because it posits that the first organisms were **heterotrophs**, organisms that cannot make their own food. Geological evidence suggests.

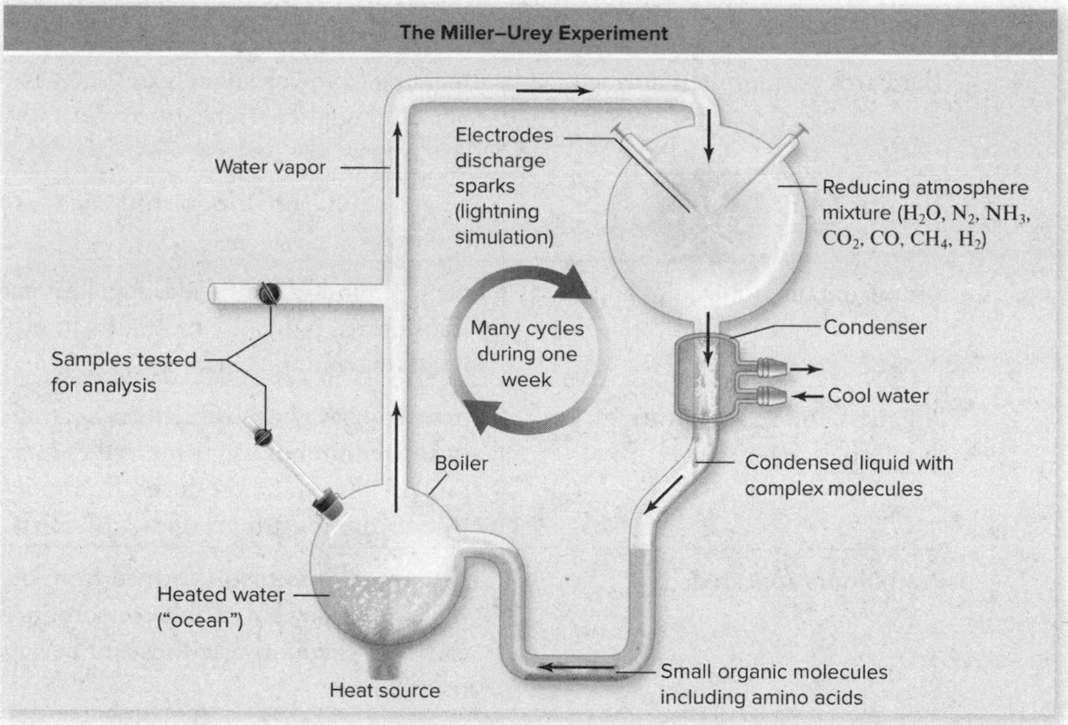

The Miller–Urey Experiment

Water vapor

Electrodes discharge sparks (lightning simulation)

Reducing atmosphere mixture (H_2O, N_2, NH_3, CO_2, CO, CH_4, H_2)

Many cycles during one week

Samples tested for analysis

Condenser

Cool water

Boiler

Condensed liquid with complex molecules

Heated water ("ocean")

Heat source

Small organic molecules including amino acids

Figure 11.13 The Miller–Urey experiment. The apparatus consisted of a closed tube connecting two chambers. The upper chamber contained a mixture of gases thought to resemble the primitive Earth's atmosphere. Electrodes discharged sparks through this mixture, simulating lightning. Condensers then cooled the gases, causing water droplets to form, which passed into the second heated chamber, the "ocean." Any complex molecules formed in the atmosphere chamber would be dissolved in these droplets and carried to the ocean chamber, from which samples were withdrawn for analysis. (*Reproduced with permission from Raven P, Johnson G, Mason K, Losos J, Duncan T; Biology, 12th ed. New York: McGraw Hill; 2020*)

First, though, it is important to understand that geological evidence provides support for the models of the origin of life on Earth (Figure 11.13) with Earth forming about 4.6 billion years ago with no signs of life due a hostile environment until 3.9 billion years ago. The earliest fossils date back to 3.5 billion years ago. The Miller-Urey Experiment demonstrated that several organic compounds could be formed spontaneously by simulating the conditions of Earth's early atmosphere.

Another theory is the RNA world hypothesis, which states that RNA could have been the earliest genetic material on Earth. A simple RNA molecule could copy itself without other molecules to help, drive chemical reactions like proteins, and be able to store genetic information just like DNA.

STEP	DESCRIPTION
The Earth's atmosphere formed.	Emerging from volcanoes, gases such as NH_3, CH_4, $H_2O(g)$, and H_2 (but not oxygen) invaded the atmosphere.
The seas formed.	The gases condensed to form the seas as the Earth cooled.
Simple organic molecules appeared.	Energy (from UV light, lightning, heat, radioactivity) transformed inorganic molecules to organic ones, including amino acids.
Polymers and self-replicating molecules appeared.	These may have been formed through dehydration, or the removal of water molecules (e.g., proteinoids can be produced from polypeptides by dehydrating amino acids with heat).
Protobionts appeared.	These are cell precursors formed from organic molecules; they are unable to reproduce, but can carry out chemical reactions and have permeable membranes.
Heterotrophic prokaryotes appeared.	Heterotrophs consume organic substances to survive (an example is pathogenic bacteria); since there was a limited amount of organic material, heterotrophs competed and natural selection occurred—these first cells were anaerobic; thus, the buildup of CO_2 from fermentation allowed for plenty of CO_2 to be available for photosynthesis.
Autotrophic prokaryotes appeared.	A heterotroph mutated and gained the ability to produce its own food using light energy, making it a photo autotroph (e.g., photosynthetic bacteria); this was a highly successful strategy compared to the heterotroph's.
Oxygen and the ozone layer appeared.	Photosynthesis produces oxygen, which interacts with UV light to form the ozone layer—this production of oxygen allowed for aerobic respiration; the ozone layer blocks UV light from reaching the Earth's surface.
Eukaryotes appeared (specifically mitochondria types and chloroplast types).	**Endosymbiotic theory** proposes that groups of prokaryotes associated in symbiotic relationships to form eukaryotes (the various organelles in cells today invaded a cell and eventually became one organism).
Life evolved.	Natural selection produced the variety of organisms that have existed throughout the Earth's history.

› Review Questions

1. Which of the following is an evolutionary process *not* based on random factors?

   A. Genetic drift
   B. Natural selection
   C. Mutation
   D. Gene flow

2. Which of the following is not a sexually selected trait?

   A. Fruit fly wings
   B. A male baboon's canine teeth
   C. Peacock tail feathers
   D. Male/female dimorphism in body size in many species

3. An adaptation

   A. can be shaped by genetic drift.
   B. cannot be altered.
   C. evolves because it specifically improves an individual's mating success.
   D. affects the fitness of an organism if it is altered.

4. Which of the following is *not* a requirement for natural selection to occur?

   A. Variation between individuals
   B. Heritability of the trait being selected
   C. Sexual reproduction
   D. Differences in reproductive success among individuals

5. Why can Hardy-Weinberg equilibrium occur only in large populations?

   A. Large populations are likely to have more variable environments.
   B. More individuals means less chance for natural selection to occur.
   C. Genetic drift is a much stronger force in small versus large populations.
   D. Large populations make random mating virtually impossible.

6. A population of frogs consists of 9 percent with speckles (the recessive condition) and 91 percent without speckles. What are the frequencies of the p and q alleles if this population is in Hardy-Weinberg equilibrium?

   A. $p = 0.49$, $q = 0.51$
   B. $p = 0.60$, $q = 0.40$
   C. $p = 0.70$, $q = 0.30$
   D. $p = 0.49$, $q = 0.30$

7. Frequency-dependent selection is

   A. particularly important during speciation.
   B. one way in which multiple alleles are preserved in a population.
   C. possible only when there are two alleles.
   D. most common in bacteria.

8. All of the following provide evidence for evolution *except*

   A. vestigial characters.
   B. Darwin's finches.
   C. homologous characters.
   D. mutations.

9. Why do we assume that oxygen was not present in the original atmosphere?

   A. The presence of O_2 would have resulted in the evolution of too many species too fast.
   B. Oxygen would have slowed down the rate of evolution.
   C. We know the ozone layer, which is formed by oxygen, has not been around that long.
   D. Inorganic molecules could not have formed in the presence of oxygen.

10. All of these are examples of random evolutionary processes *except*

    A. an earthquake divides a single elk species into two populations, forcing them to no longer interbreed.
    B. a mutation in a flower plant results in a new variety.
    C. an especially long winter causes a group of migrating birds to shift their home range.
    D. a mutation results in a population of trees that spread their seeds more widely than their peers, causing their population to grow.

❯ Answers and Explanations

1. **B**—Natural selection is the selective increase in certain alleles because they confer an advantage to their host organism. All other factors are random with respect to the alleles (a "bottleneck" is a type of genetic drift where a population is drastically reduced in size).

2. **A**—All fruit flies need to fly not only to find mates but also to survive. All the other characters listed are sexually selected, meaning that they have evolved because they confer specific advantages in mating (and not survival).

3. **D**—Adaptations are defined as traits that affect fitness if they are altered. Although adaptations may have evolved to increase mating success (answer C), they are not always intended for that function (e.g., they may have remained because they increase survival).

4. **C**—Natural selection can occur in asexually reproducing organisms, as long as the other three necessary conditions are met.

5. **C**—Genetic drift is change in allele frequencies as a result of random factors (e.g., natural disasters or environmental change). In small populations, genetic drift is a much more powerful force because each individual represents a greater percentage of the population's total genes than that person would in a much larger population. Think of it this way—if you have a population of 10 cheetahs, and 3 die, you have lost 30 percent of the genes in that pool. If you have a population of 100 cheetahs, and 3 die, you have lost only 3 percent. Since Hardy-Weinberg equilibrium depends on no genetic drift, it is much more likely to occur in very large populations.

6. **C**—Remember that p and q must add up to 1 for a population to be in Hardy-Weinberg equilibrium (this eliminates answer D). Calculate q first by taking the square root of 0.09, which is 0.30. Then simply subtract 0.30 from 1 to get $p = 0.70$.

7. **B**—Frequency-dependent selection is one process by which multiple alleles are preserved in a population. For traits that are selected for or against on the basis of frequency, an allele becomes more advantageous when it is rare, and therefore increases. In this way, it is impossible for the allele to become extinct (because as soon as it gets that low, it increases again). When it gets too high, the other allele is low, and that one then increases. Frequency-dependent selection often exhibits itself in this kind of seesaw effect.

8. **D**—Mutations in and of themselves are not evidence for evolution, although they are necessary if evolution is going to occur.

9. **D**—Inorganic molecules could not have formed in the presence of oxygen because oxygen would have taken the place of other elements in every chemical reaction (because it is such a highly reactive element).

10. **D**—This is the only answer that shows evidence of natural selection, which is the *nonrandom* process by which evolution occurs. The two elk species splitting (answer A) is an example of allopatric speciation caused by a random factor (a geologic event). A mutation is also a random event (answer B); for example, if we had said that the new variety became the dominant allele in a population because it had an advantage over other variants, then that *would* be natural selection. A home range shift (answer C) is not evolution, but rather a behavioral change within an organism's lifetime.

❯ Rapid Review

There are four modes of *evolution*:

1. *Genetic drift*: change in allele frequencies because of chance events (in small populations).

2. *Gene flow*: change in allele frequencies as genes move from one population to another.

3. *Mutation*: change in allele frequencies due to a *random genetic change* in an allele.

4. *Natural selection*: process by which characters or traits are maintained or eliminated in a population based on their contribution to the differential survival and reproductive success of their "host" organisms.

There are three requirements for *natural selection* to occur:

1. *Variation*: differences must exist between individuals.

2. *Heritability*: the traits to be selected for must be able to be passed along to offspring. Traits that are not inherited cannot be selected against.

3. *Differential reproductive success*: there must be variation among parents in how many offspring they produce as a result of the different traits that the parents have.

Adaptation is a trait that, if altered, affects the fitness of an organism; includes physical or intangible traits.

Selection types are as follows:

1. *Directional*: members at one end of a spectrum are selected against, and population shifts toward that end.

2. *Stabilizing*: selection for the mean of a population; reduces variation in a population.

3. *Disruptive (diversifying)*: selects for the two *extremes* of a population; selects against the middle.

4. *Sexual*: certain characters are selected for because they aid in mate acquisition.

5. *Artificial*: human intervention in the form of selective breeding (cattle).

Sources of *variation within populations* include the following:

1. *Mutation*: random changes in DNA can introduce new alleles into a population.

2. *Sexual reproduction*: crossover, independent assortment, random gamete combination.

3. *Balanced polymorphism*: the maintenance of two or more phenotypic variants.

Speciation is the process by which new species evolve:

1. *Allopatric speciation*: interbreeding stops because some physical barrier splits the population into two. If two populations evolve separately and change so they cannot interbreed, speciation has occurred.

2. *Sympatric speciation*: interbreeding stops even though no physical barrier prevents it.

   • *Polyploidy*: condition in which individual has a higher-than-normal number of chromosome sets. Polyploidic individuals cannot reproduce with nonpolyploidics.

   • *Balanced polymorphism*: two phenotypic variants become so different that the two groups stop interbreeding.

Other terms to remember include the following:

Adaptive radiation: rapid series of speciation events that occur when one or more ancestral species invades a new environment.

Hardy-Weinberg equilibrium: $p + q = 1$, $p^2 + 2pq + q^2 = 1$. Evolution is *not* occurring. The *rules* for this are no mutations, no gene flow, no genetic drift, no natural selection, and random mating.

Homologous character: traits similar between organisms that arose from a common ancestor.

Vestigial character: character contained by organism that is no longer functionally useful (appendix).

Gradualism: evolutionary change is a slow and steady process.

Punctuated equilibria: evolutionary change occurs in rapid bursts separated by large periods of no change.

Heterotroph theory: theory that describes how life evolved from original heterotrophs.

Convergent character: traits similar to two or more organisms that do *not* share a common ancestor; parallel evolution.

Convergent evolution: two unrelated species evolve in a way that makes them *more* similar.

Divergent evolution: two related species evolve in a way that makes them *less* similar.

Ecology

Exam Weight: 10–15%

IN THIS CHAPTER

Summary: This chapter focuses on the interaction between animals and their environments (ecology) and introduces you to some of the basic terms used in behavioral ecology and ethology.

Key Ideas

✪ Learn the bold-faced terms in this chapter well because they show up often on the multiple-choice portion of the exam.

✪ Types of animal learning: associative learning, fixed-action pattern, habituation, imprinting, insight learning, observational learning, and operant conditioning.

✪ Three major types of animal movement: kinesis, migration, and taxis.

✪ Behavioral patterns/concepts to know: agonistic behaviors, altruistic behaviors, coefficient of relatedness, dominance hierarchies, foraging, inclusive fitness, optimal foraging, reciprocal altruism, and territoriality.

✪ Types of animal communication: chemical, visual, auditory, and tactile.

✪ Three main types of dispersion patterns: clumped, uniform, and random.

✪ Two main types of population growth: exponential (J-shaped) and logistic (S-shaped).

✪ Two primary life history strategies: *K*-selected and *R*-selected populations.

✪ Three main symbiotic relationships: commensalism, mutualism, and parasitism.

✪ Defense mechanisms: aposematic coloration, Batesian mimicry, cryptic coloration, deceptive markings, and Müllerian mimicry.

✪ Biomes that come up on the AP exam: desert, savannah, taiga, temperate deciduous forest, temperate grassland, tropical forest, tundra, and water.

✪ Have a general understanding of the biogeochemical cycles (carbon, nitrogen, and water).

Behavioral Ecology

ENE-3

Timing and coordi-nation of biological mechanisms involved in growth, reproduc-tion, and homeostasis depend on organisms responding to envi-ronmental cues.

Behavioral ecology and ethology both involve the study of animal behavior. **Behavioral ecology** focuses on the interaction between animals and their environments, and usually includes an evolutionary perspective. For example, a behavioral ecologist might ask, "Why do two bird species that live in the same environment eat two different types of seeds?" **Ethology** is a narrower field, focused particularly on animal behavior and less on ecological analysis. Historically, ethology has involved a lot of experimental work, which has given us insight into the nature of animal minds.

This chapter introduces you to some of the basic terms and concepts used in behavioral ecology and ethology.

Types of Animal Learning

KEY IDEA

Associative learning is the process by which animals take one stimulus and associate it with another. Ivan Pavlov demonstrated **classical conditioning,** a type of associative learning, with dogs. As will come to be a pattern in this chapter, some poor animals were tampered with to help us understand an important biological principle. Pavlov taught dogs to antici-pate the arrival of food with the sound of a bell. He hooked up these dogs to machines that measured salivation. He began the experiments by ringing a bell just moments before giving food to the dogs. Soon after this experiment began, the dogs were salivating at the sound of the bell before food was even brought into the room. They were conditioned to associate the noise of the bell with the impending arrival of food; one stimulus was substituted for another to evoke the same response.

A **fixed-action pattern** (FAP) is an innate, preprogrammed response to a stimulus (Figure 12.1). Once this action has begun, it will not stop until it has run its course. For example, male stickleback fish are programmed to attack any red-bellied fish that come into their territory. Males do not attack fish lacking this red coloration; it is specifically the color that stimulates aggressiveness. If fake fish with red bottoms are placed in water containing these stickleback fish, there's bound to be a fight! But if fake fish lacking a red bottom are dropped in, all is peaceful.

Figure 12.1 **Innate egg-rolling response in geese.** The series of movements used by a goose to retrieve an egg is a fixed action pattern. Once it detects the key stimulus (in this case, an egg outside the nest), the goose goes through the entire set of movements: It will extend its neck toward the egg, get up, and roll the egg back into the nest by moving its neck from side to side with the egg positioned under its bill. (*Reproduced with per-mission from Raven P, Johnson G, Mason K, Losos J, Duncan T;* Biology, *12th ed. New York: McGraw Hill; 2020*)

Habituation is the loss of responsiveness to unimportant stimuli. For example, as one of us started working on this book, he had just purchased a new fish tank for his office and was struck by how audible the sound of the tank's filter was. As he sits here typing tonight about two months later, he does not even hear the filter unless he *thinks* about it; he has become habit-uated to the noise. There are many examples of habituation in ethology. One classic example involves little ducklings that run for cover whenever birdlike objects fly overhead. If one were to torture these poor baby ducks and throw bird-shaped objects over their heads, in the begin-ning they would head for cover each time one flew past them, but over time as they learned that the fake birds did not represent any real danger, they would habituate to the mean trick and eventually not react at all. One side note is that ethologists who study wild animals usually have to habituate their study subjects to their presence before recording any behavioral data.

Imprinting is an innate behavior that is learned during a critical period early in life. For example, when geese are born, they imprint on motion that moves away from them, and they follow it around accepting it as their mother. This motion can be the baby's actual mother goose, it can be a human, or it can be an object. Once this imprint is made, it is irreversible. If given an essay about behavioral ecology, and imprinting in particular, the work of Konrad Lorenz would be a nice addition to your response. He was a scientist who became the "mother" to a group of young geese. He made sure that he was around the baby geese as they hatched and spent the critical period with them creating that mother–baby goose bond. These geese proceeded to follow him around everywhere and didn't recognize their real mother as their own.

Insight learning is the ability to do something right the first time with no prior experience. It requires reasoning ability—the skill to look at a problem and come up with an appropriate solution.

Observational learning is the ability of an organism to learn how to do something by watching another individual do it first, even if they have never attempted it themselves. An example of this involves young chimpanzees in the Ivory Coast, who watch their mothers crack nuts with rock tools before learning the technique themselves.

Operant conditioning is a type of associative learning that is based on trial and error. This is different from classical conditioning because in operant conditioning, the association is made between the animal's *own* behavior and a response. This is the type of conditioning that is important to the aposematically colored organisms. For example, a brightly colored lizard with a chemical defense mechanism (it can spray predators in an attempt to escape) relies on this type of conditioning for survival. The coloration pattern is there in the hope that the predator will, in a trial-and-error fashion, associate the coloration pattern with an uncomfortable chemical-spraying experience that it had in the past. This association might make the predator think twice before attacking in the future and provide the prey with enough time to escape.

Animal Movement

There are three major types of animal movement that you should familiarize yourself with for the AP exam: kinesis, migration, and taxis.

Kinesis. This is a seemingly random change in the *speed* of a movement in response to a stimulus. When an organism is in a place that it enjoys, it slows down, and when in a bad environment, it speeds up. Overall this leads to an organism spending more time in favorable environments. In Chapter 13, Laboratory Review, an example of kinesis involving pill bugs is discussed. These bugs prefer damp environments to dry ones, and when placed into a contraption that gives them the choice of being on the dry or damp side, they move quickly toward the damp side (where the speed of their movement slows).

Migration. This is a cyclic movement of animals over long distances according to the time of year. Birds are known to migrate south, where it is warmer, for the winter. It is amazing that these animals know where to go (Figure 12.2).

Taxis. These are cars taken by people who need transportation. Hmm . . . actually, *taxis,* the biological term, is a reflex movement toward or away from a stimulus. We always think about summer evenings, sitting on the porch with the bug light near by, watching the poor little moths fly *right* into the darn thing because of the taxis response. They are drawn to the light at night (**phototaxis**).

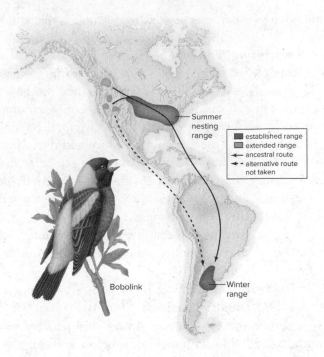

Figure 12.2   Birds on the move. The summer range of bobolinks, Dolichonyx oryzivorus, recently extended to the far western United States from their established range in the Midwest. When birds in these newly established populations migrate to South America in the winter, they do not fly directly to the winter range; instead, they first fly to the Midwest and then use the ancestral flyway, going much farther than if they flew directly to their winter range. (*Reproduced with permission from Raven P, Johnson G, Mason K, Losos J, Duncan T;* Biology, *12th ed. New York: McGraw Hill; 2020*)

Behave Yourselves, You Animals!

There are several typical behavior patterns that you should familiarize yourself with before the exam.

1. **Agonistic behavior.** Behavior that results from conflicts over resources. It often involves intimidation and submission. The battle is often a matter of who can put on the most threatening display to scare the other one into giving up, although the displays can also be quite subtle. Agonistic behaviors can involve food, mates, and territory, to name only a few. Participants in these displays do not tend to come away injured because most of these interactions are just that: displays.
2. **Altruistic behavior.** An *altruistic* action is one in which an organism does something to help another, even if it comes at its own expense. An example of this behavior involves bees. Worker bees are sterile, produce no offspring, and play the role of hive defenders, sacrificing their lives by stinging intruders that pose a threat to the queen bee. (Sounds to us like they need a better agent.) Another example involves vampire bats that vomit food for group mates that did not manage to find food.
3. **Coefficient of relatedness.** This statistic represents the average proportion of genes that two individuals have in common. Siblings have a coefficient of relatedness (COR) of 0.5 because they share 50 percent of their genes. This coefficient is an interesting statistic because it can be expected that an animal that has a high COR with another animal will be more likely to act in an altruistic manner toward that animal.
4. **Dominance hierarchies.** A dominance hierarchy among a group of individuals is a ranking of power among the members. The member with the most power is the "alpha"

member. The second-in-command, the "beta" member, dominates everyone in the group except for the alpha. It pretty much rocks to be at the top of the dominance hierarchy because you have first dibs (choice) on *every*thing (food, mates, etc.). The dominance hierarchy is not necessarily permanent—there can always be some shuffling around. For example, in chimpanzees, an alpha male can lose his alpha status and become subordinate to another chimp if power relationships change. One positive thing about these hierarchies is that since there is an order, known by all involved, it reduces the energy wasted and the risk from physical fighting for resources. Animals that know that they would be attacked if they took food before a higher-ranking individual wait until it is their turn to eat so as to avoid conflict. Keep in mind that dominance hierarchies are a characteristic of group-living animals.

5. **Foraging.** A word describes the feeding behavior of an individual. This behavior is not as random as it may seem as animals tend to have something called a **search image** that directs them toward their potential meal. When searching for food, few fish look for a particular food; rather, they are looking for objects of a particular size that seem to match the size of what they usually eat. This is a search image. In an aquarium at mealtime, if you watch the fish closely, you will see them zoom around taking food into their mouths as they swim. Unfortunately, sometimes the "food" they ingest is the bathroom output of another fish that happens to be the same size as the food and is floating nearby. Simply because the fish dropping is the appropriate size and fits the search image, the fish may take it into its mouth for a second before emphatically spitting it out.

6. **Inclusive fitness.** This term represents the overall ability of individuals to pass their genes on to the next generation. This includes their ability to pass their *own* genes through reproduction as well as the ability of their relatives to do the same. Reproduction by relatives is included because related individuals share many of the same genes. Therefore, helping relatives to increase the success of passage of their genes to the next generation increases the inclusive fitness of the helper. The concept of inclusive fitness can explain many cases of altruism in nature.

7. **Optimal foraging.** Natural selection favors animals that choose foraging strategies that take into account costs and benefits. For example, food that is rich in nutrients but far away may cost too much energy to be worth the extra trip. There are many potential costs to traveling a long distance for some food—the animal itself could be eaten on the way *to* the food, and the animal could expend more energy than it would gain *from* the food. You *know* that you have displayed optimal foraging behavior before. "Hey, do you want to go to Wendy's?" "Uhh . . . not really, it's a really long drive . . . let's go to Bill's Burgers down the road instead."

8. **Reciprocal altruism.** Why should individuals behave altruistically? One reason may be the hope that in the future, the companion will return the favor. A baboon may defend an unrelated companion in a fight, or perhaps a wolf will offer food to another wolf that shares no relation. Animals rarely display this behavior since it is limited to species with stable social groups that allow for exchanges of this nature. The bats described earlier represent a good example of reciprocal altruism.

9. **Territoriality.** Territorial individuals defend a physical geographic area against other individuals. This area is defended because of the benefits derived from it, which may include available mates, food resources, and high-quality breeding sites. An individual may defend a territory using scent marking, vocalizations that warn other individuals to stay away, or actual physical force against intruders. Animal species vary in their degree of territoriality (in fact, some species are *not* territorial), and both males and females may exhibit territorial behavior.

Animal Communication

IST-5

Transmission of information results in changes within and between biological systems.

Animals communicate in many ways. Communication need not always be vocal, and we will discuss the various communication mechanisms in this next section: visual, auditory, chemical, and tactile.

Chemical communication. Mammals and insects use chemical signals called **pheromones,** which in many species play a pivotal role in the mating game. Pheromones can be powerful enough to attract mates from miles away.

Visual communication. We mentioned a few visual communication examples earlier, such as agonistic displays. Another example of a visual display is a male peacock's feather splay, which announces his willingness to mate.

Auditory communication. This mode of communication involves the use of sound in the conveying of a message. In many parts of the United States, if one sits on one's porch on a summer night, one hears the song of night frogs and crickets. These noises are often made in an effort to attract mates.

Tactile communication. This mode of communication involves touch in the conveying of a message and is often used as a greeting (handshake in humans). A major form of primate tactile communication involves grooming behavior.

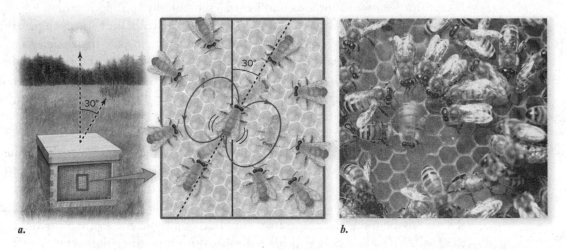

Figure 12.3 **The waggle dance of honeybees, *Apis mellifera. a.*** The angle between the food source, the nest, and the Sun is represented by a dancing bee as the angle between the straight part of the dance and vertical. The food is 30° to the right of the Sun, and the straight part of the bee's dance on the hive is 30° to the right of vertical. ***b.*** A scout bee dances on a comb in the hive. (*Reproduced with permission from Raven P, Johnson G, Mason K, Losos J, Duncan T;* Biology, *12th ed. New York: McGraw Hill; 2020*)

Bees provide an example of communication (Figure 12.3) that involves chemical, tactile, and auditory components. The beehive is a dark and crowded place, and when a worker bee returns after having found a good food source, how in the world is it going to get the attention of all of the co-workers? Unfortunately, intercom systems in hives are yet to be developed. What these bees do instead is a little dance; a dance in a tight circle accompanied by a certain wag signifies to the co-workers "Hey guys . . . food source is *right* down the street." But if the food is farther away, the bee changes the dance to one that provides directional clues as well. The bee will instead perform a different combination of funky moves. This dance provides distance and directional information to the other workers and helps them find the faraway source. The ever so pleasant chemical component to this process is the regurgitation of the food source to show the other bees what kind of food they are chasing. Imagine if humans did that . . . "Dude, I just found the greatest burger place like two miles from here . . . (burp) here . . . try this burger . . . it's delightful!"

Ecology

Ecology is the study of the interaction of organisms and their environments. This chapter covers the main concepts of ecology, including population growth, biotic potential, life history "strategies," and predator–prey relationships. The chapter will also look at within-community and between-community (intra- and intercommunity) interactions. Finally, we will talk about succession, trophic levels, energy pyramids, biomass pyramids, biomes, and biogeochemical cycles.

Population Ecology and Growth

Like many fields of biology, ecology contains hierarchies of classification. A **population** is a collection of individuals of the same species living in the same geographic area. A collection of populations of species in a geographic area is known as a **community.** An **ecosystem** consists of the individuals of the community and the environment in which it exists. Ecosystems can be subdivided into abiotic and biotic components: **biotic components** are the living organisms of the ecosystem, while **abiotic components** are the *nonliving* players in an ecosystem, such as weather and nutrients. Finally, the **biosphere** is the entire life-containing area of a planet—all communities and ecosystems.

Three more terms for you: (1) the **niche** of an organism, which consists of all the biotic and abiotic resources used by the organism; (2) **population density,** which describes how many individuals are in a certain area; and (3) **distribution,** which describes how populations are dispersed over that area. There are three main types of dispersion patterns that you should know (see also Figure 12.4):

1. **Clumped:** The individuals live in packs that are spaced out from each other, as in schools of fish or herds of cattle.
2. **Uniform:** The individuals are evenly spaced out across a geographic area, such as birds on a wire sitting above the highway—notice how evenly spaced out they are.
3. **Random:** The species are randomly distributed across a geographic area, such as a tree distribution in a forest.

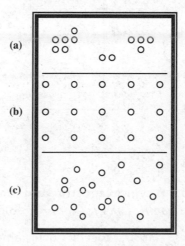

Figure 12.4   Distribution patterns: (a) clumped; (b) uniform; (c) random.

Population ecology is the study of the size, distribution, and density of populations and how these populations change with time. It takes into account all the variables we have mentioned already and many more. The size of the population, symbolized N, indicates how many individuals of that species are in a given area. **Demographers** study the theory and statistics behind population growth and decline. The following is a list of demographic statistics you should be familiar with for the AP Biology exam:

Liz (college freshman): "Know how to read these charts."

Birth rate   Offspring produced per time period. Highest among those in the middle of the age spectrum.

Death rate   Number of deaths per time period. Highest among those at two extremes of the age spectrum.

Sex ratio   Proportion of males and females in a population.

Generation time Time needed for individuals to reach reproductive maturity.

Age structure Statistic that compares the relative number of individuals in the population from each age group (Figure 12.5).

Immigration rate Rate at which individuals relocate into a given population.

Emigration rate Rate at which individuals relocate out of a given population.

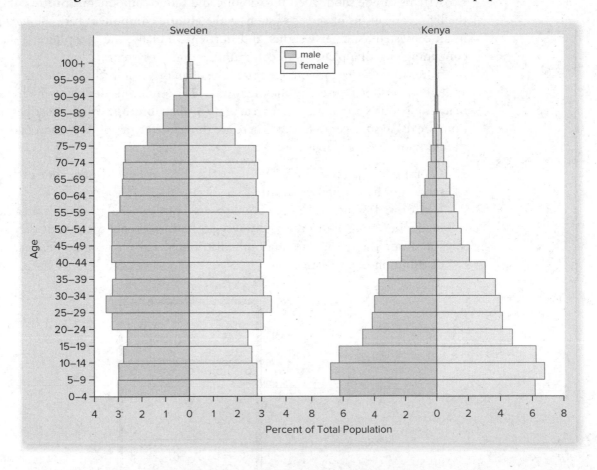

Figure 12.5 A typical age structure chart. (*Reproduced with permission from Raven P, Johnson G, Mason K, Losos J, Duncan T; Biology, 12th ed. New York: McGraw Hill; 2020*)

All these statistics together determine the size and growth rate of a given population. Obviously, a higher birth rate and a lower death rate will give a faster rate of population growth. A high female sex ratio could lead to an increase in the number of births in a population (more females to produce offspring). A short generation time allows offspring to be produced at a faster rate. An age structure that consists of more individuals in the middle of their reproductive years will grow at a faster rate than one weighted toward older people.

Population Growth and Size

SYI-1
Living systems are organized in a hierarchy of structural levels that interact.

Biotic potential is the maximum growth rate of a population given unlimited resources, unlimited space, and lack of competition or predators. This rate varies from species to species. The **carrying capacity** is defined as the maximum number of individuals that a population can sustain in a given environment.

If biotic potential exists, then why isn't every inch of this planet covered with life? Because of the environment in which we live, numerous **limiting factors** exist that help control population sizes. A few examples of limiting factors include predators, diseases, food supplies, and waste produced by organisms. There are two broad categories of limiting factors:

Density-dependent factors. These limiting factors (Figure 12.6) rear their ugly heads as the population approaches and/or passes the carrying capacity. Examples of density-dependent limiting factors include food supplies, which run low; waste products, which build up; and population-crowding-related diseases such as the bubonic plague, which just stink.

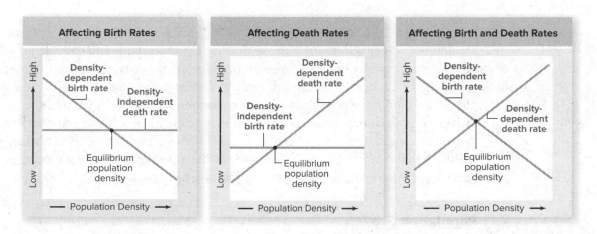

Figure 12.6   Density-dependent population regulation. Density-dependent factors can affect birth rates, death rates, or both. (*Reproduced with permission from Raven P, Johnson G, Mason K, Losos J, Duncan T;* Biology, *12th ed. New York: McGraw Hill; 2020*)

Density-independent factors. These limiting factors have nothing to do with the population size. Examples of density-independent limiting factors include floods, droughts, earthquakes, and other natural disasters and weather conditions.

There are two main types of population growth (Figure 12.8):

1. *Exponential growth:* the population grows at a rate that creates a J-shaped curve. The population grows as if there are no limitations as to how large it can get (biotic potential).
2. *Logistic growth:* the population grows at a rate that creates an S-shaped curve similar to the initial portion of Figure 12.7. Limiting factors are the culprits responsible for the S shape of the curve, putting a cap on the size to which the population can grow.

Take a look at Figure 12.7. As the population size increases exponentially from point *A* to point *C*, there seem to be enough natural resources available to allow the growth rate to be quite high. At some point, however, natural resources, such as food, will start to run out. This will lead to competition between the members of the population for the scarce food. Whenever there is competition, there are winners and losers. Those who win survive; those who lose do not. Notice that the population rises above the carrying capacity. How can this be? This is short-lived, as the

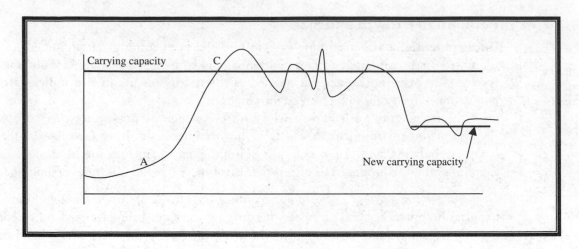

Figure 12.7   Carrying capacity.

complications of being overpopulated (lack of food, disease from increased population density, buildup of waste) will lead to a rise in the death rate that pushes the population back down to the carrying capacity or below. When it drops below the carrying capacity, resources replenish, allowing for an increase in the birth rate and decline in the death rate. What you are looking at in Figure 12.7 is the phenomenon known as a **population cycle.** Often, as seen in the figure, when the population size dips below the carrying capacity, it will later come back to the capacity and even surpass it. However, another possibility shown in this figure is that when a population dips below the carrying capacity due to some major change in the environment, when all is said and done, it may equilibrate at a new, lower carrying capacity (Figure 12.8).

Population Growth

$$\frac{dN}{dt} = B - D$$

dt = change in time

B = birth rate

D = death rate

Exponential Growth

$$\frac{dN}{dt} = r_{max}N$$

N = population size

r_{max} = maximum per capita growth rate of population

Logistic Growth

$$\frac{dN}{dt} = r_{max}N\left(\frac{K - N}{K}\right)$$

K = carrying capacity

Life History Strategies

You should be familiar with two primary life history "strategies," which represent two extremes of the spectrum:

K-*selected populations:* populations of a roughly constant size whose members have low reproductive rates. The offspring produced by these K-selected organisms require extensive postnatal care until they have sufficiently matured. Humans are a fine example of a K-selected population.

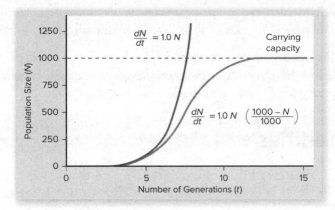

Figure 12.8 **Two models of population growth.** The red line illustrates the exponential growth model for a population with an r of 1.0. The blue line illustrates the logistic growth model in a population with r = 1.0 and K = 1000 individuals. At first, logistic growth accelerates exponentially; then, as resources become limited, the death rate increases and growth slows. Growth ceases when the death rate equals the birth rate. The carrying capacity (K) ultimately depends on the resources available in the environment. (*Reproduced with permission from Raven P, Johnson G, Mason K, Losos J, Duncan T; Biology, 12th ed. New York: McGraw Hill; 2020*)

R-*selected populations:* populations that experience rapid growth of the J-curve variety. The offspring produced by *R*-selected organisms are numerous, mature quite rapidly, and require very little postnatal care. These populations are also known as **opportunistic populations** and tend to show up when space in the region opens up as a result of some environmental change. The opportunistic population grows fast, reproduces quickly, and dies quickly as well. Bacteria are a good example of an *R*-selected population.

Survivorship Curves

Survivorship curves (Figure 12.9) are another tool used to study the population dynamics of species. These curves show the relative survival rates for population members of different ages.

Type I individuals live a long life until an age is reached where the death rate in the population increases rapidly, causing the steep downward end to the type I curve. Examples of type I organisms include humans and other large mammals.

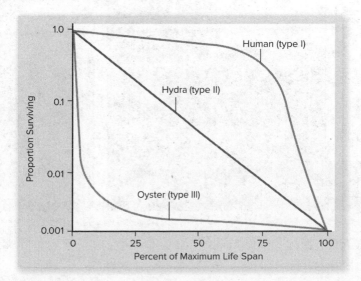

Figure 12.9 **Survivorship curves.** (*Reproduced with permission from Raven P, Johnson G, Mason K, Losos J, Duncan T; Biology, 12th ed. New York: McGraw Hill; 2020*)

Type II individuals have a death rate that is reasonably constant across the age spectrum. Examples of type II species include lizards, hydra, and other small mammals.

Type III individuals have a steep downward curve for those of young age, representing a death rate that flattens out once a certain age is reached. Examples of type III organisms include many fishes, oysters, and other marine organisms.

Biological Communities

ENE-4

Communities and ecosystems change on the basis of interactions among populations and disruptions to the environment.

Most species exist within a community. Because they share a geographic home, they are bound to interact with one another. These interactions range from positive to neutral to negative. The communities are characterized by the amount of energy they are able to produce (primary productivity) and the number of species present in the community.

Simpson's Diversity Index

$$\text{Diversity index} = 1 - \Sigma\left(\frac{n}{N}\right)^2$$

n = total number of organisms of a particular species
N = total number of organisms of all species

Ecological Niche

A niche of an organism, which was discussed earlier, represents all the biotic and abiotic resources used by organisms in a given area. However, species sometimes are not able to occupy their entire niche due to the presence or absence of other species. These interactions with other species may have harmful (negative) or helpful (positive) effects on the species. This leads to the presence of **fundamental niches**, which include all the resources and area that a species can occupy and **realized niches**, which include the actual resources and space that an organism occupies.

Competition between species for resources in a niche leads to the competitive exclusion principle: when two species compete for limited resources and one of the species uses the resources more efficiently than the other, it will lead to the elimination of the less efficient species. Figure 12.10 shows competition between two species of barnacles.

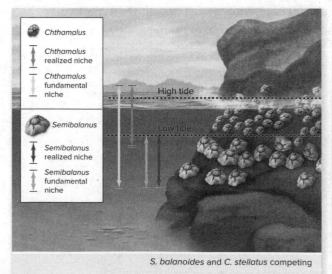
S. balanoides and C. stellatus competing

C. stellatus fundamental and realized niches are identical when S. balanoides is removed.

Figure 12.10 Competition between two species of barnacles. (*Reproduced with permission from Raven P, Johnson G, Mason K, Losos J, Duncan T; Biology, 12th ed. New York: McGraw Hill; 2020*)

Forms of Species Interaction

1. **Symbiosis**. A symbiotic relationship is one between two different species that can be classified as one of three main types: commensalism, mutualism, or parasitism.

   A. **Commensalism**. One organism benefits while the other is unaffected. Commensalistic relationships are rare, and examples are hard to find. Cattle egrets feast on insects that are aroused into flight by cattle grazing in the insects' habitat. The birds benefit because they get food, but the cattle do not appear to benefit at all.

   B. **Mutualism**. Both organisms reap benefits from the interaction. One popular example of a mutualistic relationship is that between acacia trees and ants. The ants are able to feast on the yummy sugar produced by the trees, while the trees are protected by the ants' attack on any potentially harmful foreign insects. Another example involves a lichen, which is a collection of photosynthetic organisms (fungus and algae) living as one. The fungus component pulls its weight by helping to create an environment suitable for the lichen's survival, while the algae component supplies the food for the fungus. Without each other's contribution, they are doomed.

   C. **Parasitism**. One organism benefits at the other's expense. A popular example of a parasitic relationship involves tapeworms, which live in the digestive tract of their hosts. They reap the benefits of the meals that their host consumes by stealing the nutrients and depriving the host of nutrition. Another less well-known example of parasitism involves myself and my younger brother's Playstation 2 console.

2. **Competition.** Both species are harmed by this kind of interaction. The two major forms of competition are intraspecific and interspecific competition. **Intraspecific competition** is *within*-species competition. This kind of competition occurs because members of the same species rely on the same valuable resources for survival. When resources become scarce, the most fit of the species will get more of the resource and survive. **Interspecific competition** is competition between different species.

3. **Predation.** (Figure 12.11) is one of the "negative" interactions seen in communities (well, for one half of those involved, it is negative). One species, the predator, hunts another species, the prey.

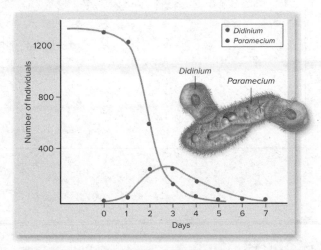

Figure 12.11 **Predator–prey in the microscopic world.** When the predatory *Didinium* is added to a *Paramecium* population, the numbers of *Didinium* initially rise, and the numbers of *Paramecium* steadily fall. When the *Paramecium* population is depleted, however, the *Didinium* individuals also die. (*Reproduced with permission from Raven P, Johnson G, Mason K, Losos J, Duncan T;* Biology, *12th ed. New York: McGraw Hill; 2020*)

Not all prey give in to this without a fight, and the hunted may develop mechanisms to defend against predatory attack. The next section describes the various kinds of defense mechanisms developed by prey in an effort to survive.

Keystone species are critical to the survival of other species in a given ecosystem. These keystone species may be predators or something as simple as a plant. But do not make the mistake of discounting their importance to the survival of the ecosystem. Without them, the ecosystem would be dramatically different.

Defense Mechanisms

Aposematic coloration is a very impressive-sounding name for this defense mechanism. Stated simply, it is warning coloration adopted by animals that possess a chemical defense mechanism. Predators have grown cautious of animals with bright color patterns due to past encounters in which prey of a certain coloration have sprayed the predator with a chemical defense. It is kind of like the blinking red light seen in cars with elaborate alarm systems. Burglars notice the red light and may think twice about attempting to steal that car because of the potential for encountering an alarm system.

In **Batesian mimicry,** an animal that is harmless copies the appearance of an animal that is dangerous to trick predators. An example of this is a beetle whose colors closely resemble those of bees. Predators may fear that the beetle is a bee and avoid confrontation.

In **cryptic coloration,** those being hunted adopt a coloring scheme that allows them to blend in to the colors of the environment. It is like camouflage worn by army soldiers moving through the jungle. The more you look like the terrain, the harder you are to see.

Some animals have patterns called **deceptive markings,** which can cause a predator to think twice before attacking. For example, some insects may have colored designs on their wings that resemble large eyes, causing individuals to look more imposing than they truly are.

In **Müllerian mimicry,** two species that are aposematically colored as an indicator of their chemical defense mechanisms mimic each other's color scheme in an effort to increase the speed with which their predators learn to avoid them. The more often predators see dangerous prey with this coloration, the faster the negative association is made.

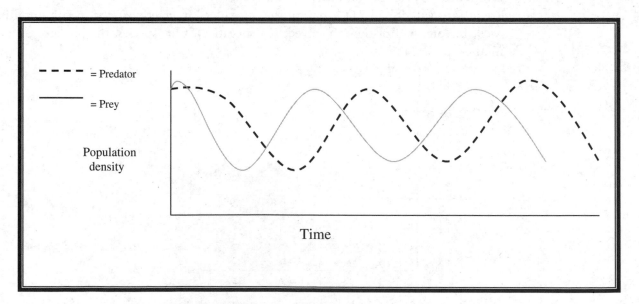

Figure 12.12   Predator–prey population curves.

Looking at Figure 12.12, we can see how the predator–prey dance plays out. When the prey population starts to decrease because of predation, there is a reactionary reduction in the predator population. Why does this happen? Because the predators run low on a valuable resource necessary to their survival—their prey. Notice in the figure that as the predator population declines, an increase in the population of the prey begins to appear because more of those prey animals are able to survive and reproduce. As the prey population density rises, the predators again have enough food available to sustain a higher population, and their population density returns to a higher level again. Unless disturbed by a dramatic environmental change, this cyclical pattern continues.

Coevolution is mutual evolution between two species and is often seen in predator–prey relationships. For example, imagine that the hunted prey adapts a new character trait that allows it to better elude the predator. In order to survive, the predator must evolve so that it can catch its victim and eat.

Succession

When something happens to a community that causes a shift in the resources available to the local organisms, it sets the stage for the process of **succession**—the shift in the local composition of species in response to changes that occur over time. As time passes, the community goes through various stages until it arrives at a final stable stage called the **climax community.** Two major forms of succession you should know about are primary and secondary succession.

Primary succession occurs in an area that is devoid of life and contains no soil. A **pioneer species** (usually a small plant) able to survive in resource-poor conditions takes hold of a barren area such as a new volcanic island. The pioneer species does the grunt work, adding nutrients and other improvements to the once uninhabited volcanic rock until future species take over. As the plant species come and go, adding nutrients to the environment, animal species are drawn in by the presence of new plant life. These animals contribute to the development of the area with the addition of further organic matter (waste). This constant changing of the guard continues until the **climax community** is reached and a steady-state equilibrium is achieved. **Bare-rock succession** involves the attachment of lichen to rocks, followed by the step-by-step arrival of replacement species up to the climax community. **Pond succession** is kicked off when a shallow, water-filled hole is created. As time passes, animals arrive on the scene as the pioneer species deposit debris, encouraging the growth of vegetation on the pond floor. Over time, plants develop whose roots are underwater and whose leaves are above the water. As these plants begin to cover the entire area of the pond, the debris continues to build up, transforming the once empty pond into a marsh. When enough trees fill the area, the marsh becomes a swamp. If the conditions are appropriate, the swamp can eventually become a forest or grassland, completing the succession process. One trivia fact to take out of primary succession is that usually the pioneer species is an *R*-selected species, while the later species tend to be *K*-selected species.

Secondary succession occurs in an area that once had stable life but has since been disturbed by some major force such as a forest fire. This type of succession is different from primary succession because there is already soil present on the terrain when the process begins.

Keystone species are critical to the survival of other species in a given ecosystem. These keystone species may be predators or something as simple as a plant. But do not make the mistake of discounting their importance to the survival of the ecosystem. Without them, the ecosystem would be dramatically different.

Trophic Levels

ENE-1

The highly complex organization of living systems requires constant input of energy and the exchange of macromolecules.

As we discussed earlier, an ecosystem consists of the individuals of the community and the environment in which they exist. Organisms are classified as either producers or consumers. The producers of the world are the autotrophs mentioned in Chapter 7 Cellular Energetics. The autotrophs you should recognize can be one of two types: photosynthetic or chemo-synthetic autotrophs. **Photoautotrophs** (photosynthetic autotrophs) start the Earth's food chain by converting the energy of light into the energy of life. **Chemoautotrophs** (chemosynthetic autotrophs) release energy through the movement of electrons in oxidation reactions.

The consumers of the world are the heterotrophs. They are able to obtain their energy only through consumption of other living things (Figure 12.13). One type of consumer is an **herbivore,** which feeds on plants for nourishment. Another consumer, the **carnivore,** obtains energy and nutrients through the consumption of other animals. A third consumer, the **detritivore,** obtains its energy through the consumption of dead animals and plants. A special subcategory of this type of consumer includes decomposers, which also consume dead animal and plant matter, but then release nutrients back into the environment. The decomposer subcategory includes fungi, bacteria, and earthworms.

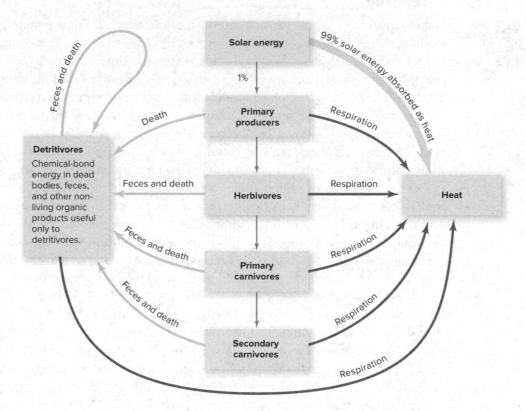

Figure 12.13 The flow of energy through an ecosystem. Blue arrows represent the flow of energy that enters the ecosystem as light and is then passed along as chemical-bond energy to successive trophic levels. At each step energy is diverted, meaning that the chemical-bond energy available to each trophic level is less than that available to the preceding trophic level. Red arrows represent diversions of energy into heat. Tan arrows represent diversions of energy into feces and other organic materials useful only to the detritivores. Detritivores may be eaten by carnivores, so some of the chemical-bond energy returns to higher trophic levels. (*Reproduced with permission from Raven P, Johnson G, Mason K, Losos J, Duncan T;* Biology, *12th ed. New York: McGraw Hill; 2020*)

Here comes another hierarchy for you to remember. The distribution of energy on the planet can be subdivided into a hierarchy of energy levels called **trophic levels.** Take a look at the energy pyramid in Figure 12.14. The primary producers make up the first trophic level. The next trophic level consists of the organisms that consume the primary producers: the herbivores. These organisms are known as **primary consumers.** The primary consumers are consumed by the **secondary consumers,** or primary carnivores, that are the next trophic level. These primary carnivores are consumed by the secondary carnivores to create the next trophic level. This is an oversimplified yet important basic explanation of how trophic levels work. Usually there are only four or five trophic levels to a food chain because energy is lost from each level as it progresses higher.

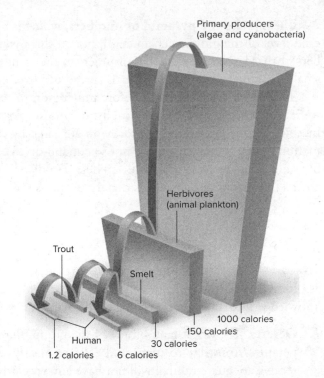

Figure 12.14 Energy pyramid, indicating decrease in energy level. (*Reproduced with permission from Raven P, Johnson G, Mason K, Losos J, Duncan T; Biology, 12th ed. New York: McGraw Hill; 2020*)

The energy pyramid is not the only type of ecological pyramid that you might encounter on the AP Biology exam. Be familiar with a type of pyramid known as a *biomass pyramid* (Figure 12.15), which represents the cumulative weight of all of the members at a given trophic level. These pyramids tend to vary from one ecosystem to another. Like energy pyramids, the base of the biomass pyramid represents the primary producers and tends to be the largest.

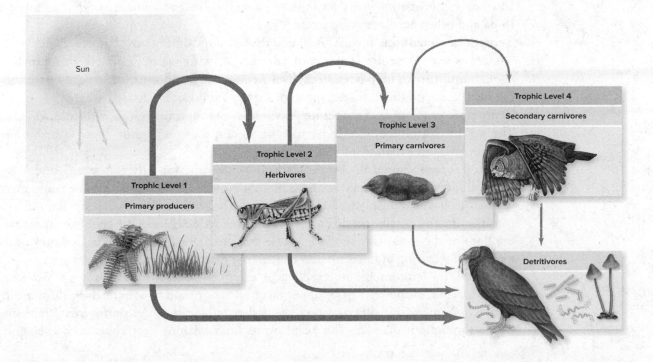

Figure 12.15 Biomass pyramid. (*Reproduced with permission from Raven P, Johnson G, Mason K, Losos J, Duncan T; Biology, 12th ed. New York: McGraw Hill; 2020*)

There is also the **pyramid of numbers,** which is based on the *number* of individuals at each level of the biomass chain. Each box in this pyramid represents the number of members of that level. The highest consumers in the chain tend to be quite large, resulting in a smaller number of those individuals spread out over an area.

Two more terms to cover before moving on to the biomes are **food chains** and **food webs.** A *food chain* is a hierarchical list of who snacks on who. For example, bugs are eaten by spiders, who are eaten by birds, who are eaten by cats. A *food web* provides more information than a food chain—it is not so cut and dry. Food webs recognize that, for example, bugs are eaten by more than only spiders. Food webs can be regarded as overlapping food chains that show all the various dietary relationships.

Biomes

The various geographic regions of the Earth that serve as hosts for ecosystems are known as **biomes.** Read through the following list so that you will be able to sprinkle some biome knowledge into an essay on ecological principles.

1. **Deserts**. The driest land biome of the group, **deserts** experience a wide range of temperature from day to night and exist on nearly every continent. Deserts that do not receive adequate rainfall will not have any vegetative life. However, plants such as cacti seem to have adjusted to desert life and have done quite nicely in this biome, given enough water. Much of the wildlife found in deserts is nocturnal and conserves energy and water during the heat of the day. This biome shows the greatest daily fluctuation in temperature due to the fact that water moderates temperature.
2. **Savanna**. **Savanna** grasslands, which contain a spattering of trees, are found throughout South America, Australia, and Africa. Savanna soil tends to be low in nutrients, while temperatures tend to run high. Many of the grazing species of this planet (herbivores) make savannas their home.
3. **Taiga**. This biome, characterized by lengthy cold and wet winters, is found in Canada and has gymnosperms as its prominent plant life. **Taigas** contain coniferous forests (pine and other needle-bearing trees).
4. **Temperate deciduous forests**. A biome that is found in regions that experience cold winters where plant life is dormant, alternating with warm summers that provide enough moisture to keep large trees alive. **Temperate deciduous forests** can be seen in the northeastern United States, much of Europe, and eastern Asia.
5. **Temperate grasslands**. **Temperate grasslands** are found in regions with cold winters. The soil of this biome is considered to be among the most fertile of all. This biome receives less water than tropical savannas.
6. **Tropical forests**. Found all over the planet in South America, Africa, Australia, and Asia, **tropical forests** come in many shapes and sizes. Near the equator, they can be rainforests, whereas in lowland areas that have dry seasons, they tend to be dry forests. Rainforests consist primarily of tall trees that form a thick cover, which blocks the light from reaching the floor of the forest (where there is little growth). Tropical rainforests are known for their rapid recycling of nutrients and contain the greatest diversity of species.
7. **Tundras**. The **tundra** biome experiences extremely cold winters during which the ground freezes completely. The upper layer of the ground is able to thaw during the summer months, but the land directly underneath, called the **permafrost,** remains frozen throughout the year. This keeps plants from forming deep roots in this soil and

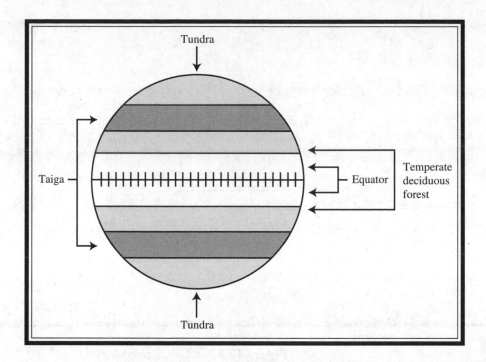

Figure 12.16   General distribution of biomes on the Earth's surface. (The other land biomes such as grassland and desert are interspersed in temperate and tropical regions with water as the limiting factor.)

dictates what type of plant life can survive. The plant life that tends to predominate is short shrubs or grasses that are able to withstand difficult conditions.

8. **Water biomes**. Both freshwater and marine **water biomes** occupy the majority of the surface of the Earth.

The general distribution of biomes on the Earth's surface is shown in Figure 12.16.

Biogeochemical Cycles

One last topic to briefly cover before we wave good-bye to ecology is that of **biogeochemical cycles.** These cycles represent the movement of elements, such as nitrogen and carbon, from organisms to the environment and back in a continuous cycle. Do not attempt to become a master of these cycles, but you should understand the basics.

Carbon cycle. Carbon is the building block of organic life. The **carbon cycle** begins when carbon is released to the atmosphere from volcanoes, aerobic respiration (CO_2), and the burning of fossil fuels (coal). Most of the carbon in the atmosphere is present in the form of CO_2. Plants contribute to the carbon cycle by taking in carbon and using it to perform photosynthetic reactions, and then incorporating it into their sugars. The carbon is ingested by animals, who send the carbon back to the atmosphere when they die.

Nitrogen cycle. Nitrogen is an element vital to plant growth. In the **nitrogen cycle** (Figure 12.17), plants have nitrogen to consume thanks to the existence of organisms that

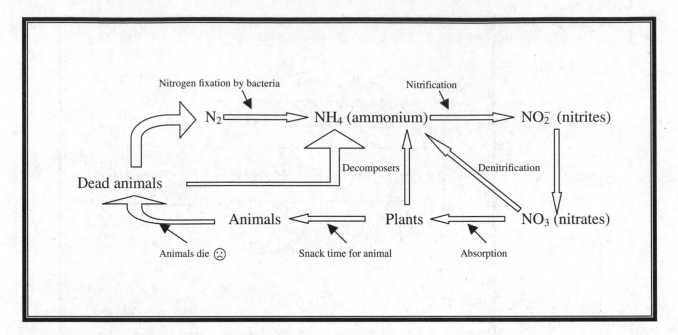

Figure 12.17 The nitrogen cycle.

perform the thankless task of **nitrogen fixation**—the conversion of N_2 to NH_3 (ammonia). The only source of nitrogen for animals is the plants they consume. When these organisms die, their remains become a source of nitrogen for the remaining members of the environment. Bacteria and fungi (decomposers) chomp at these organisms and break down any nitrogen remains. The NH_3 in the environment is converted by bacteria into NO_3 (nitrate), and this NO_3 is taken up by plants and then eventually by animals to complete the nitrogen cycle. **Denitrification** is the process by which bacteria themselves use nitrates and release N_2 as a product.

Water cycle. The Earth is covered in water. A considerable amount of this water evaporates each day and returns to the clouds. Eventually, this water is returned to the earth in the form of precipitation. This process is termed the **water cycle.**

Disruptions to Ecosystem

EVO-1

Evolution is characterized by change in the genetic makeup of a population over time and is supported by multiple lines of evidence.

SYI-2

Competition and cooperation are important aspects of biological systems.

In all ecosystems, competition and cooperation play important roles in the diversity and survival of the ecosystem. Changes to these interactions (genetic makeup change, abiotic factor change, human-caused change) could eventually lead to the evolution of the ecosystem.

An invasive species is an organism that is introduced to an area that is not native to the particular area and that leads to environmental harm to the area. While not all non-native species are invasive, invasive species are often able to outcompete native species for abiotic and biotic resources, leading to uncontrolled population growth and changes in the ecosystem. Invasive species can be introduced in many different ways, including accidently or intentionally. Either way, they negatively impact the native ecosystem.

Local and global ecosystems naturally change over time. Humans accelerate the change in many ways. These include introduction of invasive species, overpopulation, deforestation, pollution, and burning fossil fuels. These negative human impacts have caused climate change, soil erosion, and reduced air and water quality, leading to local and global ecosystem changes (Figure 12.18).

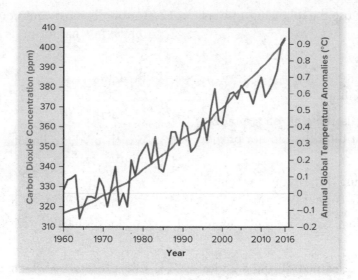

Figure 12.18 The greenhouse effect. The concentration of carbon dioxide in the atmosphere has increased steadily since the 1950s, as shown by the blue line. The red line shows the change in average global temperatures for the same period. The temperatures are recorded as anomalies relative to the mean temperature during a reference period (1951–1980). CO_2 concentration is measured as parts per million; that is, the number of CO_2 molecules compared to other molecules of gas in the atmosphere. (*Reproduced with permission from Raven P, Johnson G, Mason K, Losos J, Duncan T; Biology, 12th ed. New York: McGraw Hill; 2020*)

› Review Questions

1. When horses hear an unusual noise, they turn their ears toward the sound. This is an example of

    A. a fixed-action pattern.
    B. habituation.
    C. associative learning.
    D. imprinting.

2. Why do animal behaviorists have to account for a habituation period when undertaking an observational study?

    A. They have to make sure that the study animals do not imprint on them.
    B. They have to wait until their presence no longer affects the behavior of the animals.
    C. The animals need a period of time to learn to associate the observer with data collection.
    D. Before insight learning can be observed, the animals must practice.

3. Which of the following is an example of an agonistic behavior?

    A. A subordinate chimpanzee grooms a dominant chimpanzee.
    B. Two lionesses share a fresh kill.
    C. A female wolf regurgitates food for her nieces and nephews.

    D. A blackbird approaches and takes the feeding position of another blackbird, causing it to fly away.

4. In which of the following dyads do we expect *not* to see any altruistic behavior?

    A. Two sisters who are allies
    B. Two half-brothers
    C. Two individuals migrating in opposite directions
    D. Two group members who have frequent conflicts and reconciliations

5. Which of the following is not a requirement for reciprocal altruism to occur?

    A. Ability to recognize the other individual
    B. Long lifespan
    C. Opportunity for multiple interactions
    D. High coefficient of relatedness

6. A female tamarin monkey licks her wrists, rubs them together, and then rubs them against a nearby tree. What kind of communication is this probably an example of?

    A. Chemical
    B. Visual
    C. Auditory
    D. Territorial

For questions 7–10, please use the following answers:

    A. Habituation
    B. Imprinting
    C. Associative learning
    D. Operant conditioning

7. This type of learning is the lack of responsiveness to unimportant stimuli that do not provide appropriate feedback.

8. Trial-and-error learning important to animals displaying aposometric coloration.

9. Process by which animals associate one stimulus with another.

10. Innate behavior that is learned during a critical period in life.

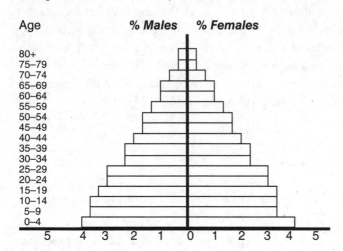

11. How would you describe the population depicted in the age structure graph shown here?

    A. Growing rapidly
    B. Growing slowly
    C. Not growing at all
    D. Experiencing slow negative growth

12. Carbon is most commonly present in the atmosphere in what form?

    A. CCl_4
    B. CO
    C. CO_2
    D. CH_2

13. Which of the following is a density-dependent limiting factor?

    A. Flood
    B. Drought
    C. Earthquake
    D. Famine

14. The process by which bacteria themselves use the nitrate of the environment, releasing N_2 as a product, is called

    A. nitrogen fixation.
    B. abiotic fixation.
    C. denitrification.
    D. chemosynthetic autotrophism.

For question 15, please use the curve below:

15. At what point on the graph does the decline in rabbit population act as a limiting factor to the survival of the foxes, leading to a decline in their population size?

    A. A
    B. B
    C. C
    D. D

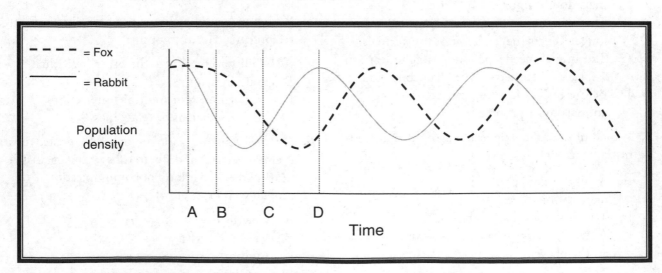

16. A collection of all the individuals of an area combined with the environment in which they exist is called a/an

A. population.
B. community.
C. ecosystem.
D. biosphere.

For questions 17–20, please use the following answer choices:

A. Aposematic coloration
B. Batesian mimicry
C. Müllerian mimicry
D. Cryptic coloration

17. A beetle that has the coloration of a yellow jacket is displaying which defense mechanism?

18. A moth whose body color matches that of the trees in which it lives is displaying which defense mechanism?

19. Two different lizard species, each possessing a particular chemical defense mechanism and sharing a similar body coloration, are displaying which defense mechanism?

20. A lizard with a chemical defense mechanism has a bright-colored body as a warning to predators that it is one tough customer is displaying which defense mechanism?

21. Which of the following is *not* a characteristic of a *K*-selected population?

A. Populations tend to be of a relatively constant size.
B. Offspring produced tend to require extensive postnatal care.

C. Primates are classified as *K*-selected organisms.
D. Offspring are produced in large quantities.

22. Which of the following would have the survivorship curve shown in the following diagram?

A. Humans
B. Lizards
C. Oysters
D. Fish

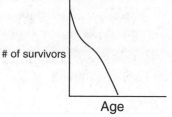

For questions 23–26, please use the following answer choices:

A. Desert
B. Taiga
C. Tundra
D. Tropical rain forest

23. This biome is known for having the most diverse variety of species.

24. This biome is the driest of the land biomes.

25. The predominate plant life of this biome is short shrubs or grasses.

26. This biome is known for its cold, lengthy, and snowy winters and the presence of coniferous forests.

› Answers and Explanations

1. A—This is a fixed-action pattern—an innate behavior that is a programmed response to a stimulus that appears to be carried out without any thought by the organisms involved.

2. B—If the scientist does not allow for a period of habituation, the behavioral observations will be inaccurate since the behavior of the animal will be altered by the presence of the scientist.

3. D—An agonistic behavior is a contest of intimidation and submission where the prize is a desired resource. In this case, the resource is the feeding position.

4. C—Altruistic behavior cannot be expected from two migrating individuals for a couple of reasons: (1) there is no reason for either of them to believe that they will see the other in the future, taking the "If I help them now, perhaps they will help me sometime in the future" element out of play; and (2) if they are migrating in different directions, it is reasonably likely that they are probably not related, which takes the "I'll help because it'll increase the chance that more of my genes get passed along" element out of play.

5. **D**—Reciprocal altruism need not occur between related individuals.

6. **A**

7. **A**

8. **D**

9. **C**

10. **B**

11. **A**—The population shown in this age structure chart is one that is growing rapidly because of the gradual increase in percentage of the population as the age approaches 0. This shows a population that has a high birth rate and a reasonable life expectancy.

12. **C**—CO_2 is the dominant form of carbon present in the atmosphere.

13. **D**—Density-dependent limiting factors show up as the population approaches and/or passes the carrying capacity. Examples of density-dependent limiting factors include availability of food resources, waste buildup, and density-induced diseases. The other three choices are examples of density-independent factors, which affect population size regardless of how large or small it may be.

14. **C**—*Denitrification* is defined as the process by which bacteria themselves use nitrates and release nitrogen gas as a product. Bacteria also perform the necessary task of nitrogen fixation, which takes atmospheric nitrogen and converts it to NH_3. They later take this NH_3 and convert it to nitrate, which plants require for photosynthetic success. (*Abiotic fixation* is a term that we made up because it sounded cool.) Chemiosynthetic autotrophs are the producers of the planet that produce energy through the movement of electrons in oxidation reactions.

15. **B**—At this point, the population of rabbits has declined to the point where the foxes are starting to feel the reduction in their food supply. The fox survival curve soon begins its decline, which leads to the revival of the rabbits.

16. **C**—An *ecosystem* consists of all the individuals in the community and the environment in which they exist. A *population* is a collection of individuals of the same species living in the same area. A *community* is a collection of all the different populations of the various species in a geographic area. A *biosphere* is the collection of all the life-containing areas of the planet.

17. **B**—An animal that is harmless copies the appearance of an animal that *is* dangerous as a defense mechanism to make predators think twice about attacking.

18. **D**—Cryptic coloration is the animal kingdom's version of army clothes. Their coloration matches that of their environment so they can blend in and hide from their predators.

19. **C**—Two species that are aposematically colored as an indicator of their chemical defense mechanism mimic each other's color scheme in an effort to increase the speed with which their predators learn to avoid them. This, of course, requires a predator that can learn based on experience.

20. **A**—This defense mechanism is warning coloration adopted by animals that possess a chemical defense mechanism. Ideally, predators will learn to avoid the species, helping the prey survive longer.

21. **D**—*K*-selected populations tend to be populations of a roughly constant size, with low reproductive rates and whose offspring require extensive postnatal care until they have sufficiently matured. *R*-selected populations tend to produce many offspring per birth.

22. **B**—Lizards follow a type II survivorship curve as illustrated in the diagram in review question 12. Humans (answer A) follow a type I curve, while oysters and fish (answers C and D) follow a type III survivorship curve.

23. **D**

24. **A**

25. **C**

26. **B**

› Rapid Review

Quickly review the following terms:

Behavioral ecology: study of interaction between animals and their environments.

Ethology: study of animal behavior.

Types of Animal Learning

- *Fixed-action pattern*: preprogrammed response to a stimulus (stickleback fish).
- *Habituation*: loss of responsiveness to unimportant stimuli or stimuli that provide no feedback.
- *Imprinting*: innate behavior learned during critical period early in life (baby ducks imprint to mama ducks).
- *Associative learning*: one stimulus is associated with another (classical conditioning—Pavlov).
- *Operant conditioning*: trial-and-error learning (aposometric predator training).
- *Insight learning*: ability to reason through a problem the first time through with no prior experience.
- *Observational learning*: learning by watching someone else do it first.

Types of Animal Movement

- *Kinesis*: change in the speed of movement in response to a stimulus. Organisms will move faster in bad environments and slower in good environments.
- *Migration*: cyclic movement of animals over long distances according to the time of year.
- *Taxis*: reflex movement toward or away from a stimulus.

Animal Behaviors

- *Agonistic behavior*: conflict behavior over access to a resource. Often a matter of which animal can mount the most threatening display and scare the other into submission.
- *Dominance hierarchies*: ranking of power among the members of a group; subject to change. Since members of the group know the order, less energy is wasted in conflicts over food and resources.
- *Territoriality*: defense of territory to keep others out.
- *Altruistic behavior*: action in which an organism helps another at its own expense.
- *Reciprocal altruism*: animals behave altruistically toward others who are *not* relatives, hoping that the favor will be returned sometime in the future.
- *Foraging*: feeding behavior of an individual. Animals have a search image that directs them to food.
- *Optimal foraging*: natural selection favors those who choose foraging strategies that maximize the differential between costs and benefits. If the effort involved in obtaining food outweighs the nutritive value of the food, forget about it.
- *Inclusive fitness*: the ability of individuals to pass their genes not only through the production of their own offspring, but also by providing aid to enable closely related individuals to produce offspring.
- *Coefficient of relatedness*: statistic that represents the average proportion of genes two individuals have in common. The higher the value, the more likely they are to altruistically aid one another.

> **Communication**
> - *Chemical*: communication through the use of chemical signals, such as pheromones.
> - *Visual*: communication through the use of visual cues, such as the tail feather displays of peacocks.
> - *Auditory*: communication through the use of sound, such as the chirping of frogs in the summer.
> - *Tactile*: communication through the use of touch, such as a handshake in humans.

The following terms are important in this chapter:

Population: collection of individuals of the same species living in the same geographic area.

Community: collection of populations of species in a geographic area.

Ecosystem: community + environment.

Biosphere: communities + ecosystems of planet.

Biotic components: living organisms of ecosystem.

Abiotic components: nonliving players in ecosystem.

Dispersion patterns: **clumped dispersion** (animals live in packs spaced from each other—cattle), **uniform distribution** (species are evenly spaced out across an area, e.g., birds on a wire), **random distribution** (species are randomly distributed across an area, e.g., trees in a forest).

Biotic potential: maximum growth rate for a population.

Carrying capacity: maximum number of individuals that a population can sustain in a given environment.

Limiting factors: factors that keep population size in check: **density-dependent** (food, waste, disease), **density-independent** (weather, natural disasters).

Population growth: **exponential growth** (J-shaped curve, unlimited growth), **logistic growth** (S-shaped curve, limited growth).

Life history strategies: **K-selected populations** (constant size, low reproductive rate, extensive postnatal care—humans); **R-selected populations** (rapid growth, J-curve style, little postnatal care, reproduce quickly, die quickly—bacteria).

Survivorship curves: show survival rates for different-aged members of a population:

- *Type I*: live long life, until age is reached where death rate increases rapidly—humans, large mammals.

- *Type II*: constant death rate across the age spectrum—lizards, hydra, small mammals.

- *Type III*: steep downward death rate for young individuals that flattens out at certain age—fish, oysters.

Forms of Species Interaction

- *Parasitism*: one organism benefits at another's expense (tapeworms and humans).
- *Commensalism*: one organism benefits while the other is unaffected (cattle egrets and cattle).
- *Mutualism*: both organisms reap benefits from the interaction (acacia trees and ants, lichen).
- *Competition*: both species are harmed by the interaction (**intraspecific** vs. **interspecific**).
- *Predation*: one species, the predator, hunts the other, the prey.

Defense Mechanisms

- *Cryptic coloration*: coloring scheme that allows organism to blend into colors of environment.
- *Deceptive markings*: patterns that cause an animal to appear larger or more dangerous than it really is.
- *Aposematic coloration*: warning coloration adopted by animals that possess a chemical defense mechanism.
- *Batesian mimicry*: animal that is harmless copies the appearance of an animal that is dangerous.
- *Müllerian mimicry*: two aposemetrically colored species have a similar coloration pattern.

Primary succession: occurs in area devoid of life that contains no soil; **pioneer species** come in, add nutrients, and are replaced by future species, which attract animals to the area, thus adding more nutrients; constant changing of guards until the **climax community** is reached and a steady-state equilibrium is achieved.

Secondary succession: occurs in area that once had stable life but was disturbed by major force (fire).

Biomes: The Special Facts

We recommend that you read the biome material in the chapter for more detail.

- *Desert*: driest land biome.
- *Taiga*: lengthy cold, wet winters; lots of conifers.
- *Temperate grasslands*: most fertile soil of all.
- *Tundra*: permafrost, cold winters, short shrubs.
- *Savanna*: grasslands, home to herbivores.
- *Deciduous forest*: cold winters/warm summers.
- *Tropical forest*: greatest diversity of species.
- *Water biomes*: freshwater and marine biomes of Earth.

Trophic levels: hierarchy of energy levels on a planet; energy level decreases from bottom to top; primary producers (bottom) → primary consumers (herbivores) → secondary consumers → tertiary consumers → decomposers.

CHAPTER 13

Laboratory Review

IN THIS CHAPTER

Summary: This chapter covers the 13 laboratory experiments that are included in the AP Biology curriculum.

Key Ideas

✪ Hands-on lab work and understanding the process of science are central parts of AP Biology. Translation—LEARN THESE WELL!

✪ Read the summaries found here and review the work that you did on the labs during the year.

✪ If you missed one of these labs in class, or just do not feel comfortable with the material even after reading this chapter, ask your teacher to go over the lab with you.

Introduction

In this chapter we take a look at each of the 13 lab experiments that are included in the AP Biology curriculum. We summarize the major objectives from each experiment and the major skills and conclusions that you should remember. This chapter is important, so do not just brush it aside if lab experiments are not your cup of tea. Experimental (data) analysis will be heavily emphasized on the exam, in both the multiple-choice and the essay sections. Of course, the questions will not be an exact duplication of the experiment, but they will test your understanding of the objectives and main ideas that are discussed in this chapter. So, only 13 experiments separate us and the end of the review material for this exam.

All of the investigations in this chapter have multiple parts, including the opportunity for you to go crazy and create your own investigation. We have no idea what kind of mad-scientist experiment you might design, so we will instead focus on the more straightforward portions of these labs, including a summary of what the key ideas are from each investigation.

Investigation 1: Artificial Selection

EVO
Evolution

This lab focuses on the role of *differential reproduction* in natural selection, meaning some organisms in a population reproduce more than others and leave more offspring. But instead of it being "natural" selection, it's "artificial" because *you* get to choose which organisms are allowed to reproduce!

Basic Setup

For natural selection to occur, first there needs to be variation in a population, right? Well, look closely at the Wisconsin Fast Plants that you'll be working with. Do you see any trait that you could easily measure (e.g., leaf color, hairiness, height)? Are there any variations in this particular trait? It should not be something that is a clear-cut yes or no, but rather a trait that exhibits a range. Now you get to make selection decisions! You will choose the top (or bottom) 10 percent of your plants with this trait, and those lucky few are the ones allowed to reproduce. You will transfer pollen between this pool of "winners" and, once the seeds develop, plant and grow your second generation of plants. Once again, you will measure your chosen trait in this second population.

Results

In this experiment you are essentially choosing which genes are passed to the next generation. By artificially selecting, say, only the purplest of the plants, you are ensuring that the next generation will have inherited those "purpley" genes. You will hopefully observe an increase (or decrease, depending on your investigation) of your chosen trait in the second population of plants. This is called *directional selection*. Considering that one of the requirements of this class is your ability to graph and analyze data, it would probably be an excellent idea for you to create a bar graph to compare the quantity of your trait between these two generations. Are the means significantly different?

Don't forget to keep this a controlled experiment! Did you measure the trait of your first-generation plants when they were nine days old? Remember to measure the second generation *at the same age, using the same method.*

Key Skills

- Graph your data.
- Explain how natural selection acts on phenotypes.
- Use data to show how a measurable trait is changing in your plant population.

Investigation 2: Mathematical Modeling: Hardy-Weinberg

EVO
Evolution

This investigation lets you build upon what you learned from Investigation 1: the idea of natural selection and how it changes a population. If you truly wanted to see if a population was evolving, you would track the frequency of alleles and how they change from generation to generation. To do so, you first need to determine what your population's alleles look like *right now*, before any funky evolutionary stuff happens. This information can then be used as a point of comparison to see if the allelic frequencies are indeed changing in your population. The Hardy-Weinberg equilibrium is used to describe a population that is in stasis, or not evolving. Your goal in this lab is to model how allele frequencies change in a generation of some imaginary population, and you will do this using a computer model.

Basic Setup

On the AP Biology exam, will you have to open up a spreadsheet file and correctly enter a formula? No. Will you have to understand how to use the Hardy-Weinberg equilibrium and how to correctly analyze the data obtained? You bet! The idea to understand is how the fitness of an allele affects its frequency in a population. For example, there are two alleles for a given gene: A and a. If a population is in Hardy-Weinberg equilibrium (i.e., not evolving), and the frequency of both alleles is 0.5 (meaning one half of the alleles in this population's gene pool is the dominant A form, whereas the other half is in the recessive a form), then it will remain that way for gazillions of generations. But how could you make that ratio change? That, my friend, is evolution, and that is the point of this lab. Using tools such as computer programs and spreadsheets, you can model how a hypothetical gene pool changes from generation to generation.

Results

Though the bulk of this lab was dedicated to creating your spreadsheet, the real investigation begins when you get to tweak your non-evolving population. The equations you have to know for this experiment are $p + q = 1$ and $p^2 + 2pq + q^2 = 1$. Chapter 11 lists the five conditions required for the existence of Hardy-Weinberg equilibrium:

1. No mutations
2. No gene flow
3. No genetic drift (large population size)
4. No natural selection (so that the traits are neutral; none gives an advantage or disadvantage)
5. Random mating

If any of these five conditions (Figure 13.1) does not hold true, then the population will experience microevolution, and the frequencies of the alleles will be subject to change.

Using your computer model, you can design an experiment to measure the effect of selection, heterozygote advantage, and genetic drift:

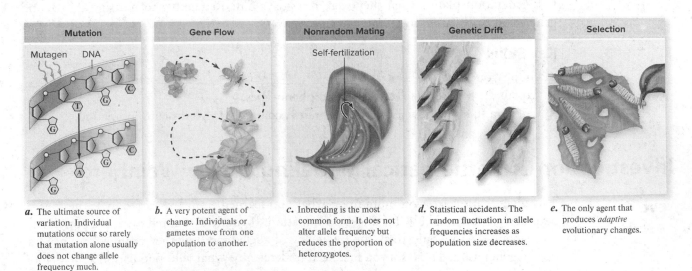

Mutation	Gene Flow	Nonrandom Mating	Genetic Drift	Selection
Mutagen DNA		Self-fertilization		
a. The ultimate source of variation. Individual mutations occur so rarely that mutation alone usually does not change allele frequency much.	b. A very potent agent of change. Individuals or gametes move from one population to another.	c. Inbreeding is the most common form. It does not alter allele frequency but reduces the proportion of heterozygotes.	d. Statistical accidents. The random fluctuation in allele frequencies increases as population size decreases.	e. The only agent that produces *adaptive* evolutionary changes.

Figure 13.1 **Five agents of evolutionary change.** (*Reproduced with permission from Raven P, Johnson G, Mason K, Losos J, Duncan T; Biology, 12th ed. New York: McGraw Hill; 2020*)

- *Selection.* Imagine that an individual homozygous recessive for a condition does not survive to reproduce. Because the aa offspring would not survive to reproduce, this will cause a shift in allele frequencies to include more A children and fewer a children.
- *Heterozygote advantage.* This is a situation in which being heterozygous for a condition provides some benefit (e.g., sickle cell allele in malarial regions). In this case, the allele will still decrease, but not as fast as in the selection example.
- *Genetic drift.* Imagine that 60 percent of your hypothetical population were killed in some horrific environmental disaster. This would leave the remaining 40 percent to continue breeding and passing on genes to the next generation. The random nature in which organisms are eliminated can lead to a shift in the allele frequency and the p and q will probably change depending on the genotype of those who are left behind.

There are two questions to ponder as you finish this experiment:

1. *Why is it so difficult to eliminate a recessive allele?* It is difficult because the allele remains in the population, hidden as part of the heterozygous condition, safe from selection, which can act only against genes that are expressed. So, although the q for a population may decline, it will not disappear completely because of the pq individuals.

2. *Why does heterozygote advantage protect recessive genes from being eliminated?* Those who are heterozygous for the condition are receiving some benefit. For example, those who have sickle trait are protected against malaria. This positive benefit for heterozygous individuals helps keep the recessive condition alive in the population.

Key Skills

- Use data from a changing population and analyze it using the Hardy-Weinberg equation.
- Explain how data from using this equation demonstrates genetic drift and the effects of selection.

Investigation 3: Comparing DNA Sequences to Understand Evolutionary Relationships with BLAST

EVO
Evolution

Say you found a brand-new fossilized creature buried in your backyard, and you want to find its closest living relative. Or maybe you identified a single gene that causes disease in hedgehogs and you want to know if that same gene is found in humans. This lab focuses on the use of BLAST (Basic Local Alignment Search Tool) as a tool to answer such questions. In addition, it incorporates the use of cladograms. A cladogram is a visual representation of the evolutionary relatedness of a species. In this investigation, you will use BLAST to generate the information needed to construct a cladogram.

Basic Setup

Given a genetic sequence, you are required to use the online BLAST software to compare it to other gene sequences already in their gigantic database. Results will show a ranking of the most closely related organisms (and what percentage of their base pairs actually match up). Just as in the previous lab, you won't have a computer available to you during the AP exam, so no, you won't have to actually know how to use BLAST while taking the test. You will, however, most likely need to analyze data obtained from a hypothetical BLAST query and, from those results, generate a cladogram depicting evolutionary relatedness.

Results

By determining the percent similarity of an unknown gene with those from other organisms, you should be able to then place your unknown creature within a cladogram to show evolutionary relatedness. For example, say you had a table showing the percent similarity of "gene X" in humans versus four other species (see Table 13.1).

Table 13.1   Percent similarity between gene X in humans and other species.

SPECIES	GENE PERCENT SIMILARITY COMPARED TO HUMANS
A	98%
B	91%
C	70%
D	52%

If you drew a cladogram showing the evolutionary relationship, it would look something like Figure 13.2.

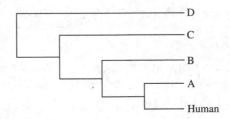

Figure 13.2   Cladogram for percent similarity between gene X in humans and other species. The closer two species reside on a clade, the closer they are genetically related.

Key Skills

- Explain the relationship between genetic sequences and evolutionary relatedness.
- Draw and/or analyze a cladogram that shows evolutionary relationships.

Investigation 4: Diffusion and Osmosis

ENE
Energetics

This investigation draws on information covered in Chapter 6, Cell Structure and Function. If you feel uncomfortable with this material, take a few moments to flip back to Chapter 6 and scan through the information about diffusion, osmosis, and cell transport. In summary, osmosis occurs from an area of high water potential to an area of low water potential. In a given solution, the higher the solute concentration, the lower that solution's water potential.

Part 1: Surface Area and Cell Size

Basic Setup for Part 1

Besides turning your fingers blue, this lab will demonstrate the relationship between surface area and volume and how this ratio affects diffusion rates in a cell. Your cell model is a block of agar that contains an indicator dye that changes color when the pH drops. You're given a chunk of this blue agar to carve into three different block sizes, each with differing surface area-to-volume ratios (SA:V). Each block is dropped into a solution, and as the liquid diffuses into the agar, the pH causes a change in agar color. This enables you to easily track the amount of time it takes for diffusion to be completed.

Results for Part 1

It's all about a large surface area-to-volume ratio. The block with the biggest SA:V ratio wins the race. For example, say you have three sizes of agar blocks:

block 1 = 1 cm × 1 cm × 1 cm
block 2 = 2 cm × 2 cm × 2 cm
block 3 = 1 cm × 1 cm × 8 cm

You should be able to calculate both the volume (cm^3) and the surface area (cm^2) for each of these blocks. (Remember: Formulas will be provided for you on the AP exam!)

BLOCK	VOLUME (cm^3)	SURFACE AREA (cm^2)	SA:V
1	1	6	6
2	8	24	3
3	8	34	4.25

Notice that even though blocks 2 and 3 have the same volume, their surface areas are different. This results in diffusion taking longer in block 2 than it does in block 3.

Key Concept

- A high SA:V ratio is important for any cell that relies on a high diffusion rate. If you were a tiny bacterium, your health and well-being would be dependent on quickly getting good stuff in (glucose for cellular respiration!) and bad stuff out (metabolic waste). The linings of your small intestine and lungs have many folds in order to create the highest surface area possible in the smallest amount of space and thereby facilitate diffusion of food monomers or oxygen molecules (Figure 13.3).

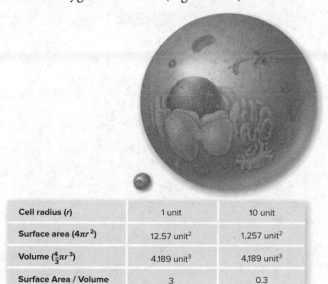

Cell radius (r)	1 unit	10 unit
Surface area ($4\pi r^2$)	12.57 unit^2	1,257 unit^2
Volume ($\frac{4}{3}\pi r^3$)	4.189 unit^3	4,189 unit^3
Surface Area / Volume	3	0.3

Figure 13.3 Surface area-to-volume ratio. As a cell gets larger, its volume increases at a faster rate than its surface area. If the cell radius increases by 10 times, the surface area increases by 100 times, but the volume increases by 1000 times. A cell's surface area must be large enough to meet the metabolic needs of its volume. (*Reproduced with permission from Raven P, Johnson G, Mason K, Losos J, Duncan T;* Biology, *12th ed. New York: McGraw Hill; 2020*)

Part 2: Modeling Diffusion and Osmosis

Basic Setup for Part 2

Now you get to create a model of a cell using dialysis tubing. Just like a real cell, the tubing is selectively permeable to water and some solutes. The point of this lab investigation is to use different solutions to model how water potential influences osmosis See Figure 13.4.

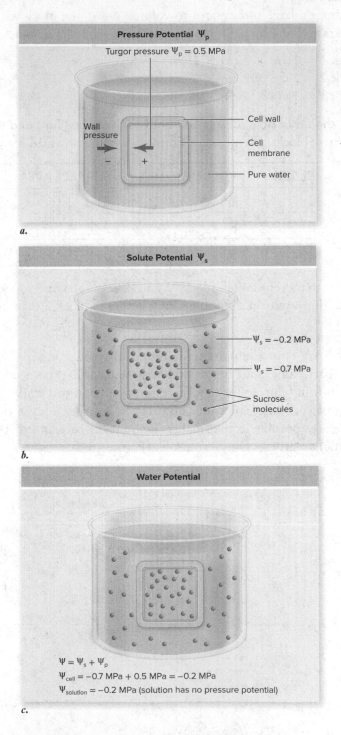

Figure 13.4   Determining water potential. *a.* Cell walls exert pressure in the opposite direction of cell turgor pressure. ***b.*** Using the given solute potentials, predict the direction of water movement based only on solute potential. ***c.*** Total water potential is the sum of ψs and ψp. Because the water potential inside the cell equals that of the solution, there is no net movement of water. (*Reproduced with permission from Raven P, Johnson G, Mason K, Losos J, Duncan T;* Biology, *12th ed. New York: McGraw Hill; 2020*)

Results for Part 2

Say you filled your dialysis bag with a 1 Molar (1 M) sucrose solution, weighed it, and placed it in a beaker of 1 M NaCl solution. After 30 minutes, you weigh the bag again and—voilà!—it got lighter! That means it lost some water, right? Can you use water potential to show why that makes sense? Recall that you can calculate the solute potential for a solution with this equation:

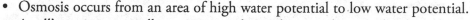

$$\Psi_S = iCRT, \text{ where } i = \text{ionization constant and } C = \text{molarity}$$

The molarities are equal for both of these solutions, so the ionization constant is the deciding factor. NaCl ionizes and sucrose does not! So for NaCl, i = 2, whereas for sucrose i = 1. Therefore, the NaCl solution has a higher solute potential; or, in other words, it is a hypertonic solution compared to your dialysis tubing "cell." Therefore, water will diffuse out of the bag into the surrounding NaCl solution.

Key Concepts

KEY IDEA

- Osmosis occurs from an area of high water potential to low water potential.
- A cell's environment allows you to make predictions about molecular movement through cell membranes.

Part 3: Observing Osmosis in Living Cells

Basic Setup for Part 3

Here you get to work with pretty, color-coded (unlabeled) sucrose solutions ranging from 0.0 M up to 1.0 M, and use potato cores to figure out the relative concentrations of these solutions. To take it one step further, you can then calculate percent change in weight of your potato cores and determine the water potential of the potato tissue. Remember that the bigger the difference in water potential between a cell and the solution, the bigger the movement of water (either into or out of the cells).

Results for Part 3

Once you calculate the potatoes' percent change in weight for each of the unknown solutions, you can arrange them from most negative to most positive. A supernegative percent change in weight indicates a significant loss of water; a highly hypertonic solution increases water loss from cells. The more negative the number, the higher the molarity of the solution! The same is true for superpositive percent change in weight. That means the potato cores gained a lot of water, which happens in a hypotonic solution. The greater the weight gain, the lower the molarity of the solution.

What if you wanted to determine the actual water potential (molarity) of the potato? It's easy, once you remember that if the water potential of the solution equals that of the cells, there is no net change in weight. If you graph your percent changes in weight, you can estimate the potato's water potential (see Figure 13.5).

The point where the line crosses the x-axis indicates the molarity when there would be no net change in weight. Therefore, 0.5 M is the approximate molarity (or, in this case, water potential) of your potato!

One final thought about your data: Although we often focus on quantitative (numerical) measurements in our labs, qualitative observations are still very important. When you removed your potato cores from the solution, did they feel different? Floppy and bendy? That would suggest that the cells lost water because they were in a hypertonic solution (the higher molarities). Was the potato core rigid, and would it snap if you bent it? That would suggest that it was in a hypotonic (low molarity) solution and water flowed into the cells, increasing their turgor pressure.

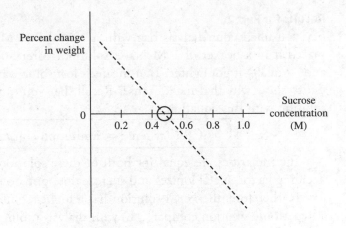

Figure 13.5   Potato core change in weight.

Key Concepts (for All Three Procedures)
- A high surface area-to-volume ratio increases diffusion rates.
- A cell that relies on diffusion would evolve to have a high SA:V ratio.
- Water diffuses from an area of high to low water potential.

Investigation 5: Photosynthesis

ENE
Energetics

Photosynthesis (Figure 13.6) is a complex (and possibly confusing) metabolic process through which autotrophs generate glucose by first converting the sun's light energy into the chemical form that all living cells use (ATP). If you wish to design a lab to track the rate of photosynthesis, how would you do it? Measure glucose production? Carbon dioxide use? Maybe focus on the light reaction's reduction of the electron carrier NAD^+ into its reduced form (NADH) as in the DPIP lab? Well, some of the best experiments are the simplest, so let's watch little pieces of a leaf float in water as oxygen is produced as a by-product of photosynthesis.

Basic Setup

This is a cool way to measure photosynthetic rates, based on the amount of oxygen produced. Little leaf disks are put in a large syringe with some slightly soapy water (this helps break surface tension). The little disks float on top of the water, which introduces the challenging part of the lab: getting them to sink. A vacuum must be created in the syringe to pull out the atmospheric gases from the spongy mesophyll layer in the leaf tissue. This takes a bit of trial and error, but once it is accomplished, the disks will slowly drift to the bottom of the syringe. The contents of the syringe are dumped into a cup filled with a sodium bicarbonate solution and put under light. As more photosynthesis occurs, more oxygen is produced:

$$6CO_2 + 6H_2O \rightarrow C_6H_{12}O_6 + 6O_2$$

If you look closely, you can see tiny bubbles forming on your leaf disks! Once enough oxygen is produced (and caught within the internal leaf space), the little disks will begin to rise to the top very slowly.

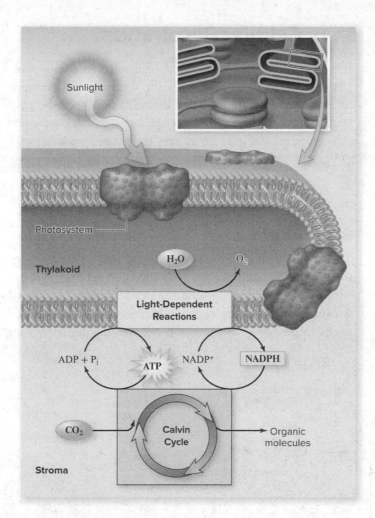

Figure 13.6   Overview of photosynthesis. Chlorophyll molecules are organized into photosystems. The light-dependent reactions begin when a chlorophyll molecule absorbs a photon of light. This light energy is used to generate ATP and NADPH. Electrons lost from chlorophyll are replaced by oxidizing water, producing O2 as a by-product. The ATP and NADPH are used to reduce CO2 via the Calvin cycle in the stroma, producing organic molecules. (*Reproduced with permission from Raven P, Johnson G, Mason K, Losos J, Duncan T;* Biology, *12th ed. New York: McGraw Hill; 2020*)

Here's a question: If your leaf pieces are photosynthesizing, where are they getting the necessary carbon dioxide? When sodium bicarbonate ionizes in water, it provides an alternative source of carbon dioxide for the plant.

Results

The investigative part of the lab allows you to explore variables that you think might influence photosynthesis in your leaf disks. Do the levels of CO_2 effect photosynthesis? How about amount of light? Regardless of your choice of variable, perform the same leaf disk analysis and compare the amount of time it takes for half of your disks to rise (ET_{50}, or estimated time it takes 50 percent of the disks to float) in both your control and experimental groups.

Key Concepts

- A lot of photosynthesis means a lot of oxygen production.
- Light increases the rate of photosynthesis.
- Carbon dioxide was provided by dissolved sodium bicarbonate.

Investigation 6: Cellular Respiration

ENE

Energetics

If you would like to see how different environmental conditions affect an organism's respiration rate, this is the lab for you! In this investigation you will use a respirometer (or microrespirometer) to track the respiration rate of seeds. Based on the equation for cellular respiration, $C_6H_{12}O_6 + 6O_2 \rightarrow 6CO_2 + 6H_2O$, how would you measure respiration rates?

There are, in fact, three ways to measure respiration:

1. *Oxygen consumption:* how much O_2 is actually consumed
2. *Carbon dioxide production:* how much CO_2 is actually produced
3. *Energy released during respiration:* how much energy is released

Basic Setup

This experiment examines germinating peas by measuring the volume of gas that surrounds the peas at certain intervals in an effort to determine the rate of respiration. Two gases contribute to the volume around the pea: O_2 and CO_2. How can we use the amount of oxygen consumed during respiration as our measuring point if CO_2 is present as well? Something needs to be done with the CO_2 released during respiration. Otherwise we would not get a

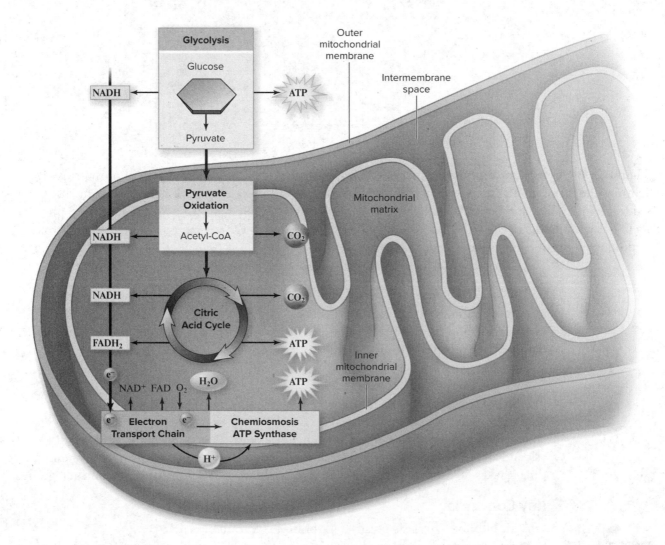

Figure 13.7 An overview of aerobic respiration. (*Reproduced with permission from Raven P, Johnson G, Mason K, Losos J, Duncan T; Biology, 12th ed. New York: McGraw Hill; 2020*)

true representation of how much the volume is changing as a result of oxygen consumption. The CO_2 would skew the numbers by making it appear as if less O_2 were being consumed.

The CO_2 problem can be handled by adding potassium hydroxide, which reacts with CO_2 to produce K_2CO_3. This reaction allows us to limit the number of variables that could be affecting the volume around our beloved peas to

1. Change in the volume of oxygen
2. Change in the temperature ($PV = nRT$)
3. Change in the pressure of the surrounding atmosphere

Aerobic respiration (Figure 13.7) requires and uses oxygen. So, one would expect the volume of oxygen around the pea to decline as respiration occurs. The reactions of interest for this experiment occur in a tubelike device known as a respirometer. To calculate the change in volume that occurs with these peas, one first has to measure the initial volume around the peas. A control group must then be set up that consists of peas that are not currently germinating and will have a rate of respiration lower than that of germinating seeds. This will give the experimenter a baseline with which to compare the respiration rate of the germinating seeds. Since temperature and pressure are also able to affect the volume around the peas, it is important to set up another control group that can calculate the change in volume that is due to temperature and pressure as opposed to respiration. Any changes in this control group should be subtracted from the changes found in the germinating seeds to determine how much of the volume change is actually due to oxygen consumption and respiration.

Just a side thought: Can you imagine how awkward it could have been if one of Mendel's lab partners had decided to run this experiment? I can see it now: Mendel walks into the lab and asks, "Has anyone seen my peas? After seven long years, I've nearly completed my research. Just need to tally up that last generation of peas. . . . Very exciting. . . . Hmm. . . . I thought my peas were sitting here on this desk by my respirometer."

Results

1. Germinating seeds consume *more* oxygen than do nongerminating seeds. This makes sense, because they have more reactions going on.
2. Seeds germinating at a lower temperature consume *less* oxygen than do seeds germinating at a higher temperature.
3. You can determine how much oxygen is consumed by watching how much water is drawn into the pipettes as the experiment proceeds. (Refer to your classroom lab manual if you are confused by the pipette portion of this lab.) This water is drawn in as a result of the drop in pressure caused by the consumption of oxygen during respiration.

Key Concepts

- A respirometer measures respiration rates by tracking the amount of oxygen being used in cellular respiration.
- Warm conditions usually speed up cellular respiration; cold slows it down.

Investigation 7: Cell Division: Mitosis and Meiosis

IST

Information Storage and Transmission

This experiment draws on information found in Chapter 8, Cell Communication and Cell Cycle, and Chapter 9, Heredity.

Part 1: Onion Roots Treated with a Mitosis-Inducing Chemical

Basic Setup for Part 1

Your goal is to see if there is a greater number of cells undergoing mitosis in root cells treated with lectin, a chemical that induces mitosis. Either you or your teacher will prepare slides of these root cells, and you will then count the number of cells either in interphase or in mitosis. Since you need a point of comparison, you will do similar counts with root cells that have not been treated with this chemical (the control).

Results for Part 1

So, how are you supposed to estimate how much time cells on a slide in front of you spend in either mitosis or interphase? Say, for example, that you record your findings and get the following breakdown: For your control, of 300 cells examined, 268 are in interphase and 32 cells are in one of the stages of mitosis (prophase, metaphase, anaphase, or telophase). This would mean that the cell spent 89.3 percent of its time in interphase. At any moment in time, 89.3 percent of the cells are in interphase. Here's how to get that number. Take the number of cells in interphase, 268, and divide that by the number of cells examined, 300. The result is 0.893. Move the decimal point two places to the right to get the percentage, 89.3 percent. By the same logic, these data also show that 10.7 percent are in mitosis. For comparison, let's say the chemically treated slide had 210 cells in interphase and 40 in mitosis (for a total of 250 cells examined).

Now, once you count your mitotic versus interphase cells for both treated and untreated roots, you need to use chi-square analysis to check if the difference is significant:

$$x^2 = \sum \frac{(o - e)^2}{e}$$

Do not panic! Even though that equation may seem intimidating, it's really not that bad. First, determine how many of your treated cells would be in mitosis *if the chemical didn't have any effect*. In other words, if 10.7 percent of your control cells were stuck in mitosis, you'd expect that same percentage in your treated group: (250 treated cells) × (0.107) = ~27 cells in mitosis. That leaves the remaining 223 cells in interphase (if you didn't expect that mitosis-inducing chemical to do its job). So now you use chi-square analysis to compare what you actually saw in your chemically treated cells (40 in mitosis and 210 in interphase) to see if there are, in fact, significantly more cells stuck in mitosis. In other words, your null hypothesis is that the treatment did not make a difference. If you find that the chi-square value is greater than the critical value, you reject this null hypothesis in favor of the experimental hypothesis (the chemical likely *did* make a difference). See Table 13.2.

As you can see, your chi-square value is 0.758 + 6.26 = 7.02. To determine your critical value, you must choose a p value (usually 0.05) and the degrees of freedom. The degrees of freedom (df) equals the number of groups minus one. In this lab, there are two groups, interphase and mitosis; therefore, df = 2 − 1, or 1. Based on the chi-square table (which will be provided for you on the AP exam), your degrees of freedom equals 3.38. Since your calculated chi-square value (7.02) was bigger than 3.38, you can reject the null hypothesis that said the treatment made *no* difference. The chemical did increase the number of cells in mitosis.

Table 13.2 Chi-Square table for investigation 7.

	# OBSERVED (o)	# EXPECTED (e)	(o − e)	(o − e)²	(o − e)²/e
Interphase cells	210	223	−13	169	0.758
Mitosis cells	40	27	13	169	6.26

Key Skill

• Analyze data using chi-square analysis. You can be sure that the AP exam will have at least one question asking you to do this. This lab is excellent practice for such a question.

Part 2: Meiosis and Crossover in *Sordaria*

Basic Setup and Results for Part 2

The title to this section makes *Sordaria* sound like some posh vacation spot in Europe. In reality it is a haploid ascomycete fungus. Anyway, the final portion of this experiment looks at the crossover that occurs during meiosis of this fungus and briefly discusses how recombination maps can be created using such data. Meiosis in *Sordaria* results in the formation of eight haploid **ascospores,** each of which can develop into a new haploid fungus. Crossover in *Sordaria* can be observed by making hybrids between wild-type and mutant strains. Wild-type *Sordaria* have black ascospores, and mutants have different colored ascospores (e.g., tan). When mycelia of these two strains come together and undergo meiosis, and if no crossover occurs, the asci that develop will contain four black and four tan ascospores in a 4:4 pattern. If crossover occurs, the ratio will change to either 2:2:2:2 or 2:4:2.

Chapter 9, Heredity, discusses gene maps constructed from crossover frequencies. You would construct the map here by first determining the percentage of asci that showed crossover. Referring to Figure 13.8, count the number of 2:2:2:2 and 2:4:2 asci and divide that sum into the total number of offspring. This result multiplied by 100 will give the crossover percentage. This number can then be used to determine how far away the gene is from the centromere. The crossover percentage is divided by 2 to determine this distance because a crossover involves only half the spores in each ascus.

Key Skill

• Explain how meiosis and crossing over leads to increased genetic diversity.

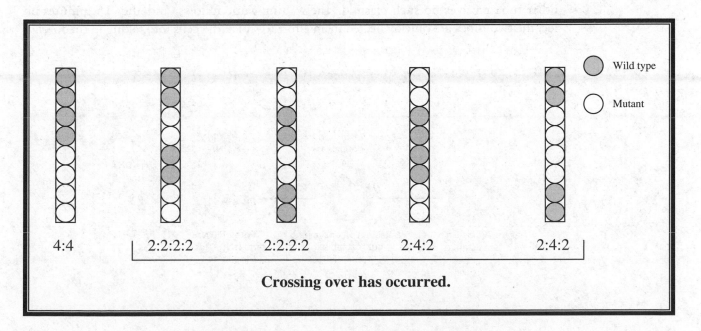

Figure 13.8 Crossover patterns in *Sordaria*.

Investigation 8: Biotechnology: Bacterial Transformation

IST

Information Storage and Transmission

This experiment deals with material from Chapter 10, Molecular Genetics. This is the kind of experiment that can make you feel like a biotech junkie. Here, you use plasmids to move DNA from one cell to another cell—**transformation.** You get to play with restriction enzymes, *E. coli* (*Escherichia coli*—eww), and gel electrophoresis.

Full understanding of this experiment requires a basic knowledge of

1. What vectors are and how they are made
2. What gel electrophoresis is and how it works
3. What a restriction enzyme is and why it is so important to the field of biotechnology

You will find all this information waiting for you in Chapter 10, Molecular Genetics. We are not going to cave in and explain to you now what those things are. That is something you should do on your own.

OK, we'll tell you now. . . . *Escherichia coli* (usually abbreviated *E. coli*) is a bacteria that is present in everyone's intestinal tract. It grows in the laboratory as well and contains extrachromosomal DNA circles called **plasmids.** This experiment deals with the process of *transformation*: the uptake of foreign DNA from the surrounding environment. This is made possible by the presence of proteins on the surface of cells that snag pieces of DNA from around the cell; these DNA pieces are from closely related species.

The goal of this experiment is to take a bacterial strain that has ampicillin resistance, and transfer the gene for this resistance to a strain that dies when exposed to ampicillin. After attempting to transform the bacteria, the experimenter can check to see if it was successful by growing the potentially transformed bacteria on a plate containing ampicillin. If it grows as if all is well, the transformation has succeeded. If nothing grows, something has gone wrong.

Basic Setup

A colony of *E. coli* is added to each of two test tubes. In one tube a solution is added that contains such a plasmid (see Figure 13.9) that carries the ampicillin-resistance gene; the other tube receives no such plasmid. The waiting game follows, and after 15 minutes on ice, the two tubes are quickly heated in an effort to shock the cells into taking in the foreign

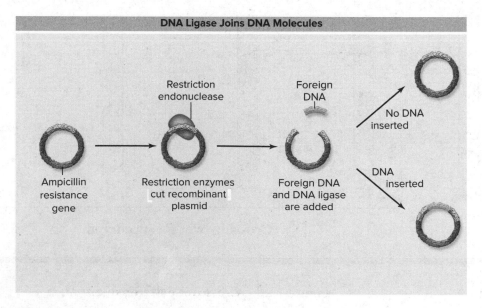

Figure 13.9 DNA Ligase at work. (*Reproduced with permission from Raven P, Johnson G, Mason K, Losos J, Duncan T; Biology, 12th ed. New York: McGraw Hill; 2020*)

DNA from the plasmid. The tubes are returned to ice and the colonies then spread out on an agar plate. They are sent to the incubator to sleep for the night and grow on the plate.

Results

Four plates are created: two with ampicillin and two without. The bacteria from both test tubes should happily grow on the plates without ampicillin. The ampicillin-coated plate that is spread with bacteria from the nontransformed tube is bare—there is, indeed, no growth. The ampicillin-coated plate that is spread with bacteria from the attempted-transformation tube shows growth . . . it may not be the greatest growth ever seen, but it is growth. This means that some of the *E. coli* originally susceptible to ampicillin have picked up the resistance gene from the surrounding plasmid and are transformed.

Important point to take from this part of the experiment: "How in the world does transformation work?" Restriction enzymes are added, which cut the DNA at a particular sequence and open the DNA so that it can be inserted into another such region in the main *E. coli* chromosome, which is treated with the *same* restriction enzyme. If the opened DNA from the plasmid happens to find and attach to DNA of the *E. coli* that is added to the tube, hallelujah, transformation occurs. In order for this transformation to succeed, the *E. coli* must be **competent,** which means ready to accept the foreign DNA from the environment. This competence is ensured by treating the cells with calcium or magnesium. Don't worry too much about how this competence business really works. Just know that bacteria must be competent for transformation to occur.

Key Concepts

- DNA works the same for all cells, both eukaryotic and prokaryotic.
- By adding a gene (changing an organism's genotype), you can change how it looks (its phenotype).
- Environmental factors can affect gene expression! If lactose is present, *E. coli*'s lac operon will turn on.

Investigation 9: Biotechnology: Restriction Enzyme Analysis of DNA

IST

Information Storage and Transmission

The three activities in this lab all work together to analyze and compare DNA sequences. For example, after cutting DNA samples from two different people with the same restriction enzymes, you would see that the RFLP patterns produced by gel electrophoresis are different. Do you have no idea what that last sentence even means? Read on . . .

Activity 1: Restriction Enzymes

Restriction enzymes are special because they are very picky about their job—they cut DNA at very specific sequences, called *restriction sites*. Many restriction sites are a 4- to 10-nucleotide base pair (bp) palindrome, a sequence that reads the same from either direction. If a restriction enzyme cuts exactly in the center of the restriction site, it will create blunt ends; if it cuts the backbone in two places, the pieces will have single-stranded overhanging "sticky" ends with exposed hydrogen bonds. If you cut two different DNA sequences with the same restriction enzyme, and if sticky ends are created, you could use ligase to then glue two sequences together, even if the DNA was not originally from the same organism! That is called a recombinant DNA molecule, and it is the basis of many biotechnological wonders. For example, if you isolate the human insulin gene with a restriction enzyme, and use that same enzyme to cut open a bacterial plasmid, you could glue the human gene into the plasmid. That's how therapeutic insulin is produced today (thank you, *E. coli*).

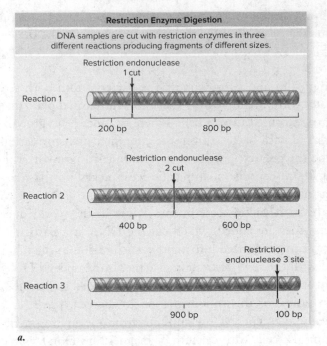

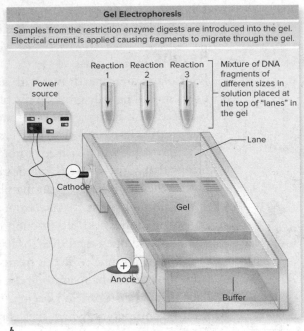

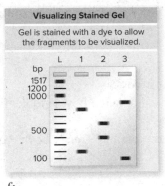

Figure 13.10   Gel electrophoresis separates DNA fragments based on size. a. Three restriction enzymes are used to cut DNA into specific pieces, depending on each enzyme's recognition sequence. **b.** The fragments are loaded into a gel (agarose or polyacrylamide), and an electrical current is applied. The DNA fragments migrate through the gel based on size, with larger fragments moving more slowly. **c.** This results in a pattern of fragments separated based on size, with the smaller fragments migrating farther than larger ones. A series of fragments of known sizes produces a ladder so that sizes of fragments of unkown size can be estimated (bp = base-pairs; L = ladder; 1, 2, 3 = fragments from piece of DNA cut with restriction endonucleases 1, 2, and 3, respectively). (*Reproduced with permission from Raven P, Johnson G, Mason K, Losos J, Duncan T; Biology, 12th ed. New York: McGraw Hill; 2020*)

Activity 2: DNA Mapping Using Restriction Enzymes

Say you wanted to identify somebody based on his or her DNA. You hear about it all the time, but how is it actually done? Using those restriction enzymes we just talked about, you can cut up a sample of DNA and look at the sizes of the distinct little pieces you have created (this requires gel electrophoresis—more on that in a bit). Everyone has a unique pattern of different lengths of DNA fragments. Restriction mapping is a way to create an organism's unique genetic "fingerprint." These unique DNA fragments are called restriction fragment length polymorphisms (RFLPs). But how do you arrange these little pieces in such a way that you can compare the DNA of two or more people? Once again, read on . . .

Activity 3: Gel Electrophoresis

Another important biotechnological tool is gel electrophoresis (Figure 13.10). Gel electrophoresis is a lab technique used to separate DNA on the basis of size. When there is an electric current running from one end of the gel to the other, the fragments of DNA dumped into the wells at the head of the gel will migrate to the other side, with the smaller pieces moving the fastest. The more voltage there is running through the gel, the *faster* the DNA will migrate. The longer the voltage is run through the gel, the *farther* the DNA will migrate. The more DNA cut by the same restriction enzymes you put into each well, the *thicker* the bands will be on the gel. If you reverse the flow of the current on the gel, the DNA will migrate in the opposite direction. The DNA just wants to go toward the positive charge . . . optimists, we suppose.

Important Facts About Electrophoresis
1. DNA migrates from negative to positive charges.
2. Smaller DNA travels faster than larger DNA.
3. The DNA migrates only when the current is running.
4. The more voltage that runs through the gel, the faster the DNA migrates.
5. The more time the current runs through the gel, the farther the DNA goes.

Key Concepts

- Understand how to use restriction enzymes and gel electrophoresis to create genetic profiles.
- The pattern made by RFLP using gel electrophoresis will look different for each individual.

Investigation 10: Energy Dynamics

IST: SYI

Systems Interactions

You will create a simple model of an ecosystem, with a single producer (plant) and a single consumer (caterpillars). Producers are so important because they capture the sun's energy and convert it into a form that can be used by us nonphotosynthetic organisms (consumers). The term **gross productivity** refers to the total amount of energy captured by producers. The **net productivity** is the amount of that energy that is actually stored by the plant (and thus is available for consumers to munch on).

As you may recall, the second law of thermodynamics says that energy transfer is never 100 percent efficient. This lab demonstrates that fact by tracking energy as it travels through a food chain. Specifically, how much of a plant's energy is actually used by the caterpillars who eat it? How much is applied to the caterpillar's growth, and how much is burned up in cellular respiration? Also, be aware that this lab has the best procedure direction of the entire year: you get to mass the frass (more on that in a bit).

Basic Setup

You will determine the total weight of all your caterpillars at the beginning of the investigation and then, after they feed for three days, weigh them again. Their change in mass was fueled by the plants they ate. The question is what percentage of that plant's energy was actually turned into caterpillar mass? If you determine the plant energy consumed by each larva, and also take into consideration the amount of their food that wasn't actually used (caterpillar poop, also called "frass"), then you're left with the amount of the producer's energy that was used for the caterpillar's metabolism. Furthermore, if you knew the amount of plant energy consumed by the larva, and subtracted from that both the energy lost in the poop and energy used for the caterpillar's increase in mass, what you're left with is the energy used in respiration. See Figure 13.11 for an example of this thought process.

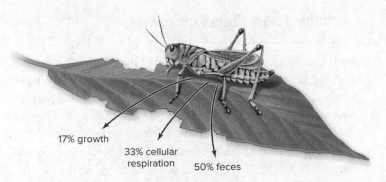

17% growth

33% cellular respiration

50% feces

Figure 13.11 **The fate of ingested chemical-bond energy:** Why all the energy ingested by a heterotroph is not available to the next trophic level. A heterotroph such as this herbivorous insect assimilates only a fraction of the chemical-bond energy it ingests. In this example, 50% is not assimilated and is eliminated in feces; this eliminated chemical-bond energy cannot be used by the primary carnivores. A third (33%) of the ingested energy is used to fuel cellular respiration and thus is converted to heat, which cannot be used by the primary carnivores. Only 17% of the ingested energy is converted into insect biomass through growth and can serve as food for the next trophic level, but not even that percentage is certain to be used in that way because some of the insects die before they are eaten. (*Reproduced with permission from Raven P, Johnson G, Mason K, Losos J, Duncan T; Biology, 12th ed. New York: McGraw Hill; 2020*)

Results

You should find that, no, energy transfer isn't perfect. All of that plant's energy was not, in fact, transferred to and used by the caterpillars.

Key Concepts

KEY IDEA

- Understand how this lab relates to the idea of how living organisms use free energy.
- Biomass is the mass of living tissue minus any water weight.

Investigation 11: Transpiration

IST: SYI

Systems Interactions

This experiment takes the concepts found in Chapter 6, Cell Structure and Function, and applies them to the material in Chapter 12, Ecology. You might want to review the material on plant anatomy and vascular tissue before you begin.

Here is just a quick reminder of how water moves from the soil to the leaves and branches of a plant (Figure 13.12). Three minor players in the transport of water are capillary action, osmosis, and root pressure. Water is drawn into the xylem (the water superhighway for the plant) by osmosis. The osmotic driving force is created by the absorption of minerals from the soil, increasing the solute concentration within the xylem. Once in the xylem, root pressure aids in pushing the water a small way up the superhighway. The main driving force for the movement of water in a plant from root to shoot is transpiration. When water evaporates from the plant, it causes an upward tug on the remaining water in the xylem, pulling it toward the shoots. The cohesive nature of water molecules contributes to this transpiration-induced driving force of water through the xylem of the plants. Water molecules like to stick together, and when one of their kind is pulled in a certain direction, the rest seem to follow.

This experiment examines various environmental factors that affect the rate of transpiration: air movement, humidity, light intensity, and temperature. The rate of transpiration increases with increased air movement, decreased humidity, increased light intensity, and increased temperature. It is not hard to remember that increased temperature leads to increased transpiration—think about how much more you sweat when it is hot. It also

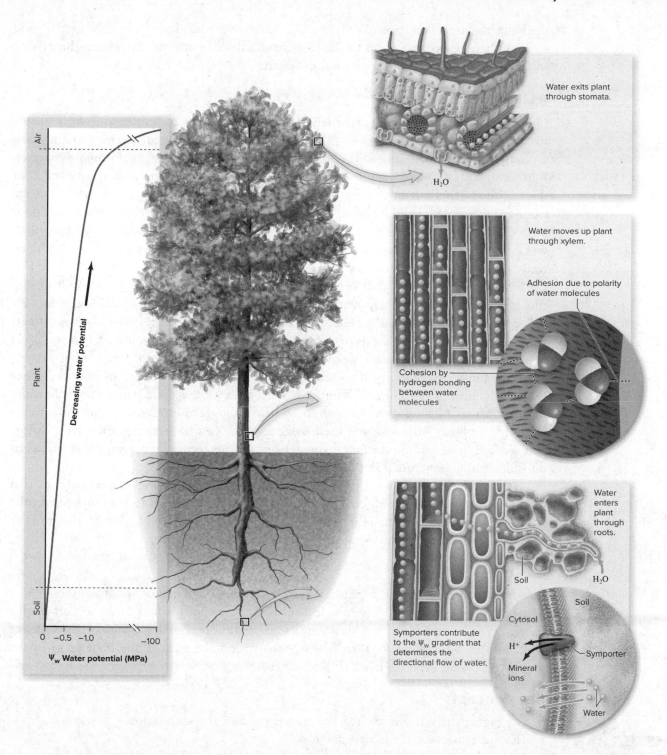

Water exits plant through stomata.

Water moves up plant through xylem.

Adhesion due to polarity of water molecules

Cohesion by hydrogen bonding between water molecules

Water enters plant through roots.

Soil H_2O

Soil

Cytosol

H^+

Symporter

Mineral ions

Symporters contribute to the Ψ_w gradient that determines the directional flow of water.

Water

Decreasing water potential

Air

Plant

Soil

0 -0.5 -1.0 -100

Ψ_w **Water potential (MPa)**

Figure 13.12   Water potential is higher in soil and roots than at the shoot tip. Water evaporating from the leaves through the stomata causes additional water to move upward in the xylem and also to enter the plant through the roots. Water potential drops substantially in the leaves due to transpiration. (*Reproduced with permission from Raven P, Johnson G, Mason K, Losos J, Duncan T;* Biology, *12th ed. New York: McGraw Hill; 2020*)

makes sense that decreased humidity would lead to an increase in the rate of transpiration. When it is less humid, there is less moisture in the air, and thus there is more of a driving force for water to leave the plant. Imagine that you are standing with a 40-watt bulb shining on your neck, and then a 100-watt bulb shining on your neck. The higher-wattage bulb will probably cause you to sweat more. The same thing with plants: the higher the intensity of the light, the more transpiration that occurs. Air movement is less obvious. If there is good airflow, then evaporated water on leaves is removed more quickly, increasing the driving force for more water to transpire from the plant.

Basic Setup

One easy and straightforward way to measure water loss is by measuring the entire plant's mass every day for about a week. This "whole plant" method requires you to tightly seal a plastic sandwich bag around the root ball so the only water loss is through the leaves. Furthermore, if the poor plant is even *thinking* about flowering, you need to ensure that it does not do so (pull off any flowers or buds). Once you understand this basic setup, the real fun begins: inquiry! Think of some variables that may affect transpiration from your poor plants. Sun? Wind? It's up to you. One plant will be your control, and every other plant will be assigned a single variable. Take the weights of your little guys as soon as they're all ready to go; this will be your *time zero* weights. Then measure the weights again 24 hours later, for as many days as your teacher indicates. Remember that if a leaf falls off during this experiment, it has to stay with the plant for subsequent weighings. When your data collection is over, you need to determine the best way to compare results between treatments. Just looking at the total change in weight doesn't really get you anywhere; it's hard to compare if the initial plant weights were different to begin with. Calculating percent change would help. But what if you need to determine the total surface area (cm^2) of your leaves? The idea of outlining each and every leaf on a piece of grid paper makes even the most dedicated AP Biology student weep, so here's a suggestion: Calculate the surface area for only one lucky little leaf, and then weigh it. Now you have a conversion ratio (SA/g) you can use to determine the (approximate) surface area for all the leaves. All you need to do is determine how much all those leaves weigh. Easy!

Another method of measuring water loss is by using a device called a potometer. This tracks transpiration from only part of a plant that has been inserted into a water-filled tube with a pipette stuck on the other end. As water evaporates from the leaves, the water is pulled down the pipette, allowing you to track changes in volume.

Results

Ideally, any treatment that increased water loss through either more photosynthesis (e.g., light) or more evaporation from the leaf surfaces (e.g., wind) would decrease your plant's weight. On the flip side, if you slow down transpiration by creating a humid environment (e.g., misting your plant) or slow down photosynthesis (e.g., stick the poor plant in the dark), you would expect water loss to be slowed.

Key Concepts

- The higher the leaf surface area, the greater the rate of transpiration.
- The more stomata, the more water loss.
- An increase in water potential of the environment would slow evaporation; a decrease in water potential would increase evaporation.

Investigation 12: Fruit Fly Behavior

IST: SYI

Systems Interactions

This experiment draws on information found in Chapter 12, Ecology. This experiment is basically an exercise in messing with fruit flies' heads. You get to stick them in a choice chamber and explore environmental factors that either attract or repel them.

Basic Setup

First, get to know your flies. For example, males have a darker abdomen, whereas females' abdomens are pale and rounder. Next, you get to create something called a choice chamber. In this experiment the chamber consists of two plastic bottles with their bottoms cut off and joined together with tape. Each end of the chamber will have one of the substances you decide to test. You can also use the chamber to investigate the flies' response to other variables, such as light or gravity. No matter what you're interested in, wrangle about 25 of those little creatures in there and let them get used to their new digs. Place a cotton ball with a few drops of water in the cap at one end (control) and a few drops of the substance you're testing at the other end. The flies will exhibit positive chemotaxis if they move toward the substance you're testing, negative chemotaxis if they move away from it.

Results

It is not important that you take away from this experiment that fruit flies enjoy the scent of one type of substance over another. What is important is that you recognize how to set up an experiment such as this one involving the choice chamber to measure chemotaxis in animals.

Key Skills

- Design a controlled experiment to determine environmental factors that either attract or repel your fruit flies.
- Analyze your data to identify the effect of environmental factors on your flies' behavior.

Investigation 13: Enzyme Activity

IST: SYI

Systems Interactions

This experiment draws on information from Chapter 5, Chemistry of Life. The experiment is designed to practice the calculation of the rate of enzyme-catalyzed reactions through the measurement of the products produced. In this particular experiment, the enzyme **peroxidase** is used to convert hydrogen peroxide to water and oxygen, and the products are measured to assist in the determination of the rate of reaction. If you do not feel comfortable with your knowledge of enzyme-substrate interactions, refer to Chapter 7, Cellular Energetics, before continuing this section.

The Nitty-Gritty About Experiment 2

The reaction of interest in this experiment is as follows:

$$2H_2O_2 \rightarrow 2H_2O + O_2$$

This reaction does indeed occur without the assistance of peroxidase, but it occurs at a slow rate. When our friend peroxidase is added to the mix, the reaction occurs at a much faster clip. Take a look at the enzymatic activity curve in Figure 13.13. Notice the constant rate of reaction in the first six minutes of the experiment.

However, after the sixth minute, the rate slows, as if the enzyme has become tired. This is because as the reaction proceeds, the number of substrate molecules remaining declines, which means that fewer enzyme-substrate interactions can occur. When calculating the **rate of reaction,** it is the constant linear portion of the curve that matters. That is the accepted rate value for the enzyme. Do not attempt to factor in the slowing portion of the curve.

Basic Setup

In this particular experiment, turnip peroxidase is added to a beaker that holds H_2O_2 and is allowed to react for a certain period of time. After the reaction stops, the amount of O_2 produced is measured using the color indicator guaiacol. Guaiacol readily grabs and binds

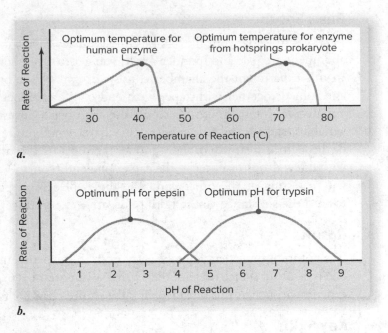

a.

b.

Figure 13.13 Enzyme-activity curve. (*Reproduced with permission from Raven P, Johnson G, Mason K, Losos J, Duncan T; Biology,* 12th ed. *New York: McGraw Hill; 2020*)

to oxygen, forming tetraguaiacol, a brown chemical. The greater the amount of oxygen produced, the darker brown your solution becomes. The relative amount of oxygen is determined by comparing the color of the tube to a turnip peroxidase color chart (a previously made series of dilutions of the oxygen-guaiacol reaction). Once you're comfortable with the experimental setup, you will investigate at what pH peroxidase works its best.

Results

You'll have six test tubes, each with a different pH buffer. Once the reaction has proceeded long enough to produce a nice color spectrum among all the different pH solutions, record the color for each tube. Once you use your lab manual's turnip peroxidase color chart to help you quantify the relative amounts of oxygen produced, you can graph your data as color intensity versus pH. Peroxidase is found in many different forms with optimum pHs ranging from 4 to 11 depending on the source. Turnip peroxidase, for example, tends to work best at pH 5.

Key Concepts

- The reaction rate can be affected by four major factors: pH, temperature, substrate concentration, and enzyme concentration.
- The rate of reaction can be found by measuring either the appearance of product or the disappearance of reactant. Either measure can provide insight into the effectiveness of an enzyme's presence.
- When calculating the rate of reaction, remember that the rate is actually the portion of the graph with a constant slope.
- To determine the ideal pH at which an enzyme functions, run the enzyme reaction at a series of different pH values and measure the various reaction rates.

› Review Questions

1. If a dialysis bag with a solute concentration of 0.6 M is placed into a beaker with a solute concentration of 0.4 M, in which direction will water flow?

   A. Water will flow from the dialysis bag to the beaker.
   B. Water will flow from the beaker into the dialysis bag.
   C. Water will first flow out of the bag, and then back into the bag.
   D. The solution is already in equilibrium, and water will not move at all.

2. What is the rate of reaction for the enzyme–substrate interaction shown in the graph below?

   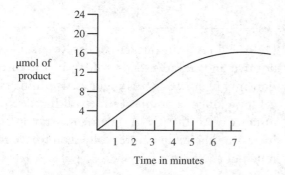

   A. 6 μmol/min (micromoles per minute)
   B. 5 μmol/min
   C. 4 μmol/min
   D. 3 μmol/min

3. In an experiment involving *Sordaria,* an ascomycete fungus, it was found that of 450 offspring produced, 58 yielded a 2:2:2:2 ratio and 32 a 2:4:2 ratio. Approximately how far apart is the gene from the centromere?

   A. 10.0 map units
   B. 15.0 map units
   C. 20.0 map units
   D. 25.0 map units

4. A plant would show the highest rate of transpiration under which of the following conditions?

   A. High humidity
   B. Low temperature
   C. High light intensity
   D. Low air movement

5. Which of the following will result in a quicker rate of DNA migration on an electrophoresis gel?

   A. Increase in temperature of the gel
   B. Increase in amount of DNA added to the well
   C. Reversal of charge of gel, switching positive and negative sides
   D. Increase in current flowing through the gel

6. A lab experiment is set up in which the participants are heterozygous individuals (Aa). After the F_1 generation is produced, 40 percent of the participants are randomly removed from the experiment and the remaining 60 percent are left to continue breeding. This experiment would be used to show what phenomenon?

   A. Natural selection
   B. Genetic drift
   C. Gene flow
   D. Mutation

7. You are studying a population of pea plants with flower colors ranging from white to dark pink. You selected only those plants with the darkest pink flowers to use in cross-pollination. Once you plant the seeds and grow your new generation of pea plants, what would you expect to see?

   A. The relative numbers of flower colors would remain unchanged.
   B. You would see disruptive selection.
   C. Your results would show directional selection.
   D. The relative numbers of white flowers would increase.

8. Which of the following would indicate you successfully transformed your *E. coli* culture with the plasmid containing the gene for ampicillin resistance?

   A. The ampicillin-containing agar plates would show growth from your control culture (*E. coli* without the plasmid), but not your transformed culture.
   B. The ampicillin-containing agar plates would show growth from your transformed culture, but not the control.
   C. The transformed culture would not grow on the agar-only plates.
   D. Both the transformed *E. coli* and the untransformed *E. coli* would grow on the plain agar plates.

› Answers and Explanations

1. **B**—The water will flow into the dialysis bag because the solute concentration in the bag is higher than that of the beaker. This creates an osmotic driving force that moves water into the bag in an effort to equalize the discrepancy in solute concentrations.

2. **D**—The rate of reaction can be approximated by calculating the slope of the straight portion of the graph. In this case it is 15 μmol of product produced in 5 minutes for an approximate rate of 3 μmoles/min.

3. **A**—The distance between the gene and the centromere in *Sordaria* is determined by adding up the number of crossovers that occur and dividing that by the number of offspring produced. This quotient should be multiplied by 100, and that product represents the percent of the offspring that experienced crossover. This percentage should be divided by 2 to obtain the distance from the centromere to the gene of interest.

4. **C**—The factors that increase the rate of transpiration are high light intensity, high temperature, low humidity, and high airflow.

5. **D**—The more current you put through the gel, the faster the DNA will migrate. Adding more

DNA will result in thicker bands. Reversing the positive and negative ends will swap the direction in which the DNA migrates. Running the gel for a longer amount of time will increase the distance that the DNA fragments travel, and increasing the temperature really won't have too much of an effect.

6. **B**—This is an example of genetic drift, in which a random chunk of the population is eliminated resulting in a potential change in the frequencies of the alleles being studied.

7. **C**—If you allow only the plants with the dark-pink flower genes to reproduce, those are the genes that will be passed on to the next generation. This will shift the average flower color towards the darker end of the spectrum, an example of directional selection.

8. **B**—By successfully transforming your *E. coli*, you are giving it the gene that enables it to survive in the presence of ampicillin (something the bacteria are unable to do otherwise). Therefore, you have successfully transformed your culture if it grows on ampicillin-containing agar, but the control culture without the plasmid dies.

› Rapid Review

Investigation 1: Artificial Selection

- To demonstrate evolution in a plant population, choose which traits are selected for and cross-pollinate only between those selected plants. Once the offspring (seeds) are planted and grown, check this trait to see if it is more prevalent in the new population.

- This is an example of directional selection, when members of a population at one end of a spectrum are selected for, whereas the trait at the other end of the spectrum becomes rarer.

Investigation 2: Mathematical Modeling: Hardy-Weinberg

- The Hardy-Weinberg equation is used to check the frequencies of alleles in a population that is not evolving. This "snapshot" of the population is used as a point of comparison, to see if evolution does occur (and changes the allelic frequencies).

- For a given gene, there is the p allele and the q allele. Therefore, $p + q = 1$.

- For that same gene, organisms can be homozygous dominant (pp), homozygous recessive (qq), or heterozygous (pq or qp). Therefore, $p^2 + 2pq + q^2 = 1$.

- By altering any of the five conditions required for a non-evolving Hardy-Weinberg population, you can cause a change in your population's gene pool.

Investigation 3: Comparing DNA Sequences to Understand Evolutionary Relationships with BLAST

- BLAST is a computer program used to compare specific genes from different organisms.

- The more similar the nucleotide base sequence between two genes, the closer the evolutionary relationship.

- A cladogram is a visual representation of the evolutionary relatedness of a species.

Investigation 4: Diffusion and Osmosis

- Water flows from **hypotonic** (low solute) to **hypertonic** (high solute).

- To measure diffusion and osmosis, take dialysis bags containing solutes of varying concentrations, place them into beakers containing solutions of various concentrations, and record the direction of flow during each experiment.

Investigation 5: Photosynthesis

- To experimentally determine the photosynthetic rate of various plants in various environments, first remove the air from leaf disk samples and add the samples to water containing sodium bicarbonate (a source of carbon dioxide). They will sink to the bottom of the cup.

- As the leaf tissue photosynthesizes, oxygen is released, causing the disks to rise to the surface. Expose different plant samples to different environmental conditions, measure how much photosynthesis occurs (ET_{50}), and then compare.

Investigation 6: Cell Respiration

- To experimentally determine the rate of respiration in peas, use a respirometer to calculate the change in volume that occurs around the peas. Set up (1) a control group of nongerminating peas that will have a lower baseline respiration rate, (2) a control group that measures the change in oxygen due to pressure and temperature changes, and (3) an experimental group that contains the group whose respiration rate you want to measure.

Investigation 7: Cell Division: Mitosis and Meiosis

- To determine experimentally the percentage of cells in a particular stage of the cell cycle, examine an onion root slide and count the number of cells per stage. Divide the number in each stage by the total number of cells to determine the relative percentages.

- To determine how far a gene for an ascomycete fungus is from its centromere, cross a wild-type strain with a mutant and examine the patterns among the ascospores. A ratio of 4:4 means no crossover occurred, whereas ratios of 2:2:2:2 or 2:4:2 indicate crossing over did occur. Total number of crossover divided by total number of offspring equals the percent crossover. Divide this by 2 to get the distance from the centromere.

Investigation 8: Biotechnology: Bacterial Transformation

- To run a transformation, add ampicillin-sensitive bacteria to two tubes, and to only one of the two, add a plasmid containing both the gene you would like to transform and the gene for ampicillin resistance. The other tube is the control. Ice the two tubes for 15 minutes, then quickly heat-shock the cells into picking up foreign DNA. Ice the tubes again, spread the bacteria out on ampicillin-coated plates, and incubate overnight. If transformation occurs, your bacteria will grow on the ampicillin plate.

Investigation 9: Biotechnology: Restriction Enzyme Analysis of DNA

- Gel electrophoresis can be used in court to determine if an individual committed a crime or if an individual is the parent of a particular child. Each person has a particular DNA fingerprint. When that individual's DNA is cut with restriction enzymes and run on an electrophoresis gel, it will show a unique pattern that only that person has. By matching a person's DNA fingerprint with that of the child of interest or the evidence from the crime scene, proper identifications can be made.

Investigation 10: Energy Dynamics

- A simple model system can be used to track how much energy is transferred from a single producer (plant) to a single consumer (caterpillars).

- By weighing the amount of plant eaten by the caterpillars (and the amount of the plant excreted), it is possible to calculate the percent of the plant's energy that was either incorporated into the caterpillar's body or used in cellular respiration.

- These are methods for estimating the efficiency of transfer of energy from producer to consumer.

Investigation 11: Transpiration

- To design an experiment to test the effects of various environmental factors on the rate of transpiration, measure the amount of water that evaporates from the surface of plants over a certain amount of time under normal conditions. You can do this using the whole-plant method or by using a piece of equipment known as a potometer, a device that measures water loss by plants. Compare the normal rate with the rates obtained when the temperature, humidity, airflow, or light intensity is altered. If you run an experiment of this nature, it is important to measure the surface area of the leaves involved because larger surface areas can transpire more water more quickly.

Investigation 12: Fruit Fly Behavior

- To study kinesis of an insect such as a fruit fly, create a contraption known as a choice chamber, which is designed to study which of two substances an organism prefers. For example, one-half of the choice chamber may contain banana extract, the other distilled water. Place the organism of interest into the choice chamber and record how many of that organism are on each side of the chamber every 30 seconds. This procedure can also be performed for a choice chamber that has differing temperatures, humidities, light intensities, salinities, and other parameters.

Investigation 13: Enzyme Activity

- Enzyme reaction rate is affected by pH, temperature, substrate concentration, and enzyme concentration.

- To test the rate of reactivity of an enzyme and the difference it makes compared to the speed of the normal reaction, run the reaction without an enzyme, then run it with your enzyme, and compare.

- To determine the ideal pH (or temperature) for an enzyme, run the reaction at varying pH values (or temperatures) and compare.

Build Your Test-Taking Confidence

AP Biology Practice Exam 1
AP Biology Practice Exam 2

Answer Sheet for AP Biology Practice Exam 1

MULTIPLE-CHOICE QUESTIONS

1 (A) (B) (C) (D)	21 (A) (B) (C) (D)	41 (A) (B) (C) (D)
2 (A) (B) (C) (D)	22 (A) (B) (C) (D)	42 (A) (B) (C) (D)
3 (A) (B) (C) (D)	23 (A) (B) (C) (D)	43 (A) (B) (C) (D)
4 (A) (B) (C) (D)	24 (A) (B) (C) (D)	44 (A) (B) (C) (D)
5 (A) (B) (C) (D)	25 (A) (B) (C) (D)	45 (A) (B) (C) (D)
6 (A) (B) (C) (D)	26 (A) (B) (C) (D)	46 (A) (B) (C) (D)
7 (A) (B) (C) (D)	27 (A) (B) (C) (D)	47 (A) (B) (C) (D)
8 (A) (B) (C) (D)	28 (A) (B) (C) (D)	48 (A) (B) (C) (D)
9 (A) (B) (C) (D)	29 (A) (B) (C) (D)	49 (A) (B) (C) (D)
10 (A) (B) (C) (D)	30 (A) (B) (C) (D)	50 (A) (B) (C) (D)
11 (A) (B) (C) (D)	31 (A) (B) (C) (D)	51 (A) (B) (C) (D)
12 (A) (B) (C) (D)	32 (A) (B) (C) (D)	52 (A) (B) (C) (D)
13 (A) (B) (C) (D)	33 (A) (B) (C) (D)	53 (A) (B) (C) (D)
14 (A) (B) (C) (D)	34 (A) (B) (C) (D)	54 (A) (B) (C) (D)
15 (A) (B) (C) (D)	35 (A) (B) (C) (D)	55 (A) (B) (C) (D)
16 (A) (B) (C) (D)	36 (A) (B) (C) (D)	56 (A) (B) (C) (D)
17 (A) (B) (C) (D)	37 (A) (B) (C) (D)	57 (A) (B) (C) (D)
18 (A) (B) (C) (D)	38 (A) (B) (C) (D)	58 (A) (B) (C) (D)
19 (A) (B) (C) (D)	39 (A) (B) (C) (D)	59 (A) (B) (C) (D)
20 (A) (B) (C) (D)	40 (A) (B) (C) (D)	60 (A) (B) (C) (D)

AP Biology Practice Exam 1: Section I

MULTIPLE-CHOICE QUESTIONS

Time—1 hour and 30 minutes

For the multiple-choice questions that follow, select the best answer
and fill in the appropriate letter on the answer sheet.

1. Which of the following characteristics would allow you to distinguish a prokaryotic cell from an animal cell?

   A. Ribosomes
   B. Cell membrane
   C. Chloroplasts
   D. Cell wall

2. Which of the following is the source of oxygen produced during photosynthesis?

   A. H_2O
   B. H_2O_2
   C. CO_2
   D. CO

3. An organism exposed to wild temperature fluctuations shows very little, if any, change in its metabolic rate. This organism is most probably a(n)

   A. ectotherm.
   B. endotherm.
   C. thermophyle.
   D. ascospore.

4. Which of the following is a frameshift mutation?

   A. CAT HAS HIS → CAT HAS HIT
   B. CAT HAS HIS → CAT HSH ISA
   C. CAT HAS HIS → CAT HIS HAT
   D. CAT HAS HIS → CAT WAS HIT

5. A researcher conducts a survey of a biome and finds 35 percent more species than she has found in any other biome. Which biome is she most likely to be in?

   A. Tundra
   B. Tiaga
   C. Tropical rainforest
   D. Temperate deciduous forest

6. On the basis of the following crossover frequencies, determine the relative location of these four genes:

m & n	→	15%
p & f	→	20%
n & f	→	30%
m & f	→	45%
n & p	→	10%

   A. f   p   m   n

   B. m   n   f   p

   C. m   n   p   f

   D. n   m   p   f

7. A man contracts the same flu strain for the second time in a single winter season. The second time he experiences fewer symptoms and recovers more quickly. Which cells are responsible for this rapid recovery?

   A. Helper T cells
   B. Cytotoxic T cells
   C. Memory cells
   D. Plasma cells

8. Which of the following are traits that are affected by more than one gene?

   A. Heterozygous traits
   B. Pleiotropic traits
   C. Polygenic traits
   D. Blended alleles

9. A lizard lacking a chemical defense mechanism that is colored in the same way as a lizard that has a defense mechanism is displaying

A. aposometric coloration.
B. cryptic coloration.
C. Batesian mimicry.
D. Müllerian mimicry.

10. Crossover would most likely occur in which situation?

A. Two genes (1 and 2) are located right next to each other on chromosome A.
B. Gene 1 is located on chromosome A, and gene 2 is on chromosome B.
C. Genes 1 and 2 are located near each other on the X chromosome.
D. Gene 1 is located on chromosome A; gene 2 is located far away, but on the same chromosome.

11. Imagine an organism whose $2n = 96$. Meiosis would leave this organism's cells with how many chromosomes?

A. 192
B. 96
C. 48
D. 24

12. A student conducts an experiment to test the efficiency of a certain enzyme. Which of the following protocols would probably not result in a change in the enzyme's efficiency?

A. Bringing the temperature of the experimental setup from 20°C to 50°C
B. Adding an acidic solution to the setup
C. Adding substrate but not enzyme
D. Placing the substrate and enzyme in a container with double the capacity

13. You observe a species that gives birth to only one offspring at a time and has a relatively long lifespan for its body size. Which of the following is probably *also* true of this organism?

A. It lives in a newly colonized habitat.
B. It is an aquatic organism.
C. It requires relatively high parental care of offspring.
D. The age at which the offspring themselves can give birth is relatively young.

14. In a certain species of plant, the allele to produce green melons (G) is dominant over the allele to produce yellow melons (g). A student performed a cross between a plant that produced green melons and a plant that produced yellow melons. When the student observed the next generation, the 94 seeds that were produced from the cross matured into 53 plants with green melons and 41 plants with yellow melons. Calculate the chi-squared value for the null hypothesis that the green-melon parent was heterozygous for the melon-color gene.

A. 0.76
B. 1.53
C. 0.50
D. 1.26

15. In a certain population of squirrels that is in Hardy-Weinberg equilibrium, black color is a recessive phenotype present in 9 percent of the squirrels, and 91 percent are gray. What percentage of the population is homozygous dominant for this trait?

A. 21 percent
B. 30 percent
C. 49 percent
D. 70 percent

16. Refer to question 15 for details on the squirrel population. Which of the following conditions is required to keep this population in Hardy-Weinberg equilibrium?

A. Random mating
B. Genetic drift
C. Mutation
D. Gene flow

17. A reaction that includes energy as one of its reactants is called a(n)

A. exergonic reaction.
B. hydrolysis reaction.
C. endergonic reaction.
D. redox reaction.

18. To which of the following labeled trophic levels would an herbivore most likely be assigned?

A. A
B. B
C. C
D. D

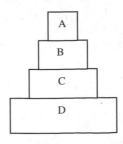

19. A population undergoes a shift in which those who are really tall and those who are really short decrease in relative frequency compared to those of medium size, due to a change in the availability of resources. This is an example of

A. directional selection.
B. stabilizing selection.
C. disruptive selection.
D. sympatric speciation.

20. Which of the following statements is correct?

A. Water flows from hypertonic to hypotonic.
B. Germinating seeds use less oxygen than do nongerminating seeds.
C. The rate of transpiration decreases with an increase in air movement.
D. Smaller DNA fragments migrate more rapidly than do larger DNA fragments on gel electrophoresis.

21. Which of the following is not a form of interspecies interaction?

A. Commensalism
B. Succession
C. Mutualism
D. Parasitism

22. Sickle cell anemia is a disease caused by the substitution of an incorrect nucleotide into the DNA sequence for a particular gene. The amino acids are still added to the growing protein chain, but the symptoms of sickle cell anemia result. This is an example of a

A. frameshift mutation.
B. missense mutation.
C. nonsense mutation.
D. thymine dimer mutation.

23. In a population of grasshoppers, the allele for tan color is dominant to the allele for green color. A drastic increase in rainfall leads to selection against the tan phenotype. When the rainy season ends, 23 percent of the remaining grasshoppers have the green phenotype. If this population is now in Hardy-Weinberg equilibrium, what will the frequency of the tan allele be in the next generation?

A. 0.52
B. 0.48
C. 0.23
D. 0.071

24. This process couples the production of ATP with the movement of electrons down the electron transport chain by harnessing the driving force created by a proton gradient.

A. Glycolysis
B. Chemiosmosis
C. Fermentation
D. Calvin cycle

25. During prophase 1 of meiosis, homologous chromosomes come together during a synapsis to form a tetrad. What does this lead to?

A. Leads to genetic variation via crossing over
B. Ensures that four daughter cells are produced
C. Creates male and female gametes
D. Separation of sister chromatids

26. The bacteria that cause pimples can be grown in the lab using a suitable nutrient broth, where they will eventually achieve exponential growth. Using the graph that follows, calculate the mean rate of growth, in millions of bacteria per hour, during their exponential phase.

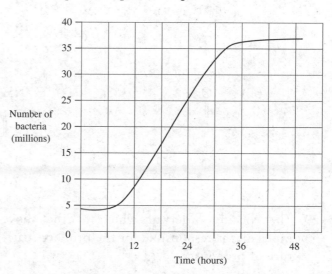

A. 1.46
B. 1.27
C. 0.83
D. 0.89

27. In a large pond consisting of long-finned fish and short-finned fish, a dam is built, splitting the large pond into two separate ponds. Fifty percent of the fish population is randomly separated into each of the smaller ponds leading to two distinct populations of long-finned and short-finned fish. This is an example of:

    A. Gene flow
    B. Bottleneck
    C. Founder effect
    D. Allopatric speciation

28. What is the water potation for a solution that is 0.1 M at 20°C? The solution is an open container of

    A. −2.4.
    B. 2.4.
    C. −1.4.
    D. 1.4.

For questions 29–30, please refer to the following answers:

(A)

(B)

(C)

(D)

29. The specific order of which of the above molecules is responsible for the primary structure of proteins?

30. Which molecule is the backbone of a structure that is vital to the construction of many cells and is used to produce steroid hormones?

31. A cell, shaped like a cube, contains sides with a measurement of 2.5 cm. Determine the surface-area-to-volume ratio for the cell.

    A. 15.6
    B. 2.4
    C. 37.5
    D. 5.2

Questions 32–34: A behavioral endocrinologist captures male individuals of a territorial bird species over the course of a year to measure testosterone (T) levels. In this population, males may play one of two roles: (1) they may stay in their natal group (the group they were born in) and help raise their younger siblings, or (2) they may leave the natal group to establish a new territory. Use this information and the two histograms that follow to answer the following questions.

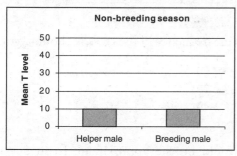

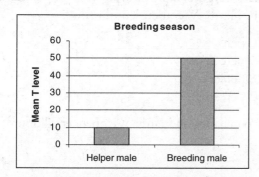

32. Testosterone level in this population may be an example of

   A. adaptive radiation.
   B. an adaptation.
   C. divergent selection.
   D. development.

33. What can you infer about the role of testosterone in reproduction in this species?

   A. It is detrimental to breeding.
   B. It aids adult males only.
   C. It ensures that all males reproduce equally.
   D. It aids in breeding.

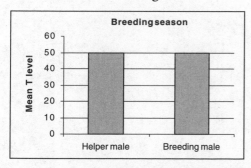

34. Which of the following is the best explanation of the results presented in the preceding graph, collected from the same population in a different year?

   A. The so-called helper males are actually breeding.
   B. The population has stopped growing.
   C. Females are equally attracted to adult and helper males.
   D. Testosterone level is affected by many processes.

Questions 35–38: A researcher grows a population of ferns in her laboratory. She notices, after a few generations, a new variant that has a distinct phenotype. When she tries to breed the original phenotype with the new one, no offspring are produced. When she breeds the new variants, however, offspring that look like the new variant result.

35. What originally caused the change in the variant?

   A. Karyotyping
   B. Balance polymorphism
   C. Mutation
   D. Polyploidy

36. What kind of speciation does this example illustrate?

   A. Allopatric
   B. Sympatric
   C. Isolated
   D. Polyploidy

37. Which of the following could possibly characterize the new variant?

   A. Adaptive radiation
   B. Divergent selection
   C. Equilibrium
   D. Polyploidy

38. Which of the following is likely to exhibit the process described earlier?

   A. Fallow deer
   B. Fruit flies
   C. Grass
   D. Spotted toads

For questions 39–41, please refer to the following figure:

39. The DNA placed in this electrophoresis gel separates as a result of what characteristic?

    A. pH
    B. Charge
    C. Size
    D. Polarity

40. If this gel were used in a court case as DNA evidence taken from the crime scene, which of the following suspects appears to be guilty?

    A. Suspect A
    B. Suspect B
    C. Suspect C
    D. Suspect D

41. Which two suspects, while not guilty, could possibly be identical twins?

    A. A and B
    B. A and C
    C. B and C
    D. B and D

Questions 42–45: The frequency of genotypes for a given trait are given in the accompanying graph. Answer the following questions using this information:

AA	Aa	aa
36%	45%	?%

42. What is the frequency of the recessive homozygote?

    A. 15 percent
    B. 19 percent
    C. 25 percent
    D. 40 percent

43. What would be the approximate frequency of the heterozygote condition if this population were in Hardy-Weinberg equilibrium?

    A. 20 percent
    B. 45 percent
    C. 48 percent
    D. 72 percent

44. Is this population in Hardy-Weinberg equilibrium?

    A. Yes
    B. No
    C. Cannot tell from the information given
    D. Maybe, if individuals are migrating

45. Which of the following processes may be occurring in this population, given the allele frequencies?

    A. Directional selection
    B. Homozygous advantage
    C. Hybrid vigor
    D. Allopatric speciation

Questions 46–48: An eager AP Biology student interested in studying osmosis and the movement of water in solutions took a dialysis bag containing a 0.5 M solution and placed it into a beaker containing a 0.6 M solution.

46. After the bag has been sitting in the beaker for a while, what would you expect to have happened to the bag?

   A. There will have been a net flow of water out of the bag, causing it to decrease in size.

   B. There will have been a net flow of water into the bag, causing it to swell in size.

   C. The bag will be the exact same size because no water will have moved at all.

   D. The solute will have moved out of the dialysis bag into the beaker.

47. If this bag were instead placed into a beaker of distilled water, what would be the expected result?

   A. There will be a net flow of water out of the bag, causing it to decrease in size.

   B. There will be a net flow of water into the bag, causing it to swell in size.

   C. The bag will remain the exact same size because no water will move at all.

   D. The solute will flow out of the dialysis bag into the beaker.

48. Which of the following is true about water potential?

   A. It drives the movement of water from a region of lower water potential to a region of higher water potential.

   B. Solute potential is the only factor that determines the water potential.

   C. Pressure potential combines with solute potential to determine the water potential.

   D. Water potential *always* drives water from an area of lower pressure potential to an area of higher pressure potential.

Questions 49–51 all use the following pedigree, but are independent of each other:

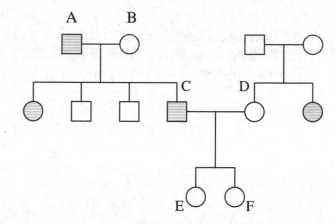

49. If the pedigree is studying an autosomal recessive condition for which the alleles are A and a, what was the probability that a child produced by parents A and B would be heterozygous?

   A. 0.0625

   B. 0.1250

   C. 0.2500

   D. 0.5000

50. Imagine that a couple (C and D) goes to a genetic counselor because they are interested in having children. They tell the counselor that they have a family history of a certain disorder and they want to know the probability of their firstborn having this condition. What is the probability of the child having the autosomal recessive condition?

   A. 0.0625

   B. 0.1250

   C. 0.2500

   D. 0.3333

51. Imagine that a couple (C and D) has a child (E) that has the autosomal recessive condition being traced by the pedigree. What is the probability that their second child (F) will have the autosomal recessive condition?

   A. 0.0625

   B. 0.1250

   C. 0.2500

   D. 0.5000

For questions 52–53, please refer to the following diagram:

52. The bold line that point *C* intersects is known as the

  A. biotic potential.
  B. carrying capacity.
  C. limiting factor.
  D. maximum attainable population.

53. On the basis of what happens at the end of this chart, what is the most likely explanation for the population decline after point *E*?

  A. The population became too dense and it had to decline.
  B. There was a major environmental shift that made survival impossible for many.
  C. Food became scarce, leading to a major famine.
  D. The population had become too large.

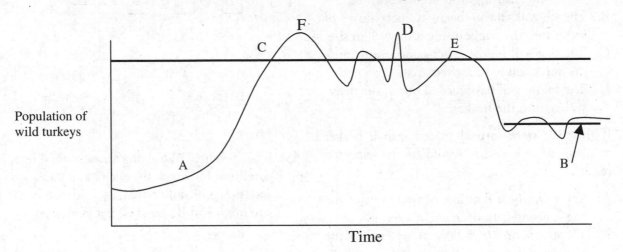

Questions 54 and 55: The solutions in the two arms of this U-tube are separated by a membrane that is permeable to water and sodium chloride, but not to sucrose. Side A is filled with a solution of 0.6 M sucrose and 0.2 M sodium chloride (NaCl), and side B is filled with a solution of 0.2 M sucrose and 0.3 M NaCl. Initially, the volume on both sides is the same.

54. At the beginning of the experiment,

  A. side A is hypertonic to side B.
  B. side A is hypotonic to side B.
  C. side A is isotonic to side B.
  D. side A is hypotonic to side B with respect to sucrose.

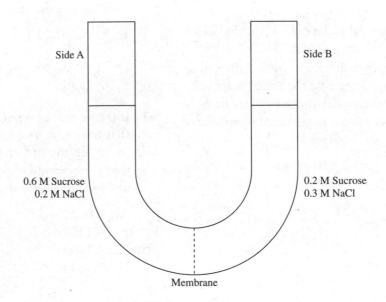

55. If you examine side A after a couple of days, you will see

    A. an increase in the concentration of NaCl and sucrose and an increase in water level.
    B. a decrease in the concentration of NaCl, an increase in water level, and no change in the concentration of sucrose.
    C. no net change.
    D. an increase in the concentration of NaCl and an increase in the water level.

56. Tay-Sachs is a disease caused by a recessive allele. Individuals with the genetic disorder usually do not survive more than a few years, and thus are not able to reproduce and pass on the gene. What would explain how this allele and its associated disease is preserved in the population?

    A. Heterozygous individuals will show no symptoms.
    B. Spontaneous mutation converts the dominant allele to the recessive form.
    C. Occasionally the gene will instead increase the fitness of the individual.
    D. Tay-Sachs is asymptomatic in people who are homozygous recessive.

57. A new plant was discovered and determined to have an unusually low number of stomata on the undersides of its leaves. For what environment would this plant most likely be best adapted?

    A. Cold and rainy
    B. Humid and sunny
    C. Hot and humid
    D. Hot and dry

58. The first simple cells evolved approximately 3.5 billion years ago, followed by the more complex eukaryotic cells 2.1 billion years ago. Which of the following statements is correct?

    A. Eukaryotic organelles helped create separate environments for metabolic reactions, thus increasing their metabolic efficiency.
    B. Prokaryotic and eukaryotic cells have no structural similarities.
    C. The organelles in larger eukaryotic cells took care of the problems of having a larger surface-area-to-volume ratio.
    D. Eukaryotic cells are able to multiply faster based on their more complex structure.

59. Easily produced genetic variation is key to the rapid evolution of viral and microbial populations. Furthermore, pathogens that need to escape the immune system rely on this variation to generate new surface antigens that go unrecognized by the host's immune system. Which of the following is an example of this antigenic variation?

    A. HIV, which can remain integrated into the host genome for many years
    B. The flu virus, which changes its envelope proteins
    C. MRSA, which has become resistant to many antibiotics
    D. Multiple sclerosis, which attacks the cells of the nervous system

60. Two species of hamster (X and Y) are in the genus *Cricetulus*, whereas a third species (Z) is instead part of genus *Mesocricetus*. Which of the following phylogenetic trees shows the correct evolutionary relatedness?

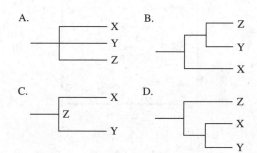

AP Biology Practice Exam 1: Section II

FREE-RESPONSE QUESTIONS

Time—1 hour and 30 minutes

(The first 10 minutes is a reading period. Do not begin writing until the 10-minute period has passed.)
Questions 1 and 2 are long free-response questions that should require about 20 minutes each.
Questions 3–6 are short-response questions that should require approximately 8–10 minutes each.
Outline form is not acceptable. Answers should be in essay form.

1. A murder trial court case ended up ruling against the defendant because of DNA evidence found at the crime scene and analyzed in the forensics lab. The following gel was produced after collecting DNA from the crime scene with A = Suspect 1, B = Suspect 2, and C = Murder.

A. **Describe** how the biotechnology in gel electrophoresis works.
B. **Identify** the independent and dependent variables used in the gel electrophoresis investigation.
C. **Explain** who is guilty of the crime? **Justify** your response.
D. When the forensics lab received the DNA evidence from the crime scene, they noticed that it was not enough to run multiple tests on. **Predict** what biotechnology the scientist would use in order to ensure they have enough DNA to work with.

2. An experiment was conducted using yeast and hydrogen peroxide to determine the effect of changing environmental conditions on the reaction rate of the catalytic enzyme in yeast (catalase) and hydrogen peroxide.

$$H_2O_2 + Catalase \rightarrow H_2O + O_2$$

A. **Describe** and **explain** the interaction between the catalase in yeast and hydrogen peroxide in the investigation.

B. **Construct** an appropriated graph of the data collected in the investigation.

C. **Identify** and **explain** the impact that the changing environmental conditions had on the reaction rate of the catalase and hydrogen peroxide.

D. Make a **prediction** on what would happen to the reaction rate if the catalase-hydrogen peroxide reaction was exposed to a pH of 14? **Justify** your prediction.

Room Temperature (25°C), pH 7	
Enzyme	Reaction Rate
1	1.24
2	1.51
3	1.33

Varying Temperature, Constant (pH)									
Enzyme	0°C	5°C	10°C	15°C	20°C	25°C	30°C	35°C	40°C
1	1.00	1.02	1.04	1.19	1.20	1.24	1.29	1.27	1.22
2	1.01	1.12	1.35	1.39	1.65	1.51	1.40	1.12	1.01
3	1.06	1.21	1.55	1.44	1.35	1.33	1.15	1.10	1.06

Varying pH, Constant Temperature (25°C)							
Enzyme	4	5	6	7	8	9	10
1	1.54	1.51	1.33	1.24	1.20	1.08	1.05
2	1.75	1.71	1.62	1.51	1.32	1.10	1.01
3	1.52	1.45	1.40	1.33	1.20	1.09	1.04

3. Life on Earth is made possible because of certain unique characteristics of water.

   A. **Describe** the characteristics of a water molecule that lead to hydrogen bonding.

   B. **Describe** and **explain** how the interaction of water molecules results in cohesion, adhesion, and surface tension.

4. Evolution is the change in allele frequencies in a population over time. This can occur through a variety of mechanisms including natural selection, genetic drift, and mutation.

   A. **Describe** the impact on a population for the mechanisms listed.

   B. A scientist is studying a population of field mice that includes individuals with light and dark brown coats. Every six months, you perform capture/recapture experiments to census the proportion of light and dark individuals. The following numbers indicate the percentage of dark-coat individuals caught in each successive census over the course of five years: 96, 94, 95, 91, 93, 95, 74, 73, 77, 76. **Explain** which of the three processes of evolution discussed in part a is most consistent with the data that supports the changes in phenotypic frequencies in the mouse population.

5. Humans maintain homeostasis in regard to blood glucose levels via the actions of insulin and glucagon. The figure below shows the pathway in detail.

   A. **Describe** how insulin and glucagon functions in the homeostasis.

   B. **Explain** the signal transduction pathway that takes places in body cells of humans in terms of blood glucose levels.

   C. **Predict** what occurs if there is a change in the pathway. **Justify** your prediction.

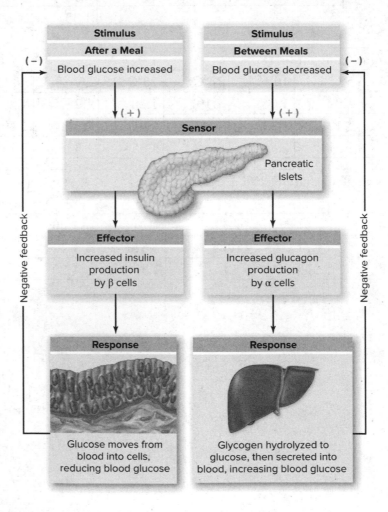

Figure is for Question 5 (*Reproduced with permission from Raven P, Johnson G, Mason K, Losos J, Duncan T; Biology, 12th ed. New York: McGraw Hill; 2020*)

6. An herbivorous grasshopper feeds on a leaf of an autotrophic plant to maintain homeostasis. For all of the energy that the grasshopper consumes 17 percent is for growth, 33 percent for cellular respiration, and 50 percent as feces.

A. **Describe** the allocation of energy by the grasshopper for homeostasis. **Explain** why all the energy consumed by the grasshopper is not available for the next trophic level.

B. A long-term drought causes a decrease in the number of autotrophic plants in the area that the grasshopper feeds. Make a **prediction** to how the grasshopper energy allocation would be different. **Justify** your prediction.

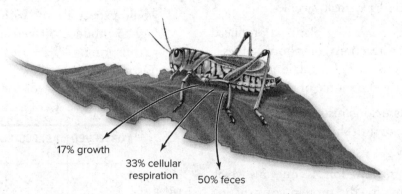

17% growth

33% cellular respiration

50% feces

Figure is for Question 6 (*Reproduced with permission from Raven P, Johnson G, Mason K, Losos J, Duncan T; Biology,* 12th ed. New York: McGraw Hill; 2020)

› Answers and Explanations for AP Biology Practice Exam 1

MULTIPLE-CHOICE QUESTIONS

1. **D**—Cell walls are present in prokaryotes but not eukaryotic animal cells. Ribosomes and cell membranes are present in both of them. Chloroplasts and large central vacuoles are not seen in either of them. Animal cells have small vacuoles.

2. **A**—The oxygen released by plants is produced during the light reactions of photosynthesis. The main inputs to the light reactions are water and light. Water is the source of the oxygen.

3. **B**—Endotherms are organisms whose metabolic rates do not respond to shifts in environmental temperature.

4. **B**—A frameshift mutation is one in which the reading frame for the protein construction machinery is shifted. It is a deletion or addition of nucleotides in a number that is *not* a multiple of 3. Often this can lead to premature stop codons, which lead to nonfunctional proteins.

5. **C**

6. **C**—We can see from the data that m and f have the highest crossover frequency. They must therefore be farthest apart of any pair along the chromosome. This leaves only answer choice C.

7. **C**—Memory B cells are able to recognize foreign invaders if they come back into our systems and lead to a more rapid and efficient attack on the invader.

8. **C**—Polygenic traits are traits that require the input of multiple genes to determine the phenotype. Skin color is a classic example of a polygenic trait; three genes combine to provide the various shades of skin tone seen in humans.

9. **C**—This is a classic example of Batesian mimicry.

10. **D**—Crossover is most likely to occur between two genes that are located far away from each other on the same chromosome.

11. **C**—Meiosis reduces the number of chromosomes in an individual by half: $96 \div 2 = 48$.

12. **D**—The volume of the container is not a major factor that affects enzyme efficiency.

13. **C**—The original question describes an organism that can be classified as a *K*-selected population.

Individuals of this class tend to have fairly constant size, low reproductive rates, and offspring that require extensive care.

14. **B**—If the green-melon parents were Gg, you would expect a cross with a yellow-melon plant (gg) to produce 50 percent Gg and 50 percent gg offspring. What you actually observed was 53 green and 41 yellow. Based on a total number of 94 offspring, your expected half-and-half ratios would be 47 of each color.

	# OBSERVED (o)	# EXPECTED (e)	(o - e)	(o - e)²	(o - e)²/e
green-melon plant	53	47	6	36	0.766
yellow-melon plant	41	47	–6	36	0.766

The chi-square value is 1.53 (less than the critical value of 3.84), so the null hypothesis is accepted.

15. **C**—If 9 percent of the population is homozygous recessive, this means that $q^2 = 0.09$, and that the square root of $q^2 = 0.30 = q$. This means that $p = 0.70$ since $p + q = 1$. Thus, the percentage of the population that is homozygous dominant: $p^2 = (0.7)^2 = 0.49$ or 49 percent.

16. **A**—All the other answer choices are violations of the Hardy-Weinberg equilibrium.

17. **C**—Exergonic reactions give off energy, and hydrolysis reactions are reactions that use water to break apart a compound. Redox reactions are reactions that involve the movement of electrons.

18. **C**—Herbivores tend to be the primary consumers of trophic pyramids, and thus would take up the first level up from the bottom.

19. **B**—Stabilizing selection tends to eliminate the extremes of a population, directional selection is a shift toward one of the extremes, and disruptive selection is the camel-hump selection in which the two extremes are favored over the middle. Sympatric speciation is the formation of new species due to an inability to reproduce that is not caused by geographic separation.

20. **D**—This is a lab experiment question based on the material in Chapter 13. We threw it in here just to remind you that you should not ignore the concepts of this very important chapter. You will be asked about these concepts on the exam.

21. **B**—Succession is an ecological process in which landforms evolve over time in response to the environmental conditions. Commensalism is when one organism benefits while the other is unaffected. Mutualism is when both organisms reap benefits from the interaction. Parasitism is when one organism benefits at the other's expense.

22. **B**

23. **A**

    tan $= p$; green $= q$

    green phenotype $= q^2 = 0.23$; frequency of green allele $= \sqrt{0.23} = 0.48$

    Since $p + q = 1$, the tan allele $(p) = 1 - 0.48 = 0.52$

24. **B**

25. **A**—Crossing over occurs when the homologous pairs match up during prophase I of meiosis. Complementary pieces from the two homologous chromosomes wrap around each other and are exchanged between the chromosomes leading to genetic variation in a population.

26. **B**—Logarithmic growth takes place during the time where the slope is the greatest, approximately between 12 and 30 hours. During that time (18 hours), the bacterial population started at 10 million and increased to 33 million (a difference of 23 million). Therefore, 23 million divided by 18 hours gives a rate of 1.27 million bacteria per hour.

27. **C**—Founder effect takes place when a new small population is created from members of a larger population resulting in reduced genetic variation for the new population.

28. **A**—The solute potential is $-(1) \times (0.1 \, M) \times (0.00831 \, \text{MPa/mole K}) \times (293 \, \text{K}) = -0.24 \, \text{MPa}$. The pressure potential is zero because the solution is in an open container. Therefore, $(-0.24) + 0 = -0.24 \, \text{MPa}$.

29. **B**—The primary structure of a protein consists of a specific order of amino acids held together by peptide bonds.

30. **A**—Cholesterol is one of the lipids that serves as the starting point for the synthesis of sex hormones.

31. **B**

    $SA = 6 \times (2.5 \, \text{cm} \times 2.5 \, \text{cm}) = 37.5 \, \text{cm}^2$
    $V = (2.5 \, \text{cm})^3 = 15.6 \, \text{cm}^3$
    $SA/V = 37.5/15.6 = 2.4$

32. **B**—Testosterone level is an adaptive trait in this population, one that has been molded by natural selection (or possibly sexual selection; we cannot determine this from the question) to aid in reproduction. Adaptive radiation is a process by which many speciation events occur in a newly exploited environment and does not apply here. This is not an example of divergent selection because both breeding and nonbreeding males have low testosterone levels during at least one part of the year; if the two male types always differed in testosterone level, this population could eventually split into two populations. Development and sperm production may be related to testosterone but are not addressed in this experiment.

33. **D**—Since testosterone levels are increased only during the breeding season, we can infer that testosterone has some role in breeding. Since reproductive males express higher testosterone levels only during the breeding season, we hypothesize that testosterone is beneficial, as opposed to detrimental, to breeding.

34. **A**—Since testosterone seems to be linked with reproduction, we infer from the new data that the "nonbreeding" males are actually breeding and therefore have elevated testosterone levels. Females, population growth, and number of offspring produced are not considered in this example. Finally, although testosterone does affect many physiological processes, none of these are discussed or illustrated in this example.

35. **C**—Although several processes can affect the frequency of a new phenotype or genotype, once it is in place, the original genetic change must have been the result of a mutation (probably a chromosomal aberration).

36. **B**—No physical barrier separated the two populations; this is therefore an example of sympatric, not allopatric speciation. The other answer choices are not types of speciation.

37. **D**—Polyploidy is the only answer that can describe an *individual*. All the others are processes or states that describe *population* events. Polyploidy is the

duplication of whole chromosomes that leads to speciation because the new variety can no longer breed with the original.

38. **C**—Polyploidy is much more common in plants; mutations such as the duplication of whole chromosomes are usually lethal to animals.

39. **C**—Gel electrophoresis separates DNA on the basis of size. Smaller samples travel a greater distance down the gel compared to larger samples.

40. **B**—His DNA fingerprint seems to exactly match that of the evidence DNA sample.

41. **B**—A and C seem to share the exact same restriction fragment cut of their DNA. Perhaps they are messing with our heads and added the DNA from the same individual twice.

42. **B**—100 – 45 – 36 = 19 percent.

43. **C**—Thirty-six percent of the population is AA. Taking the square root of 0.36, we find the frequency of the A allele to be 0.6. This means that the a allele's frequency must be 1 – 0.6, or 0.4. From these numbers, we can calculate the *expected* Hardy-Weinberg heterozygous frequency is $2pq$ = 2(A)(a) = 2(0.6)(0.4) = 48.0, or 48 percent.

44. **B**—The expected heterozygous probability does not match up with the actual. This population is not in Hardy-Weinberg equilibrium.

45. **B**—The homozygous frequency is higher than expected; one explanation for this is that the homozygotes are being selected for.

46. **A**—Water will flow *out* of the bag because the solute concentration of the beaker is hypertonic compared to the dialysis bag. Osmosis passively drives water from a hypotonic region to a hypertonic region.

47. **B**—Water would now flow *into* the bag because the solute gradient has been reversed. Now the beaker is hypotonic compared to the dialysis bag. Water thus moves into the bag.

48. **C**—Water potential = pressure potential + solute potential. Water passively moves from regions with high water potential toward those with lower water potential.

49. **D**—The mother (person B) must be heterozygous Aa because she and her husband (aa) have produced children that have the double recessive condition. This means that person B (the mother) must have contributed an a and that the cross is Aa × aa—and the probability is ½.

50. **D**—To answer this question, we must first determine the probability that person D is heterozygous. We know she is not aa because she does not have the condition. Since we know that the father *has* the condition, we know for certain that his genotype is aa. Both of mother D's parents must be heterozygous since neither of them have the condition, but they have produced a child with the condition. The probability that mother D is heterozygous Aa is ⅔. The probability that a couple with the genotypes Aa × aa have a double recessive child is ½. The probability that these two will have a child with the condition is ½ × ⅔ = ⅓ = 0.3333.

	A	a
A	AA	Aa
a	Aa	aa

51. **D**—If the couple has a child (person E) with the recessive condition, then we know for certain that mother D must be heterozygous. It is definitely an aa × Aa cross, leaving a 50 percent chance that their child will be aa.

52. **B**

53. **B**

54. **A**—The total solute potential for side A is 1.0 MPa (remember that for NaCl, i = 2), and the total solute potential for side B is 0.8 MPa. Therefore, side A has a higher concentration of solute (hypertonic).

55. **D**—Water will move from a hypotonic solution (side B) toward a hypertonic solution (side A). Sodium will diffuse from a region of more sodium (side B) to a region of less sodium (side A).

56. **A**—Heterozygous individuals carry the recessive gene but are themselves healthy.

57. **D**—Low numbers of stomata help to reduce water loss, helpful in hot and dry regions.

58. **A**—Prokaryotic and eukaryotic cells *do* have similar structures, the organelles in eukaryotic cells took care of having a *smaller* surface-area-to-volume ratio, and eukaryotic cells are not able to multiply faster.

59. **B**—Changing envelope proteins are created because of genetic variation in the genes that code for these proteins.

60. **D**—This cladogram shows a closer relationship between X and Y.

› Free-Response Grading Outline

1.

A. **Describe** how the biotechnology in gel electrophoresis works. (maximum 4 points)
   - Mentioning that smaller particles travel faster. (1 point)
   - Mentioning that the fragments of DNA are placed into wells at the head of the gel to begin their migration to the other side. (1 point)
   - Mentioning that the DNA migrates only as electric current is passed through the gel. (1 point)
   - Mentioning that the DNA migrates from negative charge to positive charge. (1 point)
   - Mentioning that when DNA samples from different individuals are cut with restriction enzymes, they show variations in the band patterns on gel electrophoresis known as restriction fragment length polymorphisms (RFLPs). (1 point)
   - Mentioning that DNA is specific to each individual, and when it is mixed with restriction enzymes, different combinations of RFLPs will be obtained from person to person. (1 point)
   - Providing a definition of a DNA fingerprint as the combination of an individual's RFLPs inherited from each parent. (1 point)
   - Mentioning that if an individual's electrophoresis pattern identically matches that of the crime scene evidence, the DNA has spoken and shown the individual to be the perpetrator, since the probability of two people having an identical set of RFLPs is virtually non-existent. (1 point)

B. **Identify** the independent and dependent variables used in the gel electrophoresis investigation.
   - Independent variable = Samples of DNA (1 point)
   - Dependent variable = Number of base pairs based on bands in gel (1 point)

C. **Explain** who is guilty of the crime. **Justify** your response.
   - Suspect 1 committed the crime. (1 point)
   - Sample A (Suspect 1) and Sample C (Murder) contain the same bands on the gel. This confirms that Suspect 1 is the murder and Suspect 2 is innocent due to the fact that two people having identical sets of RFLPs is virtually non-existent. (1 point)

D. When the forensics lab received the DNA evidence from the crime scene, they noticed that it was not enough to run multiple tests on. **Predict** what biotechnology the scientist would use in order to ensure they have enough DNA to work with.
   - Scientist would use PCR, polymerase chain reaction, to make copies of the DNA. PCR is a technology that uses original DNA sequences to amplify the original DNA sequences. (1 point)

2.

A. **Describe** and **explain** the interaction between the catalase in yeast and hydrogen peroxide in the investigation.
   - The enzyme (catalase)–substrate (hydrogen peroxide) interaction is specific between the catalase and hydrogen peroxide. (1 point)
   - The enzyme's active site has a unique confirmation (shape) that only the specific substrate is able to fit into like a lock and key. (1 point)

B. **Construct** an appropriated graph of the data collected in the investigation.
   - Independent and dependent variable correctly plotted (1 point)
   - Correctly labeled (1 point)
   - Correctly scaled axis (1 point)

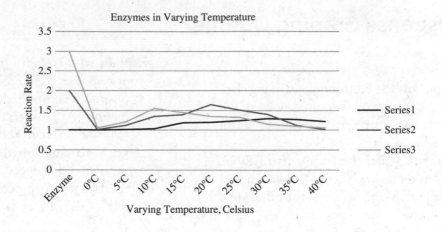

Enzymes in Varying Temperature

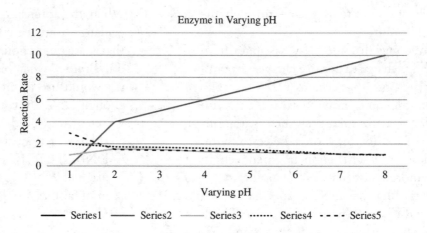

Enzyme in Varying pH

C. **Identify** and **explain** the impact that the changing environmental conditions had on the reaction rate of the catalase and hydrogen peroxide.
- Enzyme 2 functions most efficiently at 20°C, Enzyme 1 at 35°C, and Enzyme 3 at 10°C. (1 point)
- Enzyme 3 functions most efficiently at a pH of 6, Enzyme 1 and 2 at pH of 2. (1 point)
- Enzymes have optimum temperatures and pH that they function at. Enzymes are proteins which have a unique confirmation created by interactions of their R groups. These interactions are interrupted when their temperature or pH is outside their optimum range, causing them to denature. (1 point)

D. Make a **prediction** on what would happen to the reaction rate if the catalase hydrogen peroxide reaction was exposed to a pH of 14. **Justify** your prediction.

- The three enzymes would denature in a pH of 14. (1 point)
- The protein structure of each enzyme would denature, causing them to lose their shape and function. (1 point)

3.

A. **Describe** the characteristics of a water molecule that lead to hydrogen bonding.
- Water is a covalently bonded molecule. Each hydrogen molecule is covalently bonded to the oxygen molecule. (1 point)
- Water is a polar molecule. (1 point)
- The oxygen atom in water is slightly negatively charged and the hydrogen atoms are slightly positively charged due to the electrons from the hydrogen atoms being closer to the oxygen atom due to increased attraction. (1 point)

B. **Describe** and **explain** how the interaction of water molecules results in cohesion, adhesion, and surface tension.

- Water molecules form hydrogen bonds, which is an attraction between the positively charged hydrogen atoms of one water molecule and a nearby negatively charged oxygen atom of a water molecule. (1 point)
- Cohesion is when two water molecules are attracted to each other via hydrogen bonds. Adhesion is when a water molecule is attracted to a different molecule. Surface tension is when water molecules interact with each other instead of the air molecules, causing a strong tension in the water molecules at the surface of a body of water. (1 point)

4.

A. **Describe** the impact on a population for the mechanisms listed.

Definition and examples (maximum 2 points)
- Defining natural selection. (1 point)
  a. Mentioning it is the process by which certain alleles increase in frequency in a population because of the survival or reproduction benefit they give to those individuals who possess them. (½ point)
  b. Possible example: sickle cell allele persists in populations where malaria is present (having sickle-shaped red blood cells makes you less likely to contract malaria). (½ point)
  c. Defining genetic drift. (maximum 1 point)
  d. Describing how random processes can change allele frequencies. (½ point)
  e. Possible example: allele frequencies in a new population are dependent on which alleles are present in the founders of that population (founder effect). (½ point)
- Defining mutation. (1 point)
  a. Mentioning that changes in DNA create genetic variation and new alleles. (½ point)
  b. Mentioning that evolution by "neutral mutations" can occur even if the new alleles are not acted on by natural selection. (½ point)

  c. Possible example: eye color gene mutates to a different color without any change in vision or behavior as a result of the mutation. (½ point)

B. A scientist is studying a population of field mice that includes individuals with light and dark brown coats. Every six months you perform capture/recapture experiments to census the proportion of light and dark individuals. The following numbers indicate the percentage of dark-coat individuals caught in each successive census over the course of five years: 96, 94, 95, 91, 93, 95, 74, 73, 77, 76. **Explain** which of the three processes of evolution discussed in part a is most consistent with the data that supports the changes in phenotypic frequencies in the mouse population.

Explanation of data (maximum 2 points)
- Mentioning the changes could not be the gradual process of natural selection because they occurred rapidly between two censuses. (1 point)
- Indicating that the changes could be caused by genetic drift. (1 point)
- Indicating that the changes could be caused by some environmental event (flood, fire) that randomly killed many dark-coated mice. (1 point)

5.

A. **Describe** how insulin and glucagon functions in the homeostasis.
- Insulin and glucagon function as ligands or signals for blood sugar. (1 point)

B. **Explain** the signal transduction pathway that takes place in body cells of humans in terms of blood glucose levels.
- Insulin and glucagon are hormones produced in the pancreas that work to control the level of glucose in the blood. Insulin is released from the pancreatic beta cells when glucose levels are higher in the blood—insulin stimulates cellular uptake of glucose for utilization or glycogen production. On the other hand, glucagon is released from the pancreatic alpha cells when glucose levels are lower in the blood. Glucagon stimulates the release of glycogen from the liver to raise

glucose levels in the blood. The opposing effects of insulin and glucagon maintain the homeostasis of blood glucose. (2 points)

C. **Predict** what occurs if there is a change in the pathway. **Justify** your prediction.
- Diabetes occurs when the insulin/glucagon pathway is interrupted, causing the body's cells to not receive the correct amount of blood sugar. (1 point)

6.

A. **Describe** the allocation of energy by the grasshopper for homeostasis. **Explain** why all the energy consumed by the grasshopper is not available for the next trophic level.
- The grasshopper is using 100 percent of the energy it consumes to survive with 33 percent being used for cellular respiration in order to maintain homeostasis. Fifty percent of the energy is lost through waste in the form feces and heat. Only 17 percent is left over for the grasshopper to grow in terms of muscle, bones, and other tissue. (1 point)
- The grasshopper must first maintain homeostasis, which includes regulating internal and external processes. This takes an average up to 90 percent of all energy consumed by the grasshopper through cellular respiration and waste. Thus, on average, only 10 percent is left over for the grasshopper to grow, which is the energy available for the next trophic level to consume. (1 point)

B. A long-term drought causes a decrease in the number of autotrophic plants in the area that the grasshopper feeds. Make a **prediction** to how the grasshopper energy allocation would be different. **Justify** your prediction.
- The grasshopper would have to spend more energy looking for food. (1 point)
- The increased expenditure of energy looking for food would cause less energy to be available for growth, leading to less energy for the next trophic level. (1 point)

Scoring and Interpretation
AP BIOLOGY PRACTICE EXAM 1

SECTION I: Multiple-Choice Questions:

NUMBER CORRECT [　　　　　] **x 1.0000 =** [　　　　　]

WEIGHTED SECTION I SCORE

SECTION II: Free Response:

QUESTION 1 [　　　　　] **x 1.7647** [　　　　　]
(out of 9)　　　　　　　　　　　(do not round)

QUESTION 2 [　　　　　] **x 1.7647** [　　　　　]
(out of 9)　　　　　　　　　　　(do not round)

QUESTION 3 [　　　　　] **x 1.7647** [　　　　　]
(out of 4)　　　　　　　　　　　(do not round)

QUESTION 4 [　　　　　] **x 1.7647** [　　　　　]
(out of 4)　　　　　　　　　　　(do not round)

QUESTION 5 [　　　　　] **x 1.7647** [　　　　　]
(out of 4)　　　　　　　　　　　(do not round)

QUESTION 6 [　　　　　] **x 1.7647** [　　　　　]
(out of 4)　　　　　　　　　　　(do not round)

[　　　　　]

SECTION SCORE: (add 6 question totals together)

WEIGHTED SECTION II SCORE

TOTAL SCORE: (add Section I and Section II together) [　　　　　]

OVERALL SCORE

AP BIOLOGY
SCORE CONVERSION CHART

COMPOSITE SCORE RANGE	AP EXAM SCORE
94 – 120	5
76 – 93	4
54 – 75	3
30 – 53	2
0 – 29	1

Answer Sheet for AP Biology Practice Exam 2

ANSWER SHEET FOR MULTIPLE-CHOICE QUESTIONS

#	A	B	C	D		#	A	B	C	D		#	A	B	C	D
1	Ⓐ	Ⓑ	Ⓒ	Ⓓ		21	Ⓐ	Ⓑ	Ⓒ	Ⓓ		41	Ⓐ	Ⓑ	Ⓒ	Ⓓ
2	Ⓐ	Ⓑ	Ⓒ	Ⓓ		22	Ⓐ	Ⓑ	Ⓒ	Ⓓ		42	Ⓐ	Ⓑ	Ⓒ	Ⓓ
3	Ⓐ	Ⓑ	Ⓒ	Ⓓ		23	Ⓐ	Ⓑ	Ⓒ	Ⓓ		43	Ⓐ	Ⓑ	Ⓒ	Ⓓ
4	Ⓐ	Ⓑ	Ⓒ	Ⓓ		24	Ⓐ	Ⓑ	Ⓒ	Ⓓ		44	Ⓐ	Ⓑ	Ⓒ	Ⓓ
5	Ⓐ	Ⓑ	Ⓒ	Ⓓ		25	Ⓐ	Ⓑ	Ⓒ	Ⓓ		45	Ⓐ	Ⓑ	Ⓒ	Ⓓ
6	Ⓐ	Ⓑ	Ⓒ	Ⓓ		26	Ⓐ	Ⓑ	Ⓒ	Ⓓ		46	Ⓐ	Ⓑ	Ⓒ	Ⓓ
7	Ⓐ	Ⓑ	Ⓒ	Ⓓ		27	Ⓐ	Ⓑ	Ⓒ	Ⓓ		47	Ⓐ	Ⓑ	Ⓒ	Ⓓ
8	Ⓐ	Ⓑ	Ⓒ	Ⓓ		28	Ⓐ	Ⓑ	Ⓒ	Ⓓ		48	Ⓐ	Ⓑ	Ⓒ	Ⓓ
9	Ⓐ	Ⓑ	Ⓒ	Ⓓ		29	Ⓐ	Ⓑ	Ⓒ	Ⓓ		49	Ⓐ	Ⓑ	Ⓒ	Ⓓ
10	Ⓐ	Ⓑ	Ⓒ	Ⓓ		30	Ⓐ	Ⓑ	Ⓒ	Ⓓ		50	Ⓐ	Ⓑ	Ⓒ	Ⓓ
11	Ⓐ	Ⓑ	Ⓒ	Ⓓ		31	Ⓐ	Ⓑ	Ⓒ	Ⓓ		51	Ⓐ	Ⓑ	Ⓒ	Ⓓ
12	Ⓐ	Ⓑ	Ⓒ	Ⓓ		32	Ⓐ	Ⓑ	Ⓒ	Ⓓ		52	Ⓐ	Ⓑ	Ⓒ	Ⓓ
13	Ⓐ	Ⓑ	Ⓒ	Ⓓ		33	Ⓐ	Ⓑ	Ⓒ	Ⓓ		53	Ⓐ	Ⓑ	Ⓒ	Ⓓ
14	Ⓐ	Ⓑ	Ⓒ	Ⓓ		34	Ⓐ	Ⓑ	Ⓒ	Ⓓ		54	Ⓐ	Ⓑ	Ⓒ	Ⓓ
15	Ⓐ	Ⓑ	Ⓒ	Ⓓ		35	Ⓐ	Ⓑ	Ⓒ	Ⓓ		55	Ⓐ	Ⓑ	Ⓒ	Ⓓ
16	Ⓐ	Ⓑ	Ⓒ	Ⓓ		36	Ⓐ	Ⓑ	Ⓒ	Ⓓ		56	Ⓐ	Ⓑ	Ⓒ	Ⓓ
17	Ⓐ	Ⓑ	Ⓒ	Ⓓ		37	Ⓐ	Ⓑ	Ⓒ	Ⓓ		57	Ⓐ	Ⓑ	Ⓒ	Ⓓ
18	Ⓐ	Ⓑ	Ⓒ	Ⓓ		38	Ⓐ	Ⓑ	Ⓒ	Ⓓ		58	Ⓐ	Ⓑ	Ⓒ	Ⓓ
19	Ⓐ	Ⓑ	Ⓒ	Ⓓ		39	Ⓐ	Ⓑ	Ⓒ	Ⓓ		59	Ⓐ	Ⓑ	Ⓒ	Ⓓ
20	Ⓐ	Ⓑ	Ⓒ	Ⓓ		40	Ⓐ	Ⓑ	Ⓒ	Ⓓ		60	Ⓐ	Ⓑ	Ⓒ	Ⓓ

AP Biology Practice Exam 2: Section I

MULTIPLE-CHOICE QUESTIONS

Time–1 hour and 30 minutes

For the multiple-choice questions to follow, select the best answer
and fill in the appropriate letter on the answer sheet.

1. A baby duck runs for cover when a large object is tossed over its head. After this object is repeatedly passed overhead, the duck learns there is no danger and stops running for cover when the same object appears again. This is an example of

   A. imprinting.
   B. fixed-action pattern.
   C. agonistic behavior.
   D. habituation.

2. In a population of giraffes, an environmental change occurs that favors individuals that are tallest. As a result, more of the taller individuals are able to obtain nutrients and survive to pass along their genetic information. This is an example of

   A. directional selection.
   B. stabilizing selection.
   C. sexual selection.
   D. disruptive selection.

3. The relatives of a group of pelicans from the same species that separated from each other because of an unsuccessful migration are reunited 150 years later and find that they are unable to produce offspring. This is an example of

   A. allopatric speciation.
   B. sympatric speciation.
   C. genetic drift.
   D. gene flow.

4. A cell is placed into a hypertonic environment and its cytoplasm shrivels up. This demonstrates the principle of

   A. diffusion.
   B. active transport.
   C. facilitated diffusion.
   D. plasmolysis.

5. Which of the following is a biotic factor that could affect the growth rate of a population?

   A. Volcanic eruption
   B. Glacier melting
   C. Destruction of the ozone layer
   D. Sudden reduction in the animal food resource

6. Which of the following is not a way to form recombinant DNA?

   A. Translation
   B. Conjugation
   C. Specialized transduction
   D. Transformation

7. Chemiosmosis occurs in
   I. Mitochondria
   II. Nuclei
   III. Chloroplasts

   A. I only
   B. II only
   C. III only
   D. I and III

8. Which of the following theories is based on the notion that mitochondria and chloroplasts evolved from prokaryotic cells?

   A. Fluid mosaic model
   B. Endosymbiotic model
   C. Taxonomic model
   D. Respiration feedback model

9. Which of the following is *not* known to be involved in the control of cell division?

   A. Cyclins
   B. Protein kinases
   C. Checkpoints
   D. Fibroblast cells

10. Which of the following statements about post-transcriptional modification is incorrect?

    A. A poly-A tail is added to the 3′ end of the mRNA.
    B. A guanine cap is added to the 5′ end of the mRNA.
    C. Introns are removed from the mRNA.
    D. Posttranscriptional modification occurs in the cytoplasm.

11. In a certain pond, there are long-finned fish and short-finned fish. A horrific summer thunderstorm leads to the death of a disproportionate number of long-finned fish to the point where the relative frequency of the two forms has drastically shifted. This is an example of

    A. gene flow.
    B. natural selection.
    C. genetic drift.
    D. stabilizing selection.

12. During the central dogma, transcription occurs in the nucleus of eukaryotic cells by transcribing the cells' DNA. Located thousands of base pairs away from the promoter region is the transfer-affecting region on the DNA. What is that region called?

    A. Enhancer
    B. Repressor
    C. Operator
    D. Promoter

13. Which of the following statements about photosynthesis is *incorrect*?

    A. H_2O is an input to the light-dependent reactions.
    B. CO_2 is an input to the Calvin cycle.
    C. Photosystems I and II both play a role in the cyclic light reactions.
    D. O_2 is a product of the light-dependent reactions.

14. If a couple has had three sons and the woman is pregnant with their fourth child, what is the probability that child 4 will *also* be male?

    A. ½
    B. ¼
    C. ⅛
    D. ¹⁄₁₆

15. Which of the following is an *incorrect* statement about gel electrophoresis?

    A. DNA migrates from positive charge to negative charge.
    B. Smaller DNA travels faster.
    C. The DNA migrates only when the current is running.
    D. The longer the current is running, the farther the DNA will travel.

16. You are told that in a population of guinea pigs, 4 percent are black (recessive) and 96 percent are brown. Which of the following is the frequency of the heterozygous condition?

    A. 16 percent
    B. 32 percent
    C. 40 percent
    D. 48 percent

17. Which of the following is known to be involved in the photoperiodic flowering response of angiosperms?

    A. Auxin
    B. Cytochrome
    C. Phytochrome
    D. Gibberellins

18. Which of the following tends to be highest on the trophic pyramid?

    A. Primary consumers
    B. Herbivores
    C. Primary carnivores
    D. Primary producers

19. A form of species interaction in which one of the species benefits while the other is unaffected is called

    A. parasitism.
    B. mutualism.
    C. commensalism.
    D. symbiosis.

20. The transfer of DNA between two bacterial cells connected by sex pili is known as

    A. specialized transduction.
    B. conjugation.
    C. transformation.
    D. generalized transduction.

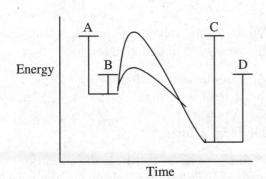

Enzyme

A

Substrate   Inhibitor #2

Active site   Inhibitor #1

For questions 21–22, please use the preceding diagram:

21. If inhibitor 1 is able to bind to the active site and block the attachment of the substrate to the enzyme, this is an example of

A. noncompetitive inhibition.
B. competitive inhibition.
C. a cofactor.
D. a coenzyme.

22. Which of the following is *not* a change that would affect the efficiency of the enzyme shown above?

A. Change in temperature
B. Change in pH
C. Change in salinity
D. Increase in the concentration of the enzyme

23. Which of the following points on the preceding energy chart represents the activation energy of the reaction involving the enzyme?

A. A
B. B
C. C
D. D

24. When an animal is harmless but has a similar appearance of a more dangerous animal, that animal is exhibiting what type of defense mechanism?

A. Aposomatic coloration
B. Batesian mimicry
C. Deceptive markings
D. Cryptic coloration

25. Twenty people decide to start a new population, totally isolated from anyone else. Two of the individuals are heterozygous for a recessive allele, which in homozygotes causes cystic fibrosis. Assuming this population is in Hardy-Weinberg equilibrium, what fraction (expressed as a decimal) of people in this new population will have cystic fibrosis?

A. 0.05
B. 0.005
C. 0.0025
D. 0.25

26. During meiosis, trisomy 21 can result from what chromosome abnormality?

A. An extra chromosome 21 from a mutation
B. An extra chromosome 21 from nondisjunction
C. An autosomal dominant disorder
D. A missing chromosome 21 from nondisjunction

27. The semiconservative model of DNA produces what complementary strand to the sequence 5′ – TTAACGAACG – 3′ during DNA replication?

A. 5′ – UUAAGCUUGC–3′
B. 5′ – AATTGCTTGC–3′
C. 3′ – AATTGCTTGC 5′
D. 3′ – UUAAGCUUGC5′

28. A local scientist has been re-creating Mendel's experiments and started by crossing a homozygous dominant yellow smooth pea plant (YYRR) with a homozygous recessive green wrinkled pea plant (yyrr). What is/are the expected F_1 genotype(s)?

A. YYrr
B. YyRr; YYRr; yyrr
C. YyRr
D. YYRR; YyRr; yyRR; yyrr

29. Describe the outcome when a carrot with an osmolarity of 0.25 M is placed in a solution of 0.45 M saltwater.

A. The saltwater will enter the cell until equilibrium is reached.
B. The saltwater and carrot are isotonic, resulting in no movement.
C. Water will enter the cell until equilibrium is reached.
D. Water will leave the cell until equilibrium is reached.

30. A certain mutation found in fruit flies (*Drosophila melanogaster*) is hypothesized to be autosomal recessive. The experimenter crossed two *Drosophila* flies that were heterozygous for the trait. The next generation produced 70 wild-type males, 65 wild-type females, 36 males with the mutation, and 40 mutant females. Calculate the chi-squared value for the null hypothesis that the mutation is autosomal recessive.

A. 3.35
B. 9.98
C. 13.33
D. 6.64

31. A recent levy has been breached, causing flooding in a local community with saltwater. A local farmer is trying to determine if his crops can survive the flooding. The saltwater has a water potential of –8.73 MPa. The farmer's crops have a molar concentration of 0.25 M with a pressure potential of –1.0 MPa at 27°C. What will happen to the crops?

A. The crops will maintain turgid pressure due to the crop's water potential being –7.23 MPa and the saltwater being –8.73 MPa.
B. The crops will become flaccid and eventually die due to the crop's water potential being –7.23 MPa and the saltwater being –8.73 MPa.
C. The pressure potential of the plant will cause the crops to gain water from the flooding saltwater.
D. The pressure potential of the plant will push the sugar out of the crops into the flooding saltwater.

32. A cell is in equilibrium with its surroundings. The molarity of the surrounding solution at 20°C is 0.8 M. Calculate the solute potential of the surrounding solution.

A. –3.90
B. –39.0
C. –19.5
D. –1.95

Questions 33–36 refer to the following pedigree.

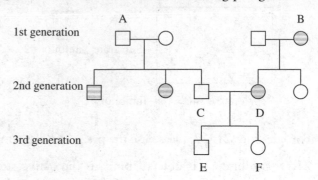

33. What kind of inheritable condition does this pedigree appear to show?

A. Autosomal dominant
B. Autosomal recessive
C. Sex-linked dominant
D. Sex-linked recessive

34. What is the probability that couple C and D will produce a child that has the condition?

A. 0
B. 0.125
C. 0.250
D. 0.333

35. Which of the following conditions could show the same kind of pedigree results?

A. Cri-du-chat syndrome
B. Turner syndrome
C. Albinism
D. Hemophilia

36. If child E does in fact have the condition, what is the probability that child F will also have it?

A. 0
B. 0.250
C. 0.500
D. 0.750

Questions 37–39: An experiment involving fruit flies produced the following results:

Vestigial wings are wild type; crumpled wings are mutant.

Gray body is dominant; black body is mutant.

525 vestigial, gray-bodied flies	V = vestigial
555 crumpled, black-bodied flies	v = crumpled
75 crumpled, gray flies	G = gray
45 vestigial, black-bodied flies	g = black

37. From the data presented above, one can conclude that these genes are

A. sex-linked.
B. epistatic.
C. holandric.
D. linked.

38. What is the crossover frequency of these genes?

A. 10 percent
B. 20 percent
C. 30 percent
D. 35 percent

39. How many map units apart would these genes be on a linkage map?

A. 5 map units
B. 10 map units
C. 20 map units
D. 30 map units

Questions 40–42: A laboratory procedure involving plants presents you with the data found in the following two charts:

Pigment	R_f
Beta-carotene	*1.251*
Chlorophyll *a*	*1.015*
Chlorophyll *b*	*0.985*
Xanthophyll	*1.125*

40. From the transpiration rate data, it appears that transpiration rate rises as

A. temperature ↑, wind speed ↓, humidity ↓
B. temperature ↑, wind speed ↑, humidity ↓
C. temperature ↑, wind speed ↑, humidity ↑
D. temperature ↓, wind speed ↑, humidity ↑

41. According to the R_f values given in the preceding smaller table, which pigment would migrate the fastest on chromatography paper?

A. Xanthophyll
B. Chlorophyll *a*
C. Chlorophyll *b*
D. Beta-carotene

42. From the transpiration rate data presented in the larger table, which of the following plants appears to be most resistant to transpiration?

A. Plant A
B. Plant B
C. Plant C
D. Plants B and C are similarly resistant.

Transpiration Rate → 1.0 = Control Rate (All Leaves Have the Same Surface Area)

PLANT	T^*10°C	T 15°C	T 20°C	HUMIDITY 20%	HUMIDITY 15%	HUMIDITY 10%	WIND 5 MPH[†]	WIND 10 MPH	WIND 15 MPH
A	1.042	1.105	1.211	1.121	1.130	1.205	1.001	1.025	1.100
B	0.600	0.800	1.000	0.851	0.910	0.950	0.760	0.785	0.810
C	1.240	1.245	1.251	1.411	1.519	1.550	1.214	1.240	1.301

*Temperature
†Miles per hour

Questions 43–45: A population of rodents is studied over the course of 100 generations to examine changes in dental enamel thickness. Species that are adapted to eat food resources that require high levels of processing have thicker enamel than do those that eat softer, more easily processed foods. Answer the following questions using this information and the curves that follow.

43. How is average enamel thickness changing in this population?

    A. There is no real change.
    B. The color and size are changing.
    C. It is increasing.
    D. It is decreasing.

44. You randomly pick one data point from all three sets of data (all three generations), and the individual's enamel thickness score is 15. Which of the following can be inferred?

    A. The individual comes from generation 1.
    B. The individual comes from generation 50.
    C. The individual comes from generation 100.
    D. The individual could be from any of these generations.

45. What inference can you make about this species' diet?

    A. Its food resources are getting softer and easier to process.
    B. Its food resources are getting harder and more difficult to process.
    C. The population is growing.
    D. The population is shrinking.

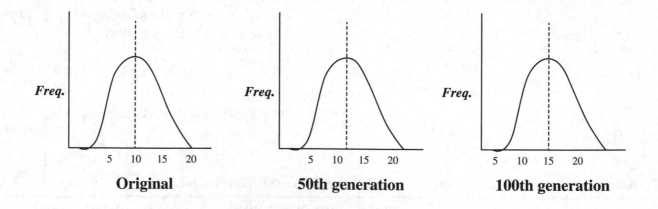

      Original   **50th generation**   **100th generation**

Questions 46–49: A student sets up a lab experiment to study the behavior of slugs. She sets up a large tray filled with soil that measures 1 square meter and has four sets of conditions, one in each quadrant:

Low salinity, high temperature	Low salinity, low temperature
High salinity, high temperature	High salinity, low temperature

She places 20 slugs in the tray, 5 in each quadrant. Use this information to answer the following questions:

46. What is this lab setup called?

    A. A gel sheet
    B. A choice chamber
    C. A potometer
    D. An incubation chamber

47. After 5 minutes, there are 5 slugs in each quadrant. Which of the following is not a viable explanation for this finding?

    A. The slugs haven't had time to move yet.
    B. The slugs have no preference for temperature or salinity conditions.
    C. The slugs can't move from one area of the tray to another.
    D. The slugs do not like to live in high-temperature areas.

48. After 20 minutes, 20 slugs are in the high-temperature, low-salinity quadrant. What kind of animal behavior has this experiment displayed?

    A. Kinesis
    B. Taxis
    C. Survival
    D. Feeding

49. A classmate has set up a similar experiment in the following manner:

Low salinity, low temperature
High salinity, high temperature

Of the 20 slugs that she puts in her tray, 18 move to the high-salinity, high-temperature section within one hour, while the other 2 move to the low-salinity, low-temperature section. She concludes that slugs prefer conditions of high salinity and temperature. What is wrong with this conclusion?

    A. She didn't specify what the two temperatures or salinities were.
    B. The slugs may not have been able to move where they wanted.
    C. Crowding may have affected the behavior of the slugs, causing the two others to move to the other section.
    D. She is measuring two variables at once with no control, and therefore can't conclude anything about slug tastes.

50. Viral transduction is the process by which viruses carry bacterial DNA from one bacterial cell to another. In what way does this process play a role in bacterial evolution?

    A. By making the bacterial cell more resistant to predators
    B. By directly creating new species of bacteria
    C. By increasing genetic variation of the bacteria
    D. By selecting for viruses better able to infect bacteria

51. ADH is a hormone secreted by the kidneys that reduces the amount of water excreted in the urine. ADH is released in times of dehydration. This is an example of

    A. innate behavior.
    B. maintaining homeostasis.
    C. failure to respond to the environment.
    D. positive feedback.

For questions 52–54, refer to the information and graph that follows.

Five dialysis bags, made from a semipermeable membrane that is impermeable to glucose, were filled with various concentrations of glucose and placed in separate beakers containing 0.5 M glucose solution. The bags were weighed every 10 minutes and the percent change in mass for each bag was graphed:

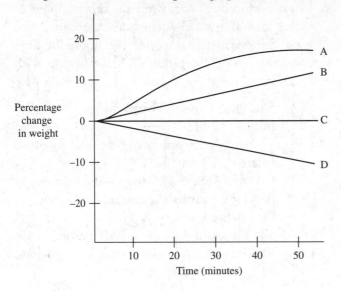

52. Which line represents the bag that contained a solution isotonic to the 0.5 M solution?

    A. A
    B. B
    C. C
    D. D

53. Which line represents the bag with the highest initial concentration of glucose?

    A. A
    B. B
    C. C
    D. D

54. Which line or lines represent bags that contain a solution that is hypertonic at 50 minutes?

    A. A and B
    B. B
    C. C
    D. D and E

55. A mutation in a bacterial enzyme changed a previously polar amino acid into a nonpolar amino acid. This amino acid was located at a site distant from the enzyme's active site. How might this mutation alter the enzyme's substrate specificity?

    A. By changing the enzyme's pH optimum
    B. By changing the enzyme's location in the cell
    C. By changing the shape of the protein
    D. An amino acid change away from the active site cannot alter the enzyme's substrate specificity.

Use the following picture of DNA to answer questions 56 and 57:

template strand   5' _____ 3'
complementary strand   3' _____ 5'

56. Based on the preceding picture, which direction would RNA polymerase move?

    A. $3' \rightarrow 5'$ along the template strand
    B. $3' \rightarrow 5'$ along the complementary strand
    C. $5' \rightarrow 3'$ along the template strand
    D. $5' \rightarrow 3'$ along the complementary strand

57. If the DNA segment is a transcriptional unit, where would the promoter be located?

    A. To the left of the complementary strand
    B. To the right of the template strand
    C. To the left of the template strand
    D. To the right of the complementary strand

58. A single gene from five related species of leafhoppers was compared, and the nucleotide differences between the genes are as shown in the table:

Nucleotide Differences

Species	1	2	3	4	5
1	—	1	8	19	7
2		—	8	20	9
3			—	19	2
4				—	18
5					—

Which of the following phylogenetic trees best shows the correct evolutionary relationship between the leafhoppers?

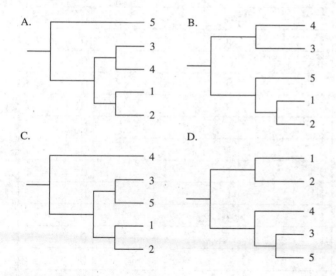

A.

B.

C.

D.

Answer questions 59 and 60 based on the following cladogram:

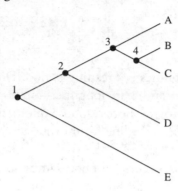

59. What is the common ancestor for B and E?

A. 1
B. 2
C. 3
D. 4

60. Which two species are most closely related?

A. A and E
B. A and B
C. B and C
D. D and E

AP Biology Practice Exam 2: Section II

FREE-RESPONSE QUESTIONS

Time—1 hour and 30 minutes

(The first 10 minutes is a reading period. Do not begin writing until the 10-minute period has passed.)
Questions 1 and 2 are long free-response questions that should require about 20 minutes each.
Questions 3–6 are short-response questions that should require approximately 8–10 minutes each.
Outline form is not acceptable. Answers should be in essay form.

1. Photosynthesis occurs in photosynthetic auto-trophs in which carbon dioxide convert light energy from the sun into chemical energy in the form of sugar such as glucose. In an investigation, leaf disks are used to assay the net rate of photosynthesis under light and dark conditions. Leaf disks normally float when placed in water but when the air spaces are infiltrated with carbon dioxide, the density of the leaf disk increases, and the leaf disks sinks. Using sodium bicarbonate dissolved in water as a carbon source for photosynthesis, which causes the leaf disks to sink, photosynthetic activity will lead to oxygen production, and the leaf disks will become less dense and begin to float. The chart at the right shows the results of the investigation with leaf disks being placed in the light and in the dark.

   A. **Explain** how carbon fixation by the leaf disks creates the oxygen needed to float when placed in light.
   B. **Identify** the independent and dependent variable used in this experiment.
   C. **Construct** an appropriately labeled graph.
   D. Make a **prediction** if the leaf disks were placed under more intense light source. **Justify** your prediction.

Time	Floating Leaf Disks	
	Light	Dark
1	0	0
2	0	0
3	0	0
4	0	0
5	0	0
6	0	0
7	1	0
8	1	0
9	1	0
10	1	0
11	4	0
12	7	0
13	8	0
14	10	0
15	10	0

2. Gila monsters are the only venomous lizard native to the United States. While they are slow and heavy, their venom is created in their salivary glands. The phenotype for scale color in gila monsters is determined by a specific locus. The dominant allele (black) is represented by G and the recessive allele (brown) is represented by g. The cross between a male gila monster with black scales and a female gila monster with brown scales produced the following F_1 generation:

- Black-scaled gila monsters: 52
- Brown-scaled gila monsters: 55
- White-scaled gila monsters: 1

The black-scaled females and brown-scaled males from the F_1 generation were then crossed to produce the following F_2 generation:

- Black-scaled gila monsters: 53
- Brown-scaled gila monsters: 54
- White-scaled gila monsters: 0

A. **Calculate** the P-generation genotypes. **Justify** your response.

B. **Describe** and **explain** the white-scaled female that was present in the F_1 generation.

C. The phenotype for scale color is claimed to be autosomal. **Support** the claim by calculating the chi-square value. **Provide** reasoning to justify the claim.

D. Coyotes are natural predators of gila monsters. During a recent drought, the coyote's population experienced a bottleneck effect. **Predict** the impact this would have on the gila monsters. **Justify** your prediction.

3. A fictional mammal called a googabear was scanned for activity every 10 minutes for 42 hours. The percentage of active behavior including feeding, moving and other social behavior, as well as in active behavior including resting or sleeping was recorded for the googabear.

A. Based on the graph below, **describe** and **explain** the pattern of activity for the googabear.

B. Winter is quickly approaching, and the scientist claims that the googabear population is a species that hibernates, requiring adaptations to reduce efficiency of cellular respiration. **Predict** the physiological and behavioral adaptations that googabear will have. **Provide** evidence that supports the scientist's claim.

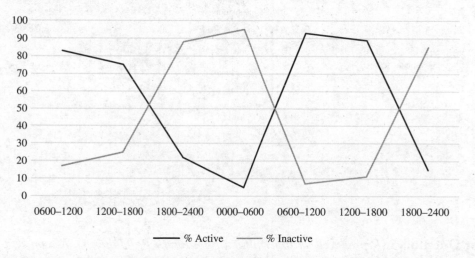

Figure is for Question 3

4. The Florida Everglades is a wet sawgrass prairie that extends from Lake Okeechobee in Central Florida to the tidal salt marshes and mangroves along the coast of southern Florida. It is made of several different types of wetlands, starting with freshwater marshes in the north moving into deep water swamps as it move south until it reaches the tidal salt marshes and coastal mangrove along the coasts of the Gulf of Mexico and the Atlantic Ocean. A scientist claims that a new plant species could thrive in the tidal salt marsh and provides the following data to help convince the community:

- Overall water potential of the soil is $\Psi_{soil} = -2.2$ MPa
- Plant cell contents: 0.08 M and 12°C (assume i = 1)
- Pressure potential of the plant cell is $\Psi_{pressure} = -1.2$ MPa

A. **Predict** the ability of the new plant species' ability to survive in the tidal salt marshes of the Everglades. **Provide** evidence to support your prediction and **justify** your response.

B. Burmese pythons, native to the tropics of Southeast Asia, which started out as a popular pet species in south Florida, is now threatening the Florida Everglades as an invasive species when pet owners release them into the Everglades' ecosystem. **Explain** how the Burmese python has affected the ecosystem of the Everglades.

5. Earth's early atmosphere was full of gases such as NH_3, CH_4, $H_2O(g)$, and H_2 from numerous volcanic activities. However, there was no O_2. Energy was abundant in the form of UV light, lightning, heat, and radioactivity. It was these characteristics that Stanley Miller and Harold Urey used to simulate Earth's primordial environment.

A. **Describe** the outcome of the Miller-Urey experiment.

B. **Explain** the significance of photosynthesis being present in simple cells before the evolution of more complex cells. **Justify** your response.

C. **Identify** the evidence that supports the evolution of the eukaryotic cell.

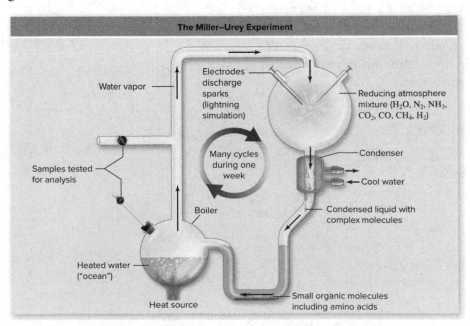

The Miller–Urey Experiment

Water vapor

Electrodes discharge sparks (lightning simulation)

Reducing atmosphere mixture (H_2O, N_2, NH_3, CO_2, CO, CH_4, H_2)

Many cycles during one week

Samples tested for analysis

Condenser

Cool water

Boiler

Condensed liquid with complex molecules

Heated water ("ocean")

Heat source

Small organic molecules including amino acids

Figure is for Question 5 (*Reproduced with permission from Raven P, Johnson G, Mason K, Losos J, Duncan T; Biology, 12th ed. New York: McGraw Hill; 2020*)

6. Sea otters, sea urchins, kelp, orcas, and other organisms live in the ecosystem along the West Coast of the United States. In the ecosystem, the orcas feed on sea otters as one of their sources of food. Graph A represents when the orcas feed mainly on sea otters, while Graph B represents when the orcas feed on a wide variety of mammals in the ecosystem.

A. **Explain** the impact of sea otters on the diversity of the ecosystem.

B. Scientists are consistently concerned by the potential loss of species due to human activity. **Identify** and **explain** one human impact that could affect the ecosystem of sea otters, sea urchins, kelp, orcas, and other organisms along the West Coast of the United States.

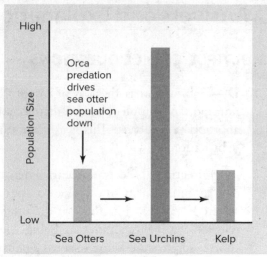

a.

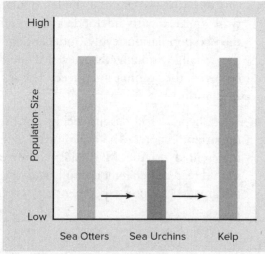

b.

Figures are for Question 6 (*Reproduced with permission from Raven P, Johnson G, Mason K, Losos J, Duncan T;* Biology, *12th ed. New York: McGraw Hill; 2020*)

› Answers and Explanations for Practice Exam 2

MULTIPLE-CHOICE QUESTIONS

1. **D**—Habituation is the loss of responsiveness to unimportant stimuli or stimuli that do not provide appropriate feedback. This is a prime example of habituation.

2. **A**—Directional selection occurs when members of a population at one end of a spectrum are selected against, while those at the other end are selected for. Taller giraffes are being selected for; shorter giraffes are being selected against.

3. **A**—When interbreeding ceases because some sort of barrier separates a single population into two (an area with no food, a mountain, etc.), the two populations evolve independently, and if they change enough, then, even if the barrier is removed, they cannot interbreed. This is allopatric speciation.

4. **D**—Chapter 13, despite being last, is a very important chapter. The experiments are very well represented on the AP Biology exam, and you should read this chapter carefully and learn how to design and interpret experiments.

5. **C**

6. **A**

7. **D**

8. **B**—The endosymbiotic theory proposes that mitochondria and chloroplasts evolved through the symbiotic relationship between prokaryotic organisms.

9. **D**—Fibroblast *growth factor* is said to be involved, but fibroblast cells are not.

10. **D**—Posttranscriptional modification actually occurs in the nucleus.

11. **C**—Genetic drift is a change in allele frequencies that is due to chance events. When drift dramatically reduces population size, it is called a "bottleneck."

12. **A**

13. **C**—Only photosystem I is involved in the cyclic reactions. Photosystem II is not.

14. **A**—Genetics has no memory. It will be ½ forever.

15. **A**—DNA migrates from a negative charge to a positive charge. The rest are true.

16. **B**—$0.04 = q^2$. Therefore, the square root of $0.04 = q = 0.20$ and $p + q = 1$. So $p + 0.20 = 1$. Therefore, $p = 0.80$, and $2pq$ is the frequency of the heterozygote condition: $2(0.20)(0.80) = 0.320 = 32$ percent.

17. **C**—Phytochrome is an important pigment to the process of flowering. Of its two forms, the active form, P_{fr}, is responsible for the production of the hormone florigen, which is thought to assist in the blooming of flowers.

18. **C**—Primary carnivores > primary consumers = herbivores > primary producers.

19. **C**—The example to know is the cattle egrets that feast on insects aroused into flight by cattle grazing in the insects' habitat. The birds benefit because they get food, but the cattle do not appear to benefit at all.

20. **B**—Conjugation is the sexual reproduction of bacteria.

21. **B**—In competitive inhibition, an inhibitor molecule resembling the substrate binds to the active site and physically blocks the substrate from attaching.

22. **C**—This is the only factor that is not a major factor affecting enzyme efficiency.

23. **B**—The activation energy of a reaction is the amount of energy needed for the reaction to occur. Notice that the activation energy for the enzymatic reaction is much lower than the non-enzymatic reaction.

24. **B**

25. **C**—For this specific gene in this specific population, there are a total of 40 alleles, two of which are the recessive cf allele ($2/40 = 0.05 = q$).

  Since you need to be homozygous recessive to have cystic fibrosis, $(q) \times (q) = q^2 = (0.05)^2 = 0.0025$. In other words, 25 out of 10,000 people (0.25 percent) will have cystic fibrosis.

26. **B**—Nondisjunction occurs during meiosis, resulting in an extra chromosome in one gamete and a missing chromosome in another gamete. trisomy 21 (Down syndrome) is a result of an extra chromosome 21 from nondisjunction.

27. **C**—During DNA replication, the semiconservative model of DNA is produced where the complementary strand is anti-parallel.

28. **C**—One hundred percent of the offspring in the F_1 generation would be YyRr.

29. **D**—When the carrot is immersed in the saltwater with a concentration of 0.45 M (a hypertonic solution), the carrot will lose water through osmosis.

30. **C**—If both parents were heterozygous and if this trait is indeed recessive, you would expect the next generation to show 75 percent normal-looking flies and 25 percent of the flies with the recessive trait. Based on a total of 211 flies, that would mean you would expect 158 normal flies and 53 recessive flies. Your observed numbers were, instead, 135 normal flies and 76 recessive flies.

	# OBSERVED (O)	# EXPECTED (e)	(o−e)	(o−e)²	(o−e)²/e
wild-type flies	135	158	−23	529	3.35
recessive flies	76	53	23	529	9.98

Since your chi-squared value (13.33) is higher than the critical value of 6.64 (based on 1 degree of freedom), you have to reject your hypothesis. Something other than an autosomal recessive trait is going on.

31. **B**—Water potential (Ψ) = −7.23 MPa (−6.23 MPa + −1 MPa)

Solute potential (Ψs) = (0.35 M)(1.0)(0.0831 liter bars/mole) (300 K) = −6.23 MPa

32. **C**—Ys = −(1)(0.8 M)(0.0831 L bars/mole K) (294 K) = −19.5 MPa

33. **B**—It is not autosomal dominant because in order for the second generation on the left to have those two individuals with the condition, one parent would need to display the condition as well. It is probably not sex-linked because it seems to appear as often in females as in males. Autosomal recessive seems to be the best fit for this disease.

34. **D**—One first needs to determine the probability that person C is heterozygous (Bb). We know that person D is double recessive because she has the condition. We know that the parents for person C must be Bb and Bb because neither of them has the condition, but they produced children with the condition. The probability of person C being heterozygous is ⅔, because a monohybrid cross of his parents (Bb × Bb) gives the following Punnett square:

	B	**b**
B	BB	Bb
b	Bb	bb

Since you know that he doesn't have the condition, he cannot be bb. This leaves just three possible outcomes, two of which are Bb. A cross must then be done between the father (person C) Bb and the mother (person D) bb. The chance of their child being bb is 50 percent, or ½. This means that the chance of these two having a child with the condition is ⅔ × ½, or ⅓.

35. **C**—Albinism is the only autosomal recessive condition on this list.

36. **C**—It is ½, because finding out that one of their children has the condition lets us know that the father (person C) is *definitely* Bb. This changes the probability of ⅔ to 1, meaning that the probability of the two having another child with this condition is simply the result of the Punnett square of Bb × bb, or ½.

37. **D**—When you see a ratio like the one in this problem—7:7:1:1 (approximately)—the genes are probably linked. The reason the crumpled, gray,

and vestigial black flies exist at all is because crossover must have occurred.

38. **A**—To determine the crossover frequency in a problem like this, simply add up the total number of crossovers (75 + 45 = 120) and divide that sum by the total number of offspring (120 + 555 + 525 = 1,200). This results in 120/1,200, or 10 percent.

39. **B**—One map unit is equal to a 1 percent recombination frequency.

40. **B**—The data in the table show you that this answer is the correct choice.

41. **D**—The larger the value of R_f for a bunch of pigments dissolved in a particular chromatography solvent, the faster the pigments will migrate. Beta-carotene has the highest R_f value.

42. **B**—Across the board it seems to have the lowest rate of transpiration. You can make this leap because, as mentioned on top of the larger chart, all the leaves have the same surface area, allowing you to compare their transpiration values.

43. **C**—The average enamel thickness started at 10, increased to 12, and then increased to 15. It is therefore increasing overall.

44. **D**—The average enamel thickness does not describe the range of possible values; an individual with a thickness of 15 could reasonably come from any of the three generations (if we took into account probability, we could say that the individual most likely came from the 100th generation because this population has the highest frequency of individuals with this thickness; however, the question does not ask for probabilities).

45. **B**—Because thicker enamel in this species indicates foods that are more difficult to process, the answer is B.

46. **B**—Experimental setups where individuals are given a choice as to where to move are called "choice chambers."

47. **D**—All the answers except D are possible, and are important things to consider when setting up an experiment. For example, it is important to allow your study animals enough time to move and/or get used to their new surroundings and conditions before drawing conclusions about their behavior. D is not a good answer because half of the slugs started in a high-temperature area and haven't moved.

48. **A**—Kinesis is the movement of animals in response to current conditions; animals tend to move until they find a favorable environment, at which point their movement slows.

49. **D**—It is important to try to measure only one variable at once. The 18 slugs may have moved to the higher-temperature, higher-salinity conditions because they need high temperatures to survive, even if they dislike high salinity, and vice versa. The original experiment circumvents this problem by giving a choice for all the possible combinations of variables.

50. **C**—New genes are introduced into the bacterium through viral transduction.

51. **B**—When the body has too little water, ADH works to increase the amount of water available. This drive to maintain a stable condition is an example of homeostasis.

52. **C**—Line C showed no net change in weight, indicating the concentration of the solution inside the bag was the same (isotonic) as the solution in the beaker.

53. **A**—The most water would diffuse into the most hypertonic solution; line A shows the biggest increase in weight.

54. **B**—Line B still shows an increase in weight at 50 minutes, whereas line A has leveled out and is isotonic at 50 minutes.

55. **C**—Even though an amino acid doesn't have direct contact with the substrate, it still plays a role in the overall shape of the enzyme.

56. **A**—As RNA polymerase adds new nucleotides to the 3′ end of the new strand, it is moving toward the 5′ end of the (antiparallel) template strand.

57. **B**—The promoter would be located upstream from where transcription would begin.

58. **C**—There are few nucleotide differences between species 1 and 2, indicating they would reside close to one another on the cladogram. The same holds true for species 3 and 5. There are large numbers of differences between species 4 and all others, indicating it would be positioned on its own branch.

59. **A**—Both B and E branches originate from point 1.

60. **C**—Species B and C reside the closest to one another.

› Free-Response Grading Outline

1.

A. **Explain** how carbon fixation by the leaf disks creates the oxygen needed to float when placed in light.
- Located in the chloroplast. (1 point)
- Light reaction transfers light energy to chemical energy via ATP and NADPH. (1 point)
- Uses CO_2 from environment, ATP, and NADPH from light reaction to create sugar, which is stored chemical energy. (1 point)
- Oxygen is the by-product of splitting of H_2O during light reaction. (1 point)

B. **Identify** the independent and dependent variables used in this experiment.
- Independent variable – exposure to light. (1 point)
- Dependent variable – number of floating leaf disks. (1 point)

C. **Construct** an appropriately labeled graph.

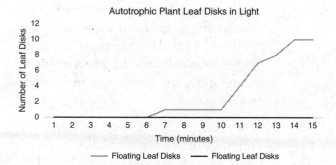

- Independent and dependent variables correctly plotted. (1 point)
- Correctly labeled. (1 point)
- Correctly scaled axis. (1 point)

D. Make a **prediction** if the leaf disks were placed under more intense light source. **Justify** your prediction.
- Predict that the leaf disk would float quicker due to an increase of photosynthetic activity in the leaves. (1 point)
- Increase in light would cause an increase of light energy being absorbed, and more oxygen would be released as a by-product of the light reaction of photosynthesis. (1 point)

2.

A. **Calculate** the P-generation genotypes. **Justify** your response.
- The P-generation is Gg × gg. (1 point)
- The P-generation results in a F_1 generation that consists of Gg (black-scaled) and gg (brown-scaled) gila monsters. Then a cross of the F_1 generation results in 50 percent black-scaled monsters and 50 percent brown-scaled monsters in the F_2 generation. (1 point)

B. **Describe** and **explain** the white-scaled female that was present in the F_1 generation.
- The white-scaled female is caused by a point mutation, which is a random event, that can lead to changes in allele frequencies. (2 points)
- The point occurred as DNA responsible for the production of protein that determines scale color was undergoing replication. (2 points)

C. The phenotype for scale color is claimed to be autosomal. **Support** the claim by calculating the chi-square value. **Provide** reasoning to justify the claim.
- $x^2 = (53 - 53.5)^2 + (54 - 53.5)^2/2 - 1 = 0.5$ (1 point)
- Null hypothesis—The phenotype for scale color is autosomal. (1 point)
- Scale color for gila monsters is, in fact, autosomal. A chi-square value of 0.5 on the F_2 generation data resulted in a failure to reject the null hypothesis. (1 point)

D. Coyotes are natural predators of gila monsters. During a recent drought, the coyote's population experienced a bottleneck effect. **Predict** the impact this would have on the gila monsters. **Justify** your prediction.
- The population of gila monsters would randomly decrease. (1 point)
- During a bottleneck effect, a population is randomly reduced, causing a decrease in the population and genetic diversity, leading to a genetic drift. (1 point)

3.

A. Based on the graph, **describe** and **explain** the pattern of activity for the googabear.
- Googabears are more active from 6 a.m. until 6 p.m. (during daylight hours). (1 point)
- Decrease activity from 6 p.m. to 6 a.m. (when it is dark). (1 point)
- Googabears' food source is available during daylight. (1 point)
- Googabear predators are nocturnal (out at night), so it is safest for googabears to remain hidden at night. (1 point)
- Googabears rely on collective body heat at night (huddling); activity of huddled group is low. (1 point)

B. Winter is quickly approaching, and a scientist claims that the googabear population is a species that hibernates, requiring adaptations to reduce efficiency of cellular respiration. **Predict** the physiological and behavioral adaptations that googabears will have. **Provide** evidence that supports the scientist's claim.

(2 Points maximum)
- Googabears are endothermic—Must maintain body temperature through increase fat storage and thick fur than when active.
- Googabears need a constant supply of ATP, which will come from a large supply of stored energy in the form of fat.
- Googabears are inactive during hibernation, during which cells require less ATP on a daily basis.

4.

A. **Predict** the ability of the new plant species' ability to survive in the tidal salt marshes of the Everglades. **Provide** evidence to support your prediction and **justify** your response.
- The plant cell's water potential (-1.39 MPa) is higher than that of the soil (-2.2 MPa). (1 point)
- Water would flow out of the plant cell (hypotonic) into soil (hypertonic). (1 point)
- The plant cell would not survive. (1 point)

B. Burmese pythons, native to the tropics of Southeast Asia, which started out as a popular pet species in south Florida, is now threatening the Florida Everglades as an invasive species when pet owners release them into the Everglades ecosystem. **Explain** how the Burmese python has affected the ecosystem of the Everglades.
- Introduction of an invasive species allows for the species to exploit a new niche free of predators and/or competitors, allowing them to outcompete other organisms for resources. (1 point)

5.

A. **Describe** the outcome of the Miller-Urey experiment.
- Organic molecules could have originated in the early atmosphere. (1 point)

B. **Explain** the significance of photosynthesis being present in simple cells before the evolution of more complex cells. **Justify** your response.
- With the first prokaryotic cells being photosynthetic, they release oxygen as a by-product, leading to an increase in atmospheric oxygen and allowing for the evolution of cellular respiration. Increased oxygen allowed cells to generate more energy and grow larger and more complex. (1 point)

C. **Identify** the evidence that supports the evolution of the eukaryotic cell.
- Chloroplasts and mitochondria have their own DNA that consists of a single, circular molecule. They replicate by a process similar to prokaryotes and have enzymes homologous to those found in prokaryotes. (2 points)

6.

A. Explain the impact of sea otters on the diversity of the ecosystem.
- The sea otter is the keystone species that keeps the sea urchin population in check, allowing kelp and other organisms to thrive. (1 point)

- Keystone species are a species that holds a habitat together by playing a pivotal role in how the ecosystem functions. It may not be the largest or most abundant species in an ecological community, but its removal sets off a chain of events that can lead to dramatic structural and diversity changes to the ecosystem. (1 point)

B. Scientists are consistently concerned by the potential loss of species due to human activity. **Identify** and **explain** one human impact that could affect the ecosystem of sea otters, sea urchins, kelp, orcas, and other organisms along the West Coast of the United States.

- Pollution, habitat degradation, or over-fishing are a few examples of human impact. (1 point)
- These human impacts on the ecosystem accelerate changes to the local ecosystem's and eventually the global ecosystem's structure and dynamics. (1 point)

Scoring and Interpretation
AP BIOLOGY PRACTICE EXAM 2

SECTION I: Multiple-Choice Questions:

NUMBER
CORRECT [   ] x 1.0000 = [   ]

WEIGHTED SECTION I SCORE

SECTION II: Free Response:

QUESTION 1 [   ] x 1.7647 [   ]
(out of 9)   (do not round)

QUESTION 2 [   ] x 1.7647 [   ]
(out of 9)   (do not round)

QUESTION 3 [   ] x 1.7647 [   ]
(out of 4)   (do not round)

QUESTION 4 [   ] x 1.7647 [   ]
(out of 4)   (do not round)

QUESTION 5 [   ] x 1.7647 [   ]
(out of 4)   (do not round)

QUESTION 6 [   ] x 1.7647 [   ]
(out of 4)   (do not round)

SECTION SCORE: (add 6 question totals together) [   ]

WEIGHTED SECTION II SCORE

TOTAL SCORE: (add Section I and Section II together) [   ]

OVERALL SCORE

AP BIOLOGY
SCORE CONVERSION CHART

COMPOSITE SCORE RANGE	AP EXAM SCORE
94 – 120	5
76 – 93	4
54 – 75	3
30 – 53	2
0 – 29	1

BIBLIOGRAPHY

Futuyma, Douglas J. *Evolutionary Biology*. 3rd ed. Sunderland, MA: Sinauer Associates, Inc., 1998.

Kotz, John C., Paul M. Treichel, and John Townsend. *Chemistry and Chemical Reactivity*. 8th ed. Stamford, CT: Brooks/Cole, 2011.

Reece, Jane B., Lisa A. Urry, and Michael L. Cain. *Campbell Biology*. 9th ed. San Francisco: Benjamin Cummings, 2011.

Starr, Cecie, Christine Evers, and Lisa Starr. *Biology: Concepts and Applications*. 8th ed. San Francisco: Brooks/Cole, 2011.

Strauss, Eric, and Marylin Lisowski. *Biology: The Web of Life*. Teacher's ed. Menlo Park, CA: Addison-Wesley Longman, 1998.

Wilbraham, Antony C. *Chemistry*. 5th ed. New York: Pearson, 2000.

WEBSITES

Here is a list of websites that contain information and links that you might find useful to your preparation for the AP Biology exam:

- http://www.collegeboard.com

- http://blast.ncbi.nlm.nih.gov

Bozeman Science

- http://www.bozemanscience.com/ap-biology

Biology with Amoeba Sisters

- https://www.youtube.com/user/AmoebaSisters

Khan Academy

- https://www.khanacademy.org/science/ap-biology

College Board YouTube

- https://www.youtube.com/user/advancedplacement

AP Classroom

- "https://myap.collegeboard.org/login"https://myap.collegeboard.org

AP Biology - The Course

- https://apcentral.collegeboard.org/courses/ap-biology/course

- https://www.biointeractive.org/

- http://www.phschool.com/science/biology_place/labbench/index.html

- https://learn.genetics.utah.edu/

- https://sciencecases.lib.buffalo.edu/

- http://datanuggets.org/

abiotic components The *nonliving* players in an ecosystem, such as climate and nutrients.

abscisic acid Plant hormone that inhibits cell growth, prevents premature germination, and stimulates closing of the stomata.

achondroplasia Autosomal dominant form of dwarfism seen in 1 out of 10,000 people.

ACTH See **adrenocorticotropic hormone.**

active site Part of the enzyme that interacts with the substrate in an enzyme–substrate complex.

active transport The movement of a particle across a selectively permeable membrane *against* its concentration gradient. This movement requires the input of energy, which is why it is termed "active" transport.

adaptation A trait that, if altered, affects the fitness of the organism. Adaptations are the result of natural selection and can include not only physical traits such as eyes and fingernails but also the intangible traits of organisms, such as lifespan.

adaptive radiation A rapid series of speciation events that occur when one or more ancestral species invades a new environment.

ADH See **antidiuretic hormone.**

adrenocorticotropic hormone (ACTH) A hormone that stimulates the secretion of adrenal cortical hormones, which work to maintain electrolytic homeostasis in the body.

aerobic respiration Energy-producing reactions in animals that involve three stages: glycolysis, the Krebs cycle, and oxidative phosphorylation; requires oxygen.

age structure Statistic that compares the relative number of individuals in the population from each age group.

agonistic behavior Behavior that results from a conflict of interest between individuals; often involves intimidation and submission.

alcohol Organic compound that contains a hydroxyl (—OH) functional group.

alcohol fermentation Occurs in fungi, yeast, and bacteria. Pyruvate is converted in two steps to ethanol, regenerating two molecules of NAD^+.

aldehyde Carbonyl group in which one R is a hydrogen and the other is a carbon chain. Hydrophilic and polar.

aldosterone Released from the adrenal gland, this hormone acts on the distal tubules to cause the reabsorption of more Na^+ and water. This increases blood volume and pressure.

allantois Transports waste products in mammals to the placenta. Later it is incorporated into the umbilical cord.

allele A variant of a gene for a particular character.

allopatric speciation Interbreeding ceases because some sort of barrier separates a single population into two (an area with no food, a mountain, etc.). The two populations evolve independently, and if they change enough, then, even if the barrier is removed, they cannot interbreed.

alternation of generations Plant life cycle, so named because during the cycle, plants sometimes exist as a diploid organism and at other times as a haploid organism.

altruistic behavior Behavior pattern that reduces the overall fitness of one organism while increasing the fitness of another.

alveoli Functional unit of the lung where gas exchange occurs.

amines Compounds containing amino groups.

amino acid A compound with a carbon center surrounded by an amino group, a carboxyl group, a hydrogen, and an R group that provides an amino acid's unique chemical characteristics.

aminoacyl tRNA synthetase Enzyme that makes sure that each tRNA molecule picks up the appropriate amino acid for its anticodon.

amino group A functional group that contains —NH_2 and that acts as a base; an example is an amino acid.

amnion Structure formed from epiblast that encloses the fluid-filled cavity that helps cushion the developing embryo.

amygdala The portion of the human brain that controls impulsive emotions and anger.

amylase Enzyme that breaks down the starches in the human diet to simpler sugars such as maltose, which are fully digested farther down in the intestines.

anaerobic respiration Energy-producing reactions, known as *fermentation,* that do not involve oxygen. It begins with glycolysis and concludes with the formation of NAD^+.

anemia Illness in which a lack of iron causes red blood cells to have a diminished capacity for delivering oxygen.

aneuploidy The condition of having an abnormal number of chromosomes.

angiosperm Flowering plant divided into monocots and dicots (monocotyledons and dicotyledons).

anion Ion with a negative charge that contains more electrons than protons.

anterior pituitary gland Structure that produces six hormones: TSH, STH (or HGH), ACTH, LH, FSH, and prolactin.

anther Pollen-producing portion of a plant.

antheridia Male gametangia in bryophytes and ferns designed to produce flagellated sperm that swim to meet up with the eggs produced by the female gametangia.

anticodon Region present at a tRNA attachment site; a three-nucleotide sequence that is perfectly complementary to a particular codon.

antidiuretic hormone (ADH) A hormone produced in the brain and stored in the pituitary gland; it increases the permeability of the collecting duct to water, leading to more concentrated urine content.

antigen A molecule that is foreign to our bodies and causes our immune systems to respond.

apical meristem Region at the tips of roots and shoots where plant growth is concentrated and many actively dividing cells can be found.

apoplast pathway Movement of water and nutrients through the nonliving portion of cells.

aposematic coloration Warning coloration adopted by animals that possess a chemical defense mechanism.

archaebacteria One of two major prokaryotic evolutionary branches. These organisms tend to live in extreme environments and include halophiles, methanogens, and thermoacidophiles.

archegonium Female gametangia in bryophytes, ferns, and gymnosperms.

archezoa Eukaryotic organism that allegedly most closely resembles prokaryotes.

arteries Structures that carry blood away from the heart.

artificial selection When humans become the agents of natural selection (breeding of dogs).

ascospores Haploid meiotic products produced by certain fungi.

A site Region on protein synthesis machinery that holds the tRNA carrying the next amino acid.

associative learning Process by which animals take one stimulus and associate it with another.

atom The smallest form of an element that still displays its unique properties.

ATP synthase Enzyme that uses the flow of hydrogens to drive the phosphorylation of an adenosine diphosphate molecule to produce adenosine triphosphate.

auditory communication Communication that involves the use of sound in the conveying of a message.

autonomic nervous system (ANS) A subdivision of the peripheral nervous system (PNS) that controls the involuntary activities of the body: smooth muscle, cardiac muscle, and glands. The ANS is divided into the sympathetic and parasympathetic divisions.

autosomal chromosome One that is not directly involved in determining gender.

autotroph An organism that is self-nourishing. It obtains carbon and energy without ingesting other organisms.

auxin Plant hormone that leads to elongation of stems and plays a role in phototropism and gravitropism.

axon A longer extension that leaves a neuron and carries the impulse away from the cell body toward target cells.

balanced polymorphism When there are two or more phenotypic variants maintained in a population.

bare-rock succession The attachment of lichen to rocks, followed by the step-by-step arrival of replacement species.

Barr bodies Inactivated genes on X chromosomes.

Batesian mimicry An animal that is harmless copies the appearance of an animal that is dangerous as a defense mechanism to make predators think twice about attacking.

behavioral ecology Science that studies the interaction between animals and their environments from an evolutionary perspective.

bile Substance that contains bile salts, phospholipids, cholesterol, and bile pigments such as bilirubin, is stored in the gallbladder, and is dumped into the small intestine on the arrival of the food.

bile salts Help to mechanically digest fat by emulsifying it into small droplets contained in water.

binary fission Mechanism by which prokaryotic cells divide. The cell elongates and pinches into two new daughter cells.

binomial system of classification System created by Linnaeus in which each species is given a two-word name: Genus + species (e.g., *Homo sapiens*).

biogeochemical cycles Cycles that represent the movement of elements, such as nitrogen and carbon, from organisms to the environment and back in a continuous cycle.

biomass pyramid *Biomass* represents the cumulative weight of all of the members at a given trophic level.

biome The various geographic regions of the Earth that serve as hosts for ecosystems.

biosphere The entire life-containing area of a planet—all ecosystems and communities.

biotic components Living organisms of an ecosystem.

biotic potential The maximum growth rate for a population given unlimited resources, unlimited space, and lack of competition or predators.

birth rate Offspring produced per a specific time period.

bivalves Mollusks with hinged shells such as oysters and clams.

blastula As a morula undergoes its next round of cell divisions, fluid fills its center to create this hollow-looking structure.

"blending" hypothesis Theory that the genes contributed by two parents mix as if they are paint colors and the exact genetic makeup of each parent can never be recovered; the genes are as inseparable as blended paint.

bottleneck A dramatic reduction in population size that increases the likelihood of genetic drift.

bronchi Tunnels that branch off the trachea that lead into the individual lungs and divide into smaller branches called bronchioles.

bronchioles Tiny lung tunnels that branch repeatedly until they conclude as tiny air pockets containing alveoli.

brush border Large numbers of microvilli that increase the surface area of the small intestine to improve absorption efficiency.

bryophytes The first land plants to evolve from the chlorophytes. Members of this group include mosses, liverworts, and hornworts.

bundle sheath cells Cells that are tightly wrapped around the veins of a leaf. They are the site for the Calvin cycle in C_4 plants.

C_4 photosynthesis Photosynthetic process that alters the way in which carbon is fixed to better deal with the lack of CO_2 that comes from the closing of the stomata in hot, dry regions.

C_4 plant Plant that has adapted its photosynthetic process to more efficiently handle hot and dry conditions.

Calvin cycle A name for the light-independent (dark) reactions of photosynthesis.

CAM (crassulacean acid metabolism) photosynthesis Plants close their stomata during the day, collect CO_2 at night, and store the CO_2 in the form of acids until it is needed during the day for photosynthesis.

capsid A protein shell that surrounds genetic material.

carbohydrate Organic compound used by the cells of the human body in energy-producing reactions and as structural material. The three main types of carbohydrates are monosaccharides, disaccharides, and polysaccharides.

carbon cycle The movement of carbon from the atmosphere to living organisms and back to the environment in a continuous cycle.

carbon fixation The attachment of the carbon from CO_2 to a molecule that is able to enter the Calvin cycle, assisted by rubisco.

carbonyl group A functional group that is hydrophilic and polar. It has a central carbon connected to R groups on either side. If both Rs are carbon chains, it is a ketone. If one R is a hydrogen and the other a carbon chain, it is an aldehyde.

carboxyl group An acidic functional group (COOH). This functional group shows up along with amino groups in amino acids.

cardiac muscle Involuntary muscle of the heart that is striated in appearance and contains multiple nuclei.

carnivore A consumer that obtains energy and nutrients through consumption of other animals.

carotenoid A photosynthetic pigment.

carrying capacity The maximum number of individuals a population can sustain in a given environment.

casparian strip Obstacle that blocks the passage of water through the endodermis of plants.

catalase Enzyme that assists in the conversion of hydrogen peroxide to water and oxygen. Found in peroxisomes.

catalysts Molecules that speed up reactions by lowering the activation energy of a reaction.

cation Ion with a positive charge that contains more protons than electrons.

cell body The main body of the neuron.

cell cycle A cycle that consists of four stages: G_1, S, G_2, and M. G_1 and G_2 are growth stages, S is the part of the cell cycle in which the DNA is duplicated, and the M phase stands for mitosis—the cell division phase.

cell-mediated immunity This type of immunity involves *direct* cellular response to invasion as opposed to antibody-based defense.

cell plate Plant cell structure constructed in the Golgi apparatus composed of vesicles that fuse together along the middle of the cell, completing the separation process.

cellular slime molds Protists with a unique eating strategy. When plenty of food is available, they eat alone. When food is scare, they clump together and form a unit.

cellulose Polysaccharide composed of glucose used by plants to form cell walls.

cell wall Wall that functions to shape and protect cells. Present in plant but not animal cells.

central nervous system (CNS) The CNS is made up of the brain and the spinal cord. The CNS controls skeletal muscles and voluntary movement.

cephalization The concentration of sensory machinery in the anterior end of a bilateral organism.

cerebellum Portion of brain in charge of coordination and balance.

cerebrum Portion of the brain that controls functions such as speech, hearing, sight, and motor control. Divided into two hemispheres and four lobes per hemisphere.

cervix The uterus connects to the vaginal opening via this narrowed region.

CF See **cystic fibrosis.**

character A heritable feature, such as flower color, that varies among individuals.

checkpoints Stop points throughout the cell cycle where the cell verifies that there are enough nutrients and raw materials to progress to the next stage of the cycle.

chemical communication Mammals and insects communicate through the use of chemical signals called *pheromones.*

chemiosmosis The coupling of the movement of electrons down the electron transport chain with the formation of ATP using the driving force provided by a proton gradient. Seen in both photosynthesis and respiration.

chemoautotrophs Autotrophs that produce energy through oxidation of inorganic substances.

chitin Polysaccharide that is an important part of the exoskeletons of arthropods such as insects, spiders, and shellfish.

chlorophyll A photosynthetic pigment.

chlorophytes Green algae that are probably the common ancestors of land plants.

chloroplast The site of photosynthesis and energy production in plant cells and algae.

choanoflagellate Accepted to be the common ancestor of the animal kingdom.

choice Refers to the selection of mates by one sex (in mammals, it is usually females who exercise choice over males).

choice chamber Chamber used in scientific experiments to study kinesis.

cholesterol Steroid that is an important structural component of cell membranes and serves as a precursor molecule for steroid sex hormones.

chorion Formed from the trophoblast, it is the outer membrane of the embryo and the site of implantation onto the endometrium. It contributes to formation of the placenta in mammals.

chromatin The raw material that gives rise to the chromosomes (genetic material is uncoiled).

chromosomal translocations Condition in which a piece of one chromosome is attached to another, nonhomologous chromosome.

chromosome duplication Error in chromosomal replication that results in the repetition of a genetic segment.

chromosome inversion Condition in which a piece of a chromosome separates and reattaches in the opposite direction.

chronic myelogenous leukemia A cancer affecting white blood cell precursor cells. In this disease, a portion of chromosome 22 has been swapped with a piece of chromosome 9.

chymotrypsin Enzyme that cuts protein bonds in the small intestine.

cilia Structures that beat in rhythmical waves to carry foreign particles and mucus away from the lungs.

circadian rhythm A physiologic cycle that occurs in time increments that are roughly equivalent to the length of a day.

class I histocompatibility antigens The surface of all the cells of the human body, except for red blood cells, have these antigens, which are slightly different for each individual. The immune system accepts any cell that has the identical match for this antigen as friendly. Anything with a different major histocompatibility complex is foreign.

class II histocompatibility antigens Antigens found on the surface of the immune cells of the body. These antigens play a role in the interaction between the cells of the immune system.

classical conditioning Type of associative learning that Ivan Pavlov demonstrated with his experiments involving salivation in dogs.

cleavage divisions Developing embryo divides; cytoplasm is distributed unevenly to the daughter cells while the genetic information is distributed equally.

cleavage furrow Groove formed in animal cells between the two daughter cells; this groove pinches together to complete the separation of the two cells after mitosis.

climax community Final stable stage at the completion of a succession cycle.

clumped dispersion Scenario in which individuals live in packs that are spaced out from each other.

codominance Both alleles express themselves fully in a heterozygous organism.

codon A triplet of nucleotides that codes for a particular amino acid.

coefficient of relatedness Statistic that represents the average proportion of genes that two individuals have in common.

coelom Fluid-filled body cavity found between the body wall and the gut that has a lining and is derived from the mesoderm.

coelomates Animals that contain a true coelum.

coenocytic fungi Fungi that do not contain septae.

coevolution The mutual evolution between two species, which is exemplified by predator–prey relationships.

coleoptile Protective structure found around a grass seedling.

collenchyma cells Live plant cells that provide flexible and mechanical support.

commensalism One organism benefits from the relationship while the other is unaffected.

community A collection of populations of species in a given geographic area.

competent Describes a cell that is ready to accept foreign DNA from the environment.

competition Both species involved are harmed by this kind of interaction. The two major forms of competition are intraspecific and interspecific competition.

competitive inhibition Condition in which an inhibitor molecule resembling the substrate binds to the active site and physically blocks the substrate from attaching.

complement A protein that coats cells that need to be cleared, stimulating phagocytes to ingest them.

compounds Two or more elements combined to form an entity.

conduction Process by which heat moves from a place of higher temperature to a place of lower temperature.

conifers Gymnosperm plants whose reproductive structure is a cone.

conjugation The transfer of DNA between two bacterial cells connected by appendages called *sex pili*.

conservative DNA replication The original double helix of DNA does not change at all; it is as if the DNA is placed on a copy machine and an exact duplicate is made. DNA from the parent appears in only one of the two daughter cells.

convection Heat transfer caused by airflow.

convergent characters Characters are convergent if they look the same in two species, even though the species do *not* share a common ancestor.

convergent evolution Two unrelated species evolve in a way that makes them *more* similar. They both respond the same way to some environmental challenge, bringing them closer together.

cork cambium Area that produces a thick cover for stems and roots. It produces tissue that replaces dried-up epidermis lost during secondary growth.

cork cells Cells produced by the cork cambium that die and form a protective barrier against infection and physical damage.

corpus callosum Bridge that connects the two hemispheres of the brain.

cortex Outer region of the kidney or adrenal gland.

cortisol Stress hormone released in response to physiological challenges.

cotyledon Structure that provides nutrients for a developing angiosperm plant.

cri-du-chat syndrome This syndrome occurs with a deletion in chromosome 5 that leads to mental retardation, unusual facial features, and a small head. Most die in infancy or early childhood.

crossover Also referred to as "crossing over." When the homologous pairs match up during prophase I of meiosis, complementary pieces from the two homologous chromosomes wrap around each other and are exchanged between the chromosomes. This is one of the mechanisms that allows offspring to differ from their parents.

cryptic coloration Those being hunted adopt a coloring scheme that allows them to blend in to the colors of the environment.

cuticle Waxy covering that protects terrestrial plants against water loss.

cutin Waxy coat that protects plants.

cyclic light reactions Pathway that produces only ATP and uses only photosystem I.

cyclin Protein that accumulates during interphase; vital to cell cycle control.

cystic fibrosis (CF) A recessive disorder that is the most common lethal genetic disease in the United States. A defective version of a gene on chromosome 7 results in the excessive secretion of a thick mucus, which accumulates in the lungs and digestive tract. Left untreated, children with CF die at a very young age.

cytokinesis The physical separation of the newly formed daughter cells during meiosis and mitosis. Occurs immediately after telophase.

cytokinin Plant hormone that promotes cell division and leaf enlargement, and slows down the aging of leaves.

cytoskeleton Provides support, shape, and mobility to cells.

death rate Number of deaths per time period.

deceptive markings Patterns that can cause a predator to think twice before attacking. For example, some insects may have colored designs on their wings that resemble large eyes, making individuals look more imposing than they are.

decomposer See **detritivore.**

dehydration reaction A reaction in which two compounds merge, releasing H_2O as a product.

deletion A piece of the chromosome is lost in the developmental process.

demographers Scientists who study the theory and statistics behind population growth and decline.

dendrite One of many short, branched processes of a neuron that help send the nerve impulses toward the cell body.

denitrification The process by which bacteria use nitrates and release N_2 as a product.

density-dependent inhibition When a certain density of cells is reached, cell growth will slow or stop. This is because there are not enough raw materials for the growth and survival of more cells.

density-dependent limiting factors Factors related to population size that come into play as population size approaches or passes the carrying capacity. Examples of density-dependent limiting factors include food, waste, and disease.

density-independent limiting factors Factors that limit population growth that have nothing to do with the population size, such as natural disasters and weather.

depolarization The electric potential becomes less negative inside the cell, allowing an action potential to occur.

desert The driest land biome on Earth, which experiences a wide range of temperatures from day to night and exists on nearly every continent.

detritivore A consumer that obtains its energy through the consumption of dead animals and plants; also known as *decomposer.*

dicot (dicotyledon) An angiosperm plant that has two cotyledons.

diffusion The movement of molecules down their concentration gradients without the use of energy. It is a passive process during which molecules move from a region of higher concentration to a region of lower concentration.

dihybrid cross The crossing of two different characters (BbRr × BbRr). A dihybrid cross between heterozygous gametes gives a 9:3:3:1 phenotype ratio in the offspring.

diploid (2n) An organism that has two copies of each type of chromosome. In humans, this refers to the pairs of homologous chromosomes.

diplomonads A phylum that is associated with the archezoan eukaryotes.

directional selection Occurs when members of a population at one end of a spectrum are selected against and/or those at the other end are selected for.

disaccharide A sugar consisting of two monosaccharides bound together. Common disaccharides include sucrose, maltose, and lactose.

dispersive DNA replication A theory that suggests every daughter strand contains *some* parental DNA, but it is dispersed among pieces of DNA not of parental origin.

disruptive selection Selection is disruptive when individuals at the two extremes of a spectrum of variation do better than the more common forms in the middle.

distribution Describes the way populations are dispersed over a geographic area.

divergent evolution Two related species evolve in a way that makes them less similar, sometimes causing speciation.

division The classification category that replaces the phylum in plant classification.

DNA methylation The addition of CH_3 groups to the bases of DNA, rendering DNA inactive.

DNA polymerase The main enzyme in DNA replication that attaches to primer proteins and adds nucleotides to the growing DNA chain in a 5′-to-3′ direction.

DNA replication The process by which DNA is copied. This process occurs during the S phase of the cell cycle to ensure that every cell produced during mitosis or meiosis receives the proper amount of DNA.

dominance hierarchy A ranking of power among the members of a group of individuals.

double helix The shape of DNA—two strands held together by hydrogen bonds.

Down syndrome A classic aneuploid syndrome affecting 1 of every 700 children born in the United States. It most often involves a trisomy of chromosome 21, and leads to mental retardation, heart defects, short stature, and characteristic facial features.

Duchenne muscular dystrophy Sex-linked disorder caused by the absence of an essential muscle protein that leads to progressive weakening of the muscles combined with a loss of muscle coordination.

ecosystem All the individuals of a community and the environment in which it exists.

ectoderm Outer germ layer that gives rise to the nervous system, skin, hair, and nails.

ectothermic animal Animal whose basic metabolic rates increase in response to increases in temperature.

Edwards syndrome The presence of trisomy 18, which occurs in 1 out of every 10,000 live births and affects almost every organ of the body.

electron transport chain (ETC) The chain of molecules, located in the mitochondria, that passes electrons along during the process of chemiosmosis to regenerate NAD^+ to form ATP. Each time an electron passes to another member of the chain, the energy level of the system drops.

element The simplest form of matter.

embryology The study of embryonic development.

emigration rate Rate at which individuals relocate *out of* a given population.

endergonic reaction A reaction that requires *input* of energy to occur. A + B + energy → C.

endocytosis Process by which substances are brought into cells by enclosure into a membrane-created vesicle that surrounds the substance and escorts it into the cell.

endoderm Inner germ layer that gives rise to the inner lining of the gut, digestive system, liver, thyroid, lungs, and bladder.

endodermis Cells that line the innermost layer of the cortex in plants that give rise to the casparian strip.

endometrium Inner wall of the uterus to which the embryo attaches.

endopeptidases Enzymes that initiate the digestion of proteins by hydrolyzing all the polypeptides into small amino acid groups.

endosymbiotic theory Proposes that groups of prokaryotes associated in symbiotic relationships to form eukaryotes (mitochondria and chloroplasts).

endothermic animal Animal whose body temperature is relatively unaffected by external temperature.

enhancer DNA region, also known as a "regulator," that is located thousands of bases away from the promoter that influences transcription by interacting with specific transcription factors.

enzymes Catalytic proteins that are picky, interacting only with particular substrates. However, the enzymes can be reused and react with more than one copy of their substrate of choice and have a major effect on a reaction.

epiblast Develops into the three germ layers of the embryo: the endoderm, the mesoderm, and the ectoderm.

epidermis (plants) The protective outer coating of plants.

epididymis The coiled region that extends from the testes. This is where the sperm completes its maturation and waits until it is called on to do its duty.

episomes Plasmids that can be incorporated into a bacterial chromosome.

epistasis A gene at one locus alters the phenotypic expression of a gene at another locus. A dihybrid cross involving epistatic genes produces a 9:4:3 phenotype ratio.

esophageal sphincter Valvelike trapdoor between the esophagus and the stomach.

esophagus Structure that connects the throat to the stomach.

estrogen Hormone made (secreted) in ovaries that stimulates development of sex characteristics in women and induces the release of luteinizing hormone (LH) before the LH surge.

ETC See **electron transport chain.**

ethology The study of animal behavior.

ethylene Plant hormone that initiates the ripening of fruit and the dropping of leaves and flowers from trees.

eubacteria One of two major prokaryotic evolutionary branches. Categorized according to their mode of nutritional acquisition, mechanism of movement, shape, and other characteristics.

eukaryotic cell Complex cell that contains a nucleus, which functions as the control center of the cell, directing DNA replication, transcription, and cell growth. Organisms can be unicellular or multicellular and contain many different membrane-bound organelles.

evaporation Process by which a liquid changes into a vapor form. Functions in thermoregulation for humans when water leaves our bodies in the form of water vapor—sweat.

evolution Descent with modification. Evolution happens to populations, not individuals, and describes change in allele frequencies in populations with time.

excision repair Repair mechanism for DNA replication in which a section of DNA containing an error is cut out and the gap is filled by DNA polymerase.

exergonic reaction A reaction that *gives off* energy as a product. A + B → energy + C.

exocytosis Process by which substances are exported out of the cell. A vesicle escorts the substance to the plasma membrane, fuses with the membrane, and ejects its contents out of the cell.

exons Coding regions produced during transcription that are glued back together to produce the mRNA that is translated into a protein.

exopeptidases Enzymes that complete the digestion of proteins by hydrolyzing all the amino acids of any remaining fragments.

exponential growth A population grows at a rate that creates a J-shaped curve.

extreme halophiles Archaebacteria that live in environments with high salt concentrations.

F_1 The first generation of offspring, or the first "filial" generation, in a genetic cross.

F_2 The second generation of offspring, or the second "filial" generation, in a genetic cross.

facilitated diffusion The diffusion of particles across a selectively permeable membrane with the assistance of transport proteins that are specific in what they will carry and have a binding site designed for molecules of interest. This process requires no energy.

facultative anaerobe Organisms that can survive in oxygen-rich or oxygen-free environments.

fallopian tube See **oviduct.**

fats Lipids, made by combining glycerol and fatty acids, used as long-term energy stores in cells. They can be saturated or unsaturated.

fatty acid Long carbon chain that contains a carboxyl group on one end that combines with glycerol molecules to form lipids.

fermentation Anaerobic respiration pathway that occurs in the absence of oxygen; produces less ATP than aerobic respiration.

ferredoxin Molecule that donates the electrons to $NADP^+$ to produce NADPH during the light reactions of photosynthesis.

fibrous root system Root system found in monocots that provides the plant with a very strong anchor without going very deep into the soil.

filtration Capillaries allow small particles through the pores of their endothelial linings, but large molecules such as proteins, platelets, and blood cells tend to remain in the vessel.

fixed-action pattern An innate behavior that seems to be a programmed response to some stimulus.

florigen Hormone thought to assist in the blooming of flowers.

fluid mosaic model Model that states that the membrane is made of a phospholipid bilayer with proteins of various lengths and sizes, interspersed with cholesterol.

fluke Parasitic flatworm that alternates between sexual and asexual reproductive cycles.

follicle-stimulating hormone (FSH) A gonadotropin that stimulates activities of the testes and ovaries. In females, it induces the development of the ovarian follicle, leading to the production and secretion of estrogen, and in males it stimulates the production of sperm.

food chain A hierarchical list of who snacks on who. For example, bugs are eaten by spiders, who are eaten by birds, who are eaten by cats.

food web Can be regarded as overlapping food chains that show all the various dietary relationships in an environment.

foraging The behavior of actively searching for and eating a particular food resource.

fossil record The physical manifestation of species that have gone extinct (e.g., bones and imprints).

F-plasmid Plasmid that contains the genes necessary for the production of a sex pillus.

frameshift mutations Deletion or addition of DNA nucleotides that does not add or remove a multiple of three nucleotides. Usually produces a nonfunctional protein unless it occurs late in protein production.

frequency-dependent selection Alleles are selected for or against depending on their relative frequency in a population.

FSH See **follicle-stimulating hormone.**

functional groups The groups responsible for the chemical properties of organic compounds.

G$_1$ phase The first growth phase of the cell cycle, which produces all the necessary raw materials for DNA synthesis.

G$_2$ phase The second growth phase of the cell cycle, which produces all the necessary raw materials for mitosis.

gametangia Protective covering that provides a safe haven for the fertilization of the gametes and the development of the zygote in bryophytes, ferns, and some gymnosperms.

gametes Sex cells produced during meiosis in the human life cycle.

gametophyte A haploid multicellular organism.

gastrulation Cells separate into three primary layers called *germ layers,* which eventually give rise to the different tissues of an adult.

gene flow The change in frequencies of alleles as genes from one population are incorporated into those from another.

generalized transduction Transduction caused by the accidental placement of host DNA into a phage instead of viral DNA during viral reproduction. This host DNA may find its way into another cell where crossover could occur.

generation time Time needed for individuals to reach reproductive maturity.

genetic code Code that translates codons found on mRNA strands into amino acids.

genetic drift A change in allele frequencies that is due to chance events.

genotype An organism's genetic makeup for a given trait. A simple example of this could involve eye color, where B represents the allele for brown and b represents the allele for blue. The possible genotypes include homozygous brown (BB), heterozygous brown (Bb), and homozygous blue (bb).

genus Taxonomic group to which a species belongs.

gibberellin Plant hormone that assists in stem elongation and induces growth in dormant seeds, buds, and flowers.

glomerular capillaries The early portion of the nephron where the filtration process begins.

glucagon Hormone that stimulates conversion of glycogen into glucose.

glycerol Three-carbon molecule that combines with fatty acids to produce a variety of lipids.

glycogen Storage polysaccharide made of glucose molecules used by animals.

glycolysis Occurs in the cytoplasm of cells and is the beginning pathway for both aerobic and anaerobic respiration. During glycolysis, a glucose molecule is broken down through a series of reactions into two molecules of ATP, NADH, and pyruvate.

glycoprotein Protein that has been modified by the addition of a sugar.

Golgi apparatus Organelle that modifies proteins, lipids, and other macromolecules by the addition of sugars and other molecules to form glycoproteins. The products are then sent to other parts of the cell.

G-proteins Proteins vital to signal cascade pathways. These proteins directly activate molecules such as adenyl cyclase to assist in a reaction.

gradualism The theory that evolutionary change is a steady, slow process.

grana Flattened channels and disks arranged in stacks found in the thylakoid membrane.

gravitropism A plant's growth response to gravitational force; auxin and gibberellins are involved in this response.

gross productivity The difference over time between the dissolved oxygen concentrations of the light and dark bottles calculated in primary productivity experiments.

growth factors Assist in the growth of structures.

guard cells Cells within the epidermis of plants that control the opening and closing of the stomata.

gymnosperm First major seed plant to evolve. Heterosporous plant that *usually* transports its sperm through the use of pollen. Conifers are the major gymnosperm to know.

habituation Loss of responsiveness to unimportant stimuli that do not provide appropriate feedback.

haploid (*n*) An organism that has only one copy of each type of chromosome.

Hardy-Weinberg equilibrium A special case where a population is in stasis, or not evolving.

helicase Enzyme that unzips DNA, breaking the hydrogen bonds between the nucleotides and producing the replication fork for replication.

helper T cell Immune cells that assist in activation of B cells.

hemoglobin Molecule that allows red blood cells to carry and deliver oxygen throughout the body to hardworking organs and tissues.

hemophilia Sex-linked disorder caused by the absence of a protein vital to the clotting process. Individuals with this condition have difficulty clotting blood after even the smallest of wounds.

herbivore Consumer that obtains energy and nutrients through consumption of plants.

heterosporous plant Plant that produces two types of spores, male and female.

heterotroph An organism that must consume other organisms to obtain nourishment. They are the consumers of the world.

heterotroph theory Theory that posits that the first organisms were heterotrophs (organisms that cannot produce their own food).

heterozygote advantage The situation, such as sickle cell anemia in malarial regions, in which being heterozygous for a condition provides some benefit.

heterozygous (hybrid) An individual is heterozygous (or a hybrid) for a gene if the two alleles are different (Bb).

histamine Chemical signal responsible for initiation of the inflammation response of the immune system.

holandric trait A trait inherited via the Y chromosome.

homeobox DNA sequence of a homeotic gene that tells the cell where to put body structures.

homeotic genes Genes that regulate or "direct" the body plan of organisms.

homologous characters Traits are said to be homologous if they are similar because their host organisms arose from a common ancestor.

homologous chromosomes Chromosomes that resemble one another in shape, size, function, and the genetic information they contain. They are not identical.

homosporous plant Plants that produce a single spore type that gives rise to bisexual gametophytes.

homozygous (pure) An individual is homozygous for a gene if both of the given alleles are the same (BB or bb).

honest indicators Sexually selected traits that are the result of female choice and signal genetic quality.

hormones Chemicals produced by glands such as the pituitary and used by the endocrine system to signal distant target cells.

host range The range of cells that a virus is able to infect. For example, HIV infects the T cells of our body.

humoral immunity Immunity involving antibodies and circulating fluids.

Huntington's disease An autosomal dominant degenerative disease of the nervous system that appears when a person is in their 30s or 40s and is both irreversible and fatal.

hybrid vigor Refers to the fact that hybrids may have increased reproductive success compared to inbred strains. This is due to the fact that inbreeding increases the likelihood that two deleterious, recessive alleles will end up in the same offspring.

hydrolysis reaction A reaction that breaks down compounds by the addition of H_2O.

hydrophilic Water-loving.

hydroxyl group A hydrophilic and polar functional group (—OH) that is present in compounds; known as *alcohols*.

hypercholesterolemia Recessive disorder (hh) that causes cholesterol levels to be many times higher than normal and can lead to heart attacks in children as young as 2 years old.

hypertonic Characterizes a solution that has a higher solute concentration than does a neighboring solution.

hypha Filament found in fungi made of chitin that separates fungi into multicellular compartments.

hypoblast Forms the yolk sac, which produces the embryo's first blood cells.

hypothalamus The thermostat and "hunger meter" of the body, regulating temperature, hunger, and thirst.

hypotonic Characterizes a solution that has a lower solute concentration than a neighboring solution.

immigration rate Rate at which individuals relocate *into* a given population.

imprinting Innate behavior that is learned during a critical period early in life.

inclusive fitness An individual's fitness gain that is a direct result of his or her contribution to the reproductive effort of closely related kin. This results from the fact that close kin share copies of identical genes.

incomplete dominance Blending inheritance. The heterozygous genotype produces an intermediate phenotype rather than the dominant phenotype; neither allele dominates the other.

induced-fit model Theory that suggests that when an enzyme and a substrate bind together, the enzyme is *induced* to alter its shape for a tighter active-site/substrate attachment, which places the substrate in a favorable position to react more quickly.

inducer Molecule that binds to and inactivates a repressor.

induction The ability of one group of cells to influence the development of another. This influence can be through physical contact or chemical signaling.

inner cell mass Portion of the blastula that develops into the embryo.

inorganic compounds For the most part, compounds containing no carbon. There are some exceptions such as carbon dioxide, carbon monoxide, and others.

insight learning The ability to do something correctly the first time even with no prior experience.

insulin Hormone secreted in response to high blood glucose levels to promote glycogen formation.

integral proteins Proteins that are implanted within the bilayer and can extend part way or all the way across the membrane.

intermediate filaments Substances constructed from a class of proteins called keratins; function as reinforcement for the shape and position of organelles in a cell.

intermediate inheritance An individual heterozygous for a trait (Yy) shows characteristics not exactly like those of *either* parent. The phenotype is a "mixture" of both of the parents' genetic input.

interneurons Function to make synaptic connections with other neurons. They work to integrate sensory input and motor output.

interphase The first three stages of the cycle, G_1, S, and G_2. Accounts for approximately 90 percent of the cell cycle.

interspecific competition Competition between different species that rely on the same resources for survival.

interstitial cells The structures that produce the hormones involved in the male reproductive system.

intraspecific competition *Within*-species competition that occurs because members of the same species rely on the same valuable resources for survival.

introns Noncoding regions produced during transcription that are cut out of the mRNA.

invertebrate Animal without a backbone.

ion An atom with a positive or negative charge.

isotonic solution Solution that has the same solute concentration as surrounding solutions.

karyotype A chart that organizes chromosomes in relation to number, size, and type.

ketone Carbonyl group in which both Rs are carbon chains; hydrophilic and polar.

kinesis A random change in the speed of movement in response to a stimulus. Organisms speed up in places they don't like and slow down in places they do like.

kingdom The broadest of the classification groups.

Klinefelter syndrome (XXY) Syndrome in which individuals have male sex organs but are sterile and display several feminine body characteristics.

Krebs cycle Energy-producing reaction that occurs in the matrix of the mitochondria, in which pyruvate is broken down completely to H_2O and CO_2 to produce 3 NADH, 1 $FADH_2$, and 1 ATP.

***K*-selected populations** Populations of a roughly constant size whose members have low reproductive rates. The offspring produced by *K*-selected organisms require extensive postnatal care.

***lac* operon** Operon that aids in control of transcription of lactose metabolizing genes.

lactic acid fermentation Occurs in human muscle cells when oxygen is unavailable. Pyruvate is directly reduced to lactate by NADH to regenerate the NAD^+ needed for the resumption of glycolysis.

lagging strand The discontinuous strand produced during DNA replication.

larynx Passageway from the pharynx to the trachea; commonly called the "voicebox."

lateral meristems Cells that extend all the way through the plant from roots to shoots and provide the secondary growth that increases the girth of a plant.

lateral roots Roots that serve to hold a plant in place in the soil.

law of dominance When two opposite pure-breeding varieties (homozygous dominant vs. homozygous recessive) of an organism are crossed, all the offspring resemble one parent. This is referred to as the "dominant" trait. The variety that is hidden is referred to as the "recessive" trait.

law of independent assortment Members of each pair of factors are distributed independently when the gametes are formed. In other words, inheritance of one particular trait or characteristic does not interfere with inheritance of another trait (in unlinked genes). For example, if an individual is BbRr for two genes, gametes formed during meiosis could contain BR, Br, bR, or br. The B and b alleles assort *independently* of the R and r alleles.

law of multiplication Law that states that to determine the probability that two random events will occur in succession, you simply multiply the probability of the first event by the probability of the second event.

law of segregation Every organism carries pairs of factors, called *alleles*, for each trait, and the members of the pair segregate out (separate) during the formation of gametes. For example, if an individual is Bb for eye color, during gamete formation one gamete would receive a B and the other made from that cell would receive a b.

leading strand The continuous strand produced during DNA replication.

LH See **luteinizing hormone.**

LH surge Giant release of LH that triggers ovulation—the release of a secondary oocyte from the ovary.

lichen A symbiotic collection of organisms (fungus and algae) living as one.

life cycle Sequence of events that make up the reproductive cycle of an organism.

limiting factors Environmental factors that keep population sizes in check (predators, diseases, food supplies, and waste).

linkage map A genetic map put together using crossover frequencies.

linked genes Genes along the same chromosome that tend to be inherited together because the chromosome is passed along as a unit.

lipase The major fat-digesting enzyme of the human body.

lipids Hydrophobic organic compounds used by cells as energy stores or building blocks. Three important lipids are fats, steroids, and phospholipids.

logistic growth A population grows at a rate that creates an S-shaped curve.

long-day plants Plants, such as spinach, which flower if exposed to a night that is shorter than a critical period.

luteinizing hormone (LH) A gonadotropin that stimulates ovulation and formation of a corpus luteum, as well as the synthesis of estrogen and progesterone.

lymphatic system Important part of the circulatory system that functions as the route by which proteins and fluids that have leaked out of the bloodstream can return to circulation. The lymphatic system also functions as a protector for the body because of the presence of lymph nodes.

lymph nodes Structures found in the lymphatic system that are full of white blood cells, which live to fight infection. These nodes often swell up during infection as a sign of the body's fight against the infectious agent.

lymphocyte White blood cell. There are two main types of lymphocytes: B cells and T cells. These cells are formed in the bone marrow of the body and arise from stem cells.

lysogenic cycle The virus falls dormant and incorporates its DNA into the host DNA as an entity called a *provirus*. The viral DNA is quietly reproduced by the cell every time the cell reproduces itself, and this allows the virus to stay alive from generation to generation without killing the host cell.

lysosome Membrane-bound organelle that specializes in digestion and contains enzymes that break down proteins, lipids, nucleic acids, and carbohydrates.

lysozyme An enzyme, present in saliva and tears, that can kill germs before they have a chance to take hold.

lytic cycle The cell actually produces many viral offspring, which are released from the cell, killing the host cell in the process.

macroevolution The big picture of evolution, which includes the study of evolution of groups of species over very long periods of time.

macronucleus A nucleus present in some protists (Ciliophora) and which controls the everyday activities of organisms.

macrospores Female gametophytes produced by heterosporous plants.

map unit Also termed *centigram*. Unit used to geographically relate the genes on the basis of crossover frequencies. One map unit is equal to a 1 percent recombination frequency.

matter Anything that has mass and takes up space.

mechanical digestion The physical breakdown of food that comes from chewing.

medulla Inner region of the kidney.

medulla oblongata The control center for involuntary activities such as breathing.

medusa A cnidarian that is flat and roams the waters looking for food (e.g., jellyfish).

melatonin Hormone that is known to be involved in our biological rhythms (circadian).

memory cells Stored instructions on how to handle a particular invader. When an invader returns to the body, the memory cells recognize it, produce antibodies in rapid fashion, and eliminate the invader very quickly.

meristemic cells Cells that allow plants to grow indeterminately.

mesoderm Intermediate germ layer that gives rise to muscle, the circulatory system, the reproductive system, excretory organs, bones, and connective tissues of the gut and exterior of the body.

mesophyll Interior tissue of a leaf.

mesophyll cells Cells that contain many chloroplasts and host the majority of photosynthesis.

methanogens Archaebacteria that produce methane as a by-product.

microevolution Evolution at the level of species and populations.

microfilaments Substances built from actin that play a major role in muscle contraction.

micronucleus A nucleus present in some protists (Ciliophora) and which functions in conjugation.

microspores Male gametophytes produced by heterosporous plants.

microtubules Substances constructed from tubulin; play a lead role in the separation of cells during cell division; are also important components of cilia and flagella.

migration This is a cyclic movement of animals over long distances according to the time of year.

mismatch repair Process during DNA replication by which DNA polymerase replaces an incorrectly placed nucleotide with proper nucleotide.

missense mutation Substitution of the wrong nucleotides into the DNA sequence. These substitutions still result in the addition of amino acids to the growing protein chain during translation, but they can sometimes lead to the addition of *incorrect* amino acids to the chain.

mitochondrion Double-membraned organelle that specializes in the production of ATP; host organelle for the Krebs cycle (matrix) and oxidative phosphorylation (cristae).

mitotic spindle Apparatus constructed from microtubules that assists in the physical separation of the chromosomes during mitosis.

monocot (**monocotyledon**) Angiosperm with a single cotyledon.

monohybrid cross A cross that involves a single character in which both parents are heterozygous (Bb × Bb). A monohybrid cross between heterozygous gametes gives a 3:1 phenotype ratio in the offspring.

monosaccharide The simplest form of a carbohydrate. The most important monosaccharide is glucose, which is used in cellular respiration to provide energy for cells.

morula A structure formed during the cleavage divisions of the zygote.

motor neurons Nerve cells that take the commands from the central nervous system (CNS) and put them into action as motor outputs.

M phase mitosis This is the stage during which the cell separates into two new cells.

Müllerian mimicry Two species that are aposematically colored as an indicator of their chemical defense mechanism; they mimic each other's color scheme in an effort to increase the speed with which predators learn to avoid them.

mutant phenotypes Characters that are not the wild-type strain in fruit flies and other organisms.

mutation A random event that can cause changes in allele frequencies. It is *always* random with respect to which genes are affected, although the changes in allele frequencies that occur as a result of the mutation may not be.

mutualism Scenario in which two organisms benefit from an interaction or relationship.

mycelium Meshes of branching filaments formed from hyphae that function as mouthlike structures for fungi.

myelinated neurons Neurons with a layer of insulation around the axon, allowing for faster transmission. They form the cable Internet of the body.

natural selection The process by which characters or traits are maintained or eliminated in a population based on their contribution to the differential survival and reproductive success of their "host" organisms.

negative feedback Occurs when a hormone acts to directly or indirectly inhibit further secretion of the hormone of interest.

nephron The functional unit of the kidney.

net productivity Difference between the concentration of dissolved oxygen for the initial and light bottle in a primary productivity experiment.

neural plate Structure that becomes the neural groove, which eventually becomes the neural tube. This neural tube later gives rise to the central nervous system.

neural tube Embryonic structure that gives rise to the central nervous system.

neuromuscular junction The space between the motor neuron and the muscle cell.

neurotransmitter Chemical released by neurons that functions as a messenger, causing a nearby cell to react and continue the nervous impulse.

niche Term used to describe all the biotic and abiotic resources used by the organism.

nitrogen cycle The shuttling of nitrogen from the atmosphere, to living organisms, and back to the atmosphere in a continuous cycle.

nitrogen fixation The conversion of N_2 to NH_3 (ammonia).

nitrogenous bases Monomers such as adenine, guanine, cytosine, thymine, and uracil out of which DNA and RNA are constructed.

noncompetitive inhibition Condition in which an inhibitor molecule binds to an enzyme away from the active site, causing a change in the shape of the active site so that it can no longer interact with the substrate.

noncyclic light reaction Pathway that produces ATP, NADPH, and O_2. Uses both photosystem I and II.

nondisjunction The improper separation of chromosomes during meiosis, which leads to an abnormal number of chromosomes in offspring. Examples include Down syndrome, Turner syndrome, and Klinefelter's syndrome.

nonsense mutation Substitution of the wrong nucleotides into the DNA sequence. These substitutions lead to premature stoppage of protein synthesis by the early placement of a stop codon. This type of mutation usually leads to a nonfunctional protein.

nonspecific immunity The nonspecific prevention of the entrance of invaders into the body.

notochord Structure that serves to support the body; found in the embryos of chordates.

nucleic acid Macromolecule composed of nucleotides, sugars, and phosphates that serves as genetic material of living organisms (DNA and RNA).

nucleoid Region of a prokaryotic cell that contains the genetic material.

nucleolus Eukaryotic structure in which ribosomes are constructed.

nucleus The control center of eukaryotic cells that is the storage site of the genetic material (DNA). It is the site of replication, transcription, and post-transcriptional modification of RNA.

obligate aerobe Organism that requires oxygen for respiration.

obligate anaerobe Organism that only survives in oxygen-free environments.

observational learning The ability of an organism to learn how to do something by watching another individual do it first.

oil Type of lipid.

Okazaki fragments The lagging DNA strand consists of these tiny pieces that are later connected by an enzyme, DNA ligase, to produce the completed double-stranded daughter DNA molecule.

ontogeny The development of an individual.

oogenesis Process by which female gametes are formed. Each meiotic cycle leads to the production of a single ovum, or egg.

operant conditioning Type of associative learning that is based on trial and error.

operator A short sequence near the promoter that assists in transcription by interacting with regulatory proteins (transcription factors).

operon A promoter/operator pair that services multiple genes.

opportunistic populations *R*-selected organisms that tend to appear when space in the region opens up due to some environmental change. They grow fast, reproduce quickly, and die quickly as well.

optimal foraging Theory that predicts that natural selection will favor animals that choose foraging strategies that maximize the differential between benefits and costs.

organic compounds Carbon-containing compounds. Important examples include carbohydrates, proteins, lipids, and nucleic acids.

osmosis The passive diffusion of water down its concentration gradient across selectively permeable membranes. It will flow from a region with a lower solute concentration (hypotonic) to a region with a higher solute concentration (hypertonic).

outbreeding Mating between unrelated individuals of the same species.

ovary The site of egg production. In animals, females often have two, one on either side of the body. Plants *usually* only have one ovary.

oviduct Known also as the *fallopian tube,* this is the site of fertilization and connects the ovary to the uterus. Eggs move through here from the ovary to the uterus (in animals only).

ovulation Stage of menstrual cycle in which the secondary oocyte is released from the ovary.

oxaloacetate Compound that plays an important role in C_4 photosynthesis of plants and the Krebs cycle in animals.

oxidative phosphorylation Aerobic process in which NADH and $FADH_2$ pass their electrons down the electron transport chain to produce ATP.

oxytocin Hormone that stimulates uterine contraction and milk ejection for breastfeeding.

P_1 The parent generation in a genetic cross.

palisade mesophyll Host to many chloroplasts and much of the photosynthesis of a leaf.

parallel evolution Similar evolutionary changes occurring in two either related or unrelated species that respond in a similar manner to a similar environment.

parasitism Scenario in which one organism benefits at the other's expense.

parasympathetic nervous system Branch of autonomic nervous system that shuts down the body to conserve energy.

parathyroid hormone (PTH) Hormone that increases serum concentration of Ca^{2+}, assisting in the process of bone maintenance.

parenchyma cells Plant cells that play a role in photosynthesis (mesophyll cells), storage, and secretion.

Patau syndrome Presence of trisomy 13, which occurs in about 1 out of every 12,000–16,000 live births and causes serious brain and circulatory defects.

pedigrees Family trees used to describe the genetic relationships within a family. One use of a pedigree is to determine whether parents will pass certain conditions to their offspring.

pepsin The major enzyme of the stomach, which breaks down proteins into smaller polypeptides to be handled by the intestines.

pepsinogen The precursor to pepsin that is activated by active pepsin (a small amount of which normally exists in the stomach).

peripheral nervous system (PNS) The PNS can be broken down into a sensory and a motor division. The sensory division carries information *to* the CNS while the motor division carries information *away* from the CNS.

peripheral proteins Proteins, such as receptor proteins, not implanted in the bilayer, which are often attached to integral proteins of the membrane.

peristalsis The force created by the rhythmic contraction of the smooth muscle of the esophagus and intestines.

permafrost Frozen layer of soil just underneath the upper soil layer, found in the tundra biome.

peroxisome Organelle that functions to break down fatty acids, and detoxify.

petals Structures that serve to attract pollinators.

PGAL (phosphoglyceraldehyde) Molecule important to energy-producing reactions photosynthesis and respiration.

phage A virus that infects bacteria.

phagocytes Immune cells (macrophages and neutrophils) that use endocytosis to engulf and eliminate foreign invaders.

pharynx Tube through which both food and air pass after leaving the mouth.

phenotype The physical expression of the trait associated with a particular genotype. Some examples of the phenotypes for Mendel's peas were round or wrinkled, green or yellow, purple flower or white flower.

phenylketonuria (PKU) An autosomal recessive disease caused by a single gene defect that leaves a person unable to break down phenylalanine, which results in a by-product that can accumulate to toxic levels in the blood and cause mental retardation.

pheromones Chemical signals important to communication.

phloem Important part of plant vascular tissue that functions to transport sugars from their production site to the rest of the plant.

phosphate group An acidic functional group that is a vital component of molecules that serve as cellular energy sources: ATP, ADP, and GTP.

phospholipid Lipid with both a hydrophobic tail *and* a hydrophilic head; the major component of cell membranes with the hydrophilic phosphate group forming the outside portion and the hydrophobic tail forming the interior of the wall.

photoautotrophs Photosynthetic autotrophs that produce energy from light.

photolysis Process by which water is broken up by an enzyme into hydrogen ions and oxygen atoms. Occurs during the light reactions of photosynthesis.

photoperiodism The response by a plant to the change in the length of days.

photophosphorylation Process by which ATP is made during the light-dependent reactions of photosynthesis. It is the chloroplast equivalent of oxidative phosphorylation.

photorespiration Process by which oxygen competes with carbon dioxide and attaches to RuBP. Plants that experience photorespiration have a lowered capacity for growth.

photosynthesis The process by which plants generate energy from light and inorganic raw materials. This occurs in the chloroplasts and involves two stages: the light-dependent reactions and the light-independent reactions.

photosystem Cluster of light-trapping pigments involved in the process of photosynthesis.

phototaxis Reflex movement toward light at night.

phototropism A plant's growth in response to light. Auxin is the hormone involved with this process.

phycobilin Photosynthetic pigment.

phylogeny The evolutionary history of a species.

phytochrome Important pigment in the process of flowering. Leads to the production of florigen.

pigment A molecule that absorbs light of a particular wavelength.

pioneer species A species that is able to survive in resource-poor conditions and takes hold of a barren area such as a volcanic island. Pioneer species do the grunt work, adding nutrients and other improvements to the once-uninhabited volcanic rock until future species take over.

PKU See **phenylketonuria.**

placenta In humans, this structure provides the nutrients for the developing embryo.

planarians Free-living platyhelminthe carnivores that live in the water.

plasma The liquid portion of the blood that contains minerals, hormones, antibodies, and nutritional materials.

plasma cells The factories that produce antibodies that eliminate any cell containing on its surface the antigen that the plasma cell has been summoned to kill.

plasma membrane Selective barrier around a cell composed of a double layer of phospholipids that controls what is able to enter and exit a cell.

plasmids Extra circles of DNA in bacteria that contain just a few genes and have been useful in genetic engineering. Plasmids replicate independently of the main chromosome.

plasmodial slime molds Nonphotosynthetic heterotrophic funguslike protists. They eat and grow as a unified clumped unicellular mass known as a *plasmodium.*

plasmodium This word has two meanings in this book. It can be the causative agent of malaria, or it can be the clumped unicellular mass that fungi form under certain feeding conditions.

plasmolysis The shriveling of the cytoplasm of a cell in response to loss of water in hypertonic surroundings.

platelet Blood cell involved in the clotting of blood.

pleiotropy A single gene has multiple effects on an organism.

PNS See **peripheral nervous system.**

polar A molecule that has an unequal distribution of charge, which creates a positive and a negative side to the molecule.

polar body Castaway cell produced during female gamete formation that contains only genetic information.

pollen Sperm-bearing male gametophyte of gymnosperms and angiosperms.

polygenic traits Traits that are affected by more than one gene (e.g., eye color).

polymerase chain reaction Technique used to create large amounts of a DNA sequence in a short amount of time.

polyp Cylinder-shaped cnidarian that lives attached to a surface (e.g., sea anemone).

polyploidy A condition in which an individual has more than the normal number of sets of chromosomes.

polysaccharide A carbohydrate usually composed of hundreds or thousands of monosaccharides, which acts as a storage form of energy, and as structural material in and around cells. Starch and glycogen are storage polysaccharides; cellulose and chitin are structural polysaccharides.

pond succession Process by which a hole filled with water passes through the various succession stages until it has become a swamp, forest, or grassland.

population A collection of individuals of the same species living in the same geographic area.

population cycle When a population size dips below the carrying capacity, it will later come back to the capacity and even surpass it. However, the population could dip below the carrying capacity as a result of some major change in the environment and equilibrate at a new, lower carrying capacity.

population density The number of individuals per unit area in a given population.

population ecology The study of the size, distribution, and density of populations and how they change with time.

positive feedback Occurs when a hormone acts to directly or indirectly cause increased secretion of a hormone.

posterior pituitary gland Structure that produces only two hormones: ADH and oxytocin.

potometer Lab apparatus used to measure transpiration rates in plants.

predation Scenario in which one species, the predator, hunts another species, the prey.

primary consumers The consumers that obtain energy through consumption of the producers of the planet; known as *herbivores.*

primary immune response When a B cell meets and attaches to the appropriate antigen, it becomes activated and undergoes mitosis and differentiation into plasma cells and memory cells.

primary oocytes Cells that begin the process of meiosis and progress until prophase I, where they sit halted until the host female enters puberty.

primary plant growth Increase in the length of a plant.

primary productivity Rate at which carbon-containing compounds are stored.

primary sex characteristics The sexual organs that assist in the vital process of procreation; include the testes, ovaries, and uterus.

primary spermatocytes Produced by mitotic division, these cells immediately undergo meiosis I to produce two secondary spermatocytes, which undergo meiosis II to produce four spermatids.

primary structure The sequence of the amino acids that make up a protein.

primary succession Succession that occurs in an area that is devoid of life and contains no soil.

primer sites DNA segments that signal where replication should originate.

prion Incorrectly folded form of a brain cell protein that works by converting other normal host proteins into misshapen proteins. Prion diseases tend to cause dementia, muscular control problems, and loss of balance.

progesterone Hormone involved in menstrual cycle and pregnancy.

prokaryotic cell A *simple* cell with no nucleus, or membrane-bound organelles; divides by binary fission and includes bacteria—both heterotrophic and autotrophic types.

prolactin Hormone that controls the production of milk and leads to a decrease in the synthesis and release of GnRH, thus inhibiting ovulation.

promoter region A recognition site that shows the polymerase where transcription should begin.

prostate gland Structure whose function in the male reproductive system is to add a basic (pH > 7) liquid to the mix to help neutralize the acidity of the urine that may remain in the common urethral passage.

protein Organic compound composed of chains of amino acids that function as structural components, transport aids, enzymes, and cell signals, among other things.

protein hormones Hormones too large to move inside a cell, and which bind to receptors on the surface of the cell instead.

protein kinase Protein that controls the activities of other proteins through the addition of phosphate groups.

provirus A virus genome that is integrated into the DNA of a host cell that can be transmitted from one generation to the next without causing lysis.

pseudocoelomate Animal that has a fluid-filled body cavity that is not enclosed by mesoderm.

pseudopods Extensions from protists (organisms of the kingdom Protist) that assist in collection of nutrients.

P site Region in protein synthesis machinery that holds the tRNA carrying the growing protein.

PTH See **parathyroid hormone.**

punctuated equilibria model Theorizes that evolutionary change occurs in rapid bursts separated by large periods of stasis (no change).

purine A nitrogenous base that contains a double ring structure (adenine, guanine).

pyloric sphincter The connection point between the stomach and the small intestine.

pyramid of numbers Pyramid based on the *number* of individuals at each level of the biomass chain. Each box in this pyramid represents the number of members of that level. The highest consumers in the chain tend to be quite large, resulting in a smaller number of those individuals spread out over a given area.

pyrimidine A nitrogenous base that contains a single ring structure (cytosine, thymine).

Q_{10} value Statistic that shows how an increase in temperature affects the metabolic activity of an organism.

quaternary structure The arrangement of separate polypeptide "subunits" into a single protein. Seen only in proteins with more than one polypeptide chain.

radiation The loss of heat through ejection of electromagnetic waves.

random distribution Random distribution of species in a given geographic area.

rate of reaction Rate at which a chemical reaction occurs.

reaction centers Control centers made up of pigments.

reciprocal altruism Altruistic behavior performed with the expectation that the favor will be returned.

recombinant DNA DNA that contains DNA pieces from multiple sources.

red blood cells Cells in body that contain hemoglobin and serve as the oxygen delivery system in the body.

red-green colorblindness Sex-linked condition that leaves those afflicted unable to distinguish between red and green colors.

redox reaction A reduction–oxidation reaction involving the transfer of electrons.

replication fork Fork opened in DNA strand that allows DNA replication to occur.

repolarization The lowering of the potential back down to its initial level, stopping the transmission of neural signals at that point.

repressor Protein that prevents the binding of RNA polymerase to the promoter site.

reproductive success A measure of how many surviving offspring one produces relative to how many the other individuals in one's population produce.

RER See **rough endoplasmic reticulum.**

respirometer Machine that can be used to calculate the respiration rate of a reaction.

restriction enzymes Enzymes that cut DNA at specific nucleotide sequences. This results in DNA fragments with single-stranded ends called "sticky ends," which find and reconnect with other DNA fragments containing the same ends (with the assistance of DNA ligase).

retrovirus An RNA virus that carries an enzyme called *reverse transcriptase* that reverse-transcribes the genetic information from RNA into DNA. In the nucleus of the host, the newly transcribed DNA incorporates into the host DNA and is transcribed into RNA when the host cell undergoes normal transcription.

reverse transcriptase Enzyme carried by retroviruses that function to convert RNA to DNA.

R_f Variable that indicates the relative rate at which one molecule migrates compared to the solvent of a paper chromatograph.

ribosomes Host organelle for protein synthesis composed of a large subunit and a small subunit. Ribosomes are built in the nucleolus.

RNA polymerase Enzyme that runs transcription and adds the appropriate nucleotides to the 3′ end of the growing strand.

RNA splicing Process that removes introns from newly produced mRNA and then glues exons back together to produce the final product.

root Portion of the plant that is below the ground.

root cap Protective structure found around the apical meristem of a root that keeps it together as it pushes through the soil.

root hairs Hairs extending off the surface of root tips that increase the surface area for absorption of water and nutrients from the soil.

root pressure Driving force that contributes to the movement of water through the xylem of a plant.

rough endoplasmic reticulum (RER) Membrane-bound organelle with ribosomes on the cytoplasmic surface of the cell. Proteins produced by RER are often secreted and carried by vesicles to the Golgi apparatus for further modification.

rRNA Ribosomal RNA, which makes up a huge portion of ribosomes.

***R*-selected populations** Populations that experience rapid growth of the J-curve variety. The offspring produced by *R*-selected organisms are numerous, mature quite rapidly, and require very little postnatal care.

rubisco Enzyme that catalyzes the first step of the Calvin cycle in C_3 plants.

saprobe Organism that feeds off dead organisms.

saturated fat Fat that contains no double bonds. It is associated with heart disease and atherosclerosis.

savanna Grassland that contains a spattering of trees found all over South America, Australia, and Africa. Savanna soil tends to be low in nutrients, while temperatures tend to run high.

sclerenchyma cells Plant cells that function as protection and mechanical support.

search image Mental image that assists animals during foraging. It directs them to food of interest.

secondary consumers Consumers that obtain energy through consumption of the primary consumers.

secondary immune response Memory cells are the basis for this efficient response to invaders.

secondary oocyte An oocyte that has half the genetic information of the parent cell, but the majority of its cytoplasm.

secondary plant growth Growth that leads to an increase in plant girth.

secondary sex characteristics The noticeable physical characteristics that differ between males and females such as facial hair, deepness of voice, breasts, and muscle distribution.

secondary spermatocyte Cells formed during spermatogenesis that give rise to spermatids and eventually sperm.

secondary structure The three-dimensional arrangement of a protein caused by hydrogen bonding.

secondary succession Succession in an area that previously had stable plant and/or animal life but has since been disturbed by some major force such as a forest fire.

second messenger Molecule that serves as an intermediary, activating other proteins and enzymes in a chemical reaction.

semiconservative DNA replication Before the parent strand is copied, the DNA unzips, with each single strand serving as a template for the creation of a new double strand. One strand of DNA from the parent goes to one daughter cell; the second parent strand goes to the second daughter cell.

seminal vesicles Structures that dump fluids into the ejaculatory duct to send along with the sperm, providing three important advantages to the sperm: energy by adding fructose; power to progress through the female reproductive system by adding prostaglandin (which stimulates uterine contraction); and mucus, which helps the sperm swim more effectively.

seminiferous tubules Actual site of sperm production.

sensory neurons Nerve cells that receive and communicate information from the sensory environment.

septae Structures that divide the hypha filaments of fungi into different compartments.

SER See **smooth endoplasmic reticulum.**

sex pili Bacterial appendage vital to process of conjugation.

sex ratio Proportion of males and females in a given population.

sexual selection The process by which certain characters are selected for because they aid in mate acquisition.

shoots Parts of a plant that are above the ground.

short-day plants Plants, such as poinsettias, that flower if exposed to nighttime conditions longer than a critical period of length.

sickle cell anemia A recessive disease caused by the substitution of a single amino acid in the hemoglobin protein of red blood cells, leaving hemoglobin less able to carry oxygen and also causing the hemoglobin to deform to a sickle shape when the oxygen content of the blood is low. The sickling causes pain, muscle weakness, and fatigue.

sieve-tube elements Functionally mature cells of the phloem that are alive.

sink Site of carbohydrate consumption in plants.

skeletal muscle Striated muscle that controls voluntary activities and contains multiple nuclei.

smooth endoplasmic reticulum (SER) Membrane-bound organelle involved in lipid synthesis, detoxification, and carbohydrate metabolism; has no ribosomes on its cytoplasmic surface.

smooth muscle Involuntary muscle that contracts slowly and is controlled by the autonomic nervous system (ANS).

sodium–potassium pump A mechanism that actively moves potassium *into* the cell and sodium *out of* the cell against their respective concentration gradients to maintain appropriate levels inside the cell.

solute A substance dissolved in a solution.

somatotropic hormone (STH) A hormone that stimulates protein synthesis and growth in the body.

somite Structure that gives rise to the muscles and vertebrae in mammals.

source Site of carbohydrate creation in plants.

Southern blotting Procedure used to determine if a particular sequence of nucleotides is present in a sample of DNA.

specialized transduction Transduction involving a virus in the lysogenic cycle that shifts to the lytic cycle. If it accidentally brings with it a piece of the host DNA as it pulls out of the host chromosome, this DNA could find its way into another cell.

speciation The process by which new species evolve.

species A group of interbreeding (or potentially interbreeding) organisms.

specific immunity Complicated multilayered defense mechanism that protects a host against foreign invasion.

spectrophotometer Machine used to determine how much light can pass through a sample.

spermatids Immature sperm that enter the epididymis, where their waiting game begins and maturation is completed.

spermatogenesis Process by which the male gametes are formed. Four haploid sperm are produced during each meiotic cycle. This does not begin until puberty, and it occurs in the seminiferous tubules.

S phase The DNA is copied so that each daughter cell has a complete set of chromosomes at the conclusion of the cell cycle.

spongy mesophyll Region of a plant where the cells are more loosely arranged, aiding in the passage of CO_2 to cells performing photosynthesis.

sporophyte The diploid multicellular stage of the plant life cycle.

sporozoite Small infectious form that apicomplexa protists take to spread from place to place.

stabilizing selection This describes selection for the mean of a population for a given allele; has the effect of reducing variation in a given population.

stamen Male structure of a flower that contains the pollen-producing anther.

starch Storage polysaccharide made of glucose molecules; seen in plants.

start codon (AUG) Codon that establishes the reading frame for protein formation.

stem cells Cells that give rise to the immune cells of the human body.

steroid hormones Lipid-soluble molecules that pass through the cell membrane and combine with cytoplasmic proteins. These complexes pass through to the nucleus to interact with chromosomal proteins and directly affect transcription in the nucleus.

steroids Lipids composed of four carbon rings. Examples include cholesterol, estrogen, progesterone, and testosterone.

STH See **somatotropic hormone**.

sticky ends Single-stranded DNA fragments formed when DNA is treated with restriction enzymes. These fragments find and reconnect with other fragments with the same ends.

stigma Flower structure that functions as the receiver of pollen.

stomata Structure through which CO_2 enters a plant, and water vapor and O_2 leave.

stop codons (UGA, UAA, UAG) Codons that stop the production of a protein.

storage diseases Diseases such as Tay-Sachs that are caused by the absence of a particular lysosomal hydrolytic enzyme.

strain Groups into which bacterial species are placed.

stroma The inner fluid portion of the chloroplast that plays host to the light-independent reactions of photosynthesis.

style Pathway in a flower that leads to the ovary.

substrates Substances that enzymes act upon.

succession Shift in the local composition of species in response to changes that occur over time.

sulfhydryl group A functional group that helps stabilize the structure of many proteins.

survivorship curves A tool used to study the population dynamics of species.

symbiosis A relationship between two different species that can be classified as one of three main types: commensalism, mutualism, and parasitism.

sympathetic nervous system Branch of the autonomic nervous system that gets the body ready to move.

sympatric speciation Interbreeding ceases even though no physical barrier prevents it. Can occur as a result of polyploidy and balanced polymorphism.

symplast pathway Movement of water and nutrients through the living portion of plant cells.

synaptic knob The end of the axon. This is where calcium gates are opened in response to the changing potential, which causes vesicles to release substances called *neurotransmitters* (NTs) into the synaptic gap between the axon and the target cell. These NTs diffuse across the gap, causing a new impulse in the target cell.

tactile communication Communication that involves the use of touch in the conveying of a message.

taiga Biome characterized by lengthy, cold, and wet winters. This biome is found in Canada and has gymnosperms as its prominent plant life. This biome contains coniferous forests (pine and other needle-bearing trees).

tapeworm Parasitic flatworm whose adult form lives in vertebrates.

taproot system System of roots found in many dicots that starts as one thick root and divides into many smaller lateral roots, which serve as an anchor for the plant.

TATA box Group of nucleotides found in the promoter region that assists in binding of RNA polymerase to the DNA strand for transcription.

taxis The reflex movement toward or away from a stimulus.

taxonomy The field of biology that classifies organisms according to the presence or absence of shared characteristics in an effort to discover evolutionary relationships between species.

Tay-Sachs disease A fatal genetic storage disease that renders the body unable to break down a particular type of lipid.

temperate deciduous forest A biome that is found in regions that experience cold winters where plant life is dormant, alternating with warm summers that provide enough moisture to keep large trees alive.

temperate grasslands Found in regions with cold winter temperatures. The soil of this biome is considered to be among the most fertile of all.

termination site Region of DNA that tells the polymerase when transcription should conclude.

territoriality Scenario in which territorial individuals defend their territory against other individuals.

tertiary structure The 3D (three-dimensional) arrangement of a protein caused by interaction among the various R groups of the amino acids involved.

test cross Crossing of an organism of unknown dominant genotype with an organism that is homozygous recessive for the trait, resulting in offspring with observable phenotypes. Test crosses are used to determine the unknown genotype.

testis The site of sperm and testosterone production in animals; males have two testes, located in the scrotum.

testosterone Sex hormone produced in testes that stimulates the growth of male sex characteristics.

thermoacidophiles Archaebacteria that live in hot, acidic environments.

thermoregulation The process by which temperature is maintained.

thigmotropism A plant's growth in response to touch.

thylakoid membrane system Inner membrane that winds through the stroma of a chloroplast. Site of the light-dependent reactions of photosynthesis.

thymine dimers Thymine nucleotides located adjacent to one another on the DNA strand bind together when excess exposure to UV light occurs. This can negatively affect replication of DNA and assist in the creation of further mutations.

thymosin Hormone involved in the development of the T cells of the immune system.

thyroid-stimulating hormone (TSH) A hormone that stimulates the synthesis and secretion of thyroid hormones, which regulate the rate of metabolism in the body.

thyroxin Hormone released by the thyroid gland that functions in the control of metabolic activities in the body.

tongue Structure that functions to move food around while we chew and helps to arrange the food into a swallowable bolus.

trachea The tunnel that leads air into the thoracic cavity.

tracheid cells Xylem cells in charge of water transport in gymnosperm.

tracheophytes Vascular plants.

transcription factors Helper proteins that assist RNA polymerase in finding and attaching to the promoter region.

transduction The movement of genes from one cell to another by phages.

transformation The transfer of genetic material from one cell to another, resulting in a genetic change in the receiving cell.

translocation Movement of the ribosome along the mRNA in such a way that the A site becomes the P site and the next tRNA comes into the new A site carrying the next amino acid.

translocation (plants) Movement of carbohydrates through the phloem.

transpiration Process by which plants lose water by evaporation through their leaves.

trichinosis Disease found in humans caused by a roundworm that infects meat products.

trophic levels Hierarchy of energy levels that describe the energy distribution of a planet.

trophoblast Forms the placenta for the developing fetus, and aids in attachment to the endometrium. This structure also produces human chorionic gonadotropin (hCG), which maintains the endometrium by ensuring the continued production of progesterone.

tropical forests These forests consist primarily of tall trees that form a thick cover, which blocks the light from reaching the floor of the forest (where there is little growth). Tropical rainforests are known for their rapid recycling of nutrients and contain the greatest diversity of species.

tropism Plant growth that occurs in response to an environmental stimulus such as sunlight or gravity.

tropomyosin Regulatory protein known to block the actin–myosin binding site and prevent muscular contraction in the absence of calcium.

trypsin Enzyme that cuts protein bonds in the small intestine.

TSH See **thyroid-stimulating hormone.**

tundra This biome experiences extremely cold winters during which the ground freezes completely. Short shrubs or grasses that are able to withstand the difficult conditions dominate.

Turner syndrome Affects females who are missing an X chromosome.

umbilical cord Structure that transports oxygen, food, and waste (CO_2) between the embryo and the placenta.

uniform distribution Scenario in which individuals are evenly spaced out across a given geographic area.

unsaturated fat Fat that contains one or more double bonds; found in plants.

uracil The nucleotide that replaces thymine in RNA.

urethra Exit point for both urine and sperm from males and urine for females.

uterus Site of embryo attachment and development in mammals.

vaccination Inoculation of medicine into a patient in an effort to prime the immune system to be prepared to fight a specific sickness if confronted in the future.

vacuole A storage organelle that is large in plant cells but small in animal cells.

vascular cambium A cylinder of tissue that extends the length of the stem and root and gives rise to the secondary xylem and phloem.

vascular cylinder Structure in plants that is composed of cells that produce the lateral roots of the plant.

vas deferens Tunnel that connects the epididymis to the urethra.

vector Agent that moves DNA from one source to another.

veins Structures that return blood to the heart.

vena cava system System of veins that returns deoxygenated blood from the body to the heart to be reoxygenated in the lungs.

vertebrate Animal with a backbone.

vessel elements Xylem cells in charge of water transport in angiosperms. More efficient than tracheid cells.

vestigial characters Characters that are no longer useful, although they once were.

viral envelope Protective barrier that surrounds some viruses but also helps them attach to cells.

viroids Plant viruses that are only a few hundred nucleotides in length.

virus A parasitic infectious agent that is unable to survive outside a host organism. Viruses do not contain enzymes for metabolism or ribosomes for protein synthesis.

visual communication Communication through the use of the visual senses.

water biomes Both freshwater and marine biomes, which occupy the majority of the surface of the Earth.

water cycle The Earth is covered in water. A lot of this water evaporates each day and returns to the clouds. This water is then returned to the earth in the form of precipitation.

water potential The force that drives water to move in a given direction. Combination of solute potential and pressure potential.

water vascular system Series of tubes and canals within echinoderms that play a role in ingestion of food, movement, and gas exchange.

wild-type phenotype The normal phenotype for a characteristic in fruit flies and other organisms.

within-sex competition Competition for mates between members of the same sex.

wobble Nucleotides in the third position of an anticodon are able to pair with many nucleotides instead of just their normal partner.

X-inactivation During the development of the female embryo, one of the two X chromosomes in each cell remains coiled as a Barr body whose genes are not expressed. A cell expresses the alleles of the active X chromosome only.

xylem The "superhighway," or important part of the vascular tissue in plants, through which water and nutrients travel throughout the plant. Also functions as a support structure that strengthens the plant.

yolk sac Derived from the hypoblast, this is the site of early blood cell formation in humans and the source of nutrients for bird and reptile embryos.

zone of cell division Region at the tip of a root formed by the actively dividing cells of the apical meristem.

zone of elongation Cells of this region elongate tremendously during plant growth.

zone of maturation Region in the plant where cells differentiate into their final forms.

5 Steps to Teaching AP Biology

TEACHER'S MANUAL

Kelcey Burris

AP Biology Teacher
Union High School in Camas, Washington

Thanks to Greg Jacobs, an AP physics teacher at Woodberry Forest School in Virginia, for developing the 5-step approach used in this teaching guide.

Introduction to the *Teacher's Manual*

Nowadays teachers have no shortage of resources for the AP Biology class. No longer limited to just the teacher and the textbook, today's teachers can utilize online simulations, apps, computer-based homework, video lectures, and so on. Even the College Board itself provides so much material related to the AP Biology exam that the typical teacher—and student—can easily become overwhelmed by an excess of teaching materials and resources.

Some of these resources you may be able to use in your class. This book is an invaluable resource for your class because it explains in straightforward language exactly what a student needs to know for the AP Biology exam and provides a review program students can use to prepare for the test.

The 5 Steps of Teaching AP Biology

This *Teacher's Manual* will take you through the 5 steps of teaching AP Biology. These 5 steps are:

▶ **Prepare a strategic plan for the course**

▶ **Hold an interesting class every day**

▶ **Evaluate your students' progress**

▶ **Get students ready to take the AP exam**

▶ **Become a better teacher every year**

I'll discuss each of these steps, providing suggestions and ideas that are things I use in my own classroom. I present them here because over the years I found that they work. You may have developed a different course strategy, teaching activities, and evaluation techniques. That's fine; different things work for different teachers. But I hope you discover in this *Teacher's Manual* something that you will find useful.

STEP 1

Prepare a Strategic Plan for the Course

Planning for AP Biology can be one of the more challenging things you do as an AP Biology teacher, regardless of whether you are brand new to the course or are a 20-year veteran. The release of the AP Biology Course and Exam Description (CED) in 2019 by the College Board has made the process so much easier. The CED provides a road map for you to follow in planning your class and preparing your students for success in the course and the exam. While not required to, it's best to follow the sequence laid out in the CED since the resources provided by the College Board in AP Classroom follow that sequence.

As I work with teachers at AP Summer Institutes and Workshops, one of the first things that I have the teachers do is establish their course calendar. Here's how:

1. Obtain your school's calendar for the year. Make sure that it includes all the early release days, teacher work days, holidays, and state testing dates. Mark those dates on your planning calendar.

2. Find out the date for the AP Biology exam in May.

3. Next, think about your school's bell schedule. Does your school have traditional scheduling? Block scheduling? This has implications for #4.

4. Consult the suggested pacing schedule from the following chart. Remember that the suggested pacing is for a traditional bell schedule with 45-minute classes. With this information, set your calendar by establishing the days you will be spending on each unit and the assessment dates for each.

5. If you plan to conduct an in-class review for your students, make sure to include it in your overall planning. For my classroom, I usually build in 1 to 2 weeks of review.

Now that you have established your calendar, you can begin to plan the instructional strategies that you will use with your students to cover the content and topics indicated in the CED. The chart below shows the units and the recommended pacing for each unit.

TOPICS	PACING	5 STEPS TO A 5
Unit 1: Chemistry of Life	5–7 class periods + 2 class periods for assessment	Chapter 5, pp. 47–60
Unit 2: Cell Structure and Function	11–13 class periods + 2 class periods for assessment	Chapter 6, pp. 61–75
Unit 3: Cellular Energetics	14–17 class periods + 2 class periods for assessment	Chapter 7, pp. 76–101
Unit 4: Cell Communication and Cell Cycle	9–11 class periods + 2 class periods for assessment	Chapter 8, pp. 102–113
Unit 5: Heredity	9–11 class periods + 2 class periods for assessment	Chapter 9, pp. 114–136
Unit 6: Molecular Genetics	18–21 class periods + 2 class periods for assessment	Chapter 10, pp. 137–169
Unit 7: Evolution	20–23 class periods + 2 class periods for assessment	Chapter 11, pp. 170–192
Unit 8: Ecology	18–21 class periods + 2 class periods for assessment	Chapter 12, pp. 193–219

Planning with *5 Steps to a 5: AP Biology*

AP Biology is a yearlong course that covers a huge amount of material; students acquire the skills and content knowledge throughout the school year in order to ultimately achieve success on the AP exam. To do this, students need to be provided the opportunity not only to learn the material during the school year, but also to review and prepare for the exam in May. *5 Steps to a 5* provides a resource for students to do either or both.

The book *5 Steps to a 5: AP Biology* is organized to mirror the AP Biology curriculum provided in the CED. To help students make connections throughout *5 Steps to a 5*, the Big Ideas and Enduring Understandings are identified with the

Big Idea abbreviation and the number associated with the Enduring Understanding. For example, in Chapter 6, "Cell Structure and Function," the organelles section is designated SYI-1. That means it is Enduring Understanding #1 ("Living Systems Are Organized in a Hierarchy of Structural Levels That Interact"), which connects with Big Idea #4, which is Systems Interact (SYI).

One of the questions that come up most often from teachers is "How do I integrate this resource into AP Biology?" The chart below includes the units from the AP Biology CED, and the corresponding Chapters and Review Questions from *5 Steps to a 5*. While this is only an outline, it paints a picture of how you can use *5 Steps to a 5* throughout the school year.

TOPICS	*5 STEPS TO A 5* READINGS	FORMATIVE ASSESSMENTS
Unit 1: Chemistry of Life	Chapter 5, pp. 47–57	Review Questions, pp. 58–60
Unit 2: Cell Structure and Function	Chapter 6, pp. 61–71	Review Questions, pp. 71–75
Unit 3: Cellular Energetics	Chapter 7, pp. 76–96	Review Questions, pp. 96–101
Unit 4: Cell Communication and Cell Cycle	Chapter 8, pp. 102–110	Review Questions, pp. 110–113
Unit 5: Heredity	Chapter 9, pp. 114–130	Review Questions, pp. 130–136
Unit 6: Molecular Genetics	Chapter 10, pp. 137–165	Review Questions, pp. 165–169
Unit 7: Evolution	Chapter 11, pp. 170–188	Review Questions, pp. 189–192
Unit 8: Ecology	Chapter 12, pp. 193–213	Review Questions, pp. 213–219

Hold an Interesting Class Every Day

AP Biology should be a course that students enjoy on a daily basis. Using a variety of instructional strategies, you will be able to help your students not only learn the content, but more important, implement the science practices that are the bedrock of the course. In my classroom, the structure of the class consists of a short bell ringer followed by an activity or investigation.

Bell Ringers

During these short mini activities, students apply the science practices to current topics we are covering. It might require the students to explain biological concepts, analyze visual representations of biological concepts, analyze the components of experiments, work with data, perform statistical tests and data analysis, or develop and justify scientific arguments using evidence.

▶ **Mini lectures.** While discussing the bell ringer, it is a great opportunity to conduct short lectures to dive deeper into challenging concepts and topics.

▶ **Interactive notebook.** In my course I use an interactive notebook, which is a "story" of the students' journey through AP Biology.

Activities and Investigations

In AP Biology it is important to realize that it is not what you do but how you do it that is the key to having success in your course. Teaching content through activities and/or investigations affords students the opportunity to practice and apply the science practices while learning the content of the course. By implementing a variety of instructional strategies in your classroom, you will allow your students to apply their understanding of course content.

▶ **Investigations.** Whether you are using the College Board's *AP Biology Lab Manual* or any other investigation resource, having students design investigations, conduct investigations, construct graphs, describe data, and develop and justify scientific arguments from the evidence collected in the investigation is a key component of the course. Remember that you should plan to have 25% of your course dedicated to investigations, with at least two investigations occurring per Big Idea.

▶ **Case studies.** Case studies are a powerful instructional tool based on contemporary science problems that students encounter in the news. These case studies make science relevant. They provide an opportunity to teach not only biological concepts and content, but also the science practices that are key to AP Biology. Case studies you can use can be found at the National Center for Case Study Teaching in Science (NCCSTS), which you can access at **https://www.nsta.org/case-studies.**

► **Data Nuggets.** Data Nuggets (**https://datanuggets.org/**) are free classroom activities that bring contemporary research and authentic data into the classroom. Each activity guides the students through the entire process of science, which includes identifying hypotheses, making predictions, visualizing and interpreting data, developing and justifying arguments using evidence, and proposing their own questions.

► **HHMI BioInteractive.** Howard Hughes Medical Institute's BioInteractive website (**https://www.biointeractive.org/**) offers students the opportunity to engage in real science. It provides stories and real data while exploring the concepts and topics in AP Biology. For the teachers, there are implementation ideas, lesson sequences, resource modifications, and quick tips for the huge collection of videos and articles.

► **Modeling.** Giving your students an opportunity to analyze visual representations of biological concepts and processes is one of the most important instructional strategies you can use in your classroom. Whether it is using Flipgrid to record the process of gene regulation, chalk markers to demonstrate the stages of cellular respiration in chalk talks, or one of your own modeling strategies, this gives students consistent opportunities to describe and explain biological concepts and processes with visual representations. This will help your students not only to learn the concepts of AP Biology, but also to improve their performance on the AP exam.

► **Flipped classroom.** I currently use a modified flipped classroom model in my course where students interact with content through screencasts, readings, Ted Talks, and so on, outside of class. This allows class time to be devoted to applied learning activities, investigations, and more higher-order thinking tasks. For AP Biology there are numerous screencasts available to students:

▷ **AP Daily videos:** https://myap.college board.org/

▷ **Bozeman Science:** http://www.bozeman science.com/ap-biology

▷ **Crash Course:** https://youtu.be/ gMOoMcsGTO4

▷ **Khan Academy:** https://www.khanacademy .org/science/ap-biology

▷ **Amoeba Sisters:** https://www.amoeba sisters.com/

Instructional Activity Ideas

The chart below shows some of my favorite activities for AP Biology by unit. You can find most of these activities at the websites cited earlier; for the investigations you can do a search online by topic to get ideas.

UNIT	INSTRUCTIONAL ACTIVITIES
Unit 1: Chemistry of Life	▶ Investigate the property of water ▶ Do the Data Nugget activity "Can Biochar Improve Crop Yields" ▶ Complete the NCCSTS case study "Do Grasshoppers Sweat?" ▶ Complete the NCCSTS case study "The Biochemistry of Curly and Straight Hair" ▶ Do the Data Nugget activity "The Ground Has Gas" ▶ Do molecular modeling
Unit 2: Cell Structure and Function	▶ Draw the fluid mosaic model with chalk markers ▶ Investigate cell surface area and volume ▶ Complete the NCCSTS case study "Water Can Kill? Exploring Effects of Osmosis" ▶ Determine osmolarity in plants
Unit 3: Cellular Energetics	▶ Measure enzyme activity with yeast spheres ▶ Do the Data Nugget activity "Urbanization and Estuary Eutrophication" ▶ Investigate photosynthesis ▶ Investigate aerobic respiration in ectotherms ▶ Complete the NCCSTS case study "A Rigorous Investigation" ▶ Complete the NCCSTS case study "The Fun in Fermentation" ▶ Investigate photosynthesis and cellular respiration with algae beads
Unit 4: Communication and Cell Cycle	▶ Draw signal transduction with chalk markers ▶ Complete the NCCSTS case study "Diabetes and Insulin Signaling" ▶ Investigate factors affecting the cell division of allium roots ▶ Investigate the signal transduction of taste
Unit 5: Heredity	▶ Simulate meiosis using chromosome models ▶ Complete the NCCSTS case study "Those Old Kentucky Blues" ▶ Complete the HHMI activity "Mendelian Genetics, Probability, Pedigrees, and Chi-Square Statistics" ▶ Investigate Mendelian genetics with fast plants ▶ Do the Data Nugget activity "Salmon in Hot Water" ▶ Do the HHMI activity "Sickle Cell Disease and Malaria"

(continued)

UNIT	INSTRUCTIONAL ACTIVITIES
Unit 6: Molecular Genetics	▶ Complete the NCCSTS case study "The Mona Lisa Molecule" ▶ Construct a model of the Central Dogma ▶ Do the Data Nugget activity "Gene Expression in STEM Cells" ▶ Do the HHMI activity "Molecular Genetics of Color Mutations in Rock Pocket Mice" ▶ Complete the NCCSTS case study "The Sound of DNA" ▶ Investigate biotechnology—transformation
Unit 7: Evolution	▶ Complete the Data Nugget activity "Why Are Butterfly Wings Colorful" ▶ Complete the NCCSTS case study "Peppered Moths and the Industrial Revolution" ▶ Investigate BLAST ▶ Investigate artificial selection with bean beetles ▶ Investigate the mathematical modeling of Hardy Weinberg ▶ Do the HHMI activity "Allele and Phenotype Frequencies in Rock Pocket Mouse Populations" ▶ Complete the NCCSTS case study "The Galapagos"
Unit 8: Ecology	▶ Investigate animal behavior ▶ Complete the NCCSTS case study "Building a More Intricate Web—a Reexamination of Trophic Levels" ▶ Do the Data Nugget activity "City Parks—Wildlife Islands in a Sea of Cement" ▶ Complete the NCCSTS case study "A Trip to the Beach—Untangling the Mystery of Algal Blooms in the Great Lakes" ▶ Do the Data Nugget activity "Invasion Meltdown"

Using *5 Steps to a 5: AP Biology* as an Instructional Resource

5 Steps to a 5: AP Biology has many different applications in the classroom. It can be used as a review tool for the teacher, or as an integral part of your instructional materials for the course, or as a review tool to help students prep for the test.

If you are new to AP Biology, you most likely are spending time learning or relearning material on a wide range of biology topics. So if you are starting a new unit that you need to learn or relearn, first read the corresponding chapter in *5 Steps to a 5* (see the chart at the end of Step 1 earlier). The book allows for efficient review because it sticks to the important points; the college-level textbooks used in AP Biology contain details that are usually beyond the scope of the course.

If you are a veteran AP Biology teacher, you can use *5 Steps to a 5* to refresh your knowledge of the material and remind yourself of specific concepts that should be emphasized. Each chapter contains a chapter summary and list of key ideas at the beginning, which is sometimes all a veteran teacher needs to prepare to teach a lesson or concept.

Chapter 13, "Laboratory Review," not only is an important review tool for students, but also serves as an additional instructional resource. Since the AP curriculum does not require any specific investigations, the chapter provides an opportunity to explore various lab setups that might be different from the ones you use in your course. For each lab, an overview is provided along with a basic setup and possible results for each lab. In your classroom you could use these labs to expose your students to different lab setups and to data sets for additional work with lab scenarios. This is important because students can expect to see different lab scenarios throughout the AP exam.

If you have a classroom set, or if students have access to the Cross-Platform edition online, *5 Steps to a 5* can be used as a learning tool on a daily basis in your class. For example, the review questions at the end of each review chapter are an efficient way for students to judge how well they have understood the material. Students who are exposed to these questions can receive immediate feedback on how well they are understanding the material, since an explanation is provided for each question. These questions can be assigned to your students as exit tickets to quickly gauge the students' progress in your course.

Another way *5 Steps to a 5* can be used in your class is by utilizing the list of key terms and concepts at the beginning of each review chapter. This list can help students quickly review difficult terms; it can also be used to create learning opportunities for your students. For example, place each term or concept on one side of a notecard with its explanation on the other side (students can use the glossary at the back of *5 Steps to a 5* if they are having difficulty). Then have the students in groups create a concept map connecting the terms and concepts to each other, only referencing the explanation when they need to. You can also have the students change groups to see if they understand the concept map created by the other group. This exercise promotes the valuable practice of connecting the concepts and terms of the course.

The 5 Steps Cross-Platform site/app can be a helpful tool for student practice. Students can use the Flashcards and the GameCenter to drill themselves or a partner. They can also use the app to study the chapter that corresponds to the unit they are studying in class. They can use practice multiple-choice questions at the end of each chapter to check their understanding of the chapter. For instructions to access the Cross-Platform site, see the back cover of this book.

The *5 Steps to a 5 Elite Edition* provides an additional bank of questions that can be used in your class. The *Elite Edition* has 180 activities and questions that require 5 minutes a day; these questions and activities cover the most essential concepts and topics from the course. While these could be used by the student throughout the school year, you as a teacher can also use these questions and activities in a variety of ways in your course. One such way is by implementing these as daily warm-ups throughout your course. To do this, you will need the chart below that lists the units that each question and activity fall under, as the questions and activities do not follow the course in chronological order.

UNIT	5 STEPS TO A 5 ELITE EDITION QUESTION ACTIVITY
Unit 1: Chemistry of Life	Days 1, 4, 5, 6, 13, 74, 114, 126
Unit 2: Cellular Structure and Function	Days 2, 3, 7, 8, 9, 10, 11, 12, 14, 15, 128, 129, 134, 154, 155, 157, 163
Unit 3: Cellular Energetics	Days 19, 20, 22, 23, 24, 25, 26, 27, 28, 29, 30, 31, 32, 33, 34, 35, 72, 73, 122, 130, 139, 151, 152, 158
Unit 4: Cell Communication and Cell Cycle	Days 16, 17, 18, 21, 36, 37, 38, 39, 40, 41, 70, 101, 102, 109, 124, 153
Unit 5: Heredity	Days 42, 43, 44, 45, 46, 47, 48, 49, 50, 51, 52, 53, 54, 106, 125, 136, 159
Unit 6: Molecular Genetics	Days 55, 56, 57, 58, 59, 60, 61, 62, 63, 64, 65, 66, 67, 68, 69, 71, 75, 77, 78, 79, 103, 104, 117, 118, 132, 137, 141, 142, 143, 146, 147, 160
Unit 7: Evolution	Days 76, 80, 81, 82, 83, 84, 85, 86, 87, 88, 89, 90, 91, 92, 93, 94, 95, 96, 97, 98, 99, 100, 105, 107, 108, 110, 111, 112, 115, 116, 119, 123, 133, 138, 148, 161
Unit 8: Ecology	Days 113, 120, 121, 127, 131, 135, 140, 144, 145, 149, 150, 156, 162, 164, 165, 166, 167, 168, 169, 170, 171, 172, 173, 174, 175, 176, 177, 178, 179, 180

STEP 3

Evaluate Your Students' Progress

Regularly assessing your students' progress is one of the most important things you can do as an AP teacher since it helps students learn. Students can use the information of how well they are doing in class as one means of determining whether or not they understand the course material. For you as a teacher, it allows you to check to see that the instructional strategies you are using are proving to be effective in your students' learning of the AP Biology material.

For my classroom, formative assessments are the key to students gaining the skills and confidence needed to do well in the course. I use a variety of techniques to provide my students with opportunities to check their understanding of the course content while also giving me feedback about individual students and the class as a whole. These formative assessments are developmental in nature, and they do not impact the student's class grade. I use various materials in the AP Classroom for the formative assessments:

- Topic questions
  - ▷ Individual topics or combined topics are assigned.
  - ▷ Students analyze their results using the feedback provided.
- Personal progress checks
  - ▷ Personal progress checks are assigned at the end of the unit to check for understanding.
  - ▷ Students analyze their results using the feedback provided.

- Practice free-response questions
  - ▷ Full or parts of free-response questions are assigned.
  - ▷ Students self- and peer-grade to get immediate feedback.

Summative assessments also play a major role in my classroom. For summative assessments, I use the question bank in AP Classroom to construct unit exams that mirror the AP exam in May. These unit exams consist of multiple-choice questions (50% of the exam grade) and free-response questions (50% of the exam grade). I use a variety of techniques to provide students opportunities to improve their performance on the exam. Some techniques I have used are letting students retake the exam after attending tutoring, allowing for exam analysis and corrections, and conducting two-stage testing. In two-stage testing, students complete and submit the exam first individually. Then working with a partner or in small groups, the students complete the exam, which provides immediate and targeted feedback for the students. Two-stage testing is explained more at this website: **https://cwsei.ubc.ca/sites/default/files/cwsei/resources/instructor/Two-stage_Exams.pdf**.

Regardless of the methods you use with your students, it is imperative that you provide regular feedback. This allows your students to grow while consistently giving you opportunities to reflect on the strategies you are using.

STEP 4

Get Students Ready to Take the AP Exam

The AP Biology exam asks students to show what they know through the application of science practices such as data analysis and argumentation. As a teacher, you have to decide how much of your instruction will be based on the AP exam, since nobody truly likes the idea of "teaching to the test." However, the reality is that students who do well on the exam provide opportunities to enhance their college applications and earn college credit. A student who is well prepared for the exam is one whose teacher implements instructional strategies and practices specifically for the AP exam.

So in my classroom, I usually complete all eight units for the course by the end of April, which leaves 1 to 2 weeks of class exclusively to review for the AP exam. This in-class review is focused on a targeted review of difficult concepts identified throughout the year, as well as practice multiple-choice questions and free-response questions. However, I start the review process with my students weeks before the in-class review starts, usually about 2 months before the test date. This 2-month review is a student-directed review where students dive into the concepts they struggled with throughout the school year. Here are some of the strategies that I use with my students to help prepare them for the AP exam:

▶ **Student review schedule.** Establishing a study schedule is one of the most important things I do for my students. By establishing the schedule early for the students, ideally approximately 2 months before the exam, you keep them from cramming for the exam, which kills learning and ultimately performance.

▶ **AP Classroom videos**

  ▷ **AP Daily videos.** I assign the AP Daily videos that go over the concepts and topics that my students found difficult throughout the year.

  ▷ **AP Live review session videos.** The eight review session videos consist of the most challenging topics and concepts in the AP Biology curriculum. However, it is important to note that they do not cover all the topics and concepts in the CED.

▶ **Review quizzes.** Using the AP Classroom Question Bank, I construct quizzes, each consisting of five multiple-choice questions, that students take on Tuesdays and Thursdays. These review quizzes start in early March and are timed (8 minutes, 90 seconds a question) just like the AP exam. Students immediately receive their results and can review the feedback provided for each question.

▶ **FRQ Fridays.** Using the AP Classroom Question Bank, students answer one long free-response question (FRQ) and one short free-response question. After answering both FRQs, students first self-grade their FRQ and then exchange with a peer in order to peer-grade.

▶ **Practice exams.** Finally, there is nothing better for your students to do in preparing for the AP exam than to take a practice exam. You can find practice exams in the AP Classroom Question Bank as well as in *5 Steps to a 5*. In my classroom, I have my students take a practice exam at the beginning of their review schedule to determine the concepts and topics they need to focus on, another practice exam in the middle of review to help students zoom in on the concepts and topics they are still struggling with, and finally a last practice exam before the official AP exam to focus on last-minute concepts and topics they need to review.

You can use *5 Steps to a 5* as an integral part of the class's review plan. If you have a classroom set or access to the Cross-Platform edition online, the students can use the book independently or in groups to check their understanding of required concepts (Chapters 5–12). In addition, students need lots of practice answering questions in AP exam–style format that *5 Steps to a 5* provides. The questions in the book mirror typical AP Biology questions in structure, content coverage, and degree of difficulty. The questions can be found in the diagnostic test (Chapter 3) and in the practice tests; furthermore, all questions are accompanied by complete explanations. By providing your students with opportunities to review difficult concepts and practice AP exam–like questions, their confidence will be enhanced leading into the AP exam.

These strategies are by no means the only strategies you can use in reviewing with your students. They are just strategies I have found to work for my students. The key is providing your students the opportunity to learn the concepts and work with the science practices throughout the school year. Then the review you do with your students will be about fine-tuning their skills and knowledge, not having to teach a year's worth of AP Biology in a couple of weeks.

Become a Better Teacher Every Year

Becoming a better AP Biology teacher involves a growth mindset. A growth mindset will allow you to seek out better instructional strategies and ideas to improve your AP classroom each and every year. The best AP teachers are not ones who believe they have "figured it out," but ones who look to improve through self-reflection and growth.

The first place to start is the yearly Instructional Planning Report (IPR) that is released each year by the College Board. The IPR, which you can find through AP Classroom, compares the performance of your students against the global population of exam takers. The IPR will allow you to identify skill gaps, determine performance between the multiple-choice and free-response questions sections, and gauge students' performance against state and global peers. This data will help you improve your instruction by identifying areas of the course that your students struggled in.

Another step to becoming a better teacher is reaching out and joining the various teaching communities that exist for AP Biology. There are various avenues to collaborate with other AP Biology teachers: You can connect with other AP Biology teachers in your geographic area to form a professional learning community; you can connect with other AP teachers in your school and discuss instructional strategies for AP courses; or you can join one of the robust online teaching communities such as the AP Biology Teaching Community provided by the College Board and the National AP Biology Teacher Group on Facebook. Each one provides a wealth of resources and ideas to improve your teaching.

Next, attending workshops is an excellent way to improve your instruction. A variety of different professional development opportunities are available to you as an AP Biology teacher. Here are some possibilities:

▶ **AP Summer Institutes**

▶ **AP One-Day Workshops**

▶ **National Association of Biology Teachers (NABT) Annual Conference**

▶ **HHMI BioInteractive Professional Development**

▶ **National Science Teaching Association Conferences**

Finally, one of the best professional development experiences that I have ever had was becoming a reader (grader) for the AP exam. It is an experience that is not only about the grading of AP exams, but about the collaboration and interaction you have with hundreds of AP Biology teachers from around the United States and the world. It has enabled me to create my own professional learning community made up of teachers from around the United States; these fellow educators have enriched my teaching in countless ways. To become a reader you apply through the College Board (**https://apcentral .collegeboard.org/professional-learning/become -an-ap-reader**) after teaching the course for at least 3 years.

Additional Resources for Teachers

Here is a list of online resources that can be used in your AP Biology classroom. Some I have already explained in this guide, but I have included them here for your convenience.

USEFUL WEBSITES

▶ **College Board AP Classroom (https://myap .collegeboard.org/):**

▷ **Biology Course and Exam Description (https://apcentral.collegeboard.org/pdf/ ap-biology-course-and-exam-description -0.pdf)**

▷ **AP Classroom**

• AP Daily videos

• Topic questions

• Personal progress checks

• AP Classroom Question Bank

▷ **AP Biology Teacher Community (Discussion Board)**

▶ **Data Nuggets (http://datanuggets.org/).** Data Nuggets are free classroom activities that bring contemporary research and authentic data into the classroom. Each activity guides the students through the entire process of science, which includes identifying hypotheses, making predictions, visualizing and interpreting data, developing and justifying arguments using evidence, and proposing their own questions.

▶ **Howard Hughes Medical Institute (https:// www.biointeractive.org/).** The Howard Hughes Medical Institute provides students the opportunity to engage in real science through stories and real data while exploring the concepts and topics in AP Biology. For the teachers, there are implementation ideas, lesson sequences, resource modifications, and quick tips for taking advantage of the huge collection of videos and articles.

▶ **National Center for Case Study Teaching in Science (https://sciencecases.lib.buffalo .edu/).** Case studies are a powerful instructional tool based on contemporary science problems that students encounter in the news. They make science relevant. The cases provide an opportunity to teach not only biological concepts and content, but also the science practices that are key to AP Biology.

▶ **PhET Interactive Simulations (https://phet .colorado.edu/).** PhET Interactive Simulations are free science simulations that give students the opportunity to learn concepts through exploration and discovery.

▶ **Jon Darkow Simulations (https://sites.google .com/site/biologydarkow/).** A collection of computational models for biology and ecology where students are able to hypothesize, test, and review computer models of difficult concepts in biology and ecology.

▶ **Genetic Science Learning Center** (https://learn.genetics.utah.edu/). An interactive website consisting of a collection of videos, supplementary practice exercises for students, and materials for teachers.

▶ **Khan Academy—AP Biology** (https://www.khanacademy.org/science/ap-biology). An interactive website consisting of a collection of videos, supplementary practice exercises for students, and materials for teachers.

▶ **Amoeba Sisters** (https://www.amoebasisters.com/). A collection of videos and other resources for students and educators designed to help in understanding difficult biology concepts with humor.

▶ **Bozeman Science** (http://www.bozemanscience.com/ap-biology). A series of short science videos focused on specific topics and concepts for AP Biology.

▶ **Crash Course** (https://youtu.be/gMOoMcsGTO4). A collection of high-quality educational videos covering specific topics and concepts for AP Biology.